Conceptualizing Mass Violence

Conceptualizing Mass Violence draws attention to the conspicuous inability to inhibit mass violence in myriad forms and considers the plausible reasons for doing so. Focusing on a postcolonial perspective, the volume seeks to popularize and institutionalize the study of mass violence in South Asia.

The chapters explore and deliberate upon the varied aspects of mass violence, namely revisionism, reconstruction, atrocities, trauma, memorialization and literature, the need for Holocaust education, and the criticality of dialogue and reconciliation. The language, content, and characteristics of mass violence/genocide explicitly reinforce its aggressive, transmuting, and multifaceted character and the consequent necessity to understand the same in a nuanced manner. The book is an attempt to do so as it takes episodes of mass violence for case study from all inhabited continents, from the twentieth century to the present. The volume studies "consciously enforced mass violence" through an interdisciplinary approach and suggests that dialogue aimed at reconciliation is perhaps the singular agency via which a solution could be achieved from mass violence in the global context.

The volume is essential reading for postgraduate students and scholars from the interdisciplinary fields of Holocaust and Genocide Studies, History, Political Science, Sociology, World History, Human Rights, and Global Studies.

Navras J. Aafreedi is Assistant Professor of History at Presidency University, Kolkata, and Research Fellow at the Institute for the Study of Global Antisemitism and Policy, New York. His publications include his monograph *Jews, Judaizing Movements and the Traditions of Israelite Descent in South Asia.*

Priya Singh is Associate Director at Asia in Global Affairs (www.asiainglobalaffairs.in). Priya is a political scientist with an interest in issues pertaining to geo-politics, nationalism, post-nationalism, identity, state formation and gender. She has authored, edited, and co-edited books on Israel and the Middle East.

Mass Violence in Modern History

Edited by Alexander Korb (University of Leicester, United Kingdom) and Uğur Ümit Üngor (Utrecht University, the Netherlands)

Despite the horrors of nineteenth-century conflicts including the US Civil War and the Napoleonic Wars, it was not until the twentieth century that mass killing was conducted on an industrialized scale. While the trenches of Flanders and the atomic bomb were major manifestations of this, mass violence often occurred outside the context of conventional war or away from the traditional battlefield. Research has understandably tended to focus on major events and often within a binary superpower narrative. In fact, instances of mass violence are often hard to pin down as well as being little known, and involving civilians and citizens of a wider range of territories than is publicized. The books in this series shed light on mass violence in the modern era, from Armenia to Rwanda; from Belarus to Bosnia-Herzegovina and many points in between.

For more information about this series, please visit: https://www.routledge.com/Mass-Violence-in-Modern-History/book-series/MASSVIOLENCE

Conceptualizing Mass Violence
Representations, Recollections, and Reinterpretations

**Edited by Navras J. Aafreedi and
Priya Singh**

LONDON AND NEW YORK

First published 2021
by Routledge
2 Park Square, Milton Park, Abingdon, Oxon OX14 4RN

and by Routledge
52 Vanderbilt Avenue, New York, NY 10017

Routledge is an imprint of the Taylor & Francis Group, an informa business

British Library Cataloguing-in-Publication Data
A catalogue record for this book is available from the British Library

Library of Congress Cataloging-in-Publication Data
Names: Aafreedi, Navras Jaat, editor. | Singh, Priya, editor.
Title: Conceptualizing mass violence : representations, recollections, and reinterpretations / edited by Navras J. Aafreedi and Priya Singh.
Subjects: LCSH: Genocide. | Genocide--South Asia. | Violence--South Asia.
Classification: LCC HV6322.7 .C653 2021 | DDC 304.6/63--dc23
LC record available at https://lccn.loc.gov/2020050905

ISBN: 978-0-367-69997-0 (hbk)
ISBN: 978-0-367-70406-3 (pbk)
ISBN: 978-1-003-14613-1 (ebk)

Typeset in Times New Roman
by SPi Global, India

To
Professor Mahavir Singh
With respect and warm regards

Contents

Figures

Tables

Contributors

Navras J. Aafreedi is an Assistant Professor in History at Presidency University, Kolkata, where he teaches an MA course "A History of Mass Violence, the Twentieth Century to the Present" among several other courses. He is the author of the monograph *Jews, Judaizing Movements and the Traditions of Israelite Descent in South Asia* (New Delhi, 2016), several papers in peer-reviewed journals, and chapters in edited books published by prestigious publishing houses. He has also published in quasi-academic publications, leading newspapers, and popular media, and guest edited four special thematic issues for the online magazine *Café Dissensus*. Other than English, his writings have also appeared in German, Spanish, and Urdu. He writes on Genocide Studies, Indo-Judaic Studies, Interfaith Relations, Antisemitism Studies, and Jewish Literary History, with focus on South Asia. He has spoken at scholarly forums in all continents except South America and held visiting fellowships at the universities of Tel Aviv and Sydney, and at the Woolf Institute, Cambridge, UK. He was a scholar-in-residence at St John's College, Oxford, for the ISGAP Summer Institute on Curriculum Development in Critical Antisemitism Studies in July 2017. He received his entire tertiary education at the University of Lucknow, from where he earned the degrees of BA, MA, and PhD.

Tutku Ayhan is a PhD Candidate in Security Studies at the University of Central Florida. Her research interests include gender-based violence, gender and conflict, and political violence, with a regional focus on Middle East. Her dissertation project focuses on post-genocide gender dynamics among the Yezidi community. Adopting an intersectional approach, she examines the impact of violence, displacement, and immigration on post-conflict experiences of Yezidi women. She currently is conducting multisite fieldwork in northern Iraq, Germany, and the US. She received her MA in Sociology in EHESS, Paris, and wrote her master's thesis on femicide in Turkey.

Charles E. Ehrlich has served as a Program Director at Salzburg Global Seminar, in Salzburg, Austria, since May 2014. He has particular responsibility for designing, developing, and implementing programs on justice, rule of law, public administration, and governance including Salzburg Global Seminar's Holocaust Education and Genocide Prevention work. He has practical experience in legal development working in over a dozen countries, including in the Balkans, the Caucasus, and the Russian Federation, advising governments and public institutions on strategic planning, drafting legislation, and implementing comprehensive reforms in the justice sector, public administration, property rights, freedom of the media, and constitutional law, including in post-conflict contexts. Dr Ehrlich has also worked as legal counsel for the Organization for Security and Cooperation in Europe in Kosovo, in Georgia, and at its Secretariat in Vienna. At the Claims Resolution Tribunal in Switzerland, he adjudicated claims to Nazi-era bank accounts. He remains affiliated with Wolfson College, University of Oxford, and has published a book, *Lliga Regionalista – Lliga Catalana, 1901–1936* (in Catalan), and numerous academic articles on constitutional law, justice, and political history. Dr Ehrlich holds an AB in history and classics (Latin) from Harvard University, a JD from the College of William and Mary, an MSEcons in European studies from the London School of Economics, and a DPhil on contemporary Spanish history from the University of Oxford.

Reuven Firestone is the Regenstein Professor in medieval Judaism and Islam at Hebrew Union College, Los Angeles, and affiliate professor of religion at the University of Southern California. His books include *Journeys in Holy Lands: The Abraham-Ishmael Legends in Islamic Exegesis*; *Jihad: The Origin of Holy War in Islam*; *Holy War in Judaism: the Fall and Rise of a Controversial Idea*; *Who Are the* Real *Chosen People: The Meaning of "Chosenness" in Judaism, Christianity and Islam*; *An Introduction to Islam for Jews*, and *An Introduction to Judaism for Muslims; Learned Ignorance: Intellectual Humility among Jews, Christians and Muslims*, with James Heft and Omid Safi. Firestone received rabbinical ordination from Hebrew Union College and his PhD in Arabic and Islamic Studies from New York University. He has served as Vice President of the Association for Jewish Studies and President of the International Qur'anic Studies Association. Firestone is chair of the International Abrahamic Forum of the International Council of Christians and Jews, and lectures at universities in Europe, Asia, and the Middle East as well as throughout North America. He is active on the boards of numerous scholarly journals and community commissions treating interreligious relations and dialogue.

Daniela Gleizer is an associate researcher at the Institute of Historical Research, of the National Autonomous University of Mexico (UNAM). Her work has focused on the relationship between the Mexican state and foreigners, particularly on immigration and naturalization policies. Gleizer earned her PhD in History from El Colegio de México, in Mexico City, and has received various awards for her work. Her book *Unwelcome Exiles, Mexico and the Jewish Refugees from Nazism 1933–1945* (Brill, 2014) analyzes the Mexican stance towards Jewish refugees during Nazism, questioning the country's "open door" myth, by pointing to the limitations placed by the Mexican immigration policy on a number of nationalities, religious and political groups, including the Jews. She has also worked on the relationship between Mexico and the Third Reich, and the role of Mexico´s consuls in granting visas during the Second World War. Gleizer is currently working on two projects: one on the limits of citizenship policy in Mexico and the other on witness´s accounts of Holocaust survivors who arrived to Mexico. She teaches several graduate and postgraduate history courses at the UNAM. She belongs to the National System of Researches, to the Latin American Jewish Studies Association, and she is Affiliate Researcher at the Center for Advance Genocide Research of the University of Southern California.

Suzanne Hampel OAM holds a master's in Holocaust and Genocide Studies (2010) from Monash University. She is co-president of the Jewish Holocaust Centre in Melbourne and she has been appointed as a member of the National Archives of Australia Advisory Council. Sue is working as a teaching associate and research assistant in the Arts faculty at Monash University. She has received many teaching awards and is passionate about education. As the daughter of a Holocaust survivor, her work has been centred on the importance of memory and its transmission to future generations. Sue has led and organised numerous student groups on study tours to Poland and Rwanda. This year, Sue joined the State Government's Holocaust Education Working Group, to assist with development and implementation of mandatory Holocaust Studies for Years 9 and 10 across Victoria. In 2021, she will serve as the International Chair of the Education Working Group for the International Holocaust Remembrance Alliance (IHRA).

Dennis B. Klein is Kean University Professor of History and director of the Jewish Studies program and the Master of Arts in Holocaust and Genocide Studies program. He is the author or editor of five books, including *Jewish Origins of the Psychoanalytic Movement* (University of Chicago Press, 1985), *Hidden History of the Kovno Ghetto* (Little, Brown in cooperation with the US Holocaust Memorial Museum, 1997), *The Genocidal Mind* (Paragon, 2005), *Survivor Transitional Narratives of Nazi-Era Destruction: The Second Liberation* (Bloomsbury, 2017), and *Societies Emerging from Conflict: The Aftermath of Atrocity* (Cambridge Scholars Publishing, 2017). He is founding editor-in-chief of *Dimensions: A Journal of Holocaust Studies* and founding director of the Anti-Defamation League's Braun Center for Holocaust Studies. He is a recipient of numerous research awards, most recently, an NEH award for leading a 2021 seminar for higher education faculty on "The Search for Humanity after Atrocity". At present he is exploring the incrimination of the bystander in the late twentieth century. He frequently presents his research abroad, as well as in the US, including in Cape Town, Jerusalem, Oxford, London, New Delhi (by Skype), Poznan, Tel Aviv, and Wenzhou, China (by Skype).

Nancy Nicholls Lopeandía is a lecturer in the Institute of History, Faculty of History, Geography and Political Sciences of the Pontificia Universidad Católica de Chile, teaching courses on Memory and Oral History, Chilean Contemporary History and Holocaust. Recent publications include: (with Yael Siman and Lorena Avila) "Migration Narratives of Holocaust Survivors in Chile, Colombia, and Mexico", in: *Lessons and Legacies* XIV, *The Holocaust in the Twenty-First Century: Relevance and Challenges in the Digital Age*

(Northwestern University Press, 2020); in 2019, "Defensa de Derechos Humanos en Chile en el contexto transnacional del movimiento de defensa de los derechos humanos, 1973–1990" in *Estudos Ibero-Americanos*, Rio Grande do Sul, Brasil, 45, no. 1.

Tali Nates is the founder and director of the Johannesburg Holocaust & Genocide Centre and chair of the South African Holocaust & Genocide Foundation. She is a historian who lectures internationally on Holocaust education, genocide prevention, reconciliation, and human rights. Tali has presented at many conferences including at the United Nations in New York (2016) and is a fellow of the Salzburg Global Seminar (2014–2020). She published many articles and contributed chapters to different books, among them *God, Faith & Identity from the Ashes: Reflections of Children and Grandchildren of Holocaust Survivors (2015)* and *Remembering The Holocaust in Educational Settings (2018)*. Tali serves on the Academic Advisory Group of the School of Social and Health Sciences, Monash University (IIEMSA), South Africa. Born to a family of Holocaust survivors, Tali's father and uncle were saved by Oskar Schindler.

David Patterson holds the Hillel A. Feinberg Distinguished Chair in Holocaust Studies at the Ackerman Center for Holocaust Studies, University of Texas at Dallas. He is a commissioner on the Texas Holocaust and Genocide Commission, a member of the Executive Board of Academic Advisors for the Institute for the Study of Global Antisemitsm and Policy (ISGAP), and a member of the Executive Board of the Annual Scholars' Conference on the Holocaust and the Churches. He has lectured at universities on six continents and throughout the United States. A winner of the National Jewish Book Award, the Koret Jewish Book Award, and the Holocaust Scholars' Conference Eternal Flame Award, he has published more than 35 books and more than 220 articles, essays, and book chapters on topics in literature, philosophy, the Holocaust, and Jewish studies. His most recent books are *Shoah and Torah* (SUNY, forthcoming), *Elie Wiesel's Hasidic Legacy* (SUNY, forthcoming), *The Holocaust and the Non-Representable* (SUNY, 2018), *Anti-Semitism and Its Metaphysical Origins* (Cambridge, 2015), *Genocide in Jewish Thought* (Cambridge, 2012), and *A Genealogy of Evil: Anti-Semitism from Nazism to Islamic Jihad* (Cambridge, 2010).

Md. Muddassir Quamar is associated with the Manohar Parrikar Institute for Defence Studies and Analyses, New Delhi. He holds a PhD in Middle East Studies from Jawaharlal Nehru University. His doctoral thesis focused on social dynamics in Saudi Arabia in the context of the tensions between two seemingly non-harmonious trends; Islamization and modernization. He has wider interest in Gulf societies, political Islam, Middle East geopolitics and India's relations with the Middle East. His research papers have appeared in leading international journals. He has co-authored three books including *India's Saudi Policy: Bright to the Gulf* (Palgrave Macmillan, 2019), co-edited four anthologies including *Changing Security Paradigm in West Asia:*

Regional and International Responses (Knowledge World, 2020) and contributed numerous chapters published in anthologies across the world. Dr Quamar regularly contributes opinion articles on developments in the Persian Gulf, Middle East, and India's relations with the region. In 2014–2015, he was Visiting Fellow at the King Faisal Center for Research and Islamic Studies, Riyadh. Since its inception Dr Quamar has been associated with the Middle East Institute, New Delhi, in various capacities including serving as Associate Editor of its flagship journal, the *Contemporary Review of the Middle East*.

David Rosen KSG CBE, former Chief Rabbi of Ireland, is AJC's International Director of Interreligious Affairs and director of AJC's Heilbrunn Institute for International Interreligious Understanding. Rabbi Rosen is a member of the Chief Rabbinate of Israel's Committee for Interreligious Dialogue. He is an International President of the World Conference on Religion and Peace, Honorary President of the International Council of Christians and Jews, and the only Jewish member of the Board of Directors of the King Abdullah International Center for Interreligious and Intercultural Dialogue, established in 2012 by the King of Saudi Arabia together with the governments of Austria and Spain with the support of the Holy See. In 2005, Rabbi Rosen received a knighthood from the Pope in recognition of his contribution to promoting Catholic–Jewish reconciliation and in 2010 he was awarded a CBE (Commander of the British Empire) by Queen Elizabeth II.

Stephanie Shosh Rotem is an independent scholar of architectural history and museum studies. She was a Visiting Professor of Israel Studies at UC Berkeley (2019–2021) and the University of Virginia (2018–2019) teaching courses on Israeli art, architecture, and culture. Rotem is an architect, who after ten years of fieldwork, returned to graduate school at Tel Aviv University. She received her PhD in 2010 in the Program for Interdisciplinary Arts, and her doctorate was published as "Constructing Memory: Architectural Narratives of Holocaust Museums" (Peter Lang, 2013). Between 2011 and 2017, Rotem was Head of the Museum Studies Program at Tel Aviv University. She also taught graduate courses in Tel Aviv's Faculty of the Arts and in the International Program for Holocaust Studies at the University of Haifa. Rotem lectures and publishes on architectural history, museum history and architecture, and Holocaust museums.

Anubhav Roy is a PhD candidate at the Department of Political Science, University of Delhi. He has conducted research for projects of the Hebrew University of Jerusalem, a veteran Indian diplomat, and the United Service Institution of India, and has volunteered as a Senior Commissioning Editor for *E-International Relations*.

Rituparna Roy is Assistant Professor of English at The Heritage College, Kolkata. She is the author of *South Asian Partition Fiction in English: From Khushwant Singh to Amitav Ghosh* (AUP, 2010) and co-editor of the ICAS Volume *Writing India Anew: Indian English Fiction 2000–2010* (AUP, 2010). She is "Initiator" of the Kolkata Partition Museum Project (KPMP) and

"Managing Trustee" of the KPM Trust, which aims at the establishment of a Partition museum in Kolkata (https://kolkata-partition-museum.org/). Roy is also a writer. Her first collection of shorts, *Gariahat Junction*, was published in January 2020 by Kitaab International, Singapore. She writes reviews and features for Scroll.in, The Wire.in and other online portals; and blogs at www.royrituparna.com/category/kolkata-diaries/.

Suzanne D. Rutland MA (Hons) PhD, Dip Ed., OAM is Professor Emerita in the Department of Hebrew, Biblical and Jewish Studies, University of Sydney. She has published widely on Australian Jewish history, as well as writing on issues relating to the Holocaust, Israel, and Jewish education. Her latest books are *The Jews in Australia* (Cambridge University Press, 2005) and co-author with Sam Lipski of *Let My People Go: The Untold Story of Australia and Soviet Jews, 1959–1989* (Hybrid Publishers, 2015), which was co-winner of the Australian Prime Minister's Literary Awards, Australian History, 2016. She received a government grant from the Australian Prime Minister's Centre for Research on Australia for this project. In January 2008 she received the Medal of the Order of Australia for services to Higher Jewish Education and interfaith dialogue.

Srimanti Sarkar is Assistant Professor in the Department of Political Science, West Bengal State University. Previously she has been a Full-time Researcher at the Maulana Abul Kalam Azad Institute of Asian Studies Kolkata, an autonomous institute under the Ministry of Culture, Government of India (2012–2015). Her areas of research interests include theoretical postulates of democracy and democratization in South Asia with special focus on India and Bangladesh. She has specialized in "Peace and Conflict Studies" from Kulturstudier (Culture Studies) and Oslo and Akershus University College, Norway, and has been a Salzburg Global Fellow participating in the Salzburg Global Seminar at Salzburg, Austria, in 2017. She has several articles and book chapters to her credit and has widely presented papers in various national and international seminars and conferences. She has co-edited a book titled *The Political Future of Afghanistan: Issues and Perspectives* (Knowledge World Publishers, 2016).

Anita Sengupta is an area studies specialist and has been involved with research on the Central Asian region with Uzbekistan being her area of special interest. She has also worked extensively on Turkish politics and on the Syrian refugees in Turkey. Her areas of interest include issues of identity politics, migration, gender, borders, critical geopolitics, and logistics from an Asian perspective. She is the author of *Symbols and the Image of the State in Eurasia* (Springer, 2016), *Myth and Rhetoric of the Turkish Model: Exploring Developmental Alternatives* (Springer, 2014), *Heartlands of Eurasia: The Geopolitics of Political Space* (Lexington Books, 2009), *The Formation of the Uzbek Nation-State: A Study in Transition* (Lexington Books, 2003). Her most recent publication is Ranabir Samaddar and Anita Sengupta (eds), *Global Governance and India's North-East; Logistics, Infrastructure and Society* (Routledge, 2019). She is a regular commentator on debates on Asian affairs and is part of Asia in Global Affairs, an independent research forum that looks at a wide range of global issues from an Asian perspective. She is currently Senior Fellow, Indian Council of Social Science Research, New Delhi, India.

Fuzail Asar Siddiqi is a PhD research scholar at the Centre for English Studies, Jawaharlal Nehru University, New Delhi. He works as a freelance copyeditor with Oxford University Press, India, and Cambridge University Press, India. He is also the Founder and Editor-in-Chief of *Scriber*, an editorial services company. He has also been Assistant Professor of English, Gargi College, New Delhi.

Yael Siman is Associate Professor at the Department of Social and Political Sciences, Iberoamericana University, Mexico City. She is part of the National Scientific Research System in Mexico. She has a PhD in Political Science from the University of Chicago. Her research interests concern the connections between the Holocaust and Latin America, and the narratives of victims of genocide and mass violence. She has taught courses on genocide and the Middle East at Iberoamericana University, Anáhuac University, and Instituto Tecnológico Autónomo de México. She participated in the Global Salzburg Conference on Holocaust Education and Genocide Prevention and in the International Conference on Holocaust Education organized by USHMM and UNESCO. Dr Siman is currently working on two research projects: the displacement, migration and integration of Holocaust survivors in Latin America; and the forced disappearances and emergence of collectives of families of victims since the "War on Drugs" in Mexico. Her latest publication (2020) is: "Migration Narratives of Holocaust Survivors in Chile, Colombia and Mexico" in *Lessons and Legacies XIV: The Holocaust in the 21st Century: Relevance and Challenges in the Digital Age*, Tim Cole and Simone Gigliotti, eds, Evanston, IL: Northwestern University Press (with: Nancy Nicholls and Lorena Ávila).

Priya Singh is Associate Director and Programme Coordinator at Asia in Global Affairs (AGA), a non-profit, independent forum for research. She is the author of the monograph *Foreign Policy Making in Israel: Domestic Influences* (2005) and editor of the books *Perspectives on West Asia: The Evolving Geopolitical Discourses* (2012) and *Democracy in Asia: Discourses and Counter-Discourses* (2012). She has also co-edited several books that include *Corridors of Engagement* (2019), *Protest and the State in Eurasia and West Asia* (2016), *Re-envisaging West Asia: Looking Beyond the Arab Uprisings* (2016), *Asia in Transition* (2015), *Beyond Strategies: Cultural Dynamics in Asian Connections* (2014), *The Dilemma of Popular Sovereignty in the Middle East: Power from or to the People?* (2014), and *Interpreting the Arab Uprisings: Significance of the New Arab Awakening?* (2013). She has also published in prestigious peer-reviewed journals and serves on the editorial boards of a few of them. A political scientist, Singh has been Fellow at the Maulana Abul Kalam Azad Institute of Asian Studies, Kolkata, an autonomous institute under the Ministry of Culture, Government of India (2002–2016) and a Researcher at the Calcutta Research Group, for a Rosa Luxemburg Stiftung project on "Asian Connectivity" (2017–2018). She taught at the Loreto College, Kolkata from 1998 to 2001. She has also delivered lectures at several institutions in India and abroad. Her academic engagements and scholarly pursuits have taken her to Afghanistan, Egypt, Israel, Kyrgyzstan, Sri Lanka, and Turkey.

Güneş Murat Tezcür PhD (University of Michigan, 2005) is the Jalal Talabani Endowed Chair and Professor at the School of Politics, Security, and International Affairs at the University of Central Florida (UCF). He also directs the UCF's Kurdish Political Studies Program, the first and only such program in North America. His research on politics of identities, violence, and democratic struggles has appeared in many leading scholarly journals. He is also the author of *Muslim Reformers in Iran and Turkey* (University of Texas Press, 2010) and the editor of several books and volumes including *The Oxford Handbook of Turkish Politics* (Oxford University Press, 2020).

Acknowledgements

We are most grateful to all the scholars who have contributed to this volume and are indebted to them for their immense patience and the trust reposed in us. We would like to express our sincere gratitude to Alvin H. Rosenfeld, Professor of English and Jewish Studies, Irving M. Glazer Chair in Jewish Studies, and Director of the Institute for the Study of Contemporary Antisemitism, Borns Jewish Studies Program, Indiana University, for his interest in, encouragement towards and support for this academic initiative. We greatly appreciate the help we received from Rob Langham, Senior Publisher (History), Eve Setch, Publisher, and Emily Irvine, Editorial Assistant at Routledge. We must also acknowledge the anonymous peer reviewers for their invaluable feedback.

Introduction

1   Reading mass violence

Navras J. Aafreedi and Priya Singh

Contending terminologies

By and large, there appears to be no consensus with respect to the vocabulary pertaining to the deliberate annihilation of a significant number of civilians. The most commonly used term to describe the same is "genocide", which has been critiqued for its inadequacy in terms of its comparatively limited connotation, both with respect to its origin and with regard to who comprise the victims. The expression "genocide" conceived by Raphael Lemkin in 1944 is an amalgamation of *"genos"* (Greek) implying "race or tribe" and *"cide"* (Latin), which denotes "to kill".[1] Lemkin (1944) explicated genocide as "a coordinated plan of different actions aiming at the destruction of essential foundations of the life of national groups, with the aim of annihilating the groups themselves".[2] The United Nations Genocide Convention of 1948, restricts the victims of genocide to "national, ethical, racial or religious" groups.[3] The Cambridge English Dictionary describes genocide as "the murder of a whole group of people, especially a whole nation, race, or religious group".[4] However, history is replete with instances of large-scale violence akin to genocide wherein the altercation has not been premised on ethnic, racial, religious or national identities. Moreover, the phrase, loaded with an intense ethical approbation as well as political backing, has been employed to encompass a wide variety of activities by various pressure groups to fulfil their objectives, which fall beyond the realm of deliberate, instigated large-scale violence.[5] Holocaust/Shoah, on the other hand, is the phrase designated to refer to as the *Encyclopaedia Britannica* puts it,

> The systematic state-sponsored killing of six million Jewish men, women, and children and millions of others by Nazi Germany and its collaborators during World War II ... *Sho'ah* ("Catastrophe") is the term preferred ... by people who speak Hebrew and by those who want to be more particular about the Jewish experience or who are uncomfortable with the religious connotations of the word Holocaust. Less universal and more particular, *Sho'ah* emphasizes the annihilation of the Jews, not the totality of Nazi victims.[6]

The other term in contention to explicate the intentional and planned annihilation of a large number of civilians, "mass killings", has been defined as the intentional killing of a massive number of noncombatants ...Victims of mass killing may be members of any kind of group (ethnic, political, religious, etc.) as long as they are non-combatants and as long as their deaths were caused intentionally.[7]

While Holocaust and Holocaust centric academic studies have evolved systematically, genocide and the umbrella term mass killings/violence have predominantly followed the Holocaust archetype and have more than often been categorized together, reiterating the ambiguity of the expressions. Even as scholarship pertaining to the subject, inclusive of all categories has proliferated, concomitantly, the accessibility of Holocaust/genocide literature has increased humungously with the initiation of online platforms such as the electronic version of encyclopaedia of genocide/Holocaust, Facebook/Twitter groups and specialized literature on specific case studies. In the non-virtual world, universities and research centres specializing on the Holocaust gradually have broadened their ambit to incorporate genocides, albeit clearly highlighting the difference between the two terms. While Holocaust studies have by and large, reiterated their uniqueness in terms of the political ideology that constituted their basis, genocide studies, the more recent of the two have predominantly adopted a theoretical and comparative stance.[8] In terms of public policy, makeshift international and criminal courts of inquiry have been constituted to adjudicate in instances of genocide encompassing different continents whereas the International Criminal Court (ICC) undertakes similar responsibilities on a more enduring and ubiquitous scale, in addition, the European Union and the United States likewise have constituted apparatuses committed to assist in thwarting probable genocides or arbitrate in the continuing ones. The cumulative repercussion of these developments has been the evolution of an inclusive corpus of material pertaining to common law, legislation, and international politics. Moreover, with the culmination of the Cold War and the dawn of the age of globalization with its emphasis on an interlinked world, an additional focus was on the urge to contextualize incidents of genocide/mass violence, both historically and spatially.[9] Furthermore, in contemporary times, as articulations of dissent towards globalization are on an upsurge with the call for de-globalization or conversely, globalization, the tendency to interpret acts of mass violence through a combination of the meta and micro lens/narratives could be the focal point of academics and policy making.

The resurgence of genocide

The twentieth century came to be called the "The Age of Genocide".[10] In the aftermath of the Holocaust/Shoah, we raised the slogan "Never Again!", but it proved to be hollow, for it was followed by several genocides. It is not surprising given the fact that the five permanent member states of the United Nations Security Council are among the top six arms exporters of the world. According to the data released by the Stockholm International Peace Research Institute (SIPRI), just two countries, the United States, with 34 per cent, and Russia, with 22 per cent, accounted for more than half of the global arms exports for the period 2014–2018.[11] Some of the major crises the Security Council currently grapples with, such as Yemen, have been attributed to the actions of its own members involved in selling arms to the conflicting parties.[12] An end to genocides would be detrimental to the arms industry. It does not seem the twenty-first century would be any better if we fail to prevent mass violence as miserably as we have in its first two decades. In fact, we have witnessed a Nobel Peace Prize winner, Aung San Suu Kyi, indulge in genocide denial[13] and a genocide denier, Peter Handke, win a Nobel Prize for literature.[14] The United Nations Convention on Genocide expects all states that are signatories to "prevent and to punish" genocide. Yet the global record at both is extremely dismal. It is so primarily because more often than not political and financial/commercial interests take precedence over human life. Omar al-Bashir, President of Sudan, who has had an arrest warrant against himself from the International Criminal Court for a decade now, continues to travel to countries that are signatories to the International Criminal Court without being arrested.[15] The International Court of Justice observed in its ruling of 23 January 2020 that "the Fact Finding Mission concluded in September 2019 that the Rohingya people remained at serious risk of genocide." It asked Myanmar to "take effective measures to prevent the destruction and ensure the preservation of evidence to allegations of genocide".[16] Yet, there is nothing that the court can do against Myanmar should it defy. The measures ordered by the ICJ are binding, but it lacks the means of enforcement.[17]

Most at risk of genocidal violence are those who are stateless and their population at 12 million in 2020[18] is more than it has ever been. The number is only bound to increase should the present government in India go ahead with its plan to implement the exercise for the formation of a National Register of Citizens (NRC) across India in spite of the nationwide agitation against it. The Genocide Watch has already released a genocide alarm for two places, Assam in north-eastern India and India administered Kashmir. The stateless are invariably always a religious/ethnic/linguistic minority or all three at once wherever they are stripped of citizenship. It would be a fallacy to be indifferent to the plight of people even in the remotest corner of the world for what happens anywhere in the world eventually affects us all, dwelling as we are in connected and interdependent global spaces. An example is how the conflict in Syria and Levant led to a refugee crisis in Europe.

All this only goes to prove that the scourge of mass violence deserves far more attention than it has received if we are sincere in our efforts to prevent its occurrence. This attention has to come from politicians, world leaders, lawyers, activists, scholars, and academics. There are scholars who have devoted their entire lives to its study, but there are few institutions beyond Western academia where mass violence studies exist as an independent academic discipline. As the world marks 70 years of the liberation of the Auschwitz concentration camp at a time when we are witnessing a resurgence of antisemitism, we attempt to make a small contribution through this volume to enhancing our understanding of mass violence and its varied dimensions.

Reading mass killings

Although modest in its scope, this volume takes a global, national, as well as local approach, and tries to explore a number of aspects of mass violence: differences of narratives, betrayal, propaganda, revisionism, reconstruction, marginalization, trauma, remembrance, memorialization, education and awareness, dialogue, and our efforts to overcome hatred and achieve reconciliation. In doing so, it draws our attention to cases from all inhabited continents and brings together scholars from these continents to contribute to this anthology of papers. As for its time frame, the volume discusses cases from the Holocaust/Shoah (1933–1945) to the genocidal violence perpetrated against the Yezidis (2014–16).

Narratives

Dennis B. Klein provides insight into how narratives of betrayal figure in accounts of atrocities given by Holocaust survivors. He draws attention to how survivor testimonies were often regarded as merely subjective and sentimental when they came into wide circulation in the 1960s. The perception changed only in the 1990s with the emergence of "deep-memory" theorists who came to value them as emotional expressions from the "inside" deserving of greater attention, as according to them they revealed dimensions of persecution otherwise missed by empirical and schematic interpretations. These accounts more often than not point that the enemy was once an ally: a friend or a neighbour, bringing into sharp focus the cruelty of indifference and betrayal. Klein finds that both retribution and resentment coexist in survivors' accounts. He looks at mass violence from below, from the perspective of witnesses only to find that this optic challenges the classic, empirical standard of documented, objective, and verifiable truth, a standard in the tradition of historical and legal positivism that exalted historical reconstruction. His argument seeks to preserve the victim's voice and aspires to mine it for historical insight. Serving as witnesses to atrocity, victims disclose such dimensions of persecution that empirical and schematic interpretations miss.

Daniela Gleizer and **Yael Siman** analyse the conflicting testimonies given by Holocaust survivors settled in Mexico that either complement or contradict national and community narratives of open doors and welcoming society, based primarily on the experiences of other asylum seekers, such as Republican Spaniards (1930s–1940s) and, years later, the political exiles from the Southern Cone. They also point out that this narrative is in conflict with what the existing studies have established; did the Mexican government, driven by notions of miscegenation and antisemitism that prevailed then, pursue a highly restrictive and selective immigration policy towards Jewish immigrants? Their study includes stories of Jews who fled Europe in three different phases: during the rise of Nazism, during the war, and after the war. It takes into account testimonies and memoirs of a diverse population of survivors that exist in several oral history collections, as well as other bibliographic and archival sources. This chapter combines archival historical research and oral history to analyse the construction of a discourse of gratitude in Mexico by Holocaust survivors – in spite of prevailing difficulties – based on historical context, structural factors, and individual memories. It considers historical sources from the Immigration Mexican Archive, testimonies from the USC Shoah Foundation's collection, memoirs, and interviews that the authors conducted with survivors in Mexico.

Reuven Firestone provides us with an insightful and comprehensive analysis of the work of Vamık Volkan. How through the preservation of particularist narratives for generations in latent state, national or community trauma can be eternalized and preserved in varied ways, only to erupt into mass violence when conditions are ripe is what Volkan probed. Commemorative rituals and the formulation of particular types of historical narrative are the means to the maintenance and preservation of the experience of communal trauma. But it need not be. Firestone analyses the work of Volkan in order to consider four aspects of the phenomenon:

1. How communal trauma influences historical perspective, encouraging the formulation of highly problematic communal narratives.
2. How historical narrative and commemorative practice preserve and perpetuate communal trauma in the memory of victimized communities.
3. How the memory of communal trauma is activated to motivate mass violence against innocent victims.
4. How unresolved anxiety and tension brought about by communal trauma preserved by historical narrative can:
   a. be perpetuated and later discharged through violence, or alternatively
   b. be reduced and even relieved through constructive processes that thwart the release of violence.

Revisionism and reconstruction

Charles Ehrlich takes an overview of the propaganda and the distortion of Holocaust history in Eastern Europe and the former Soviet Union. He investigates how post-Holocaust historical memory of Jewish presence in Eastern Europe has been erased twice, first by communists and later by countries that belonged to the Soviet sphere of influence. These countries asserted their national identities after the disintegration of the USSR but erased the Jewish presence for it did not fit into their historical narratives. False moral equivalence enables them to justify atrocities, equate victims with perpetrators, and obfuscate justice. While abusing distorted narratives, the Holocaust is often used as a buzzword. Ehrlich became interested in the specific theme in the course of his own professional work (in public international law and development) in the former Soviet Union and other post-Communist nations. He witnessed the misuse of the Holocaust within the current state (primarily Russian) propaganda and in false narratives in nations where the Holocaust took place which were re-establishing their own independence – many of these narratives themselves deriving from decades of communist party-line contextualization of the Holocaust. Being attentive to the issue as a result of his personal experiences, he selected key countries (so as not to cast the net too widely) and focused his review of the literature on those. What is new with his approach in his chapter is the cross-examination of different narratives. There is a plethora of literature that focuses on individual country contexts or communist propaganda at large, but what he attempts to do is to illustrate how the former Soviet propaganda infected the discourse in the Eastern European space and how it has resulted in conflicted false narratives from Russia (primarily) on one hand and the former occupied states on the other.

Srimanti Sarkar contends that if forgetting or ignoring a bleak history of genocide makes us susceptible to repeating the misdemeanour, then accepting a "constructed" history of genocide is perhaps more likely to lead to a similar or even a graver kind of transgression. She holds a cautious de-construction and subsequent re-construction of the widely professed historiography imperative for drawing a pragmatic lesson from a history of genocide, considering every risk of fallacious elucidation. She takes the genocide of 1971 in Bangladesh for case study and adopts a critical approach as she aims to de-construct the dominant historiography of Bangladesh that is enduringly woven around the Genocide of 1971. Her study blends field research with an analysis of texts, documents, and artefacts to draw three distinct issue-specific case-studies that capture three significant time-frames: (a) the plight of the *Biranganas* (the women war-victims of Bangladesh) in the immediate aftermath of the Liberation War of Independence 1971; (b) the systemic marginalization of the hill dwellers of the Chittagong Hill Tracts (CHT) throughout the 1970s, 1980s, and 1990s; and (c) the growing popular discontent over the lacklustre trial of the war criminals of 1971 reaching its zenith through a mass uprising in Dhaka's Shahbag Square in 2013. Methodologically, her chapter adheres to a distinct sub-type of the Historical–Comparative Research that takes up a single nation (Bangladesh) as the key riposte for analysis and attempts to examine a particular phenomenon (the impact of the history of genocide and the spirit of the Liberation War of Independence) across time periods using qualitative databases. It justifiably allows a nation's historical, cultural, and political sensitivities to be taken into consideration ahead of making any broad theoretical propositions.

Md. Muddassir Quamar makes a thoughtful attempt to understand the phenomenon of Holocaust denial and minimization in the Urdu language press in India. Urdu is the lingua franca of linguistically diverse South Asian Muslims. India is home to the world's second largest Muslim population. They form the largest minority segment in the world with their proportion in India's total population estimated to be around 14 per cent. The Urdu print press in India is the third largest, both in terms of the number of publications and their readership. It largely caters to Muslims and plays a pivotal role in shaping their perceptions and forming their opinions on issues. He tries to understand in his chapter why and how the Urdu press in India denies and minimizes the Holocaust and the impact it has. The chapter is based on content analysis of nearly 15 Urdu newspapers published in different cities in India based on four to five years of monitoring of their editorial content and coverage. Newspapers include *Rashtriya Sahara* (Delhi edition), one of the largest circulated Urdu dailies in India with nine editions; *Dawat* (Delhi), the mouthpiece of Jamat-e-Islami Hind, an Islamist organization founded by Abul Ala' Maududi; *Sahafat* (Lucknow edition), a pro-Iran daily; *Urdu Times*

(Mumbai); *Étémād, Siāsat, Munsif* (all Hyderabad); *Akhbāre-e-Mashriq* (Kolkata) with socialist leanings; *Qaumi Tanzīm* (Patna); *Qaumi Raftār* (Lucknow); *Hamāra Samāj* (Delhi); *Daily Roshni* (Srinagar); *Inquilab* (Mumbai); *Hindustan Express* (Delhi); and *Nai Duniya*, a popular tabloid. These newspapers are chosen on the basis of their popularity reflected in circulation numbers and at least one newspaper from each region of India is taken for analysis so as to have a pan-India view. Hence, it is not only newspapers from Delhi or Mumbai but many other cities, including those from southern and eastern India that have been included for analysis. At the same time, Quamar has kept in mind while choosing the newspapers that they reflect the diversity schools of thought and political inclinations among Indian Muslims. The chapter limits its focus to newspapers and excludes the Urdu news television because of its small reach in comparison to the print medium. However, he has benefited from the digital medium for monitoring the content.

Education

Suzanne Rutland and **Suzanne Hampel** give a brief overview of the Australian Holocaust survivor community, analyse the concept of "the silence" and explore the initial memorialization within the survivor community, which at first focused on the unique aspects of the Holocaust. They also trace the emergence of Holocaust museums and their educational programs. They examine the major generational changes that have taken place both in terms of trips to the killing sites in Poland and particularly the move to include a broader universal message of human rights and prevention of mass violence, described by Yehuda Bauer as *Rethinking the Holocaust* (2001). They are convinced that the introduction of Holocaust Studies into Australian state curricula and Australia's acquirement of the membership of the International Holocaust Remembrance Alliance has made these new approaches evident. According to them, it only goes to prove the central role Holocaust education can play in combatting prejudice. Their chapter is an historical analysis, so it is based on historical methodology, rather than social science methodology. As a result, their research is based on archival research starting with Rutland's doctoral research in the 1980s, discourse analysis of Australian Jewish literature relating to Holocaust memory, and surveys of the main Jewish institutions contributing to Holocaust memory and education in Australia as well as policies of the different Australian state governments to the teaching of the Holocaust, undertaken with the assistance of a doctoral student who is researching Holocaust education in New South Wales.

Tali Nates provides us an insight into the opportunities and challenges that Holocaust and genocide education offers in South Africa, through the teachings of the Johannesburg Holocaust & Genocide Centre. She updates us on the new developments in Holocaust and genocide education in South Africa. She explains how they have engaged with the question of how to teach about the Holocaust and genocide and use these histories as tools to understand human rights and democracy in a country still recovering from the legacy of Apartheid. She elaborates upon how it is possible to make connections between the Holocaust and current issues in South Africa, such as xenophobia. She draws attention to how it is beneficial to use another country's history to understand South Africa's own reality and tells how it will help to build its future. She identifies in her research the key historical developments in the creation of the Johannesburg Holocaust and Genocide Centre as a museum for public learning and remembrance in South Africa. She also recognizes the significant means of drawing lessons from Holocaust and Genocide history for the South African society as a whole through connections between history and human rights issues today.

Anubhav Roy reports on the dismal state of secondary education in India when it comes to lessons on the Holocaust, where it is more often than not hardly anything more than a mere passing reference. He blames the structural bottlenecks for this situation. He surveys the staple history textbooks of India's prominent secondary education boards – central and provincial – in a two-tier investigation. In his investigation of the provincial boards of education he focuses on states like, Tripura in the northeast and Gujarat on the western coast. In the process he also examines the nuances of politicizing fundamental historification in India. Roy looks beyond conventional assessments of the problematic phenomenon to trace its roots in India's education curricula. He indulges in a critical reinvestigation of the historical and political rationales usually flagged to explain away India's persisting misbeliefs about Hitler and Nazism. Following which he samples the history textbooks at the secondary level of education in India to ascertain if it is the contemporary intellectual, instrumental, and systemic holes in the country's formative education that cause the present manifestations of the phenomenon. For the purpose of locating its contemporary perpetuators, he analyses the contents of the high school-level history textbooks approved by the National Council of Education Research and Training (NCERT) as well as the state (or provincial) governments of several Indian states, to gauge their seriousness, accuracy, and depth vis a vis the Holocaust.

Navras J. Aafreedi emphasizes the relevance of Holocaust commemoration and studies for India and laments the absence of Holocaust education in the country. He refers to historical records to draw our attention to how India responded to the Holocaust and identifies Holocaust denial, particularly in the Muslim discourse, and the trivialization of the Holocaust in the Hindu nationalist discourse as some of the important challenges for raising Holocaust awareness in India. He makes suggestions as to how those challenges can be overcome and updates us on the current state of Holocaust education at the tertiary level in India.

Reflections

David Patterson offers a graphic image of the urgency attached to memory and testimony through his analysis of four photographs, with particular attention to the one often omitted at displays because of its poor picture quality. These are photographs that were taken under the most dangerous and severe of conditions at Crematorium V, one of the four crematoria at the Birkenau concentration camp by one of the one thousand-strong *Sonderkommando*, using a camera acquired from Jews' stolen goods and smuggled out in a tube of toothpaste. He points out that in the matter of the Holocaust it is realized, "most urgent for memory is the utterance of the ineffable and the portrayal of the invisible. There lies not only the evil of Auschwitz but also the Good that summons us to remember and bear witness". The methodology adopted for this chapter entails a close analysis of the photographs taken at Crematorium 5 of Birkenau in August 1944 by the Sonderkommando member known as Alex. The aim of the analysis is to determine how the photographic image transmits what is not visible to the eye. So the method is guided by the question of what the photographic image reveals about what cannot be "shown" with regard to the Holocaust.

Güneş Murat Tezcür and **Tutku Ayhan** probe if the genocidal violence against Yezidis, a religious group in northern Iraq, and mass enslavement of their women and children was a rupture with past practices of their persecution or an outburst of deep-seated communal hatreds. They base their findings on original archival materials in primary languages and extensive fieldwork involving dozens of in-depth interviews with a diverse group of Yezidis. They identify both similarities and discontinuities characterizing anti-Yezidi violence to inform scholarly understandings of religious coexistence. They conducted several fieldworks among the Yezidis, in Iraqi Kurdistan (September 2017, May–June 2018, and May 2019) and Germany (June 2017 and October 2019). The fieldworks primarily involved more than a hundred in-depth interviews with a variety of individuals including Yezidi leaders, displaced survivors, local and international activists, NGO staff, and Iraqi Kurdish authorities. They also recorded some participant observation during their fieldwork.

Anita Sengupta attempts to examine how the modern Turkish state continues to exclude certain groups from its definition of who constituted its "relevant" citizen and thereby creates new notions of marginality. In spite of a secular definition of "Turk" in the 1924 constitution, it was only the Hanafi Muslims who spoke Turkish who came to be seen as the "real2 Turks. This understanding risked marginalizing not only the non-Turkish speaking Kurds, who belonged to the Shafi branch of Sunni Islam, but also Arabs and Alevis who constitute the second largest religious community in Turkey. The AKP tried to redress some of these issues but with the state recognition of a sharp distinction between supporters and adversaries of AKP new definitions of the "margin" have come into existence. Thus, marginality has acquired political overtones that define belonging in terms of ideological convergence. It is a "margin" that is subject to change depending on electoral performance. With the transformation of the definition of the "margin" in Turkey, Sengupta questions whether the changing notions of marginality will develop into a wider West Asian trait. She examines the emergence of a new "marginality" in Turkey, a marginality that it sets against the more cosmopolitan reality of Ottoman times. She uses qualitative and interpretive methods and examines a range debates and opinions about the issue in contemporary Turkey. The research is deductive in nature and based on secondary literature but also experiences and conversations about marginality in recent times in Turkey.

Trauma

The dictatorial regime that followed the coup d'état of the Chilean armed forces in September 1973 that overthrew the democratic government of Salvador Allende traumatized a number of Chileans, radically disrupting their lives. The dissidents were particularly preyed upon – tortured, executed, and "disappeared". From 1990 as a result of initiatives by both civil society and the state Chileans have bravely confronted this extremely painful recent past. **Nancy Nicholls Lopeandía** hypothesizes that in the post-dictatorship period, Chilean society has engaged in a process of reflection on this trauma – produced by the coercive policies of the military regime – which has implied a consensual recognition of the veracity of the violations to human rights committed by the dictatorship, and a condemnation of them. However, the sustained violation of human rights by police and army during the social uprising between October 2019 and March 2020 only proves that Chile has failed to incorporate the traumatic memory of the repression and its devastating effects on citizens as a means of societal learning for the strengthening of democracy. She refers to primary sources such as the Truth and Reconciliation Reports of the post dictatorship, including the human rights reports of various organizations that visited the country to monitor the social uprising and state-led responses, such as the Inter-American Commission on Human Rights and Amnesty International.

Memorialization

Stephanie Rotem presents various examples of non-traditional Holocaust museums, which she terms "Grassroots Holocaust Museums", and questions how they reflect contemporary Israeli society and studies their impact on Holocaust commemoration. She sees these small, non-institutional museums that have sprung up in Israel to display overlooked or unrecognized aspects of the Holocaust, challenging the hegemonic narrative of Holocaust memory and commemoration ingrained in Israel since the establishment of the modern Jewish state in 1948. The chapter is based on interdisciplinary research, which includes historical and visual analyses of the exhibitions. Information on their establishment museums was gathered from interviews of the founders and/or curators, catalogues, newspaper articles, and websites. These primary materials are supported by academic texts to understand the dynamics of these grassroots museums and their place in society.

Rituparna Roy narrates the story of her late mother's wardrobe full of sarees. Among the ones she prized the most is a "Dhakai", a muslin that originates from and is a speciality of Dhaka. Her family cook – a Bangladeshi who lived and worked in India for a long time without a passport – swears by "Padma'r ilish", saying the hilsa of the Ganges she has here are no match to it. When Kalikaprasad, a popular Indian folk singer/composer/scholar, died an untimely death in 2016, he was equally mourned on both sides of the India–Bangladesh border that divides Bengal. Even after more than seven decades there is still much that binds the two Bengals in everyday life, in terms of fabric, food, and song. To her they represent the quiet continuities in Bengali life, as opposed to the rupture of the political division. Although richly documented in history-writing, literature, and cinema, the public memorialization of this partition had been lacking. The Amritsar museum addresses that lacuna with respect to the Punjab. In Kolkata, Roy has initiated a project that focuses on Bengal: aiming at both memorializing the specificity of its partition history and aftermath, and emphasizing the continuities between the two Bengals – in an effort to promote tolerance between a divided people and make a conscious attempt to remain humane. In her chapter, she discusses how the said project intends to execute the latter. Roy gives the genesis of and highlights/elaborates on an important aim of a museum project-in-progress (the Kolkata Partition Museum Project) – viz, the continuities in the living heritage of the people on both sides of the Bengal border. Fabric, food, and music are some of the integral aspects of quotidian life: hence the data found in her chapter relates primarily to personal experiences sourced from blog posts in websites. That apart, the career of a popular folk singer–composer has been traced from available internet sources. The chapter is essentially speculative in nature, as it predicts a hopeful outcome – the promotion of tolerance between a divided people and the ways in which they can remain humane in an increasingly communalized atmosphere – instead of arriving at a scientific conclusion after quantitative/qualitative research.

Literature

How secular and religious publics have failed to address issues of genocide and violence is what **Fuzail Asar Siddiqi** strives to understand by focusing on Nathan Englander's stories. He draws our attention while doing so to the need to rethink public discourse that, according to him, should be post-religious and perhaps even post-secular, if there can be such a thing. His chapter tries to understand how Nathan Englander's collection of short stories *For the Relief of Unbearable Urges* attempts to participate in a discourse regarding the position/location of the modern subject vis-à-vis the political public sphere. The paper uses the Habermasian notion of the public sphere as a means to interrogate the shortcomings of articulation of the modern subject in a world that is not only constantly changing but is also hostile to democratic articulation itself, and uses the stories to highlight the powerlessness of both secular and religious publics to provide a counter argument against discourses of mass violence.

Dialogue and reconciliation

David Rosen reports on a significant attempt to achieve amity and harmony among the three Semitic monotheistic religious communities that make up half of the global population. The Alexandria Summit was held in 2002 precisely to explore as to how religion may be a vehicle for promoting tolerance and peace rather than a tool of violence. An outcome of the summit was the Council of the Religious Institutions of the Holy Land – incorporating the Chief Rabbinate of Israel, the Palestinian Authority Ministry of Waqf and Sharia Courts, and the Patriarchates and Bishoprics in Jerusalem, established with three purposes: to maintain open lines of communication between the religious leadership; to stand together against the defamation/disrespect or any attack on any one of the three faith communities; and to support appropriate political initiatives for the resolution of the conflict and the promotion of peace. The methodology is based on the author's personal involvement in the events and process he describes as well as personal observations.

At the present juncture, as we contend with a global pandemic, which could perhaps be read (though currently, strictly at a conjectural level) as a possible emerging instrument of mass killings, the language, content, and characteristics of mass violence/genocide explicitly reinforces its aggressive, transmuting, and multifaceted character and the consequent necessity to understand the same in a nuanced manner. The volume embodies a modest endeavour to study "consciously enforced mass violence" through an interdisciplinary approach, (albeit, not the first) with the belief that dialogue aimed at reconciliation is perhaps the singular agency via which an enduring solution could be achieved from mass violence in the global context. At the same time, purely from an academic level it seeks to popularize as well as institutionalize the study of mass violence in South Asia, focusing as it would be on a postcolonial perspective.

Notes

1 Benjamin A. Valentino, *Final Solutions: Mass Killing and Genocide in the Twentieth Century* (Ithaca and London: Cornell University Press, 2004) p. 9.
2 Raphael Lemkin, *Axis Rule in Occupied Europe: Laws of Occupation, Analysis of Government, Proposals for Redress* (Washington, DC: Carnegie Endowment for International Peace, 1944), p. 79.
3 Lawrence J. LeBlanc, *The United States and the Genocide Convention* (Durham, NC: Duke University Press, 1991), pp. 245–249; Valentino, *Final Solutions*, p. 9.
4 Meaning of genocide in English, Cambridge English Dictionary, Accessed 24 February 2020. https://dictionary.cambridge.org/dictionary/english/genocide
5 Valentino, *Final Solutions*, p. 9.
6 Meaning of Holocaust in English, *Encyclopaedia Britannica*, Accessed 24 February 2020. www.britannica.com/event/Holocaust,
7 Valentino, *Final Solutions*, p. 10.
8 Dirk Moses, "Toward a Theory of Critical Genocide Studies." *SciencesPo*, Updated on 18 April 2008 Accessed 24 February 2002. www.sciencespo.fr/mass-violence-war-massacre-resistance/en/document/toward-theory-critical-genocide-studies.html
9 Donald Bloxham and A. Dirk Moses, *The Oxford Handbook of Genocide Studies* (Oxford and New York: OUP, 2010), pp. 2–3.
10 Genocide Studies and Prevention: An International Journal, The International Association of Genocide Scholars, Publications, Accessed 26 January, 2020. https://genocidescholars.org/publications/
11 *SIPRI Yearbook Summary*, Stockholm International Peace Research Institute, Stockholm, 2019, p. 9.
12 Lyndal Rowlands, "UN Security Council Seats Taken by Arms Exporters." *Inter Press Service New Agency*, 23 January 2020. Accessed 25 January 2020. www.ipsnews.net/2016/11/un-security-council-seats-taken-by-arms-exporters/
13 Christina Lamb, "Tale After Tale of Horror in Burma, Aung San Suu Kyi Didn't Bat an Eyelid." *The Sunday Times*, 15 December 2019. www.thetimes.co.uk/article/tale-after-tale-of-horror-in-burma-aung-san-suu-kyi-didnt-bat-an-eyelid-2gfwq2nx5
14 Alexander Hemon, "The Bob Dylan of Genocide Apologists." *The New York Times*, 15 October 2019. www.nytimes.com/2019/10/15/opinion/peter-handke-nobel-bosnia-genocide.html; Alex Marshall and Christopher F. Schuetze, "Genius, Genocide Denier, or Both?" *The New York Times*, 10 December 2019. www.nytimes.com/2019/12/10/books/peter-handke-nobel-prize.html; Peter Maas, "How the Nobel Prize Succumbed to the Literary Art of Genocide Denial." *The Intercept*, 26 October 2019. https://theintercept.com/2019/10/26/nobel-prize-literature-peter-handke-genocide/;   Johannes

Anyuru, "Peter Handke's Nobel Condones Violence." *The Nation*, 18 October 2019. www.thenation.com/article/johannes-anyuru-peter-handke/

15 "How Do You Define Genocide?" *BBC*, Accessed 26 January 2020. www.bbc.com/ news/world-11108059

16 International Court of Justice Press Release No. 2020/3, 23 January 2020. www.icj-cij.org/files/case-related/178/178-20200123-PRE-01-00-EN.pdf

17 Mia Swart, "Will Myanmar Respect ICJ Order to Protect Rohingya from Genocide?" *Al Jazeera*, 24 January 2020. www.aljazeera.com/news/2020/01/myanmar-respect-icj-order-stop-genocide-rohingya-200123144204115.html

18 "Stateless People: Searching for Citizenship", The UN Refugee Agency, 8 October 2019. Accessed 26 January 2020. www.unhcr.org/ceu/78-enwho-we-helpstateless-people-html.html

Part 1
Narratives

2 Violence and violations[1]

Betrayal narratives in atrocity accounts

Dennis B. Klein

The unseen

The standard scholarly account of assault goes something like this: "The Germans brought along with them a Ukrainian battalion that had been set up by an intelligence officer called Theodor Oberländer and was known as the Nightingale unit ... Together with local hooligans, the troops went on a rampage" (Segev 2010, 44). In their reports, as primary sources, scholars commit themselves to describing the scene, noting the brutality and carnage.

Unlike secondary documentation, witnesses' accounts have had a difficult reception as sources of reliable information. From the time their accounts entered popular circulation in the 1960s, scholars and jurists often regarded them as merely subjective and sentimental, at best as derivative confirmation of their empirically validated arguments. This view was exemplified by the political philosopher Hannah Arendt, who covered the 1961 Eichmann trial for *The New Yorker*. The proceedings provided a major platform for survivors of Nazi-era destruction. Though they offered little evidence in support of the case for the prosecution, they succeeded at drawing worldwide attention to atrocity victims' emotional ordeal. Arendt disparaged their testimony as "embroidery" (Arendt 2006, 229). Their testimonies did not meet the classic, empirical standard of objective and verifiable truth, a standard in the tradition of historical and legal positivism that exalted historical reconstruction.

A new wave of scholars pushed back against this rationalist standard that they felt silenced the victim's voice. Noteworthy was the emergence in the 1990s of "deep-memory" theorists who championed attention to emotional expressions from the "inside", where they claimed to harvest authentic truths (Langer 1991; 1994, 79; Felman 2002; Hirsch and Spitzer 2009, 151–170). In *The Era of the Witness*, Annette Wieviorka criticized the over-attention to what she claimed were ahistorical emotions that decontextualized and deracinated the expressive emotions in survivors' accounts and robbed them of their historical immediacy. She argued for a resurrection of historical reconstruction as the legitimate alternative and best practice – history authorized by historians (Wieviorka 2006).

Our argument seeks to preserve the victim's voice but aspires to mine it for historical insight. Victims, who serve as witnesses to atrocity, disclose dimensions of persecution that empirical and schematic interpretations miss. These subjective dimensions, which valuably include the interpersonal and intercultural dynamics of persecution, are what Primo Levi termed the "unseen from the outside" (Levi 1988, 82). For Levi, the "unseen" was what he called the "gray zone" – in his iteration, the surprising convergence, and not only divergence, of "masters and servants" in the Lager where the oppressed pandered to the authorities for privilege (Levi 1988, 36–39). He observed new codes of behaviour that required "that you take care of yourself first of all" (Levi 1988, 78–79). The offer to help another inmate, he observed, simply didn't exist (Levi 1988, 78). This kind of conduct was not limited to time or place or party: All were implicated (Levi 1988, 86–87). Levi concluded that the obsessive behaviour abetted the summary collapse of moral order; his remarkable analysis also helps us to recognize the historical immediacy of victims' subjective negotiations.

Scholars have since come to recognize the historical disclosures of victims' accounts. Geoffrey Hartman noted "The psychological and emotional milieu of the struggle for survival" that factual, documentary evidence ignores (Hartman 1996, 142). Dominick LaCapra used this principle against Raul Hilberg's notorious critical assessment of Jewish Council members. Hilberg's evaluation of SS-appointed *Judenrat* leaders exemplified the compromised perspective of outsiders, LaCapra argued. Though the evidence indicates their responsibility for implementing Nazi orders often at the expense of fellow Jews, witnesses' testimonies assert another reality: they were implicated in a hopeless dilemma (Lacapra 1998, 100). (See for comparison (Davidson 1964, 191–194).) Omer Bartov argued that conventional documentation "distorts and ultimately falsifies the historical record". It is helpless, for example, to deal with the fog of hostilities, imposing on extraordinary chaos a tripartite victim–persecutor–bystander schema that failed to reflect actors' frequently indistinguishable roles: "The distinction between rescue and denunciation was often blurred and at times nonexistent, as was the distinction between perpetrators and victims" (Bartov 2013, 403). In one instance, a survivor recounted that a Ukrainian nationalist, who hid him and his mother, was responsible for killing Jews and Poles (Bartov 2013, 407). The enemy, he affirmed, was often once an ally: "I would say that 80 percent [of my family] were killed by the Ukrainians who were our friends" (Bartov 2013, 407).

In citing witnesses' accounts, Bartov refers to a crucial historical dynamic. The Ukrainian killing fields were spaces where Jews were historically in close contact with their ethnic Polish and Ukrainian neighbours. "While there were periods of strife – both domestic and with external forces – and although we should not idealize their relations, these groups knew only the reality of coexistence" (Bartov 2007, 116). Interaction was constant in schools, at marketplaces, in common spaces, and even in state and military service. The relative comity did not last into the twentieth century as Ukrainian nationalism and Soviet interference marginalized "foreigners", including ethnic Poles as well as Jews. But even as terror mounted in the 1930s interethnic relationships remained close, closer than the term "coexistence" suggests. Bartov is especially poignant when he investigated relationships in the severe climate of racial antagonism. Killing, he showed, often occurred among residents who had cared for each other; provocatively, it was "intimate". The parties in conflict, he asserted, knew each other well: As he documented, Jewish victims identified their assailants as their school friends and Christian neighbours before the war. One survivor, Alicia, told the story of her friend's father who became a Ukrainian police official. Before arresting her, she recalled, he said "he loved me like a daughter" (Bartov 2013, 406).

These accounts "from below" refer to an intercultural affliction in circumstances of intense conflict we will identify as the phenomenon of betrayal. As Wiesel reflected, "The further I go, the more I learn of the scope of the betrayal by the world of the living against the world of the dead" (Elie Wiesel 1982, 191). This is a reality often unseen that deserves our attention – it is a sovereign truth and a stark emotional reality of atrocity. "The cruelty of the enemy would have been incapable of breaking the prisoner", Wiesel continued. "It was the silence of those he believed to be his friends – cruelty more cowardly, more subtle – which broke his heart" (Elie Wiesel 1982, 189).

Narratives: retribution and resentment

Survivors' accounts are commonly distinguished by their commitment to bearing documentary witness: Survivor Jean Améry recriminated his assailants for their physical brutalization and its effect of overwhelming the victim and destroying life. This is typical of survivors' manifest narratives: They record and they condemn. So strong was his reaction to the torment and the terror that he wrote about wanting the "vile satisfaction" of punishing his enemy (Améry 1980, 69). What was important for him was to keep "a moral chasm … wide open" (Améry 1980). In this voice, his expression of anger was divisive leaning toward retaliation. Retribution, he said, was the reason for reissuing in 1977 the collection of essays he published as *At the Mind's Limits* a decade before.

At the other end of the spectrum, in an account dedicated to finding alternatives to retribution, Simon Wiesenthal's *The Sunflower*, published in 1969 as *Die Sonnenblume*, also evoked the victim's abjection: hunger, exhaustion, anxiety, the cruelty of SS officers in charge, forced hard labour, and ambient death. He, too, reviled the mistreatment: "I still clung to the belief that the world one day would revenge itself on those brutes" (Wiesenthal 1998, 35). Victims, he added, were helpless and "defenseless" (Wiesenthal 1998, 35). Damaged by "mental paralysis" (Wiesenthal 1998, 68) "fate" alone (Wiesenthal 1998, 13; 55) seemed to determine the outcome: The prisoner "had to learn to let himself be driven without a will of his own" (Wiesenthal 1998, 68).

Wiesenthal wrote boldly about his ghettoized ordeal: I lived from day to day, he wrote, "savoring hunger, exhaustion, anxiety for my family, humiliations … most of all humiliations" (Wiesenthal 1998, 9). In fact, it was "shocking humiliation" that demanded his attention (Wiesenthal 1998, 57). In recounting his return with other prisoners from a work detail, the observations he made of local citizens who were staring at them overshadowed his passing reference to the day's ruinous labour. He was appalled by what he believed was their brutal indifference: "Of what concern were we to them?" (Wiesenthal 1998, 56). Comparing this encounter with the infliction of persecution and grim privation, he asked, "Was it not just as wicked for people to look on quietly and without protest at human beings enduring such shocking humiliation? But in their eyes were we human beings at all?" (Wiesenthal 1998, 57).

Nested in this question is a presumption of a common, bedrock moral obligation. Expecting aid or assistance, instead he felt "alone" (Wiesenthal 1998, 22). Indifference and abandonment became increasingly salient in his personal life before the war when he was denied admission to the University of Lvov, then in Poland, where an infamous numerus clausus imposed a quota that limited the admission of Jews.

Wiesenthal wrote about an incident that occurred 30 years before he wrote *The Sunflower* at another local university in Lvov (in German, Lemberg) where he was working toward a Polish diploma. With depressing regularity, a number of students – the "'gilded youth' of Lemberg" (Wiesenthal 1998, 18) – brandished ribbons with the words "the day without the Jews". It wasn't so much the slander and its consequences that disturbed him, however, as the desertion by those whom he looked to for support. The school's Rector failed to call in the police. Other students, who, he observed, were in the vast majority, stood by out of "cowardice and laziness. The great mass of the students were unconcerned about the Jews or indeed about order and justice" (Wiesenthal 1998, 19). Those students, who caused the most disturbances and were eventually arrested, "emerged from prison as heroes" (Wiesenthal 1998, 19), martyrs "for their country's cause!" (Wiesenthal 1998, 20).

These episodes contributed to an erosion of his faith in the unspoken bond of social relationships. His world of normative expectations would no longer be the same: "I was consumed by a feeling that the world had conspired against us and our fate was accepted without a protest, without a trace of sympathy" (Wiesenthal 1998, 13), adding, vindictively, "I don't want their sympathy" (Wiesenthal 1998, 69). Améry referred to normative expectations as a "social contract" – "the certainty that by reason of written or unwritten social contracts the other person will spare me" (Améry 1980, 28). Their violations demanded his attention as well, remarking that the land and the people he called "our homeland" became a "racial disgrace" (Améry 1980, 50).

Notably in East Europe, where Jewish life before its collapse was characteristically interethnic and intercultural, betrayal is a prominent refrain against the grain of accounts bearing witness to lethality. In one vehement account written toward the end the war, Tadeusz Obręski wrote, while in hiding in Warsaw, about the misguided decision of the Polish government-in-exile to pay tribute to a victim of the Warsaw ghetto uprising.

> Why are they awarding a medal of honor to the dead, but refraining from helping the living? ... I have been following the behavior of the Polish population from the very beginning [and] this posthumous decoration arouses in me [only] feelings of contempt. Now the Polish government decides to raise its voice? Now, when no Jews are left? ... Where was it ... during the four and a half years of occupation? Why... didn't it order the Poles, back in 1939, to help Jews hide from the German murderers? Why did they keep silent? Why did they let, and why are they still letting, us be destroyed, here on the Aryan side?

The question, "Where was it?" – the leadership comprising his worthy compatriots – presumes that Obręski expected a better response than a useless medal. He believed that the government-in-exile possessed the potential to save Jewish lives but violated the promise by remaining silent.

> This is where the main crime of the [Polish] government and of Polish society stems from: this hostility [to Jews] and this complete indifference. All of Polish society helped exterminate Jews … The Polish people betrayed three and a half million Jews. This is a fact that will be discussed in [future] history.

Havi Ben Sasson, who unearthed Obręski's "Memories and Diary", is on point in her interpretation. For Polish Jews, there existed an "unbearable gap between the positive image they had created and the reality – as they experienced it – in the later years [of the war]. As high as their hopes had soared, so deep was the depth of their disappointment". As the war entered its third year, Jews began to see their neighbours as their primary persecutors. Polish Jews from that point on saw no reason to change again their view of their neighbours or their relationships with them. Their "shattered hopes and beliefs about Polish society during the Holocaust" would "shape [the] discourse" for years to come, perhaps, she wonders, up to the present moment (Ben-Sasson 2014, 9–12).

In a Hebrew edition of *Night* that he never published, Wiesel assailed the turncoat behaviour of his Hungarian neighbours: They all "stood at the entrances of their homes, with faces filled with happiness at the misfortune they saw in their friends of yesterday" (Eliezer Wiesel 2016). Lawrence Langer argued that comments like these, referring to the cruelty of indifference and betrayal, could hardly compare with evocations of "meaningless deaths" that represented the singularly authentic victims' voice. Indeed, he felt they were a puzzling distraction (Langer 1994, 133). But in Wiesel's expressions, like Obręski's, was a true assertion and, importantly, a valuable historical observation: the moral collapse of social trust and mutuality. A vital part of humanity, Wiesel lamented, died in the camps.

In his chronicle of degradation in Polish–Jewish relations written and preserved clandestinely in the Warsaw ghetto, Emanuel Ringelblum intoned in 1943 the new reality of chastening surprise. Before the war, when the occupying German authorities compelled Jews to register whatever possessions they did not already plunder, Jews made the decision to hand over their belongings to Polish Christians for safekeeping. As a measure of what he characterized as their reliance on their associates before the war, he added that Jews surrendered their valuables "on condition that the Jew should be a partner in the business". In characteristic understatement, he remarked, "It usually turned out very badly for the Jew". Ringelblum commented that Polish–Christians "had been decent and honest all their lives". There were even some "noble individuals" who refused any benefits from the transaction and who exhibited extraordinary courage in hiding Jews and who, moreover, "to this day are still saving the lives of Jews on the Aryan side". But he recognized that something seismic was taking place. Their number was small, he wrote: "As happens in war, baseness predominates."

The war "demoralized" people, though he permitted himself on occasion to use somewhat stronger terms: They "appropriated Jews' possessions unscrupulously" (Ringelblum 1974, 77–78),

Germans and Polish Christians were clearly culpable in his account, but the story's expressive features belonged to Polish Jews – to them, for sure, but also to the radical and remarkable subversion of their social relationships. Ringelblum preferred to observe events from a reflective distance, but he could hardly suppress his awakening to the new regime of betrayal.

An inscription in the memorial book for Jedwabne (sometimes transliterated as Yedwabne), written some 40 years after residents in this Polish village destroyed its Jewish community, mourned the conclusions drawn by community leaders, in the days leading up to the 1941 pogrom, after imploring a Catholic bishop for protection. The reporter recalled that he had warned family members about heedlessly trusting the bishop's pledge of intervention: "The Jews placed too much confidence in his promise [to help] and refused to listen to the constant warnings that came from friendly Gentile neighbors." Once again, we are reminded about the impossible dilemmas facing Jews at each turn, for whom were they to believe – the bishop or their friendly neighbours? Even though the story's details are in dispute, the recorded memory is a tableau of pathos. "We here in Yedwabne are safe", he recalled his own family members saying, "because the Bishop promised to protect us" (Gross 2002, 42).

It is tempting to regard betrayal as a constituent survivor narrative, a part of what every Holocaust survivor must have experienced. Indeed, as Tony Judt and Jan Grabowski, among other scholars, make clear, local collaboration with fascist authorities, including acts that exposed Jews in hiding or in flight, were endemic (Judt 2006, 803–31; Grabowski 2013).

Ancestral memories: betrayal

What explains the stories of betrayal that interrupted the manifest narratives of condemnation? If their hopes didn't soar, would betrayal have preoccupied survivors as a cruelty that finally broke their hearts? In counter-narratives that swerve away from manifest narratives of rupture, we see passages that hint at anterior expectations of intimate Jewish relationships with their Christian neighbours, attachments that survived experiences of exorbitant assault and lingered as lived memory in survivors' otherwise bitter accounts.

Wiesenthal's discussion of his famous encounter with a dying SS officer reveals the historical traces of longing for human connections. Woven into references to Karl's repugnant behaviour are offbeat expressions of "sympathy" for him (Wiesenthal 1998, 47, 87). We get this impression in the details of the account: Calling the officer by his first name (a pseudonym), he often referred to Karl's eyes, offhanded remarks that inflect a search for a deeper communication with him than mere interlocution. The importance of the search is especially poignant when we learn that Wiesenthal couldn't really see Karl's eyes; they were covered with bandages. Yet, "I had the feeling that he was staring at me" (Wiesenthal 1998, 29), adding inexplicably that his eyes "looked at me through small holes in the bandages" (Wiesenthal 1998, 78). Karl appeared capable of a human response even as he recalled his participation in his unit's slaughter of helpless Jews. As Wiesenthal wanted to relate, Karl could never forget the incident, "least of all" one child with "dark eyes" (Wiesenthal 1998, 43).

It is incredible that Wiesenthal would want to rescue Karl's humanity in a world he had come to resent for its inhumanity, but that is an apparent contradiction we need to explore. Whether or not he took liberties in telling the story, *The Sunflower* is at bottom an account that accommodated in the same text two distinctive views of humankind, one that looked back to a sinister period, the other that represents a foundation for the future: "Were we truly all made of the same stuff? If so, why were some murderers and other victims? Was there in fact any personal relationship between us, between the murderers and their victims?" (Wiesenthal 1998, 7). The violence that Wiesenthal endured was indelible and augured a world sundered by considerable transgression, and yet parallel undercurrents simultaneously resisted the triumph of malevolence. Leavening recrimination was a search for the "same stuff" that tethered strangers and enemies to a common bond.

What is the source of these surprising affirmations, these references to a common humanity? The answer resides at the heart of the modern Jewish experience: the post-emancipation aspiration to belong to mainstream society, to assimilate. Wiesenthal occasionally referred to Jews' historical attachments: "We adored the emperor and we were ardent patriots of the Austro-Hungarian Empire" (Segev 2010, 31). It is a sentiment expressed by poet Alfred Margul-Sperber, who lived in Czernowitz (now in western Ukraine): "Emancipated from the ghetto, Jewish youth sat at the feet of German teachers from the West and eagerly absorbed everything new, great, and beautiful that Western culture and civilization could procure for them" (Hirsch and Spitzer 2009, 93). For emancipated Jews, the allure of the West was irresistible. "Our fathers had crept out of the confines of the [premodern] ghetto into the open world", Wiesenthal remarked. "They had worked hard and done all they could to be recognized by their fellow creatures." High hopes collided with violent betrayal: "But it was all in vain" (Wiesenthal 1998, 70).

Améry devoted significant, counter-narrative space to the emotional social attachments he had cultivated. He recalled how much he once had in common with his neighbours: "I could not say today which of my acquaintances at that time was a Jew and which was not" (Améry 1980, 97). All, in fact, were German, which for many Jews had represented a moral community. For Améry, "memories of Alpine valleys and folk rituals" (Améry 1980, 84) was an evocation of fellow feeling. The desire of a Jew who "took such pains" to belong and who, by speaking and looking like Germans, believed he did – mutated as vivid and precious memories fuelling accounts of melancholy betrayal. But it also pointed to the future: "Mother tongue and native world grow with us, grow into us" (Améry 1980, 48). For him, "the simple summation of early experience" is what it means to be "Something": "Everyone must be who he was in the first years of his life, even if later these were buried under. No one can become what he cannot find in his memories" (Améry 1980, 84). Violence, alone – the province of manifest narratives – could not prevail as the legacy of mass destruction. For Améry there must be something else – indeed, to be "Something". Fellow feeling grew into him and he would continue to long for it no matter how eternally elusive it would be.

Améry's longing for a common humanity colonized his counter-narratives as dreams. He dreamt that the Nazi criminal would someday experience "the moral truth of his crimes" and would "once again become a fellow man" (Améry 1980, 70). Even the German revolution "would be made good" (Améry 1980, 78), he fancied in "an extravagant moral daydream I have abandoned myself to!" (Améry 1980, 79). Germans, "as I sometimes hope" (Améry 1980, 78) would seek to negate their acquiescence in the Third Reich, integrate it in their moral education, and come to eradicate criminal inclinations (Améry 1980, 78) – a "negation of the negation: a highly positive, a redeeming act" (Améry 1980, 79). He eventually reawakened to his senses: "Nothing of the sort will happen ... The German revolution? Germany will not make it good" (Améry 1980, 79). But there it is – a dream he could have erased but significantly delivered as a matter of public expression. Not only did he not silence the dream; he elaborated on it in two significant passages. He could no longer expect Germans to "become a fellow man", but he still reached out to them in a spirit of fellow feeling.

Recalling an encounter with the Gestapo just before his arrest in exile for his resistance activities, Améry clarified how "my homeland followed after me" (Améry 1980, 49). He and other members of his resistance group were meeting secretly in an apartment that felt safe to them even though German soldiers were living on the floor below. Disturbed one day by the noise they made, one of the Germans climbed the stairs and, entering the room, demanded quiet. Apologies apparently appeased him and he left, but the point of his story centred on the petitioner's manner of speech, a dialect he recognized from his native region. Even though he noticed that the soldier was an SS man whose task included arresting state enemies and deporting them to death camps, evocations of homeland eclipsed for the moment "fear and the control of reason": "There stirred within me the mad desire to answer him in his own dialect." He felt he actually knew him, and recognized feelings of "intimate cordiality". The "good comrade" whose mission was "to wipe me out" "appeared to me suddenly as a potential friend" (Améry 1980, 49). The suddenness is important, for it betrays the primal attraction of kinship, and it was spontaneity like this that ignited a glimmer of homeland fellowship (Améry 1980, 48). His German identification was, of course, imaginary. His "intellectual function", "the control of reason" that existed in his manifest narratives dismissed the national impulse as "abstractive" and risible. As dreams or wishes, however, they possess something deeply emotional and affective. In them inhabits lived experience fostering an orientation to worldly engagement. Engaging the world *après le déluge* would be nothing like the antediluvian world predicated on a social contract; he recognized that it was prone to internecine virulence. But the urge to belong remained vivid.

In another passage, Améry lamented his "pretentious nostalgia" for his homeland, but when he let his guard down, "relaxed by alcohol", he affectionately recalled "the mountains and rivers (*heimischen Bergen and Flüssen*) back home ... in tearful bliss ... [We] secretly wiped our eyes" (Améry 1980, 50–51; 2014, 97). Much as he tried "dismantling our past piece by piece" – he twice asserted the paramount value of emotional suppression (Améry 1980, 44, 61) – *Heimat,* a term connoting a deep, childhood sense of belonging, would have a lasting hold. (See Applegate 1990.) Home "still penetrates through the eye ... and is assimilated in a mental process we call remembering" (Améry 1980, 57). It was not only a matter of remembering; it appears he was still searching: "What we urgently wished, and were socially bound to hate, suddenly stood before us and demanding our longing" (Améry 1980, 51). Améry knew he couldn't go back; home would no longer mean belonging the same way. But his love of home, even if it were forbidden love, was still intense: "Now and then traditional homesickness (*Heimweh*) also welled up and claimed its place" (Améry 1980, 51; 2014, 98).

Survivors' lived experiences "from below" tell us a great deal about the ravages of atrocity. Their subjective expressions of betrayal offer a different and more nuanced understanding of violence than objective accounts of wholesale destruction. For many survivors, the violence they bear witness to in manifest narratives receives a second-person reconsideration in counter-narratives – examined memories of encounters with assailants who were their neighbours and compatriots. They surely dedicated their accounts to condemning criminality, but they also mourned the unexpected violations of a faith they had in mutual human obligations, a faith intensified historically by Jewish-ancestral, post-emancipation aspirations and expectations. Expressions of resentment, the emotion that responds to broken expectations, surfaced in accounts otherwise given over to primitive emotions responding to harm: retaliation and retribution. We observe narratives of betrayal in accounts as rancorous as Améry's and as sympathetic as Wiesenthal's.

What is particularly noteworthy in these betrayal narratives is their forward-looking orientation. This surprises us, since survivors' accounts, often characterized as memoirs, are strikingly backward-looking in witnessing the crimes they endured. But unlike references to revenge and inclinations to condemnation and prosecution, betrayal is a permeable and dynamic emotion. As Améry noted, it recalls antecedent relationships, or at least relationships Jews wished for and aspired to, that demanded "our longing". It recalled Wiesenthal's personal relationships anterior to their historical polarization into murderers and victims, making possible his discernment of, or more likely his search for, Karl's basic humanity. Retribution, in Améry's words, tends to keep "a moral chasm ... wide open". Resentment, on the other hand, evokes memories of intimate relationships or aspirations to belong and is open to possibilities of transforming an enemy into what Améry called "a potential friend". Both emotions – retribution and resentment – coexist in survivors' accounts. Recrimination of historical injustices oscillates with their re-evaluation and predilections toward negotiating successor relationships. Arendt and other historical and legal positivists dismissed the emotional truths of the unseen as mere sentiment or embroidery, yet these truths significantly possess insights that reorient our understanding of mass violence from static, objective conceptions of persecution to include transitional conceptions of betrayal and the prospects they inspire of the negotiated, post-atrocity society.

Note

1 This article is based on Dennis B. Klein's 2018 book, *Survivor Transitional Narratives of Nazi-Era Destruction: The Second Liberation* (Bloomsbury) and revised for the present volume.

References

Améry, Jean. *At the Mind's Limits: Contemplations by a Survivor on Auschwitz and Its Realities*. Bloomington: Indiana University Press, 1980.
Améry, Jean. *Jenseits von Schuld und Sühne: Bewältigungsversucheeines Überwältigten*. Stuttgart: Klett-Cotta, 2014.
Applegate, Celia. *A Nation of Provincials: The German Idea of Heimat*. Berkeley: University of California Press, 1990.
Arendt, Hannah. *Eichmann in Jerusalem: A Report on the Banality of Evil*. New York: Penguin Books, 2006.
Bartov, Omer. "Communal Genocide: Personal Accounts of Destruction of Buczacz, Eastern Galicia, 1941–1944." In *Shatterzone of Empires: Coexistence and Violence in the German, Habsburg, Russian and Ottoman Borderlands*, edited by Eric D. Weitz and Bartov Omer. Bloomington: Indiana University Press, 2013.
Bartov, Omer. "On Eastern Galicia's Past and Present." *Daedalus* 136 (2007), 115–118.
Ben-Sasson, Havi. *Polish-Jewish Relations During the Holocaust: A Changing Jewish Viewpoint.MS*, 2014.
Davidson, Basil. *The African Past*. Boston: Little, Brown, and Company, 1964.
Felman, Shoshana. *Juridical Unconscious: Trials and Traumas in the Twentieth Century*. Cambridge: Harvard University Press, 2002.
Grabowski, Jan. *Hunt for the Jews: Betrayal and Murder in German-Occupied Poland*. Bloomington, IN: Indiana University Press, 2013.
Gross, Jan T. *Neighbors: The Destruction of the Jewish Community of Jedwabne*. Poland, New York: Penguin Books, 2002.
Hartman, Geoffrey. *The Longest Shadow: In the Aftermath of the Holocaust*. Bloomington: Indiana University Press, 1996.
Hirsch, Marianne, and Leo Spitzer. "The Witness in the Archives." *Holocaust Studies/ Memory Studies* 2 (2009), 151–170.
Judt, Tony. *Postwar: A History of Europe Since 1945*. New York: Penguin Books, 2006.
Lacapra, Dominick. *Writing History, Writing Trauma*. Baltimore: Johns Hopkins Press, 1998.
Langer, Lawrence L. *Holocaust Testimonies: The Ruins of Memory*. New Haven: Yale University Press, 1991.
Langer, Lawrence L.. "Remembering Survival." In *Holocaust Remembrance: The Shapes of Memory*, edited by Geoffrey H. Hartman. Cambridge: Blackwell Publishers, 1994.
Levi, Primo. *The Drowned and the Saved*. New York: Summit Books, 1988.
Ringelblum, Emanuel. *Polish-Jewish Relations During the Second World War*. Jerusalem: Yad Vashem, 1974.
Segev, Tom. *Simon Wiesenthal: The Life and Legends*. New York: Doubleday, 2010.
Wiesel, Elie. *Legends of Our Time*. New York: Schocken Books, 1982.
Wiesel, Eliezer. *Ofer Aderet, Newly Unearthed Version of Elie Wiesel's Seminal Work Is a Scathing Indictment of God*, 2016. http://www.haaretz.com/jewish/news/.premium-1.717093.
Wiesenthal, Simon. *Sunflower: On the Possibilities and Limits of Forgiveness*. New York: Schocken Books, 1998.
Wieviorka, Annette. *The Era of the Witness*. Ithaca: Cornell University, 2006.

3 Holocaust survivors in Mexico

Intersecting and conflicting narratives of open doors, welcoming society and personal hardships

Daniela Gleizer and Yael Siman

Debórah Dwork and Robert Jan Van Pelt wrote about the need to bring the stories of Jewish refugees from the margins to the centre of Holocaust historiography more than a decade ago.[1] Since then, more space has been given to individual experience and memory, other social actors – beyond victims and perpetrators – have been incorporated, and geographical regions long unaddressed, such as Latin America, have been included. In a recent study, *Journeys from the Abyss*, however, Tony Kushner reminds us that most studies of Nazi Germany still focus on anti-Jewish policies and to a lesser degree on the victims and their destiny.[2]

Although there are many memoirs and literary works, the experiences of Holocaust survivors remain largely understudied. This is even more the case in Latin America, where little research has been conducted on the victims, their plight, and their social agency. Some studies examine specific cases or attempt to bring forth a comparative perspective, but they are still very few.[3] This article's objective is to analyse the experience of Holocaust survivors who immigrated to Mexico, placing at the centre the survivor and his/her testimony. Our study is based on oral history collections, memoirs, and archives.[4]

It is fundamental to consider that Latin America was not a marginal site of refuge during Nazism and the post-war period. It is estimated that between 1933 and 1943 close to 100,000 Jewish refugees immigrated to Latin America and the Caribbean.[5] Several studies have shown that Latin American governments adopted different attitudes towards Jewish refugees. This depended on their immigration policies, internal political situations, external pressures, antisemitism, the agency of local Jewish communities and less evident factors such as corruption. Although there were some similarities, the result was significant variations in the numbers of Jewish refugees and survivors: fewer than 2,000 Jewish refugees went to Mexico between 1933 and 1945 while only a few hundred in the post-war years.[6] This contrasts with the much higher numbers who went to Brazil (23,500) and Argentina (between 34,000 and 39,000), but also with the contribution made by smaller countries such as Bolivia or Chile, which during the same period accepted about 10,000 Jews escaping Nazism, respectively.

Mexico's closed doors to Jewish refugees and survivors

In April 1934, the Ministry of Interior circulated a confidential memorandum that prohibited the entry of Jews to Mexico. It sought to limit not only the immigration of Jews but also of all foreigners considered "non-assimilable" to the Mexican population who were seen as "undesirable". But there were two important differences in relation to other groups listed in this document: Jewish immigration was characterized as the most undesirable of all, even though the Jews were those with the most need for refuge.[7]

In a context of strong nationalism and mistrust towards foreigners, resulting from the long experience of external interventions in the country, the closing of borders to foreign immigration seemed to be coherent with the intention of post-revolutionary governments to protect national workers. Furthermore, it responded to racial conceptions. The government sought two goals: to preserve the homogeneity of the population, even if this resulted from miscegenation ("mestizaje"), and to "protect" Mexicans from foreign influences.[8]

It should be remembered that Mexico is not, and it has not been, a country of immigration. On the contrary, it has consistently pushed out a great proportion of its population to the United States. At the same time, however, Mexico has offered political asylum to several groups in different historical moments. The support by the Mexican government to the Spanish Republic during the Civil War, and the generous reception of Republican Spaniards since 1939, after their defeat, is noteworthy. Following Mexico's participation at the refugee conference in Evian in July 1938, and the position presented by Mexican diplomats at the League of Nations to condemn the invasions of weak countries by stronger ones (in particular, the *Anschluss*), applications for asylum to Mexico by Jewish refugees significantly increased.[9]

Nevertheless, the majority of the applications were denied. Furthermore, the ships that arrived at the port of Veracruz with small numbers of Jewish refugees who travelled with their own means were denied entry and returned to Europe: the case of the *Orinoco* (1938) generated the greatest number of protests internationally; but the *Quanza* (1940) got more attention because its passengers, not allowed to disembark, had received visas from the Minister of Mexico in Lisbon.[10] Mexico's immigration policy towards Jewish refugees was not planned from the outset, but rather adapted to circumstances. It took into account the level of international pressure, especially from the United States, which was actually not significant.

Several proposals were advanced in the 1930s so that Mexico would welcome a certain number of refugees, but they all failed. These proposals included projects of rural colonization, plans to rescue children, initiatives to improve unpopulated areas that required investments, as well as attempts to attract talented scientists and academics. Governmental approval was not achieved for any of them.[11] The strong opposition to welcome Jewish refugees by members of the Cárdenas government (1934-1940), the public opinion's xenophobic position, and the lack of external pressure ended any possibility of opening Mexico's doors.

It should be mentioned that the country's position towards political exiles was very different: the Mexican government was willing to allow entry of certain well-known international figures such as Leon Trotsky as well as anti-fascists, "combatants for freedom and democracy." In this case, it did not matter if they were Jews. It was a small (between 100 and 300) but notable group of exiled German-speaking people: Paul Merker, Ludwig Renn, Bodo Uhse, Anna Seghers, Bruno Frei, Alexander Abusch, Egon Erwin Kisch, Victor Serge, Leo Zuckermann, etc. The decision to open the doors to internationally recognized individuals played two roles. On the one hand, it reinforced the independent and sovereign character of the Mexican government vis-à-vis the United States, where the communists could not stay. On the other hand, it turned out to be very effective because it helped to build the international progressive image of Mexico, portraying it as a country of asylum. The leading cultural role of exiled individuals who continuously thanked Mexico for its solidarity in their publications contributed to consolidating the discourse of Mexico as a country of asylum.

As we mentioned earlier, during the Nazi period Mexico received fewer than 2,000 Jewish refugees. But even if only a small number of Jewish refugees were able to enter Mexico and thus did not constitute a critical mass, they represented an important percentage of the total number of local Jews. The Jewish community in the 1930s was formed by about 10,000 people and close to 18,000 by the 1940s. Thus, in relative terms, the number of Jews escaping or surviving Nazism was not negligible. Receiving and assisting this population required great efforts and State-like functions: negotiating with governmental agencies, including the Ministry of Interior, and with Jewish agencies abroad, paying the associated costs (of visas but also bribes), transporting the refugees from the port of Veracruz to Mexico City, giving them loans and advice as they looked for jobs, and hiring lawyers to help them normalize their migratory status.[12]

Most of the testimonies of survivors who immigrated to Mexico show that it was not only the institutions of the Jewish community that had a fundamental role in leading to the opening of doors for some refugees. Mexico's law allowed the entry of close relatives and thus the actions of uncles, aunts, brothers, sisters, cousins, friends, and acquaintances were central. To obtain the granting of entry to relatives and friends by the Immigration Department of the Ministry of Interior, they developed a series of strategies that included the submission of letters and documents, hiring legal representatives, identifying economic benefactors and relevant political contacts, and sending travel tickets and money. Given that authorization processes were very slow and visas expired six months later, they had to follow up and, in some cases, renew them because of the scarcity of transatlantic transport. When visas were finally granted and reached their recipients, family members and friends welcomed survivors in Mexico City's airport, train stations, or the port of Veracruz. Thus, these "immigration helpers" also became "hosts" providing housing, first meals, loans, access to education and support to find a job. In some cases, agencies collaborated; in others, family members acted independently.

The narrative of open doors

Mexico is known for being a country of open doors, a country of asylum. This narrative refers to an unquestionable historical reality, the country did open its doors to some groups of exiles: Spanish Republicans since 1939; a small number of German speaking anti-fascists in the 1940s and Argentineans and Chileans who escaped military dictatorships in their countries in the 1970s.[13] Based on these asylum experiences, the narrative of open doors consolidated and extended over time, and included the case of Jewish immigration and refuge, although this experience was completely different. Jews were racialized and purposefully excluded.

If we review the sources from that period, it is clear that in that moment Mexican authorities explicitly recognized that they followed different policies towards Spanish Republicans, German-speaking political exiles, and Jewish refugees. On this matter there is wide evidence.[14] But this clear distinction made by the government between "political" and "racial" refugees (as the latter were eventually called) together with the demonstration that racial refugees would not be welcomed, diluted over the years. At the same time, the memory of Mexico's position towards the Jewish refuge was also modified, to include the idea that they were welcomed.

When the war ended and the Holocaust was known about, countries tried to justify their "politically correct" behaviour. In this sense, in a message to the world, the Mexican government declared in 1945 that "it had always combatted racial discrimination" and that the international policy of Mexico had been based mainly on the equality of all men and races. Nevertheless, the most intense moments of this narrative reconfiguration occurred later.

The first instance of this took place in 1947, when the UN resolution to partition Palestine was voted and Mexico abstained. In the discourse through which the government justified its position, it declared, referring to the Holocaust, that it "had not only raised its voice in a timely manner against such barbaric procedure" but that it had also "opened its doors to millions of refugees, overcoming great economic and demographic difficulties that opposed, and continued to oppose a growing immigration".[15] It was fundamentally a discourse framed for an external audience given that Jewish immigration to Mexico was still prohibited, and many of the refugees who had tried to enter the country continued to be "conditional immigrants" without work permits and risking deportation. The Jewish Mexican community was the only one that felt offended with the government's discourse, but did not officially deny it.

The second moment was in 1975 when the Mexican government supported UN resolution 3379, which equated Zionism with racism. As a result, the Jews of the United States organized a touristic and economic boycott against Mexico that was severely criticized by the Mexican government. It conveyed to the Jewish community its lack of loyalty and reminded it of its "historic debt" towards the country for having provided asylum to Jewish refugees during Nazism.[16] Since then, there have been multiple references to Mexico's open doors towards the Jewish refuge by the Mexican government as well as by academics, journalists, historians, and the leaders of the Jewish community.

To understand why the Jewish community of Mexico did not deny the government's declaration we need to consider the way in which power was conducted by the Institutional Revolutionary Party (PRI) during several decades of authoritarianism (1929–2000).[17] It was very difficult to question the government and even more so by minority groups that, like the Jews, were trying to build a good relationship with the government to guarantee their safety.

In 1938 the *Comité Central Israelita de México* (Central Jewish Agency, CCIM) was founded to negotiate the entry of a certain number of refugees with the Mexican government. It then knew that attempts to support Jewish immigration had failed.[18] The closed doors were also experienced by families with relatives in Europe for whom they were unable to obtain visas. In many cases, this situation was felt as a personal failure, not the result of a State policy.[19]

Nevertheless, Zionism played a fundamental role in the downplaying of the issue of Jewish refugees. Given the big effort to mobilize the support of the Mexican government towards the creation of the State of Israel, complaints against the closed doors policy were put in a second place. The strategy was the opposite: to applaud the Mexican government's humanitarianism. But it was not only a Mexican phenomenon: in the Assembly of the World Jewish Congress in 1944 the issue of Jewish immigration to Latin America was not on the agenda. Moisés Glikowski, executive secretary of CCIM, criticized this omission, considering that it was intended not to hinder the goal to gain support for the creation of the state of Israel.[20] But in addition to politics, other factors help understand the absence of a collective memory in the Jewish Mexican community regarding the country's closed doors policy. The silence regarding the Holocaust that prevailed in the first years after the war might have also contributed to this inaccurate representation.

With the passing of time, the Holocaust was gradually remembered as a European phenomenon, disassociated from the country's position of "closed doors". Finally, the government's narrative and the discourse of the Jewish community converged: both recognized a reality that, even if non-existent, excluded some from guilt, legitimized the government's "politically correct" behaviour, and provoked acceptance among the Jews of Mexico, which was needed for their own process of integration to the country.

The testimonies

The group of testimonies analysed includes the experiences of refugees and survivors who immigrated to Mexico mostly in the second half of the 1940s and, to a lesser extent, in earlier years and subsequent decades. While the category of refugee generally refers to a particular legal and political condition, we use it interchangeable with "survivor" in the sense that both those who immigrated before the war and the creation of ghettos and camps, as well as those who came later, were potential victims of Nazism and its genocidal policies. However, when we use the term refugee we are aware of the specific temporality and context in which these individuals came to Mexico.

These testimonies show how difficult it was to obtain visas to Mexico, transit visas, and other required documents, as well as a place in the ship. They also speak to the strong impressions upon arrival to the port of Veracruz, and the cultural shock of finding completely different people. But they frequently express great gratitude to the country.

To understand the confluence of these two discourses of difficulties and gratitude, it is important to provide some context: first, the interviews only included those who were able to enter the country, not those who were rejected and thus could have told a very different story. Second, together with Mexican society, the Jewish community experienced significant economic growth, especially between the 1950s and 1970s, which gave them widespread opportunities for social mobility. Third, most interviews were conducted in the 1980s and 1990s when the moment of arrival to Mexico might have felt distant, but the experience of having had a peaceful life in Mexico was present. Finally, even if they faced difficulties to immigrate and adapt, Mexico represented a strong contrast with their previous Holocaust experience. Thus, testimonies refer to the country as a safe place, a refuge, a site of liberty and progress, all characteristics of the country at the time.

Immigration and arrival

Survivors came to Mexico from very different European villages, cities, and countries: Poland (in larger numbers), Germany, Hungary, Lithuania, France, Belgium, Italy, Romania, Greece, Austria and Yugoslavia. They also had very different Holocaust experiences: some fled Europe in the early years of Nazism, while others were sent to ghettos, forced labour, concentration camps and death camps (mainly Auschwitz). Some were hidden while others were rescued by Catholic families or nuns in convents; a few participated in resistance activities or were forced into death marches. In the post-war period, some were in DP camps or returned to their place of origin while others lived in other European countries, or left to Palestine, the United States or Latin American countries before settling in Mexico.

Reasons for escaping Europe depended on the moment of immigration and the political and social context. For Jews who left in the late 1930s and until 1942, Nazism and the outbreak of war were the main factors leading them to leave. After the war, it was very difficult for them to live in destroyed Jewish communities and cities where they did not envision a promising future. Some survivors also refer to antisemitism and communism as significant reasons to emigrate.

Survivors followed different paths to Mexico. Alberto Bejarano's family survived hiding in villages in rural Bulgaria but returned to the city of Varna after the war. A few years later his parents decided to emigrate, traveling to Paris and Bordeaux, and stopping in the Azores islands, Curaçao, Habana, and finally, the port of Veracruz. After surviving Auschwitz and Bergen Belsen, Miriam Stillmann did not return to her home in Transylvania. Instead, together with her sister Itsu, she left for Sweden with the aid of the International Red Cross. A few years after the war the two young women immigrated to Mexico to reunite with Bella, their older sister. Following his liberation in Günskirchen, Avraham Avigdor – born in Poland and a survivor of several camps – stayed in two different DP camps until he was able to board a ship to New York. Several years later, he went with his father to Mexico City.

Mexico did not generally appear as a preferred option, but rather as a non-expected destination. This is similar to the experiences of Jewish immigrants after 1924, who preferred the United States as their journey's end, but unable to immigrate there went to Mexico instead, and founded the present Jewish community in the country. Many communists, for instance, found a temporary refuge in the United States but could not stay because of their political affiliations; they were welcomed in Mexico, an act that could be seen as defiance to its northern neighbour. Other survivors remember how the US or Palestine were desired destinations but a visa from Mexico came first. For some of them, Mexico remained a temporary place in their journey to the United States. In contrast, some early refugees often regarded post-revolutionary Mexico as culturally and politically vibrant. For some left-wing refugees, the Cárdenas era was a continuation of the struggle that had begun in Europe ("For us Cárdenas was the best" – "Para nosotros Cárdenas era lo mejor"). In other cases, instrumental factors were considered as having a central weight in their decision to immigrate to Mexico: speaking Ladino and thus being able to learn Spanish easily, or having a Spanish (Republican) passport that allowed them to immigrate under the "Cárdenas Law".[21]

Almost all who immigrated to Mexico had a relative living in the country that applied for an entry visa, often with great effort, and paid related costs. A few arrived as political refugees thanks to the support from members of left-wing parties and networks. Without family or friends, or without the aid of a political group or a "good contact" in the government it was practically impossible to enter Mexico.

Difficulties to arrive and settle

While the discourse of gratitude is prevalent among survivors who went to Mexico, they also speak of several difficulties during their immigration and arrival process. Some remember that to enter Mexico one had to know "the President".[22] Many survivors describe that they had to visit Mexican consulates and embassies in Europe many times, although their visas were available from the onset. Others remember that they stayed a long time in a transit location waiting for their entry visa, although they had relatives in Mexico trying to help them. In a letter he wrote in Paris (1947) to his brother in Palestine, Bronislaw Zajbert's father said that he wanted to leave Poland and emigrate with his family to Mexico where his wife's brother lived. He thought their journey would begin very soon. Nevertheless, we know from Bronislaw's testimony that they left Paris a few months later and stayed in New York for three additional months. Their final destination was Venezuela, not Mexico. It is unclear why Bronislaw's uncle was unable to take his family to Mexico.[23]

Noemi Nickin, an orphaned little girl who was rescued from the Warsaw ghetto, arrived in Mexico about a year after her two uncles, Chijel and Abraham, who already lived in this country, submitted an official request to the Mexican government. On 6 September 1945, Chijel Nickin, the brother of Noemi's father, wrote a letter to the Minister of the Interior requesting the entry of his "orphaned niece of 12 years" who was living in Warsaw in a friend's home. It seems that in building her case it might have helped, or this was Noemi's uncles' thought, that both of them were Mexicans by naturalization, and that they had the capacity to become her economic benefactors. Such requirements were accompanied by humanitarian arguments and appeals addressed to the Minister of the Interior. Additionally, the language used, specifically the terms of affection ("little girl" – "niñita") showed an attempt to persuade and sensitize public functionaries. Anguish and despair might have been felt more acutely when official requirements could not be fulfilled (e.g. proving a direct family link between Noemi and her uncles in a context in which families had been annihilated and personal documents were destroyed).[24]

Bruno Schwebel tells how following his liberation from a concentration camp in 1940, his father Theodor wanted to escape France. "It became a priority to obtain visas, no matter for which country."[25] In their case, high hopes were put on the aid efforts by organizations such as The Jewish Labor Committee, The Emergency Rescue Committee, or the Centre Américain de Secours in Marseille. Bruno remembers several Americans who became potential sponsors in the United States. In May 1940, the American Consulate in Marseille granted the Schwebel family a visa to the United States but, unable to fulfil the required conditions, this offer was annulled. The only route left was emigration to Mexico. Congruent with the dominant national narrative, Bruno writes that the Mexican Embassy in Paris, under the supervision of Luis I. Rodríguez "granted a very large number of visas [July–December 1940] for Spanish Republicans and for many refugees of Central European origin, primarily Germans and Austrians, no matter what their religion". Nevertheless, his memoir also tells of the "frequent" visits of his father to Marseille and his stays for "a certain time" given the "countless required documents" that had to be obtained "in strict sequence".[26] While his family faced a "paper war", uncle Oskar's visa was denied. Families such as the Kurzweils were not secured a visa at all: they were arrested in 1942 and deported to several camps including Auschwitz. The fact that Bruno's family obtained a visa explains his gratitude to the Mexican consul in Marseille, expressed in his memoir's dedication to "Don Gilberto Bosques".

In a similar way, the German writer Anna Seghers, who obtained a Mexican visa in Marseille but faced the "paper wall"[27] explains, through the voice of Marie, the main character in her book *Transit*: "How could the consuls make a mistake? Not a detail is left out from your passport, not even a sentence in your file. If only one word were missing, they would prefer to retain here one hundred righteous before letting pass a mistaken one."[28] References to the difficulties to immigrate to Mexico can also be found largely in archival sources, particularly in the letters exchanged by exile organizations that sought to rescue their fellow members, such as the League for German Culture or the Society for Culture and Aid, in Mexico, and organizations based in the United States such as The Jewish Labor Committee, the Unitarian Service Committee or The League of American Writers.[29]

Those who arrived: mixed emotions

For those who were able to immigrate to Mexico, sites of departure, routes and means of transportation diversified after the war. Marseilles and Lisbon remained the main ports for leaving Europe and travel to Latin America until 1943 and after 1945, but in the post-war years survivors also travelled by air from London, Paris, or Stockholm to Panama or New York; and then by train to Monterrey or Mexico City. Ships were boarded at ports in France, Portugal, Italy, or Greece making several stops in Puerto Cabello, Venezuela, and La Habana, Cuba. Survivors travelled in cargo, commercial, or military ships: *Queen Elizabeth II, Serpa Pinto, Nyassa, St. Thome.*

Some knew only the geographical location of Mexico or fragments of its history because they had studied it in school,[30] or they had read about the country; some did not know even that. Remembering his trip from Lisbon to Veracruz on the *Nyassa*, Bruno Schwebel tells:

I had not the slightest idea what to expect … Notions of pistols, of horses and Indians with huge hats had captivated me, which was about the extent of what most Europeans with very little exposure to cultures on another continent knew. I remember my mother getting a letter from a … relative with a warning to watch out for Indians lurking in the jungle … [During the trip] all of us were moved by the announcement that we were coming so close to the United States, the country to which so many had wanted to emigrate. It was of great importance to all of us to see the port with what certainly would be magnificent installations. It was an ambivalent feeling to see but not be able to enter a longed-for and yet inaccessible land.[31]

First impressions of Mexico were ambivalent. Some emphasize the light, the sun, the transparent air, colours and smells, fruits, plants, the exuberance of Veracruz. Looking back at their arrival from a later moment in their lives, some survivors remember Mexico in idyllic terms: a "paradise"[32] or "first love". Some also talk of the country's "warm people" and "nice weather". For others, however, light blinded them and caused infections; they recall unbearable smells, and terrible dirt. The poverty of rural areas was astonishing and the walking without shoes, or with sandals ("huaraches") by the policemen gave them the sense that they had not arrived at a serious place. Probably these sensations of "otherness" slightly diminished in Mexico City, a cosmopolitan urban centre that by then had already almost two million inhabitants.

Upon arrival, Mexico was also experienced through its ports, train stations, neighbourhoods, public plazas, and hotels. The first impression of Mexico by Nitsa Revah Modiano, originally from Salonika, Greece, refers to the train station of Buena Vista (in Mexico City): "A change from sun to night … poor, Indians, beggars. Everything was grey" ("Cambio de sol a noche … pobres, indios, mendigos. Todo era gris").[33] Nitsa's brother, Freddy, shares his first memories of the "ugly" train station. However, other spaces of Mexico City are remembered in a positive light: through the main public plaza (the zocalo), Freddy remembers feeling a "sensation of liberty" (En México había una "sensación de libertad"). Luis Stillmann remembers the very cheap hotel ("hotel de paso") where he stayed the first night as "delightful" and "luxurious": it had a bathroom, a bed, and a telephone on the table.[34]

Arrival was difficult in relation to language. Indeed, the need to learn Spanish is the factor most frequently mentioned by survivors of the Holocaust in Mexico. Language was fundamental to communicate, relate, and exchange. It was easier for both children and Sephardic survivors who knew Ladino, or Romance languages such as Italian or French. Some survivors felt out of place given their clothes and accents. This created a sense of otherness (*extrañeza*)[35] and put them in a disadvantaged position as foreigners:

> In Mexico ... no one welcomes you in Veracruz, or in the station or at the airport with a silver plate (*charola de plata*), and tells you: since you are a foreigner, you are destined to be prosperous. These are lies. It is much harder for you. You need to learn the language, travel to work in public transportation, experience hunger and anxiety. At work, local Mexicans are afraid of you taking away their jobs. Only gradually you prosper.[36]

As we mentioned previously, families had a particularly important role in the rescue of refugees/survivors. Memories of families, however, are not homogenous. As immigration helpers they are generally represented in positive ways, but initial encounters and co-habitation were often difficult. Noemi Nickin (a hidden child during the Holocaust) and Bernardo Galek (an Auschwitz survivor) remember their families in Mexico as welcoming and supportive. First encounters with families at the main entry points are generally portrayed as "warm" and "emotional". But in some instances, survivors express disappointment given the lack of cultural understanding or personal empathy on the part of their host families. This was strongly felt by children or adolescents, although it was also present among adult survivors. Elena Zondowicz, a child survivor hidden with a Polish family, was finally brought to Mexico in 1950 by her (maternal) uncle, Mr Glezer. But Elena did not adapt well in her uncle's home. Thus, when returning from a short trip, she was forced to move out and live with her mother's brother. Although they treated her nicely, she still remembers having cultural differences with them. In her view, they were "too superficial". Other survivors refer to how their relatives made them work in their stores in downtown Mexico City while expecting their daily gratitude for providing them with housing and food; others worked with relatives without getting a salary, or were made to do housekeeping work, and felt uncomfortable in their homes. While some survivors talk openly about this, others purposefully don't mention their bitter memories, and instead emphasize their gratitude towards their hosts.

Mixed experiences may coexist within one individual's memories of arrival. Abraham Majzner was born in Krasnik, Poland, and survived the Holocaust in several concentration camps. After the war, Abraham returned home looking for any surviving relatives only to find out that they had all perished. He then decided to leave Poland. He tells in his testimony that while he had the "offer" of emigrating to Mexico, he preferred becoming a "jalutz" (pioneer) in Israel and help "build a State". He lived in a kibbutz, got married and had a child, staying in Israel from 1946 until 1957 when "difficult times" led him to finally immigrate to

Mexico. Aaron Gutfraind, his maternal uncle, helped with the formal request and submission of documents, but also with his later adaptation:

> He was already a settled man, he had money, he had a location where to place me, he brought us, he gave me a job, he helped us settle down … We arrived by plane, he sent us the documents … We arrived late, it was Passover, the uncle waited for us at the airport, he welcomed us after we were registered.

Nevertheless, Abraham also describes how uneasy it was to adapt to each other:

> living together was not easy when we arrived to his house. One comes to a new country, it is not easy with a child, without the language … one thing is the uncle from far away and a different thing is when we were in his house and with a small child … they were not used to it, it was hard.[37]

These stories contrast with totally positive remembrances of relatives and friends. The Revah family survived the war hidden near Athens. Shortly after the war ended, they decided to emigrate. They went to Mexico in 1946 with the help of Jack Benusillo, a close friend of their father. In their testimonies, the three survivors mention the kindness of this man. He received them at the train station, provided them with housing, and made them feel at home where beds were made, food was found in the refrigerator, bananas (a luxury in Greece) and flowers were set on the table.[38]

Isaac Kelerstein's story represents the painful situation of relatives in Mexico who survived the Holocaust but lost their family. His father emigrated to Mexico in 1936 due to a permission that was obtained on his behalf by his uncle, who had arrived earlier. The war made it impossible for the rest of the family to leave Europe, a large part of which perished in the Holocaust. Only Isaac and his brother Israel survived. The family's women died. Isaac remembers the re-encounter with his father: "Having just arrived, overwhelmed still by the tragedy that occurred, he told us: 'My children … help me.' We never saw him make a joke or smile again. He was also a victim of the Holocaust."[39]

Survivors gave priority to their recovering of "normality" thus postponing addressing their trauma. For some, their survival meant: "starting all over again". When arriving to Mexico, they also had other priorities and they were not necessarily understood by locals. Through their gradual insertion into the local Jewish community and adaptation to Mexican culture, survivors acquired a material base that helped them rehabilitate but only partially given that the recognition of their victimhood was delayed.

Most interviewees in Mexico say that they decided not to tell their stories either not to sadden their spouse or children, or in response to the community's imposed silence. Relatives also told survivors to repress their experiences to move on. Some spoke to their children but did so only in fragments and without details, while only a few say that they always felt they had the obligation to share. One survivor remembers that the warm welcome he received by his relatives in Mexico was followed by not asking him about his past. Even loving relatives were reluctant to listen.[40] Another survivor recalls the reunion in her cousin's home during her first night in Mexico. While having dinner her relatives told her "Forget everything that happened to you, new life … Who could I talk to if they did not let me talk?"[41] In her experience, this was an attitude more prevalent among adult Jews, and less so among the young. One woman felt shame for telling her friends she was a Holocaust survivor. "People saw it as something ugly. My middle school mates told me that it had not happened; that it was impossible for me to have survived, that I was telling silly stories (*tonterías*) … I then began silencing my past."[42]

Different scholars have shown that following liberation, survivors were "victims of a pervasive societal reaction" of "obtuseness, indifference, avoidance, repression and denial of their Holocaust experiences".[43] Whether survivors wanted or did not want to speak about their past, such communal and societal reactions guaranteed their silence and their feeling of frustration. This made it more difficult to mourn their massive losses.[44] Dori Laub reminds us that survivors do not find peace in silence, even when it is their choice.[45] By not telling their story, they turn into "victims of a distorted memory", and the more prolonged the silence, the greater the doubts regarding the veracity of the events thus affecting their self-perception. In extreme cases, "despite survivors' willingness and determination to get settled, their past came back to haunt them and undermine their great efforts".[46]

Throughout the years, survivors found some ways to partially address their trauma, either by marrying and having children, focusing one's mind on working long hours, receiving psychological assistance, doing volunteer work, meditating, or creating art, among other strategies. By marrying and having children, they sought to re-create life and challenge the legacies of Nazism, filling the void left by their lost relatives. Some survivors describe their therapeutic work as opening a window into a very deep "precipice" or as a way to unlock the memories that had been "swallowed". In this they found "liberation" and "relief".[47] It was only then that they began sharing their grief with others. Several decades later, journeys to their place of birth, or to sites of murder, helped them give closure to their pain. Collective responses by the Jewish community and Mexican society came many years after their immigration, through their inclusion in commemoration events, their interviewing for oral history projects, their visibility in museums, and the local support given to economic reparations and aid.

Many survivors arrived in Mexico stateless. For some of them, it took several years or decades to obtain their Mexican nationality. The reasons for not acquiring the citizenship vary significantly. But many survivors who permanently stayed in the country finally became Mexicans through naturalization, several years or even some decades later.

Conclusion

Incorporating survivors' testimonies in the historiography of Jewish immigration to Mexico during Nazism and in the post-war years allows us to have a better and deeper understanding of the experiences of those who were able to arrive. These testimonies narrate a more complex history than the one told by romanticized and idealized stories of immigration and arrival, adaptation, and integration that are at the core of the Mexican open doors policy myth. Indeed, survivors faced multiple difficulties to get to Mexico, adapt to a new landscape and host families, learn a new language, and become part of a society based on totally different cultural codes. This contrasts with long constructed and dominant narratives that not only framed Mexico as a country that opened its doors to refugees but also as a society that was particularly hospitable to newcomers. The mosaic of diverse experiences reveals an extraordinarily rich horizon that includes positive encounters and solidarity, surprise, and awe, as well as negative moments and emotions. In fact, some Jewish immigrants adopted Mexico as their new homeland while others failed to adapt, thus emigrating again to other places, mostly to the United States.

The testimonies analysed are framed by place and time. Many Holocaust survivors recall their experiences from later positions of professional and personal success, as integrated members of the Jewish community and citizens of Mexico. But even from a post-fact situation they refer with pain and emotion to the difficulties they initially faced as newcomers and victims/survivors. They adapted only gradually, a process that needs to be studied further. The interviews only include those who were able to immigrate and not those who were denied entry. This particular set of testimonies also involves a large group of survivors who chose to belong to the Jewish community, but not those who remained unaffiliated. Many of the interviewees were children or adolescents during the Holocaust, thus not knowing or remembering clearly the hardships endured by their parents to immigrate to Mexico.[48]

Although we do not refer to the issue of gender roles, it is interesting to consider that women, particularly professionals, had to face a Mexican traditional society with rigid gender norms. Women were housewives and mothers but were ill regarded and stigmatized if they worked. Many chose to do volunteer work in Jewish and non-Jewish organizations. Others did not adapt and looked for social relations outside the Jewish community or emigrated. A small number continued to conduct their professional careers or studied at the university adopting new roles.

The socio-economic means of survivors and their relatives together with ethnic Jewish and political networks, in the country and abroad, influenced the possibilities of Jewish immigrants to prosper. They were given loans to start workshops, trades, or businesses. Additionally, their Holocaust experience impacted their possibilities to build "normality" in daily life in profound ways. But more research is required to identify the particular ways in which age, gender, class, and the trauma of the Holocaust interacted to shape these different experiences.

The testimonies were not rendered in a "vacuum of memory". When the interviews were conducted, Mexico's discourse as a country of open doors was well established in the Mexican social imaginary, one that the Jewish community internalized and reproduced. It is well understood that survivors also adopted this narrative; ultimately, they were the ones who experienced these hardships. It is possible that the narrative of gratitude and love for Mexico resonated with this discourse, reinforcing it, while the most difficult episodes were only privately told to the interviewers. This was particularly evident during the interviews when many survivors had internalized the principle that "one should not criticize the government". When they had to tell conflictive stories that questioned the government, they requested the conversation to be off the record. Evidently, it was not something that was told publicly in comfortable ways. Neither was it easy to discuss hardships in their relatives' homes or workspaces, although some decided to open up.

Finally, we should consider the role of the discourse of acceptance and openness by the country to Jewish refugees and survivors in relation to their adaptation to Mexico. We believe that adopting this discourse vis-à-vis the one of closed doors must have had an instrumental function: it would be easier to integrate if they felt welcomed. This narrative crystallized as their memories became increasingly distant from their homes in Europe, their Holocaust experiences, and their immigration and arrival. We should also mention that, in general, survivors tell their histories of adaptation as happy endings. For most, Mexico was indeed the country that allowed them to recover normality expressed through work, studies, freedom of movement, making their own choices, falling in love, marrying, and having families. This is likely to have influenced the way they told their post-Holocaust life stories.

In the process of recreating "normal" life in Mexico, survivors showed great resilience. To some extent they reveal that they recovered a sense of dignity and agency, perhaps at the cost of a prolonged silence of their Holocaust experiences, whether resulting from external pressures or internal fears. This certainly might have also postponed addressing their traumatic memories. A recognition of their victimhood came many years later in very different global and national contexts.

Notes

1 Debórah Dwork and Robert Jan Van Pelt, *Flight from the Reich: Refugee Jews, 1933–1946* (New York: W. W. Norton & Company, 2009).
2 Tony Kushner, *Journeys from the Abyss: The Holocaust and Forced Migration from the 1880s to the Present* (Liverpool: Liverpool University Press, 2017).
3 On Mexico, *El Rostro de la Verdad: Testimonios de Sobrevivientes del Holocausto en México*, edited by Esther Shabot (Mexico: Memoria y Tolerancia, 2002); Vilia Mam Gmora, "Proyecto de Investigación sobre el Libro Testimonial de Sobrevivientes Judeo-Mexicanos durante el Holocausto" (M.A. Thesis), Mexico: Universidad del Claustro de Sor Juana, 2003. On comparative studies, see Lorena Avila, Nancy Nicholls, and Yael Siman, "Migration Narratives of Holocaust Survivors in Chile, Colombia and Mexico." In *Lessons and Legacies XIV: The Holocaust in the 21st Century: Relevance and Challenges in the Digital Age*, edited by Tim Cole and Simone Gigliotti (Evanston: Northwestern University Press, 2020).
4 We consider testimonies mainly from the Visual History Archive at University of Southern California-Shoah Foundation, as well as a smaller number from the Jewish Documentation Center in Mexico (CDIJUM). We also include some interviews conducted by us since 2017. While this group of testimonies reveals diversity in the profile of survivors, it is not a representative sample.
5 *Entre la aceptación y el rechazo. América Latina y los refugiados judíos del nazismo*, edited by Avraham Milgram (Jerusalem: Yad Vashem, 2003).
6 Haim Avni, "La guerra y las posibilidades de rescate." In *Entre la aceptación y el rechazo* 13–36; Judit Bokser Liwerant, "Cárdenas y los judíos: entre el exilio y la inmigración." In *Entre la aceptación y el rech*azo, 248–276; Judit Bokser Liwerant, Daniela Gleizer, and Yael Siman, "Conceptual and Methodological Clues for Approaching the Connections between Mexico and the Holocaust: Separate or Interconnected Histories?" *Contemporary Review of the Middle East*, no. 3 (2016): 279–315; Daniela Gleizer, *Unwelcome Exiles. Mexico and the Jewish Refugees from Nazism, 1933–1945* (Boston: Brill, 2014); *Entre la aceptación y el rechazo*, 2003 (There are no precise estimates for the number of survivors who came to Mexico in the postwar period. Our research shows only a few hundred).

7 Archivo Histórico del Instituto Nacional de Migración (AHINM), file 4-350-2-1933-54, Confidential Circular n° 157, April 27, 1934.
8 The Director of the Mexican Society of Eugenics had declared, for example, that "Not all races [can] mix compatibly; from the biological or social point of view not all can fuse into a desirable mixture; there are families who degenerate with mixing or cross-breeding, while others improve". Alfredo M. Saavedra, *Eugensia y Medicina Social*, 119, quoted in Alexandra Stern, "Mestizofilia, biotipología y eugenesia en el México posrevolucionario: hacia una historia de la ciencia y el Estado, 1920–1960." *Relaciones XXI*, no. 81 (2000): 57–92, 67.
9 See Gleizer, *Unwelcome Exiles*, 2014.
10 Gleizer, *Unwelcome Exiles*, 2014, 112–116 and 182–189.
11 The only exception was a project to rescue children of parents in internment camps in France, but it took so much time to be approved that by then there were no Jews to be rescued anymore. Gleizer, *Unwelcome Exiles*, 2014, 211–213.
12 Gleizer, *Unwelcome Exiles*, 2014.
13 Pablo Yankelevich, *México país refugio. La experiencia de los exilios en el siglo XX* (Mexico: INAH-Plaza y Valdés, 2002); Clara Lida, *Inmigración y exilio. Reflexiones sobre el caso español* (Mexico: Siglo XXI Editores – El Colegio de México, 1997); José Antonio Matesanz, *Las raíces del exilio. México ante la guerra civil española 1936–1939* (Mexico: El Colegio de México-UNAM, 1999).
14 For instance, Ignacio García Téllez, the Minister of Interior in the government of Lázaro Cárdenas, declared in 1938 that the country would only accept persecuted immigrants considered "prominent fighters for social progress, valiant defenders of Republican institutions, or select expositors of science and the arts […] being careful, on the other hand, that disorganized or fraudulent immigrations, which were a danger as a social burden or competition that would displace our working classes, were not allowed in." Gleizer, *Unwanted Exiles*, 2014, 88.
15 Rafael De la Colina, "Declaración de abstención en torno al problema de Palestina", in *Rafael de la Colina, Sesenta años de labor diplomática* (Mexico: Secretaría de Relaciones Exteriores, 1981), 192.
16 Judit Bokser, "Fuentes de legitimación de la presencia judía en México: el voto positivo de México a la ecuación sionismo-racismo." *Judaica Latinoamericana*, III (1997): 319–349, 339; Ariela Katz, "El boicot turístico a México. Controversias político-diplomáticas a raíz del voto mexicano en la Resolución 3379 de la ONU." *Historia Mexicana*, LXVI, no. 2 (2016).
17 An illustrative example is the situation of Mexico's vote in favor of UN resolution 3379 in 1975, and the late cautionary response of the Jewish community which justified it by saying that the leadership wanted to prevent a critique of the government that could be interpreted as interfering with the political situation. See Katz, "El boicot turístico", 2016. It is important to consider that foreigners face, and still do, a prohibition to participate and even providing an opinion on domestic political issues of the country, while Mexican can do so. By then, the majority of the Jewish community had been born in Mexico, or had naturalized, but the notion of foreignness was still prevalent.
18 In 1939, CCIM considered that in Mexico there was almost no problem with Jewish refugees because they were not allowed in. Proceedings of the CCIM, September 5, 1939. Quoted in Daniela Gleizer, "Recordar lo que no pasó: memoria y 'usos del olvido' en torno a la recepción de refugiados judíos del nazismo en México." *Revista de Indias*, no. 72 (2012): 465–494, 478.
19 Given the widespread corruption, and that great amounts of money opened many rescue possibilities, there were some who felt guilt throughout their life for not having had enough money to rescue their loved ones.
20 Letter from Moises Glikowski to the CCIM, 29 February 1944. Quoted in Gleizer, "Recordar lo que no pasó", 2012, 484.
21 Cárdenas's government facilitated the immigration of Spanish refugees, and also of those recognized by the Spanish government as Spaniards because of their

participation in the civil war, particularly in the International Brigades. Spanish refugees did not require visa; when they arrived, they were allowed to work, and naturalization was easier.

22 Elena Zondowicz. Visual History Archive (VHA). 25 October 1996. Mexico City.
23 Bronislaw Zajbert. VHA. 20 March 1996, Mexico City. We have conducted several interviews with B. Zajbert between 2017 and 2019 in Mexico City.
24 Noemi Nickin. VHA. 4 October 1996, Mexico City. Also, 27 October 2017. Mexico City.
25 Bruno Schwebel, *As Luck Would Have It. My Exile in France and Mexico. Recollections and Stories* (Riverside, CA: Ariadne Press, 2004), 82.
26 Schwebel, *As Luck Would Have It*, 83.
27 Her real name was Netty Reily de Radvanyi, but the visa came out with her pseudonym Anna Seghers, and as such, it did not include her husband, Laszlo Radvanyi, and their two sons. She had to wait in Marseille in a very difficult situation for several months until the Ministry of Interior sent her a visa with her name. Daniela Gleizer, "Gilberto Bosques y el consulado de México en Marsella. La burocracia en tiempos de guerra (1940–1942)." *Estudios de Historia Moderna y Contemporánea de México*, no. 49 (2005): 54–76, 64.
28 Seghers, *Transit*, 2005, 195. Quoted in Gleizer, "Gilberto Bosques", 2005, 64.
29 Gleizer, *Unwelcome Exiles*, 2014; Gleizer, "Gilberto Bosques", 2005.
30 Interview with Ruth Goldstein. 10 November 1987. Mexico City. Oral History Archive, Centro Documentación e Investigación Judío de México (CDIJUM). Bokser Liwerant, Gleizer, and Siman, "Conceptual and Methodological Clues", 2016; Daniela Gleizer, "Recordar lo que no pasó", 2012.
31 Schwebel, *As Luck Would Have It*, 2004, 101–103.
32 Salvador Gilbert. VHA. 1 May 1996, Mexico City.
33 Nitsa Modiano. VHA. 5 March 1997, Mexico City.
34 Luis Stillmann. VHA. 29 January 1996, New York.
35 Alberto Bejarano. VHA. 24 November 1997, Mexico City.
36 Julio Botton. VHA. 13 November 1998, Mexico City.
37 Abraham Majzner. VHA. 3 November 1997, Mexico City.
38 Freddy Revah. VHA. 15 May 1997, Mexico City; Nitsa Modiano, *Op. Cit.*; Lilette Rubinstein. VHA. 5 November 1998. Mexico City.
39 Isaac Kelerstein, *Cuando el sol se avergonzaba* (Mexico: n.p., 1994).
40 Max Daniel. VHA. 6 February 1997, Mexico City.
41 Ida Benadon. VHA. 23 July 1996, Mexico City.
42 Dolly Hirsch. VHA. 29 April 1998, Mexico City.
43 Tom Segev, "Zion's Ambivalence", In *How Was It Possible? A Holocaust Reader*, edited by Peter Hayes (Lincoln & London: University of Nebraska Press, 2015), 775–788; Adara Goldberg, *Holocaust Survivors in Canada: Exclusion, Inclusion, Transformation, 1947–1955* (Manitoba: University of Manitoba Press, 2015).
44 Yael Danieli, "Essential Elements of Healing After Massive Trauma: Complex Needs Voiced by Victims/Survivors." In *Handbook of Restorative Justice*, edited by Dennis Sullivan and Larry Tifft (London & New York: Routledge, 2008), 343–354.
45 Dori Laub, "Truth and Testimony: The Process and the Struggle." In *Trauma: Explorations in Memory*, edited by Cathy Caruth (Baltimore: John Hopkins University Press, 1995), 61–75.
46 Beth Cohen, "America's Incomprehension" In *How Was It Possible? A Holocaust Reader*, edited by Peter Hayes (Lincoln & London: University of Nebraska Press, 2015), 790–798.
47 Andrés Bogati. VHA. 13 March 1997, Mexico City.
48 In the Visual History Archive's testimonies, the percentage of time devoted to the immigration journey and arrival to Mexico is often limited.

4 Historical narratives, the perpetuation of trauma, and the work of Vamık Volkan

Reuven Firestone

The subject of conflicting historical narratives is not merely a topic of academic interest. Competing narratives between communities can and do cause mass violence of great and abiding horror. A classic example is the Srebrenica genocide in which Serbs "saw fourteenth-century Ottomans" when they engaged in the mass slaughter of twentieth-century Bosnian Slavs. At some very deep level, Serbs involved in the massacres were engaging in vengeful retribution for the loss of the Serbian kingdom to Ottoman Muslims at the Battle of Kosovo 500 years earlier. One scholar treating the dangers associated with historical narrative and communal trauma is Dr Vamık Volkan, who studied the ways in which national or community trauma can be eternalized and maintained through the preservation of particularist narratives for generations in latent state, only to erupt into mass violence when conditions are ripe. The experience of communal trauma can be maintained and perpetuated through commemorative rituals and the formulation of particular types of historical narrative. But it need not be. This paper will analyse the work of Volkan in order to consider four aspects of the phenomenon:

1. The ways in which communal trauma can influence historical perspective and encourage the formulation of highly problematic communal narratives.
2. The ways in which communal trauma is preserved and perpetuated in the memory of victimized communities through historical narrative and commemorative practice.
3. The ways in which the memory of communal trauma can then be activated to motivate mass violence against innocent victims.
4. The ways in which unresolved anxiety and tension brought about by communal trauma preserved by historical narrative can (a) be perpetuated and later discharged through violence, or alternatively (b) be reduced and even relieved through constructive processes that thwart the release of violence.

When children get into a schoolyard fight, they always seem to offer the same excuse: "He hit me first!" It seems obvious that one child began swinging before the other. Is it simply childhood invention that we are observing in these blame-the-other scenarios, or may there be something deeper behind the inevitable contradictory claim?

Let's consider a typical playground battle between two children. One of them certainly swung the first punch. Let's call the puncher Child A. But perhaps Child B pushed Child A before he began swinging, and perhaps Child A called Child B names or purloined his lunch before Child B pushed him. And that behaviour too, may have been triggered by something else that Child B did to Child A the day before. One question of interest when trying to determine "who started it" is, how far back into history can one (or *should* one) go when probing the origin of a conflict. This is a major issue when considering the problem of conflicting narratives. How far back must one go in the search for truth?

It is also possible that Child A did nothing intentionally to provoke Child B. He may have done nothing "wrong" according to his personal playbook of behaviours. Nevertheless, it could be perceived as an injustice by Child B.

Who is guilty of starting the conflict? Who is guilty of escalating it?

These are natural questions and are quite reasonable. But of greater importance for this conference even in relation to a childish schoolyard fight, and in fact for all cases of violence, is the deeper background. What in an individual's history might trigger, sanction, enable or even encourage recourse to violence in settling a perceived hurt or injustice? Mistreatment from an abusive parent can trigger a response in a child that directs violence outward onto another. Many other possible triggers can prompt acts of violence.

A corollary exists between individual and communal violence, and this observation has triggered various social scientists to look into it in the past few decades. One researcher, Vamık Volkan, has applied psychoanalytic theory to mass violence undertaken by large groups.[1] I use Volkan's term "large group violence" rather than "mass violence" because I am concerned with issues of large group identity that are associated with the release of violence by large groups. In what follows I will consider the work of Volkan in relation to communal perceptions of grievance, victimization, and humiliation that are often at the core of large groups' recourse to engage in mass violence.

I will not try to determine whether any side is "at fault" as I did in my brief example of the playground incident. It is, of course, possible that one side is entirely victimized. Two examples immediately come to mind from my personal frame of reference: the genocide of Jews and the genocide of Sinti and Roma peoples in mid-twentieth-century Europe. I know that one could cite other such cases of innocence, and I have no intention to exclude them. But for the purpose of this chapter, I am not concerned with the determination of guilt or innocence. I am, rather, interested in considering how communities that have suffered trauma and depredation can absorb the pain and humiliation of suffering and retain them for generations, only to release them onto another community (or communities) in a way that not only can cause horrific harm but can move forward the cycle of violence without resolution in a manner that will cause even more suffering as history unfolds. I am also interested in examining methods that may remove or at least reduce the sense of suffering, humiliation, and grievance of a victimized community to a manageable level that can avoid or even put an end to the perpetuation of violence.

Large-group identity and historical narrative

As noted above, one of the pioneers in this endeavour is Vamık Volkan. Through his Center for the Study of Mind and Human Interaction (CSMHI), he and the Center staff have applied theoretical and field-tested knowledge to violent ethnic, racial, and religious conflicts in the Baltic Republics, Former Yugoslavia, Central Asia, Turkey and Greece, and elsewhere. Eighty-eight years old at the time of this writing, Volkan has written dozens of books and many more articles on his findings.[2] These are immensely helpful in suggesting some of the reasons why communities can engage in what would appear to any outsider as senseless and irrational acts of violence. They treat why and how large group violence occurs, how tensions can fester among large groups for generations and even centuries, how that tension can be released in horrific violence, and what can be done to help communities heal in such a way that they will not feel the need to vent their rage violently against innocent victims. He establishes his argument by citing dozens of his and his centre's experiences working with communities engaged in violent conflict.

Volkan does not often use the term "historical narrative" in his work, but he works with the same issues when he treats a large-group's dedication to what he terms "chosen trauma" and "chosen glories".[3] These are core aspects of a group's constructed historical narrative, which are often at odds with the historical narratives of neighbouring communities. In fact, one community's "chosen trauma" may be another's "chosen glory". A most obvious case in point would be the Israelis' *Yom Ha`atzma'ut* ("Independence Day"), which coincides exactly with Palestinians' "Nakba Day" or *Yawm al-Nakba* – the "Day of Disaster" that marks the trauma of Palestinian victimhood and displacement with the establishment of the modern State of Israel in 1948.[4]

What we are considering here is large-group identity-related conflicts. The pivots of large-group identity can be ethnic, religious, national, or ideological.[5] It is not any particular aspect of national culture that promotes large-group violence. Neither is it some feature of a particular ethnicity or religion (or of religion in general). It is, rather, the notion of *distinction* between in-group and out-group, and the particular *manner* in which the large group responds to its own collective pain, triumph, and trauma. Most communities experience collective pain and trauma sometime in their history. In many cases, they are able to heal from it. When they are not able to heal, however, the collective pain can be directed outward and released through mass violence against absolutely innocent victims.

At the root of many group conflicts are what Volkan calls "bloodlines", a form of identity distinction that establishes a kind of impassable border in times of crisis.[6] Yet these bloodlines are not biological or genetic. They are, rather, deeply held convictions of difference. Whether large groups are identified by religion, ethnicity, nation, or ideology, they tend to believe that they hold a set of features in common that are unique, a defining aspect that is not shared by others with whom they are in contact.

Volkan refers to the relationship between an individual and the group with which the individual identifies through an analogy of protective clothing. Every individual has two layers of clothing. The first fits snugly. This is one's personal identity. The second layer is an ethnic or religious layer that binds the individual to a large group. That second layer is a loose covering that protects the individual in the way that a parent, close family member or other caregiver protects a member of the family. "Because this garment is not formfitting, it also shelters other members of the group and resembles, in a sense, a large canvas tent."[7] Volkan goes on to describe the leader of the community as the "tent pole" that holds the tent erect and the community together under his leadership and protection.

What Volkan does not note in his schema is that individuals usually fit into a number of different "tents" determined by religion, region, dialect, culture, age, gender, etc. One can belong to different groups and overlap with many different people by sharing particular perceived commonalities. For example, individuals identifying with different religions or races can be a part of the same "national tent", or individuals identifying with different ethnicities or language communities can be a part of the same "religious tent", etc. In the cosmopolitan world we inhabit today, all of us who live anywhere but in a completely isolated village travel in our "individualness" between multiple variations of "tentedness", and these overlapping tents (or identities) allow us to live in multi-cultural, multi-religious, and multi-ethnic communities.

Large-group identity in times of stress

Under certain conditions, this flexibility between multiple identities can become static. Times of stress can encourage regression to a single tent of identity. This is especially true when anxiety or trauma causes individuals who once felt an aspect of shared identity with a variety of groups to regress to a single identity tent in which they can feel more secure because they feel that they are surrounded by the protective shelter of a single, secure community. This kind of regression can be encouraged by certain types of tent-pole leaders who identify other community tents as threatening and dangerous. Those now dangerous and foreboding tents may have once been shared by the individuals who have since regressed into their single, large-group tents of opposition.

Under certain conditions, such groups who have been neighbours for generations may appear to have suddenly transformed into merciless enemies.[8] Individual ethical values can then be entirely jettisoned and give way to a collective will in response to the commands of a charismatic leader under a defensive single-identity tent. A classic example of how this can occur is the case of the former Yugoslavia.

In the former Yugoslavia, Serbs, Croats, and Bosnians were large groups within a nation that shared the same language (with some dialectical differences), the same ethnic attributes, and the same basic migratory history. Shared language, ethnicity, and history are often cited as unifying factors in the formation of national identities. Yet the three groups, nevertheless, hold major differences in large-group narrative that have come to be defined in terms of religious difference. Serbs are overwhelmingly Orthodox Christians, Croats are chiefly Catholic, and Bosnians are mostly Muslim. In fact, the actual religious and theological differences between Orthodox Christians and Catholic Christians are relatively minor, and significantly less important than the difference between Christians and Jews and Muslims or even Catholics (or Orthodox Christians) and Protestants. Orthodox and Catholic Christians were a single religious community for over a thousand years, yet the perceived differences between them can become points of intense contention that, in the 1990s as during other periods of history, tolerated a level of "othering" that allowed for horrific mass-violence.[9]

Large-group identities are, in the final analysis, constructed identities. Benedict Anderson has shown how national identities are constructed under conditions of need, when groups organize around certain perceived traits that may be centred on regional issues or even dialect.[10] Often, the actual centralizing point of group identity is "not them". Any number of constructed differences can be used to define borders between groups.

One of the earliest well-known cases is that which produced the "shibboleth" phenomenon in the Hebrew Bible (Old Testament). The Book of Judges (chapter 12) records a large-group conflict between two communities of ancient Israelites, those from the tribe of Ephraim, and those from the Gilead, a region situated south of the Ephraimites. The conflict became a bloody battle, which the Gileadites won under the leadership of a powerful tribal chieftain named Jephthah. The two communities were both Israelite groups that belonged to the same religious community and shared a common language, communal history of redemption from Egyptian slavery, shared covenantal relationship with God, and so forth. There was, however, one small linguistic distinction that was highlighted in a bloody and horrific way. When survivors among the defeated Ephraimites tried to cross fords of the Jordan River controlled by the Gileadites, the latter required them to pronounce the word, *shibboleth*. The Ephraimites had a distinctive way to pronounce it, not as *shibboleth*, but with a sound that resembled more of an "s", as in *sibboleth*. That slight pronunciation difference was enough to identify them as Ephraimites, so when they said *sibboleth* they essentially pronounced their own death sentence. Similar tests have been carried out between communities in more recent history in which dialectical differences or even accents have been used to distinguish members of particular out-groups, identifying them as "enemy", with parallel gruesome results.[11]

Human communities constantly define themselves as *different* (and therefore, ultimately, *better*) than other human communities. This appears to be a common and a natural phenomenon of human nature. In fact, this trait fuels a huge, multi-billion-dollar international sports industry through which people identify with sports teams – an obviously constructed identity – that battle against other sports teams. In the case of sports, the battles are symbolic and controlled in a manner that prevents most injuries – and certainly many fewer than would occur if the teams were squads of warriors setting out to capture territory for permanent possession rather than goals for a trophy.

The distinction between in-group and out-group in human communities has often been defined as "human" versus "non-human", and, in fact, the distinction may have even originated when Homo sapiens and Neanderthals or other competing humanoid species existed simultaneously in pre-history. The distinction between one's own group, which is human, and other groups, which are non-human or subhuman, is sometimes called *pseudospeciation*.[12] An attempt to define opposing human groups as subhuman is a move that can lead to violence because it removes the community from the most basic and universal "tent" of humanness.

Community loss and community mourning

One of Volkan's primary emphases is that large groups may experience trauma in ways that are similar to the experience of individuals. This is part of his view of layered identity in which individuals have, as it were, two layers of clothing: one personal, the other communal. Just as individuals mourn loss, so do large groups.

When an individual mourns the loss of a loved-one, the mourning process heals the grieving person as it advances in stages. The first stage is crisis grief, which occurs in the immediate aftermath of loss. "It includes shock, denial, bargaining, and the sadness and pain of losing access to the deceased. Feeling anger in the first stage is important ... This anger is often displaced and directed toward others – relatives, for example, or a physician who treated the deceased person. Anger marks the realization that what is lost will never come back."[13]

The second stage, sometimes called "the work of mourning", is a time when the mourner adapts to the change in his/her reality. The mourner engages in an internal review of memories along with their accompanying feelings. This period also includes painful feelings, but when it develops properly it is accompanied by a gradual acceptance of loss as the mourner "convert[s] the relationship with the dead person into a memory that no longer eclipses other thoughts". This is part of a process "like the healing of a wound: it takes time and it occurs gradually ... If there are complications during any of the stages of the mourning process, they may prevent adaptive resolution of the loss".[14]

If proper mourning does not occur, a person can become a "perennial mourner". Perennial mourners cannot move away successfully from the loss. They continue to live, as it were, in the world of the dead.[15] They may have silent conversations with the dead person long after they are gone. Mourners may have "linking objects" that serve to connect the mourner with the dead. A linking object is something that becomes symbolic of the person or thing that is lost. It could be a personal item of the dead person, or perhaps a photograph of the lost individual. Linking objects can interfere with the mourning process by focusing one's emotional attention on the object in a manner that does not allow for the mourner to come to terms with the finality of loss. Certain kinds of attachment to the linking object can make the mourner into a perennial mourner. In some cases, however, linking objects can help a mourner move through the mourning process in positive fashion.[16] A grave can be a positive linking object because it can enable a mourner to review the connection and love for the dead person while also reminding the mourner that the deceased is truly gone. The grave stone marks where the remains of the dead person lie. But a grave can be a negative linking object if the mourner cannot get beyond the loss and returns obsessively to the graveside. In this case, obsessive attachment to the grave keeps the mourner from completing the process.

Or more accurately, the mourner uses the grave as a means of holding on because of their inability to work through the mourning process.

As with individuals, large groups also mourn losses that they experience as a community.[17] The loss can be caused by a natural or a human-caused disaster, for example. The unexpected killing of national heroes such as Mahatma Gandhi, John F. Kennedy, and Martin Luther King caused trauma in national communities that required community mourning in order to heal. The Vietnam War is another national trauma that, for many Americans, required mourning for fellow citizens. Successful mourning in these situations can take place through engagement in large-group rituals and anniversaries that are repeated over time with decreasing intensity. When a national hero dies of natural causes, the mourning is easier than if the hero is assassinated.

Sometimes a national failure requires mourning. The Vietnam War is one example, and ambivalence about the war among the American public hindered full mourning from taking place, leaving many individuals and parts of the American public in a state of incomplete mourning. The construction of the Vietnam War Memorial in 1982 is one example of a linking object that assisted the large group in mourning, helping the American public to move beyond the grief and humiliation associated with the war.[18]

Severe calamities suffered by a large group can arouse extensive feelings of helplessness and a general breakdown of community. When severe calamities occur from natural disasters such as a typhoon or earthquake, or human failure in a dam-break or a nuclear plant such as at Chernobyl, there is often great suffering and loss. Particularly in the case of human failure, that loss may be accompanied by anger against those who are perceived as being responsible for the loss. In such cases, mourning may take some time, but it can generally play itself out in a manner that brings eventual healing, even if after some years.

In the case of a severe calamity caused by another group of people, however – that is, by an enemy – the suffering, loss and anger is often accompanied by humiliation and the loss of human dignity. These kinds of severe calamities can remain unhealed and can fester for generations and even centuries.[19] One example cited by Volkan is the suffering of the Navaho Indians at the hands of the US government in the horrific experience of the "Long Walk", actually a series of forced marches from Arizona to eastern New Mexico in the 1860s in which thousands of people were humiliated and hundreds died.[20]

Another is the destruction of the Serbian kingdom in the fourteenth century by the expanding Ottoman Turks at the Battle of Kosovo. The Battle of Kosovo was an important battle, but it did not cause the destruction of the Serbian kingdom. Through the chosen trauma of the Battle of Kosovo a complex historical narrative of heroism and destruction developed among Serbs that perpetuated a feeling of group loss and humiliation through its regular retelling in epic poetry, song, literature, music, dance, and the plastic arts. The loss was never fully mourned, and the deep wound that it left became embedded in Serbian culture. Regular ritual perpetuating the trauma of the Battle of Kosovo helped to keep alive a powerful identity, but it did so through the transmission of unresolved emotions from generation to generation.[21]

In situations such as the chosen trauma of the Battle of Kosovo, the healing of mourning is not allowed to occur. This is similar in the case of a large group to the case of individuals who are unable to heal from the trauma and humiliation, for example, of rape or incest, or the humiliation of a person who perceives himself as a failure in life. In the individual case, the victim who is unable to mourn may externalize the traumatized self onto a developing child. "A child then becomes a reservoir for the unwanted, troublesome parts of an older generation. Because the elders have influence on the child, it absorbs their wishes and expectations and is driven to act on them. It becomes the child's task to mourn, to reverse the humiliation and feelings of helplessness pertaining to the trauma of its forebears."[22] But if the child is unable to work through those emotions, it can transfer the unwanted feelings of humiliation and rage onto yet another generation.

A severe, humiliating group calamity forges a link between the psychology of the individual experience of suffering with the psychology of the group.

> In the wake of such an event, a mental representation of it, common to all members, begins to shape. This mental representation is the consolidated collection of the shared feelings, perceptions, fantasies, and interpretations of the event ... When the mental representation becomes so burdensome that members of the group are unable to initiate or resolve the mourning of their losses or reverse their feelings of humiliation, their traumatized self-images are passed down to later generations in the hope that others may be able to mourn and resolve what the prior generation could not ... [T]he traumatized self-images passed down ... become part of the group identity, an ethnic marker on the canvas of the ethnic tent.[23]

The memory of the past trauma can remain dormant for generations,

> kept in the psychological DNA of the members of the group and silently acknowledged within the culture – in literature and art, for example – but it reemerges powerfully ... under certain conditions ... [N]ew enemies involved in current conflicts may be perceived as extensions of an old enemy from a historical event.[24]

The contemporary generation may then attempt to reverse their ancestors' humiliation by taking revenge on people who represent for them the original perpetrators of the calamity generations or even centuries before. This is what occurred with the massacres of Bosnian Muslims by Serbs, who often referred to the victims as "Turks" despite the fact that they were south Slavs like the Serbs themselves.

Prior to the breakup of Yugoslavia, the power of the state was used to prevent such horrific actions from occurring. Yugoslavia functioned under the ideological dream that socialist aspiration for the common good would cause ethnic and religious difference to fade away. This ideological position inhibited leaders from devoting resources to educating the multi-layered large group population of Yugoslavia to work on resolving perceived conflicts between communities. Unfortunately, this shortsightedness allowed serious perceived grievances to fester and lie dormant until the opportunity presented itself for release through violent revenge.

As noted above, large-group communities often maintain a sense of cohesion through what Volkan calls "chosen traumas" and "chosen glories".[25] These are historical events that are remembered collectively. Chosen glories recall great success or victory, and chosen traumas recall collective suffering. Both reinforce group identity. Chosen trauma reinforces a sense of victimization and can impel a group to avenge its ancestors' perceived hurts.

Let us imagine large-group communities we are familiar with. It seems to me that many, if not most, large-group communities have their own chosen traumas and chosen glories through which they build a sense of group cohesion and identity. Many religious communities in the West perceive themselves as emerging into history through horrific trauma, what I call "birth-pangs" of religious emergence.[26] The Jews suffered under the slavery of ancient Egypt and were redeemed by God via the Exodus, given the divine law at Mt Sinai, and enabled by God to conquer the "Land of Israel". With the horrific destruction of the Jerusalem Temples, the Jews were exiled throughout the world. These are all chosen traumas and glories, and their collective commemoration has forged a strong sense of Jewish communal identity. But the traumas have been exploited by leaders in various periods of Jewish history, including the present, in order to motivate mass movements and sometimes mass-violence against perceived enemies.[27]

Christianity emerged into history through the horrific trauma of the suffering of Christ and the glory of his resurrection. These are chosen traumas and glories that came to epitomize the very identity of Christians. Christian leaders have exploited the trauma to mobilize violence against perceived enemies of Christ generations and centuries later.[28] Islam has also experienced birth-pangs through the resistance by Jews and Christians and indigenous Arabians, all of whom opposed the Prophet Muhammad and tried to force his failure.[29] The Qur'an, like the Hebrew Bible and the New Testament before it, contains much anger directed against its perceived enemies at the time.[30] Shi'a Islam is especially affected by its perceived trauma of emergence at the hands of fellow Muslims who opposed what they believe to be the true desire of God to ensure leadership of the Muslim community through the family of the Prophet.[31] Similarly, national communities often commemorate their birth, independence, or re-independence that were experienced through revolution, struggle or war.[32]

Virtually all ethnic and national communities remember and memorialize their own traumas and glories. It is especially the traumas that concern me, for if the loss experienced by the trauma and passed down generation after generation is not allowed to heal, it can be released through the explosion of horrific violence.

Some new tools have been found that have been at least partially successful in releasing some of these tension in a positive way. One is the truth and reconciliation commissions carried out in South Africa.[33] The South African case provided a culturally appropriate means of mourning and public statement of regret. But it has proven almost impossible to replicate in other cultural and national contexts.[34] There may be other ways to enable mourning to take place so that people can get beyond the humiliation and rage that can be released generations hence.

Non-governmental organizations are working on solutions in some contexts, such as Israel/Palestine, but they are often thwarted by short-sighted governments.

One means suggested by Volkan is through the erection of monuments around which communities can work through the group mourning process. He cites the example of the Vietnam War Veterans' Memorial, which did enable healing. But Volkan also cites examples where memorials, as linking objects, can block the mourning process. One such example is the Crying Father Monument in Tskhinvali, South Ossetia, which perpetuates a sense of victimization among South Ossetians by their Georgian neighbours.[35]

Volkan has literally written volumes about his and his colleagues' experience working with large groups to help them move out of the cycle of repression and subsequent release of humiliation and rage through violence. In these dozens of books and articles, the reader is invited to vicariously experience the group feelings and behaviours that are so crucial to the cycle, and the efforts of the CSMHI to help communities work through the emotions that perpetuate the violence. Understanding the healing process through these examples requires patience for the reader, since there are so many case studies, and each one adds important data to the overall process of healing. Volkan's experiential writing style tends to avoid over-systematizing and over-intellectualizing the processes, since every situation is different and calls for individual treatment. But that can be frustrating for the reader who is interested in isolating patterns of large-group behaviour because Volkan tends to present his analysis through individual narrative descriptions. He nevertheless does summarize occasionally, and it is from one such summary that I draw the conclusion to this short chapter.[36]

The "Tree Model" for bringing opposing groups together

Volkan likes to use images and metaphors to develop his ideas. In his summary here he uses a tree.

> Briefly, the roots of a tree stand for a psychopolitical assessment of the conflict, the trunk represent(s) a years-long series of psychopolitical dialogues between high-level representatives of the opposing groups, and the branches refer to taking what has been learned from the psychopolitical dialogues to both the grassroots level and the official level in order to institutionalize peace coexistence.[37]

A team of experts is formed that comprises psychoanalysts, psychiatrists, psychologists, former diplomats, political scientists, historians, and individuals from other disciplines when necessary. The historians need not be experts on the particular history of the target conflict and large groups involved; it is enough to bring a methodology and way of thinking that will help to understand the data that are gathered. What he calls the clinicians – the psychoanalysts, psychiatrists, and psychologists – bring an understanding of the way in which individuals create mental images of historical events and how large groups share those images. Diplomats evaluate the economic, legal, and related issues as they are reflected in political processes. The team must do its homework before the initial engagement by studying the history and culture of the large groups involved. It must also collect information about the immediate situation out of which the current manifestation of conflict is occurring. The team must travel to the location of the conflict and engage the players in the environment.

The main tool for assessment is in-depth interviews by the clinicians with a variety of people from both sides of the conflict. These should include ordinary adult citizens, children, and government officials, though not at the highest level of government. It is the nature of high governmental positions to place officials under political pressure that inhibits their ability to change their attitudes. Government officials at the next level below such political positions have proven to be more accessible to change while remaining politically influential.

The process consists of three parts. In the first, interviews are conducted over a period of up to four days. The second consists of visiting "hot places", which are the locations of battles, monuments established to commemorate chosen traumas or glories, and other places that are loaded with meaning and that can trigger emotions.[38] The visit(s) occur after the beginning of the interview phase. The third part is the assessment phase, which includes collecting and reviewing the data, after which an overall psychopolitical "diagnosis" is formulated along with a compilation of the real world issues to be addressed, as well as shared feelings, thoughts, and perceptions that lie beneath the surface.

The style of interviews, the nature of the meetings in larger and smaller groups, the flow of the program, and other factors are very carefully developed by the team, which has been working together for many years and in a variety of situations in order to develop its skills. Because of the complexity of the process and the fact that I have neither experienced it nor been trained for it, I will make no attempt to walk through it here; I nevertheless reproduce here some of the observations voiced by Volkan in his description of the Tree Model.

Meetings are carefully planned, as are the location of the meetings. Meetings should be held at least three times per year and over a period of two or three years if not more. The process cannot be rushed. The same team and local participants should take part in all the meetings. An ideal size is 30–40 participants, made up equally of members or representatives of each side in conflict. Initially, each meeting begins with a plenary session at which representatives summarize what had preceded from their perspectives, after which the group splits into small groups of eight to ten persons, each led by two or three members of the facilitating team. The make-up of the facilitating team will vary. As the dialogue progresses, there are fewer plenary sessions and more small-group sessions.

Volkan describes the usual processes and perspectives that members of the opposing camps experience during the sequence of meetings. Throughout the series of meeting, the facilitating team makes no recommendations but helps the participants on both sides of the conflict to remove their resistances to hearing one another so that realistic negotiations can take place. There are no pre-assigned agendas for any of the meetings. They develop naturally and participants are invited to give "free associations", similar to the process of an analysand in individual therapy. In addition to the formal meetings, participants and facilitators eat meals together and have other occasions for informal social interactions. This helps the group members know what goes on in each small group in which they do not participate. The goal is for the representatives of opposing groups to come together and discuss conflicts between them in an unofficial capacity, negotiate possible solutions, and strategize together to suggest positive actions that may produce positive outcomes.

Volkan notes that two parallel processes take place. One is the evolution that occurs within each four-day meeting. The other is the larger process that takes shape over the entire two to four-year series. It is crucial that an environment be established that is psychologically safe for dialogue. That is accomplished by demonstrating the neutrality of the facilitators (through a variety of ways outlined by Volkan) and by choosing a neutral location, which may be outside (though nearby) the actual area of conflict.

This entire process is located within what diplomats now call "Track Two Diplomacy".[39] This is a process of non-governmental, informal, and unofficial contacts and activities that take place outside the framework of "Track One" official governmental channels. It can lead to a less encumbered understanding of the perspectives of opposing sides and can positively influence the official governmental diplomacy. As such, it is organized by non-governmental organizations (NGOs) and funded outside of the framework of official government diplomacy.

Postscript

Volkan's work centres on large-group conflicts that appear to be unresolvable through the usual diplomatic channels. He has contributed greatly toward understanding the problem of large-group trauma and for developing programs to help large groups get beyond the barriers to full healing and healthy relationships. That healing process often requires some kind of large-group mourning that can move communities out from being stuck with internalized pain and humiliation that can be released in dangerous and unrestrained ways. Large group pathologies need to be successfully treated, he would contend, in order for communities to normalize and resolve conflicts successfully and conclusively.

The cases that he and the Center for the Study of Mind and Human Interaction studied and treated were all identified because they were yet unresolved. That is, he and his team were invited to contribute to the resolution of conflict that was already raging and causing suffering. It would be preferable for intervention to occur *before* there is a need to call in the emergency team – before the outbreaks of violence require outside intervention.

Since so many large groups, whether they be religious, national, or ethnic communities, self-identify at least partly on the basis of chosen traumas that are internalized and become basic aspects or even pillars of group identity, it would seem that many if not most large groups have the potential to act out their traumas in negative and destructive (and self-destructive) ways. Is it possible for perceptive members of large-group communities to work with artists, social activists, intellectual, and educational leaders and government in order to re-frame the narratives of suffering and trauma that seem to be so ubiquitous? Can insightful individuals and groups work to build positive linking objects to facilitate large-group healing from their chosen traumas? It would seem to me that this is an area in which we should consider investing so that we can avoid the vicious release of violence as a reaction to the humiliation and suffering that so many of our communities experience as part of their identity.

Notes

1 Vamık Volkan is a Turkish-Cypriot American psychiatrist, Emeritus Professor of Psychiatry at the University of Virginia, Charlottesville, and founder of the Center for the Study of Mind and Human Interaction (CSMHI) at the University of Virginia School of Medicine (www.vamikvolkan.com/About-Vam%FDk-D--Volkan.php).

2 Op. cit.

3 Vamık D. Volkan, "Bosnia-Herzegovina: Chosen Trauma and Its Transgenerational Transmission," in *Islam and Bosnia: Conflict Resolution and Foreign Policy in Multi-Ethnic States*, ed. Maya Shatzmiller (Montreal: McGill University, 2002); *Enemies on the Couch: A Psychopolitical Journey through War and Peace* (Durham, North Carolina: Pitchstone, 2013), 17–168.

4 On conflicting narratives between Israelis and Palestinians, see Robert Rothberg (ed.), *Israeli and Palestinian Narratives of Conflict: History's Double Helix* (Bloomington: Indiana University, 2006); Neil Caplan, *The Israel-Palestine Conflict: Contested Histories* (London: Wiley-Blackwell, 2009); Sami Adwan, Dan Baro-On, and Eyal Naveh, *Side by Side: Parallel Histories of Israel-Palestine* (New York: The New Press, 2012).

5 Vamık D. Volkan, *Blood Lines: From Ethnic Pride to Ethnic Terrorism* (New York: Farrar, Straus and Giroux, 1977), 17; ibid., "What Some Monuments Tell Us about Mourning and Forgiveness," in Elazar Barkan and Alexander Karn (eds.), *Taking Wrongs Seriously: Apologies and Reconciliation* (Stanford, CA: Stanford University), 115–131.

6 Vamık D. Volkan, *Blood Lines: From Ethnic Pride to Ethnic Terrorism* (New York: Farrar, Straus and Giroux, 1997).

7 *Blood Lines* 27–28; ibid. *Killing in the Name of Identity: A Study of Bloody Conflicts* (Charlottesville, VA: Pitchstone, 2006), 69–70.

8 *Blood Lines* 20.

9 One classic example is the (Catholic) Crusader sack of (Orthodox) Constantinople in 1204.

10 Benedict Anderson, *Imagined Communities* (London: Verso, 2006 [1981])

11 For a classic case of identifying French occupiers for slaughter in the city of Bruges in Flemish Belgium, see Edward Le Glay, *Schild En Vriend, 1302–1303* (Paris: Magen et Comon, 1842 (repr. 2012). In 1918 Finland, locals identified Russians who changed to civilian clothing to avoid detection, by demanding that they count to three. Russians were unable to pronounce the Finish *yksi* for the number "one," but said, rather, *uksi*, after which they were immediately shot (Heinrich Pesch, "A Dog Trained to Bite: Finish War Culture and its Image of the Enemy," (www.schneeland.com/web/stites.html). Many other examples can be cited.

12 The term was coined by Eric Erikson "to refer to the fact that mankind, while one species, has divided itself throughout its history – territorially, culturally, politically – into various groupings that permit their members, at decisive times to consider themselves, more or less consciously and explicitly, the only truly human species, and *all* others (and especially *some* others) as less than human"(Kai Erikson, "On Pseudospeciation and Social Speciation," in Charles B. Strozier and Michael Flynn (eds) *Genocide, War, and Human Survival* (Lanham, MD: Rowman and Littlefield, 1996), 51.

13 *Blood Lines* 36.

58   *Reuven Firestone*

14 *Blood Lines* 37.
15 *Enemies*, 94–95.
16 *Enemies*, 95–98.
17 Volkan, "The Next Chapter: Consequences of Societal Trauma," in Pumla Gobodo-Madikizela and Chris Van Der Merwe, *Memory, Narrative and Forgiveness: Perspectives on the Unfinished Journeys of the Past* (Cambridge: Cambridge Scholars, 2009), 8–12.
18 *Killing,* 144–145.
19 *Killing*, 108, 157–172; *Enemies*, 101.
20 *Blood Lines,* 40–42.
21 *Blood Lines*, 57–80
22 *Blood Lines*, 43.
23 *Blood Lines*, 45.
24 *Blood Lines*, 46–7. See also, Volkan, "Transgenerational Transmissions and Chosen Traumas: An Aspect of Large-Group Identity," *Group Analysis*, vol. 34, 2001, 79–97.
25 *Enemies*, 157–160.
26 Reuven Firestone, "A Common Word and Love of Neighbor in the Face of Religious Trauma," in Yazid Said (ed.) *A Common Word ...* (Cambridge: Cambridge University Press, 2017).
27 Reuven Firestone, *Holy War in Judaism: The Fall and Rise of a Controversial Idea* (Oxford University Press, 2012.)
28 David Nirenberg, *Communities of Violence* (Princeton: Princeton University, 1996), 200–231.
29 Reuven Firestone, "A Phenomenology of Monotheism in Relationship: Jews, Christians and Muslims," in *Current Dialogue* 58 (2016): 21–24.
30 Q. 2: 61, 75–91; 9:30, etc.
31 Mahmoud Ayoub, *Redemptive Suffering in Islām* (Berlin: De Gruyter, 1978).
32 For a study of this phenomenon in Eastern Europe since the fall of the USSR, see Igor Torbakov, "History, Memory and National Identity: Understanding the Politics of History and Memory Wars in Post-Soviet Lands," in *Demokratizatsiya* 19 (2011), 209–232 (www2.gwu.edu/~ieresgwu/assets/docs/demokratizatsiya%20archive/GWASHU_DEMO_19_3/J773U5477844263L/J773U5477844263L.pdf).
33 Erik Doxtader, *Truth and Reconciliation in South Africa: The Fundamental Documents* (Cape Town: David Philip Publishers, 2007); Muhammad Haron, *South Africa's Truth and Reconciliation Commission: An Annotated Bibliography* (Hauppauge, NY: Nova Science Publishers, 2009).
34 Lyn S. Graybill, *Truth and Reconciliation in South Africa: Miracle or Model?* (Boulder: Lynne Rienner Publishers, 2002).
35 Volkan, "What Some Monuments Tell Us…", Volkan, *Killing*, 155.
36 Volkan, *Killing*, 198–227: "From Theory to Practice: The Tree Model."
37 Volkan, *Killing*, 198.
38 Volkan, *Killing*, 137–142; Volkan, "What some Monuments Tell Us…", 2006.
39 Joseph Montville, "Track Two Diplomacy: The Work of Healing History," *The Whitehead Journal of Diplomacy and International Relations* 7.2 (2006), 15–26.

Part 2

Revisionism & reconstruction

5 Holocaust, propaganda, and the distortion of history in the former Soviet space

Charles E. Ehrlich

What distinguished the Holocaust (and genocides) from other mass violence is its commission: although perpetrated by individuals, it utilized the mechanisms of a state, including official propaganda. This propaganda justified the commission of crimes, either directly by the state apparatus or indirectly through incitement of citizens to violence against the victims. Massive propagandistic falsifications led a supposedly civilized country with an educated citizenry to commit the murder of six million Jews.

The notion of state propaganda underscores the importance of studying the history, both to ensure lessons are learned to not repeat tragedies, and to guard against intentional distortions and false narratives serving new political objectives. Differences of opinion can and do exist among scholars, but if there is a wilful distortion of the history then the lessons will go unlearned.

Prevalence of Soviet propaganda in the post-Soviet world

Some current political narratives, primarily in the post-Soviet space, have emerged as consequences of earlier distortions of history leading to new narratives based on incorrect "facts". The continued prevalence of Soviet propaganda actually makes understanding the Holocaust and learning its lessons more difficult in this part of the world.

Soviet propaganda, still-prevalent in Russia, set out the narrative of the "Great Patriotic War" as victory over "fascism" without actually applying critical thought to define "fascism", beyond the nominal enemy against which the Soviet Union fought, and by analogy anything deviating from the Communist Party line.[1] It was even Soviet policy to downplay the fact that the victims were murdered *because* they were Jews, as this fact interfered with the political framing.[2] But not understanding this key element means that people in these countries do not appreciate the causes of the Holocaust nor how it happened in their countries.

The Soviet Union under dictator Josef Stalin was, in terms of total numbers, more murderous than Nazi Germany, and also targeted entire peoples. Although Stalin's crimes are taught today in Russian schools, it remains acceptable in public discourse to admire Stalin's perceived attributes.[3] Soviet Russia's formal pact with Nazi Germany in 1939 and its alliance with Germany to start the Second World War, the reasons for the disastrous unpreparedness when Germany did invade the Soviet Union in 1941, and then the brutal way in which the Russians themselves carried out the war are often ignored. While some people may admit that Stalin "made mistakes" along the way, his leadership role in the victory over Nazi Germany outweighed those "mistakes" and vindicated the brutality of the Soviet regime.[4]

The eventual collapse of the Soviet Union – in practice the Russian Empire under a new name and regime[5] – left its successor state, the Russian Federation, reduced and with revisionist territorial ambitions. After the chaos of the 1990s, a re-assertive Russia could pick up in this propaganda where its predecessors had left off.[6] In the process, the shrunken Russia remains as the core of a "*Russkii Mir*" ("Russian World" akin to German-speaking or -influenced people living outside the *Reich*).[7]

Russian propaganda thus needs to undermine neighbouring states in order to justify Russian regional hegemony. So distinct Ukrainian and Byelorussian identities are called into question, and the Baltic States are portrayed as "failed states" that are too small to survive. And, anyway, the propaganda holds, they were all fascist collaborators.[8] The current ongoing war in Ukraine is marked by repeated Russian propaganda that Ukraine has no history (reminiscent of Marxist dogma about "peoples without history" who could be eradicated or absorbed). These states can also be described in the same blink as somehow "Jewish".[9]

The post-Soviet rehabilitation of Russia as a distinct entity, combined with a desire to restore a greater Russian empire, required absolving Russians of complacency in mass violence. Within Russia, this amnesia has led to the failure to memorialize the victims of the Soviet regime combined with a rehabilitation of perpetrators (including Stalin – so, for example, during the restoration of Moscow's Kursk Metro Station in 2009, a previously removed poem of praise to Stalin was restored to the wall, justified by historical accuracy from the original station; prominent portraits of Stalin were also displayed across Moscow at the 2010 Soviet Victory Day celebrations, also justified by Stalin's role presiding over that victory).[10]

To argue that Russians are victims today, as well as victims of previous aggressions, then they need perpetrators. These must be exploitative Jews inside Russia linked to some global Jewish conspiracy, and fascist collaborators in the near abroad. Even without needing to deny the Holocaust, or the mass murders committed by the Soviet regime, there could be calls for "mutual understanding" – a moral equivalence blurring victims and perpetrators.[11]

Soviet symbols, meanwhile, can be retained because they represent the achievements of the (Russian-led) Soviet Union before 1991 and are thus part of Russia's historical legacy. Even if official Russia could admit that the Soviet Union may have been less than ideal, this could not impact the glory of Russian achievement in that period.[12]

The continuing legacy of the Molotov–Ribbentrop Pact

Conversely, if newly independent states remove Soviet symbols as representative of their persecutors, Russian propaganda would say this must itself represent anti-Russian sentiment, and by association fascist collaborationism in 1941–1945 (as the enemy of Soviet communism – again ignoring Russia's own pre-1941 alliance).[13] This highlights a long Russian resistance to equating Nazism and communism, remembering Soviet crimes against humanity and even the Molotov–Ribbentrop pact – reminders of all of that are seen as attacks on Holy Russia.[14] Even if the Soviet and Nazi regimes arose from different circumstances, there is still a value in comparing them. But the way in which the USSR ended in 1991 compared to Nazi Germany's total defeat in 1945 has made starting over to address the past more difficult in Russia.[15]

The issue is not whether there were antisemites, and indeed collaborators with the Germans, in carrying out the Holocaust, in these various countries before 1945 (there were). But Russian propaganda has imputed that this makes those entire countries guilty by association *today*.[16] Also by association, anything challenging the Russian position is, in this dichotomy, "fascist". This propaganda, often aimed at Western ears, is easier to digest. But it underscores the need for these countries to openly address their own histories – and to openly address Russia's.

Ironically, this same perverse logic has twisted the Molotov–Ribbentrop pact into a positive event for Russia. In May 2015, at a press conference with German Chancellor Angela Merkel, Russian President Vladimir Putin praised the Pact, explaining that the West had abandoned Russia, and this pact with Nazi Germany therefore represented peace for Russia – and peace, by definition, must be a good thing (Russia's culture minister called it a "colossal achievement of Stalin's diplomacy".).[17] In a narrow sense, this was, of course, true. But Hitler's interest in *Lebensraum* in the east at the expense of the Slavic peoples was well known[18]; Russia had purged its general staff and was unprepared for war, making a delaying tactic certainly in order[19]; and the demarcation of a line in Eastern Europe to mark the border of German and Russian zones at the exclusion of the countries in the middle (which might have survived, but only at the tolerance of the two signatory powers).

The legacy of the Pact lived on longer than the Pact itself. By denying the territories it occupied in 1939–1941 any recognition, and classifying them and their citizens as Soviet, the Soviet Union retained these conquests after the end of the War. With Germany vanquished, Russia could pact further West, sliding the effective boundary of puppet states deep into Central Europe, again without any legitimacy among the subject peoples.

The "Great Patriotic War" is a mythologized historic and popular struggle, surpassing the first "Patriotic War" (Napoleon's invasion of Russia). It is explicitly *not* the "Second World War".[20] Russian propaganda would insist that this aspect was underestimated in the West as part of Cold War positioning, of course ignoring that much of the suffering in these countries was caused by the Soviet regime. The unwillingness of Russia to consider that aspect – and indeed to consider non-Russian narratives completely – has hardened other attitudes in formerly Russian-occupied territories. Russia also dates the beginning of the war to the German invasion of 1941, ignoring its own complicity in the war which began in 1939.[21]

The second Soviet occupation from the late stages of the war until 1991, had to become a "liberation" from fascism, and not itself an "occupation". Those who had protected Jews (often those who did have an ideology connected to state-hood and who therefore defied occupation by Germans and by Russians) must therefore have been "fascists" as well, in the sense that anyone who opposed the Soviet Union, and especially someone the Soviets claimed as a citizen, must by definition be fascist.[22]

Since the USSR had integrated locals in occupied territories as its own citizens during the period before the German invasion in 1941, they ended up with additional consequences. First, that the local (non-Jewish) populations became victims of two occupations. Second, these populations themselves collaborated varyingly with the Russians and the Germans. Where they collaborated with the Russians between 1939 and 1941, they had to cleanse their guilt, which made killing Jews for the Germans easier.[23] They were also willing to accept the German "Judeobolshevik" myth as a way to exonerate themselves, so that if they had cooperated with the Soviets it was part of a Jewish plot.[24]

But when they collaborated with the German occupation forces, it also meant that the Soviet Union had to account for the actions of its own citizens (the interwar states and borders having been, according to the Russian view, illegitimate). This required externalizing an enemy, so downplaying the Jewishness of the Holocaust, on one hand, and exaggerating the "nationalist" and therefore fascist identity of the captive peoples, on the other.[25]

Soviet historiography wished to highlight collaboration first and foremost. The relation of those "collaborators" to Jews and the Holocaust was secondary (if it was relevant at all).[26] Most important was the implementation of Soviet state policy, rather than the truth, so some topics did not require discussion.[27]

Russia today uses distortion of history to support its own foreign policy. This means both to augment supposed collaboration with Nazi Germany by former captive nations to tarnish those countries' challenges to Russian hegemony today; as well as to downplay mass atrocities carried out by Russia. Russia can thus portray an independent Ukraine seeking to escape Russian hegemony as a fascist state, and subsequently to claim Crimea from Ukraine based on the peninsula's "historic" Russian identity, casually ignoring that Russia had deported the entire indigenous Crimean Tatar population leading to the death of half of them.[28]

Large-scale stirring up of ethnic hatred, making entire populations into villains, and accusing entire classes of people as enemies of the state (or "fascists") continues. This is especially clear in the recent events in Ukraine, where Russian propaganda has misused the legacy of the Second World War to incite hatred and violence. Similarly, in 2008, Russia simply invented stories that Georgia was committing "genocide" against Ossetians as part of Russia's justification for invading Georgia.[29]

Rather than addressing the facts on the ground in Georgia in 2008 and in Ukraine since 2013 – which are subject to legitimate debate – Russian mouthpieces created false narratives rooted in earlier Soviet propaganda either about the events of the Second World War or echoes thereof. If the Holocaust, genocides, mass murder, and similar crimes become details, and are then used to colour invented genocides of the present, then it becomes difficult to learn any lessons.

Ukraine and the Holocaust

In context, it is entirely understandable that many Ukrainians initially welcomed the Germans as liberators in 1941. They were not the only people to do so, and it in no way implies that these people were "fascists".[30] This happened despite the fact that Nazi ideology was also anti-Slav, and Hitler had made his plans for Ukraine and Ukrainians very clear (and it was not going to be much better than the way Ukraine was treated under the Soviet Union), and it was the Nazis who ultimately rounded up the Ukrainian nationalist leadership. Yet some Ukrainians were more than happy to collaborate in the Holocaust then, and since independence after the collapse of the Soviet Union, Ukraine has continued to follow Soviet trends to erase the historical memory of the Jewish population, almost as if there had never been many Jews living there. Some of this erasure is due to Soviet ideology, but some is due to Ukrainian nationalism or national myth.[31]

The lack of proper education and understanding about the Holocaust has resulted in the misuse of history by people today in Ukraine. A better memory or historical understanding would make it harder for Russian propaganda to take hold. This gap has had direct repercussions in Ukraine, presenting conflicting distorted narratives by both Ukrainian nationalists and Russia. Avoiding the issue of whether the Great Famine would meet the definition of genocide under international law, it still involved state-organized mass starvation, deportation, and murder. Partly as a result of this experience, some Ukrainians collaborated with the Nazis. Official Russia has thus mostly perpetuated a Soviet position to accuse Ukrainians as Nazi collaborators, while Ukrainian nationalists downplay involvement by some Ukrainians in the Holocaust. The appraisal of the Holocaust and genocide in general has thus become more emotional than historical.

In 2005, at the height of the *Holodomor* controversy,[32] the Ukrainian authorities inflated the number of deaths to 10 million, in part to exceed the magnitude of the Holocaust, as though numbers of dead alone constituted a marker for genocide.[33] With respect to "comparative genocide" or "comparative atrocities", it does not really matter who suffered more, only that people suffered. That Nazi Germany saw Slavs as a lower category of human fit only for labour can still represent a negative without trying to relativize it. Acknowledging that Germany singled Jews out for extermination does not deny the Ukrainian (or other) narrative. Furthermore, recognizing the role of Ukrainians (and others), who participated in the extermination of the Jews, sometimes not because the Germans compelled them to but actually willingly, becomes politicized – if the countries admit that their people played a role in the crime, this does not negate the victimhood of their people. Indeed, it is the opposite: recognizing history strengthens their narrative. And while it was true that Jews were not the majority of the dead in Eastern Europe, most people who were killed in Eastern Europe were killed because they were physically present. Jews were killed because they were Jews.[34]

Memorialization (of whom?) in Poland

Here, Poland also has a relevant history. In September 1939, with the joint invasion of Poland by Germany and Russia, both occupying forces sought to eliminate
the same targets: the Polish elites. But the methods differed. Both sides believed
Poland had no right to exist. The Russians made Poles living in their zone of
occupation into Soviet citizens (and added the territory to Soviet Byelorussia and
Ukraine), whereas Germany excluded Poles as citizens of a state. As for Jews, the
Germans concentrated them before determining the Final Solution; the Russians
saw them as capitalists (and after 1941 ironically therefore as potential German
collaborators), which led to expropriations and deportations.[35]

The history of Poland especially is unique because the Russo-German dismantling of the Polish state in September 1939 meant that it had no collaborationist
government nor civil authorities. But this also meant that after 1945 antisemitism
had not become discredited as it was elsewhere. So, antisemitism remained, and
required justification – leading to both a Polish communist and a Polish post-communist narrative. Communists used historical antisemitism in Poland to consol-
idate power after 1945. Since the pre-War Communist Party had included Jews
when other parties discriminated against them, one post-war result was a need for
the Party to exclude Jews in order to legitimize itself.[36]

In the period 1945–1948, tensions were still unresolved at the time of the
communist takeover of Poland. This both submerged the dialogue and added a
new layer of official antisemitism. Eventually, this would make Israel, as the
representation of the "disloyal" Jews, into an enemy as well, an act of externali-
zation, particularly after the 1968 unrest.[37]

In the post-communist context, there was also a double-counting of victims
(e.g. 6 million Poles – but 3 million of those were Jews; 6 million Jews were
murdered, of which 3 million had come from pre-War Poland).[38] The nature of
the Holocaust and the treatment of Poland were different. It has been easier for
Poland to consider its own victimization, in a story in which Jews collaborated
with the Russians.[39] In the communist world, where the Jewish element had been
downplayed anyway and the death camps were merely sites for the murder of
"victims of fascism", it became easier to deny the Holocaust as a specifically
Jewish tragedy – but rather make it one of "Polish" suffering.[40]

Poles supporting the installation of Catholic crosses at Auschwitz on two
major occasions did so for Catholic and Polish nationalist reasons. The Catholic
position – that this was a sacred memorial site and the cross represented Christian
prayers for the dead – harked back to Christian "supersessionist" doctrine and
the primacy of Christianity over Judaism.[41] The nationalist version explained that
10 per cent of those killed in Auschwitz were Polish Catholics, who deserved a
memorial.[42] Of course, "Auschwitz" had become shorthand for the Holocaust, in
part because people survived Auschwitz.[43] More Jews were killed elsewhere, but no
one survived to tell their story.[44] But antisemitic voices used Jewish objections as
an excuse to enter the debate openly. These boiled over afterward the controversy
over the historical memory of events in Jedwabne (in which Poles had brutally
murdered their Jewish neighbours without prompting by the German occupiers),

as elaborated in Jan Gross' 2001 book *Neighbors*, and have continued under the current Polish government, which has brought in legislation to criminalize perceived insults to Polish identity, in which it is clear this means anyone who might confront Polish antisemitism in this period.[45]

Indeed, Auschwitz I (the site of the crosses) had initially been used for Polish elite and military prisoners, and later for Soviet prisoners of war. Auschwitz II at Birkenau was the death camp (and mostly for non-Polish Jews deported from elsewhere in German-occupied Europe). So the Polish nationalist portrayal of Jewish reactions to the cross controversies were of the Jews trying to appropriate Auschwitz, then the Catholic convent on the site, and finally all of Poland.[46] This too has its origins in communist memorialization at Auschwitz as a "Monument of the Martyrdom of the Polish Nation and of Other Nations" as a fascist aggression against Poland (and other Warsaw Pact allies) in the past rather than a memorial of the Holocaust and its Jewish character.[47]

Post-communist memorialization often considers how Jews were killed, or where they came from to be killed within the pre-war boundaries of Poland – including parts of Ukraine and Byelorussia today – and not how they had lived in those places for centuries. It is convenient for modern narratives if they were never there.[48] In many cases, post-Holocaust expropriations were opportunistic – the Germans had murdered or deported the Jews but the property remained, and while Poles and others took advantage of the opportunity, they had not themselves sought the opportunity, owing as it did to German (or Russian) occupation.[49] But as Gross has pointed out, the concept of "formerly Jewish property" requires there to be no more Jews – if they survived and returned, they came into direct conflict with the local non-Jewish population regardless of their situation prior to the Holocaust.[50]

Other models of memory

This also had the knock-on impact that the countries under Russian captivity before 1991 were not in a position to honestly address their own histories.[51] So where there had been involvement in the Holocaust, this too was not fully understood nor accepted, and where known could even be written off as Russian propaganda. Eastern European countries cast themselves merely as victims of the Germans or of the Russians, or of both. But the difficulty that these various countries have had in addressing what happened on their territories – and how much their own populations were involved, and how willingly – has instead opened the door for Russian propaganda.

In Estonia, for example, 99 per cent of its pre-Holocaust Jewish population did not survive. According to Soviet propaganda (continued by the Russians after 1991), this was because of Estonian antisemitism and collaborationism. But the overwhelming majority of Estonian Jews perished in the early stages of the German invasion, at the hands of Germans (albeit with some Estonian collaborators) without local pogroms. The Estonian state had already been destroyed by Russia – since it did not exist, it could not protect its Jewish citizens, and the Germans acted quickly to prove a political point to Estonians that they would not recover their independence.[52]

Post-Holocaust historical memory of Jewish presence in Eastern Europe has been erased twice because it did not fit into historical narratives – first by communists and later by countries after independence who asserted identities outside Russian domination. When evaluating some individuals' war record, it becomes important to distinguish between cooperation and collaboration, and whether there is guilt by association.[53] This is, after all, how individual Germans (and Austrians) are evaluated, or indeed anyone who has ever lived in a totalitarian state. It is one thing to join the Party (or the Hitler Youth, or Komsomol) because not to do so would open the family up to persecution and close off access to education and careers. It is another thing entirely to use the position to commit atrocities.

The Germans did indeed co-opt anti-Russian resistance units for their own use during occupation. The question remains what those individuals did. In many cases, people did commit mass violence, for which they should be condemned. But how indicative are they of the occupied people as a whole at the time, not to mention of those people or countries today?

Germany (or at least the Western portion) could rehabilitate itself quickly after the Nazi period by honestly addressing its own collective and individual past. Where countries have not done this, it becomes doubly easy for Russia to tarnish their motives: first by using the former Soviet narrative that all in the captive nations who resisted the Russians were by definition fascists and Nazi collaborators, and second by pointing to real collaboration that these countries may not have fully addressed.

In Austria, the myth of Austria as Nazi Germany's "first victim" grew out of the fact that Austria as a state did not exist between 1938 and 1945, thus it could not be responsible for crimes – as a *state*.[54] While true, this is very different from saying the Austrians themselves were not responsible, and that the reconstituted Austrian state should not be responsible for its former Jewish citizens. Austria allowed denazification to lapse (including under the Western occupying powers).[55] But the myth was useful propaganda in 1943, hence Stalin's insistence on declaring Austria the "first victim". Stalin also wished to deflect blame from citizens of what had been Austria in order to get their cooperation and to stake his own claims for when the war finished.[56]

Conclusion

Therefore, the former Soviet space requires (1) more emphasis on critical understanding of the Holocaust within its German context; (2) an improved understanding of the crimes against humanity committed by the Soviet Union (mass murder, deportation of entire ethnic groups, etc.) whether or not these meet the legal definition of "genocide"; (3) a much less sentimental view and a more honest appraisal of Stalin; and (4) proper lessons learned from the Holocaust, so that the memory of the Holocaust is not thrown around and abused by demagogues today but actually informs dialogue.

Lack of these steps suggests that many people in the former Soviet space have not learned the lessons from the Holocaust, and that some leaders know these lessons very well but use those lessons dishonestly in order to manipulate the emotions of the population, making the leadership fit more into the category of perpetrators than victims. So studying the Holocaust becomes relevant – not because it is forgotten, but because it is misused.

Notes

1 Olga Baranova, "Politics of memory of the Holocaust in the Soviet Union," in P. Marczewski & S. Eich (eds.), Dimensions of Modernity: The Enlightenment and its contested legacies (Vienna 2015), available on www.iwm.at (Vienna Institute of Human Sciences).

2 Baranova, in Marczewski and Eich (eds.), *op. cit.* Cf. Tomas Sniegon, *Vanished History: The Holocaust in Czech and Slovak Historical Culture* (New York, 2017), 60–62, and Robert Gellately, *Stalin's Curse: Battling for Communism in War and Cold War* (New York, 2013), 187–192.

3 Indeed, even after the Soviet Union had removed the cult of personality surrounding Stalin and rehabilitated many of his victims, the Soviet Union still failed to memorialize victims or address the regime of terror, as Stalin was simply indicative of that terror and to do otherwise would have opened up internal criticism of Soviet communism. Polly Jones, *Myth, Memory, Trauma: Rethinking the Stalinist Past in the Soviet Union, 1953–1970* (New Haven, 2013), 134f.

4 David Satter, *It Was a Long Time Ago and it Never Happened Anyway: Russia and the Communist Past* (New Haven, 2012). On Russia's pre-1939 preparations for a war of aggression, and Stalin's incompetent military leadership both before and after 1941, see Bernd Bonwetsch, "Stalin, the Red Army, and the 'Great Patriotic War'", in Kershaw and Lewin (eds.), *Stalinism and Nazism: Dictatorships in Comparison* (Cambridge, 1997), 185f. Cf. Andrei Kolesnikov, "Why Russia is Making Stalin Great Again", Carnegie Moscow Center (13 March 2019), available at https://carn-egie.ru/2019/03/13/why-russia-is-making-stalin-great-again-pub-78590.

5 Russia, uniquely among the Soviet Socialist Republics, did not have its own separate party apparatus or republican government, which serves as the clearest indication equating Russia as the central and dominant identity within the entirety of the Soviet Union, with the other republics and nationalities being at best junior partners if not internal colonies or long-term occupied territories to be absorbed under Russian hegemony. The fact that the communist party apparatus was not closed to non-Russians (Stalin himself was a Georgian of Ossetian descent) does not reduce the predominance of Russia as the state identity within the Soviet Union.

6 An inexact parallel with Russia today and with Weimar Germany produces a narrative that combines a "humiliation myth" of disloyal people inside Russia who collaborated with anti-Russian forces from outside to undermine the Soviet Union. Andrew Wilson, *Ukraine Crisis: What It Means for the West* (New Haven, 2014), vii and 11f.

7 Ibid., 157

8 Ibid., 175f. Here, the target of the propaganda is the European Union: if the EU regards these states as outside post-Second World War European values, then it will slow or halt the integration process (a Russian objective).

9 Timothy Snyder, *Black Earth: The Holocaust as history and warning* (London, 2015), 333f. The "Jewishness" of a state without a legitimate identity (in the eyes of the propagandist) also ties directly to the antisemitic communist buzzword for Jews as "rootless cosmopolitans." For Marxist theory regarding "peoples without history", see Roman Rosdolsky, *Zur Nationalen Frage: F. Engels und das Problem der "geschichtslosen Völker"* (Berlin, 1979).

10 Satter, *op. cit.* The manner of Soviet Russia's defeat in the Cold War was altogether different than the defeat of Nazi Germany, and this made a difference in how the two

countries have come to deal (or not) with their respective pasts. Ian Kershaw and Moshe Lewin, "Introduction", in Kershaw and Lewin (eds.), *op. cit.*, 5.

11 Satter, *op. cit.*, 169f. This also whitewashed centuries of official Russian antisemitism that spanned multiple regimes and rulers.

12 Ibid., 188f. Even the idea that the War established the Soviet Union (and thus, by rightful succession, also the Russian Federation) as one of the world's two super-powers is therefore also a positive achievement. Mark von Hagen, "From 'Great Fatherland War' to the Second World War: New Perspectives and Future Prospects", in Kershaw and Lewin (eds.), *op. cit.*, 248.

13 Satter, *op. cit.*, 217f.

14 Ibid., 226f.

15 Ian Kershaw and Moshe Lewin, "Introduction: The Regimes and their Dictators, Perspectives of Comparison", in Kershaw and Lewin (eds.), *op. cit.*, 3–4.

16 Inasis Feldmanis, "Waffen SS Units of Latvians and Other Non-Germanic peoples in World War II: Methods of Formation, Ideology, and Goals" in Commission of the Historians of Latvia, *The Hidden and Forbidden History of Latvia under Soviet and Nazi Occupations, 1940–1991* (Riga, 2005), 122f. Cf. Sofi Oksanen, "How History Is Falsified – Deportations in the Politics of Russia and the Soviet Union", speech at the Toronto Conference on Repressions and Human Rights: Commemorating the 1949 Baltic deportations", 27 March 2015, available at www.sofioksanen.com/how-history-is-falsified-toronto-2015/.

17 "Putin Defends Ribbentrop-Molotov Pact in Press Conference with Merkel", in *The Moscow Times*, 11 May 2015. Cf. Satter, *op. cit.*, 212f.

18 Hitler said as much in *Mein Kampf.* See also Andrew Wilson, *The Ukrainians: Unexpected Nation* (New Haven, 2002), 133f.

19 For Stalin's inadequate preparation for war with Germany, see Simon Sebag Montefiore, *Stalin: The Court of the Red Czar* (London, 2003), 307–366.

20 By narrowing the War's official descriptor, Russian mythology would insist that instead of a global conflict the War was really a defense of Mother Russia from inva-sion, making every other country's fate irrelevant (including, of course, even the fates of those countries Russia had occupied before and after the German invasion). For example, compare Ukrainian and Russian visions in Nolan Peterson, "Ukraine purges symbols of its communist past", *Newsweek*, 10 April 2015, available at www.newsweek.com/ukraine-purges-symbols-its-communist-past-321663.

21 Von Hagen, "From 'Great Fatherland War' to the Second World War: new perspec-tives and future prospects", in Kershaw and Lewin (eds.), *op. cit.*, 238f.

22 Snyder, *Black Earth*, 282f. Indeed, the destruction of the Jews, especially in Ukraine, matched Soviet objectives, but the narrative had to be negated afterwards. Kershaw and Lewin in Kershaw and Lewin (eds.), *op. cit.*, 6.

23 Snyder, *Black Earth*, 152f.

24 Snyder, *Black Earth*, 158f. Cf. Fabio Belafatti, "On Russian propaganda, anti-Semitism, and Lithuania's lessons", 16 December 2016, at https://en.delfi.lt/poli-tics/on-russian-propaganda-anti-semitism-and-lithuanias-lessons.d?id=73205166. Hitler set out the "Judeobolshevik" myth already in *Mein Kampf.* For an analysis of the Nazi view of – and propaganda for – a global Jewish conspiracy, see Jeffrey Herf, *The Jewish Enemy: Nazi propaganda during World War II and the Holocaust* (Cambridge, MA, 2006).

25 In this case, they made no distinction between cooperation and collaboration with the Germans. Yet the understandable desire to cooperate in order to rid their countries of Russian occupiers (even if, in the end, the Germans would have been unwill-ing to restore local sovereignty), without committing crimes against humanity in the process, is altogether different than collaborating with the German occupying forces to commit those crimes (albeit sometimes both motives influenced individuals). Cf. Inesis Feldmanis, "Waffen SS Units of Latvians and Other Non-Germanic Peoples in World War II: Methods of formation, Ideology, and Goals" in Commission of the

Historians of Latvia, *op. cit.*, 122f. and Aivars Stranga, "The Holocaust in Occupied Latvia, 1941–1945" in Commission of the Historians of Latvia, *op. cit.*, 163f., and, for Ukraine specifically, Gellately, *op. cit.*, 206f.

26 Aivars Stranga, "The Holocaust in Occupied Latvia, 1941–1945" in Commission of the Historians of Latvia, *op. cit., 1940–1991*, 170f.

27 Rudīte Vīksne, "Members of the Arājs Commando in Soviet Court Files: Social Position, Education, Reasons for Volunteering, Penalty" in Commission of the Historians of Latvia, *op. cit.* 206.

28 See, *inter alia*, Leonid Ragozin and Max Seddon, "Threatened, Raided, and Exiled: Opposing Putin in Crimea" 27 September 2014 at www.buzzfeed.com/leonidr2/threatened-raided-and-exiled-opposing-putin-in-crimea.

29 Ronald D. Asmus, *A Little War that Shook the World: Georgia, Russia, and the Future of the West*, 41–42. For example, see comments by Russian Foreign Minister Sergei Lavrov, available on the website of the Permanent Mission of the Russian Federation to the United Nations at http://russiaun.ru/en/news/200808121712, and reports on Russia's international propaganda channel Russia Today at https://web.archive.org/web/20080813023856/http://russiatoday.com/news/news/28732 and https://web.archive.org/web/20080826120543/http://www.russiatoday.com/news/news/29428.

30 Since the Soviet Union regarded these people as citizens – whether they lived in the pre-1939 Soviet Union or were in territories incorporated into the Soviet Union under the Molotov–Ribbentrop Pact, it had to explain their actions as treason, negating that they may have been motivated by their own identity independent of Russian domination and not for any love of Germany or Nazi ideology. But the Soviet propaganda, carried on by Russia today, would see their decision as individual choices and not subject to a different experience of their respective countries vis-à-vis Russia. Von Hagen, in Kershaw and Lewin (eds.), *op. cit.*, 247.

31 In contrast to the Poles, who are secure in their own identity, the Ukrainians, who have not had a sustainably independent state in their modern history, have a more extreme need to define what they are not. This makes Jews more foreign by necessity – both responsible for Communism (and hence crimes including the communist-induced mass starvation) as well as the capitalist exploiters of Ukrainian peasants. Bartov, *Erased: Vanishing Traces of Jewish Galicia in Present-day Ukraine* (Princeton, 2007), 208f.

32 The *Holodomor* controversy had to do with official Ukrainian attempts to define the mass starvation of Ukrainians during the Soviet Union not as a tragic consequence of communist ideology but rather as a genocide perpetuated on ethnic Ukrainians by Russia. On this controversy and its justification by Russia, see Satter, *op. cit.*, 214.

33 Ibid., 220f. Cf. Snyder, *Bloodlands: Europe between Hitler and Stalin* (London, 2011), 404.

34 Snyder, *Bloodlands*. Cf. Baranova, in Marczewski and Eich (eds.), *op. cit.*

35 Snyder, *Black Earth*, 123f.

36 Jan Gross, *Fear: Anti-Semitism in Poland after Auschwitz* (New York, 2006), 241. Gross points out that the Jews did not bring Communism to Poland but rather Poland brought Jews to Communism through exclusion from much of Polish society.

37 Bożena Szaynok, "The Role of Anti-Semitism in Postwar Polish-Jewish Relations" in Robert Blobaum (ed.), *op. cit.*, 279f.; Jews, in this setting, became in some ways less of an ethnic group and more of an "organization" in the spirit of the classic Russian antisemitic forgery *Protocols of the Elders of Zion*. As an example, Polish communist propaganda characterized even West German reparations as part of a Jewish plot. Since West Germany paid, Jews sought to absolve Germans and needed someone else to blame: this would be the Poles. Dariusz Stola, "Fighting Against the Shadows: the Anti-Zionist Campaign of 1968" in Robert Blobaum (ed.), *Anti-Semitism and Its Opponents in Modern Poland* (Ithaca, 2005), 291f. This latter logic (blaming Poles supposedly to absolve Germans who had paid off the Jews) emerged again in public discourse after the publication of *Neighbors: the Destruction of the Jewish Community in Jedwabne, Poland* (Princeton, 2001) by Jan Gross.

38 Bartov, *Erased*, 204f. Snyder, *Bloodlands*, 406f.
39 Gross, *Fear*, 252.
40 Janine P. Holc, "Memory contested: Jewish and Catholic views of Auschwitz in contemporary Poland" in Blobaum (ed.), *op. cit.*, 303.
41 Blobaum, "Introduction", in Blobaum (ed.), *op. cit.*, 15–16. Cf. Carroll, *Constantine's Sword: The Church and the Jews* (Boston, 2001), 3f.
42 Holc, "Memory Contested: Jewish and Catholic Views of Auschwitz in Contemporary Poland" in Blobaum (ed.), *op. cit.*, 301f.
43 Communist mythology actually obscured the importance of the site in the West until several decades later, so that the primacy of Auschwitz in Holocaust memory is relatively recent – and itself ironically a triumph of Communist propaganda. Tim Cole, *Images of the Holocaust: The Myth of the "Shoah" Business* (London, 1999), 98f.
44 Snyder, *Bloodlands*, viii.
45 Blobaum, "Introduction", in Blobaum, *op. cit.*, 17; Gross, *Neighbors*. Cf. Cole, *op. cit.*, 102f.
46 Holc, "Memory Contested" in ibid., 314f.; Snyder, *Black Earth*, 210f.
47 Cole, *op. cit.*, 99.
48 Bartov, *Erased*, xi.
49 Gross, *Fear*, 249.
50 Ibid., 245.
51 Rehabilitations of one wartime leader or another who committed atrocities in collaboration with the Germans, albeit in the name of the former state which had been destroyed by the prior Russian occupation, without context does not help these countries, and indeed further enables Russian propaganda by equating assertions of identity against Soviet Russia (and now against post-Soviet Russia) as equivalent to fascism. These countries would be better off addressing these problematic figures head-on, but often lack the critical tools to do so. Cf. Belafatti, *op. cit.* Ironically, until 1990, Russian policy was often to cover up the existence of these leaders, as it showed Soviet citizens collaborating – post-Soviet Russia has become more interested in reviving their memories, in parallel with the nationalists in the respective countries which may not fully understand the criminal activities of these figures. Cf. Baranova, in Marczewski and Eich (eds.), *op. cit.*
52 Snyder, *Black Earth*, 212f. On the recovery of the history of Estonia's twentieth-century occupation by Russia in conjunction with the recovery of Estonia's post-Soviet independence, see Oksanen, *op. cit.*
53 Inesis Feldmanis, "Waffen SS Units of Latvians and Other Non-Germanic peoples in World War II: Methods of Formation, Ideology, and Goals" in Commission of the Historians of Latvia, *op. cit.*, 122f.
54 Hella Pick, *Guilty Victim: Austria from the Holocaust to Haider* (London, 2000), 5.
55 Ibid., 20f.
56 Ibid., 16f. When it recovered its independence in 1955, a so-called "responsibility clause" was removed from an earlier draft of the Austrian State Treaty with the four occupying powers, on the logic that a "new state" could and should not be responsible for earlier crimes. In practice, this also absolved individual Austrians of official responsibility. Ibid., 31.

6   The Genocide of 1971 in Bangladesh

Lessons from history

Srimanti Sarkar

Those who forget the past are doomed to repeat it
George Santayana[1]

Introduction

What is the lesson that a history of genocide teaches us? A simplistic avowal may
be that it teaches us one of the most punitive lessons for practising intolerance,
towards other fellow beings, in the meanest possible way. It thereby underscores
the absolute need for tolerance (social, political, ideological, religious, or cultural)
as quintessential for the prevention of the generic destruction of the human society.
But, reiterating what has been stated above, one may ask: If "those who forget the
past are doomed to repeat it" (Charny 1999: lvii) – what will it amount to recollect
a past which is differentially "constructed"? That is, if forgoing a bleak history of
genocide is susceptible to repeated misdemeanour, then reminiscing about a "constructed" history of genocide is perhaps more likely to account for a similar or even
a graver kind of transgression. A cautious de-construction and subsequent re-construction of the widely professed historiography, given every risk of fallacious elucidation, is thus imperative to draw a pragmatic lesson from a history of genocide.

Recollecting the history of genocide in Bangladesh

An act of genocide is perhaps the most terrible crime that humankind can commit. However, drawing a definite lesson out of a distinct history of genocide is
nothing short of a perplexing affair, as any attempt to study genocides has to
deal with the endless definitional contestations and subjective relativities that
it brings along. For instance, there exists a considerable difference of opinion
among scholars worldwide regarding the very definition of "genocide."[2] The
United Nations defined "genocide" as an act committed with an intent to debil-
itate a national, ethnic, racial, or a religious group using means such as killing
members of the group; causing serious bodily or mental harm to members of the
group; deliberately inflicting on the group conditions of life calculated to bring
about its physical destruction in whole or in part; imposing measures intended
to prevent births within the group; or forcibly transferring children of the group
to another group. However, this legal definition is only an operational one and is
not devoid of its limitations. It leaves much space for ambiguities while judging

the "intent" to destroy,[3] or "mental harm"[4] caused, or while prosecuting the "state"[5] or "non-state"[6] actors for carrying out such an act.[7] Estimates of genocide are also uncertain, confusing and significantly propagandist as it is difficult to separate the battle-dead or those dying in the wake of war from those who are mass murdered.[8] Furthermore, accounts of genocide are invariably blurred by denials and cross-accusations. Therefore, given these larger contestations, defining an act of genocide – either on the basis of moral dictates (essentially relative) or in terms of sheer numerical totalities (essentially varying) – is testing. As a clear tension with regard to the conceptual purity and totality of genocide do remain; only contextual analyses, wherein one can move backward and forward between the various opposing positions, may prove to be helpful to surmise a reasonable lesson out of it. Accordingly, this chapter will attempt to put forth the case of Bangladesh – the South Asian nation that has witnessed one of the worst kinds of genocide in the late twentieth century – to highlight some of the immanent challenges that prevent one to draw an encompassing lesson from a history of genocide. Considering a "reasonable" lesson as more inclusive and effectual, the Bangladeshi experience is expected to highlight some of the nuanced aspects of the blasé historiography of genocide that unfolds in this part of the world.

The history of Bangladesh is essentially one of her Liberation War of Independence, which recounts incessantly the perilous violence and bloodshed that accompanied it. The Liberation War of 1971 has been a horrifying exemplar of extreme intolerance, more semitic[9] than political, which marked the history of the sub-continent forever. The nascent state of Bangladesh emerged from the remnants of the carnage that was carried out by the West Pakistani armed forces on East Pakistan as the latter demanded secession and rose against the systematic subjugation by its western counterpart. Post 1947, relations between the two wings of Pakistan became increasingly stressed over issues concerning land reforms, state language, provincial autonomy, defence, and inter-wing economic and administrative disparities. Systemic inconsistencies and political indisposition conjoined with extreme ethno-cultural divergences ultimately culminated in a barbaric act of genocide, which continued for nine months starting from 26 March to 16 December 1971 during the course of which around 3 million of the population were literally annihilated.[10] It speckled the history of Pakistan forever – then united as West and East Pakistan, and now divided as present Pakistan and Bangladesh respectively – the burden of which neither of the two states could sufficiently obliterate.

For Pakistan, recollection of 1971 has always been an arduous episode of genocide denial; whereas for Bangladesh, to date, the recollection of 1971 is as much a celebration of its struggle for independence as it is an anguished rumination of its national devastation. The recollection of the memories of the Liberation War and that of the Genocide of 1971 in Bangladesh takes place in a number of ways. Bangladesh still looks back at its brutal past and takes a definite recourse to its stained history of genocide, which neither the emergent state nor its people can overlook. Apart from the wide range of literature that vividly captures the history of Bangladesh, nooks and corners of the city further help one to significantly recount the war-time memories in a passionate way. A conscious attempt to keep alive the history of the liberation takes place either through a gallant display of the pictures, photographs, or artefacts that are preserved in the various war museums; or through the symbolic monuments, sculptures, or even the poignant mass graves that spread all across the country.[11] However, this passionate recollection of the much eulogized nationalist history, impregnated with barbaric violence, is rather problematic. The problem does not lie in the commemoration of the much-warranted independence, which was achieved with great toil, but in the recollection of a history that was arguably "constructed" over the period of time. It hints at a lurking danger upon the prospective future of the country calling for a critical appraisal of the same.

Three illustrative examples will help explain better the way the dominant historiography of Bangladesh taking constant recourse to the Genocide of 1971 got "constructed" with evident gender, ethnic, and political biases: (1) If one carefully charts the way memories of the Liberation War of 1971 are being recollected especially by the women victims of the genocide – a perceptible gender bias can be seen at work. (2) If one attempts to gauge the rationale behind the struggles of the hill people of the Chittagong Hill Tracts (CHT) in post-independence Bangladesh – an associated ethnic bias, rooted into the country's much professed nationalism, can be perceived. (3) In light of the recent furore with regard to the trial of the war criminals of 1971 that culminated into a mass movement, namely the Shahbag Movement in 2013 – a definite political bias can be noticed. While it arguably leaves scope for much apprehension, it calls for a careful de-construction and a subsequent re-construction of the dominant historiography of Bangladesh that is incessantly linked to the history of the Genocide of 1971. The following section will thereby adopt a case-centric approach to highlight the plausible biases that "construct" the history of Bangladesh (rooted in the history of the Genocide of 1971) and buttress the need for a re-construction of history to draw a reasonable lesson out of it.

Constructed history of Bangladesh with gender bias

Recollecting the memories of the Genocide of 1971 is invariably a difficult task as it painstakingly makes one recount the immutable loses that were suffered. Out of the 3 million people who were killed, nearly all were women who were victimized under the "Operation Searchlight"[12] conducted by the West Pakistani armed forces upon its Eastern counterpart. From a humanist perspective, it may seem inappropriate to subscribe to a gendered view of human suffering during the war; but given the wider societal practice of bigotry it becomes imperative to render special attention towards the cause of the women victims of the war, who are almost always doubly persecuted.

Rape, murder, brutal torture, abduction, or forcible prostitution were some of the primary means of persecution, during the course of the nine-month long war, from which the women suffered. However, the plight of the women victims of the Genocide of 1971 was never addressed adequately even after independence. Social victimization of the war-ravaged women continued with all persistency, for which, scholars often (almost justifiably) put part of the blame upon the patriarchal state that had emerged out of the liberation struggle.[13]

The state policies of the newly independent state of Bangladesh failed to capture some of the vital aspects of victimhood. "Social death," for instance, was one of the central evils of genocide, to which the persecuted women had to succumb. It amounted to the loss of their social life, their social identity, and the meaning for their existence.[14] It may be noted here, that the title "*Birangana*" symbolizing "war heroines" or "national heroines" was given to the rape victims of the 1971 Genocide as a means to officially recognize their sufferings and to re-integrate them into the mainstream society. However, such measures proved largely ineffective as they could not prevent the victimized women from incurring relentless social deaths on a regular basis. Nayanika Mookherjee in her article explained how discrepancies remained between a raped women's national position as icons of "honour" and their local reception, which was subjected to "*khota*" (sarcastic/censorious remarks expressing scorn and evoking the unpleasant events) or lewd social sanctions.[15] She highlighted the plights of the *Biranganas* through a brief story of three poor, landless women – Kajoli, Moyna, and Rohima from the Enayetpur village in western Bangladesh. She narrated the social reactions they and their family members had to face after their photographs were printed on the front page of the national newspapers with the caption: "Birangonas [war heroines] from Kushtia demand trial of Gholam Azum [a well-known collaborator of the war of 1971]" on 28 March 1992. Kajoli's husband, Rafique, was ridiculed in public for his wife's testimony against Gholam Azum, the collaborator. He was told that by publicly acknowledging that they had been raped by "the military" (the term used to refer to the Pakistani soldiers of 1971), the news had spread all over the world to add to their dishonour.[16]

While countless such stories, as the one mentioned above, can be recounted, it simply projects the way women's national position as icons of "honour" largely mismatched with the conformist and patriarchal society that subsisted. Bangladesh being a country where female chastity and the practice of purdah isolation have been one of the cardinal principles, such false eulogization of the rape victims as "war heroines" was nothing but "a trope" for the symbolic evocation of the dynamism of the new nation. Through it, the State tried to show its progression out of the taboos, dogmas, and traditions of a Muslim society – but the reality simply proved it otherwise.[17]

It was only with the eventual progression of the feminist scholarship that a nuanced study of the history tilted prominently against the women, wherein the State tried to impose its patriarchal preponderance, came to the fore. Mention may be made of the path-breaking work by Susan Brownmiller, who in her work titled *In Against Our Will: Men, Women and Rape* highlighted the faulty government policies towards the women victims of war.[18] She affirmatively pointed out that, rape, abduction, and forcible prostitution during the nine-month war proved to be only the first round of humiliation for the Bengali women. Prime Minister Mujibur Rahman's decision of regarding the war victims of rape as national heroines was the opening shot of an ill-starred campaign to reintegrate them into the society. Initiatives were taken on part of the State to facilitate the return of the victimized women to their husbands and attempts were made to find bridegrooms for the unmarried or the widowed ones, especially from among the *Mukti Bahini* (freedom fighters). But, in actuality, this initiative could not get off the ground as a successful rehabilitation policy or a measure; since, only few prospective bridegrooms stepped forward, and those who did, made it plain that they expected the government to present them with handsome dowries. Thus, the initiative simply turned into a "marry them off" campaign, which was more condescending and socially demeaning in nature.[19]

Furthermore, even amidst all the futilities, the State-led measures proved to be no less draconic and devoid of moral sanctions. Neelima Ibrahim, for example, in her voluminous documentary *Ami Birangona Bolchi* pointed out the way the State, presuming itself as the final authority to define the fate of the women victims, took the decision to give away the war babies for adoption despite protests and pleadings from their mothers. The most striking response regarding the fate of these children came from the "Father of the Nation" Sheikh Mujibur Rahman himself, who said: "Send the children, who have no identity of their father abroad. Let the children of human beings grow up like proper humans. Besides I do not want to keep that polluted blood in the country".[20]

These accounts clearly express the utter insensitiveness on the part of the State towards its women victims of war and which was allegedly not a mere overlooking. It may be added here that no exhaustive victims lists accounted adequately for the women victims of war who lost their lives or died during the war; the 14 volumes of the officially documented history of the Liberation War carried only few testimonies of rape and among the category of *Shaheeds* (martyrs who sacrificed their lives for the cause of their country) the names of only two women, that too belonging to the intellectual class, were included and the rest of the majority were excluded.[21] This epitomizes the hegemonic preponderance and the essentially gendered attitude of the State towards its women victims of the War and the Genocide of 1971.

Thus, while the feminist accounts espouse the agonies of the persecuted women – that of their "parched souls", their "silenced voices" and "marked fates" – they provide the much required cue to trace the inherent "gender bias" in the glorification of the history of the Liberation War and the Genocide of 1971. The bias makes the recollection of the war memories not only problematic but also symptomatic: "problematic" because it reminds of the horror of the genocide as well as highlights the associated discrimination that the State conjointly inflicted upon its women victims; and "symptomatic" since it constructed the history in its own gendered way thereby silencing or abating the women's question away from the public discourse.

Constructed history of Bangladesh with ethnic bias

The second case study that I wish to put forth in this context is that of the hill dwellers of the Chittagong Hill Tracks (CHT). Bangladesh is home to around 45 different ethnic communities who find no substantial representation in the political, institutional, or cultural arenas of the state. Located in the south-eastern part

Bangladesh, the CHT forms a part of the mountain range that stretches north for some 1,800 km from western Burma to the point where it meets the eastern Himalayas in China. Apart from the narrow strip of roughly 280 km by 60 km, now administered from Dhaka, and the Chinese-administered northern tip, this mountain range is divided almost equally between India and Burma. It is subdivided into three districts – Bandarban, Khagrachari and Rangamati, and is inhabited by 12 ethnic groups who comprise a bewildering mass speaking a wide range of languages, adhering to various creeds and organized socially in different ways.

Anthropological accounts affirm that there existed no uniform category such as "hill people" or "hill dwellers" as such prior to the colonial encounter in 1860[22]. It was only under systematic socio-economic and political exploitation, during the colonial and post-colonial period, that the region began to take on a separate identity.[23] During the colonial period different parts of this mountainous range were colonized and administered separately. As the British rule came to an end in 1947 followed by the partitioning of British India, the Chittagong Hills were awarded to Pakistan.[24] When Bangladesh seceded from Pakistan in 1971, the Chittagong Hills became part of the new country. The newly independent state of Bangladesh, imbued with its spirit of nationalism, went ahead with its agenda of creating a homogeneous Bengali state in which language, culture, and religion became the basis of imposing Bengali nationalism. The State subsequently imposed latent compulsions for identifying with the dominant cultural group upon the people belonging to the "other" ethnic groups. This naturally encroached upon the autonomy of the hill people and put them on a disadvantageous position.

The CHT being the homeland of people belonging to varied and multi-lingual nationalities demanded for special entity status to protect their separate communal identity in independent Bangladesh. In view of their traditional ethnic lineages and past experiences of exploitation under the colonial and West Pakistani rule, on 15 February 1972 a hill people's delegation, led by Manobendra Narayan Larma,[25] called on the State to provide political and economic autonomy to them with constitutional guarantee for the continuation of their traditional system. But their demands were rejected by Sheikh Mujibur Rahman on the grounds that it would threaten the national unity and oneness of the newly independent state. Subsequently, the 1972 constitution not only made no provision for rendering special status to the natives of CHT and to protect its ethno-cultural plurality; but, instead, with the passage of a bill on 23 January 1974 the parliament declared Bangladesh as a uni-cultural and uni-lingual nation-state. Furthermore, on his first (and last) visit to Rangamati, Sheikh Mujibur Rahman declared: "From this day onward the tribals are being promoted into Bengalis".[26] Sheikh Mujib's speech aroused many misgivings among the hill people as it implied that the Bengalis belonged to some higher echelons of civilization unlike the non-Bengali "others" making them feel all the more marginalized. Threatened by Sheikh Mujib's conception of a culturally homogeneous state, a regional political platform – the United People's Party of CHT (PCJSS), along with its armed wing, *Shanti Bahini* (Peace Force) – was formed on 7 March 1972. The PCJSS emerged as the main mouthpiece for the hill people and its formation signalled the formal break of the CHT from the state-sponsored model of nationhood.

The subsequent history of systemic marginalization of the hill people of CHT is not unknown. They were not only asked to forget their separate identities but were even threatened by the State to turn them into minorities by sending Bengalis to the CHT. The "political" migration in the name of re-settling landless Bengali families on the government owned *Khas* land since 1979, did greater harm to the hill people (especially to the *Jhumias* or the *Jhum* cultivators) as they were snatched from their natural habitat, culture, and resources. As the government ignored the indigenous views and attempted to superimpose its preponderance through developmental projects, it was considered a gross violation of the inalienable rights of the hill people. Social economic and political vulnerability ultimately turned the region into a battle ground where the seeds of *Jumma* nationalism (an identity that was claimed by the hill people) were sown as against the version of Bengali nationalism that was championed by the State. Escalating insurgency ultimately led to the militarization of the CHT and in the name of counter-insurgency massive human rights violations were committed by the military itself. Cases of forced religious conversions, persecution, evictions, arrests, tortures, and kidnappings were rampant and the region remained a hot bed of socio-political tension for over two decades. Though the CHT Peace Accord signed on 2 December 1997 could only put a formal end to the armed insurgency in the region, it failed to establish "peace" (for absence of war does not ensure peace alone), "equity" (for special status as "tribal" inhabited region did not necessarily reflect equality, but subordination to the dominant construction of a "state-nation"),[27] or "justice" (for there existed no provisions for compensation for the excesses committed by the State-led military) to the ethnic minority communities living in this embattled region[28].

This besetting history of ethnic determination or "ethnicity"[29] in Bangladesh can be linked, in a way, to the history of the Liberation War and that of the Genocide of 1971, which has allowed an eulogized concept of "nationalism" – more "exclusive" rather than "inclusive" in nature – to foster. This version of nationalism is essentially a "construction" of the State's hegemonic power and control, which has permitted the pre-domination of one ethnic group (the majority Bengalis) over the numerous ethnic "others" (the non-Bengali populace that includes the indigenous populace of the CHT). Accordingly, the lesson that one can draw from it is that: if the Genocide of 1971 in Bangladesh was predicated upon the non-tolerant and ethno-religious brand of nationalism or "semitism" (as one may term it) professed by West Pakistan, then the whole host of repression and systemic excesses committed by the State towards its indigenous population, amounting to nothing short of an "ethnocide", can be blamed upon the post-independence state of Bangladesh, which had adopted an equally non-assimilationist brand of nationalism.

Constructed history of Bangladesh with political bias

The third case study, to put forth in this context, is the issue of the trial of the war criminals of 1971 that culminated into a striking popular movement, namely the Shahbag Movement in 2013. This study may be considered relevant to highlight the vicious political predilection in Bangladesh.

The Shahbag Uprising in Bangladesh was one of the most important developments that marked the country's socio-political scenario over the last few years. The popular movement at Dhaka's Shahbag Square had started on 5 February 2013 with the demand of capital punishment for the perpetrators of the Genocide of 1971. It all happened when the ever-bustling Shahbag Square, which is the key transport hub of Dhaka, struck the news headlines for protests, counter-protests, and violence as the International Crimes Tribunal (ICT) of Bangladesh sentenced the Jamaat-e-Islami leader Abdul Quader Mollah to life imprisonment. Soon, a war of words took place over the cyber space among the bloggers, twitterati, and social networkers, and violence broke out as Jamaat activists took to the streets following the indictment of their leaders. While a section of Bangladeshis gathered on the streets to celebrate the tribunal's verdict of life imprisonment for Quader Mollah, a *Rajakar*[30] and a prominent war criminal accused of committing heinous crime against humanity during the Liberation War of 1971, another section of activists virulently protested against the verdict considering it as meek compared to the propensity of crimes committed by him. They insisted on the death sentence for Quader Mollah for corroborating the genocide in Bangladesh together with the Pakistani (West) armed forces during 1971. Active protests continued uninterruptedly for 17 days; thereafter, a blogger-activist named Ahmed Rajib Haider was brutally murdered in Mirpur on 15 February 2013 for writing against the Jamaat radicals. The blogger's death re-ignited violence and took the movement to a crucial level whereby the contentious issue of separating religion from politics was raised. The intermittent clashes that took place thereafter assumed a characteristic nature, as the so-called Islamist and the Secularist forces clashed with each other propelling the nation into an unanticipated low of societal disarray[31].

Here, one needs to note, for Bangladesh was born out of a reprehensible bloodbath – confronted with the formidable task of nation-building and immediate recovery of its war-ravaged economy amidst a highly unstable socio-political state of affairs – the trial of the convicts of war crimes of the 1971 Genocide remained a big task wanting its due fulfilment. While the immediate post-War years was the best time to hold to account those who committed war crimes, the 1970s was a decade of death and deluge for Bangladesh, which saw successive governments coming into power and getting overpowered with existential crises and thereby refraining from holding proper trials. The new constitution that was adopted by the Constituent Assembly on 4 November 1972 stated in its Preamble that nationalism, socialism, democracy, and secularism would be the main principles of state policy.[32] Through these principles it was expected that the past indignations will be meted out and social justice will be realized – but, inadequacies remained.

The newly independent government of Bangladesh promulgated the Bangladesh Collaborators (Special Tribunals) Order in 1972 and passed the International Crimes (Tribunals) Act 1973 to try, investigate, and prosecute the persons responsible for the genocide and crimes against humanity committed during the Genocide of 1971. But the Act had its drawbacks. Through a general amnesty declared by Sheikh Mujibur Rahman on 30 November 1973, most of the convicts barring those found guilty for rape, murder, and arson were pardoned.[33]

Furthermore, with Sheikh Mujib's assassination in 15 August 1975, the trial of the war criminals was stalled by the military rulers. President Ziaur Rahman after assuming power repealed the very act and the trial procedures were muted. As a result, many of the leaders of the Jamaat-e-Islami who had collaborated with the Pakistani armed forces to carry out the genocide during the Liberation War of Independence either went underground or fled to other countries.

Under General Ziaur Rahman's rule, the constitution of Bangladesh was amended to remove and prevent the realization of the principle of secularism.[34] "Islam" was declared the state religion and thereby the gradual process of Islamization relegated the followers of every other religion – Hindus, Christians, or Buddhists – to the backdrop and rendered them into a subservient position.[35] The process further enabled the war criminals to rehabilitate and participate openly in politics. For instance, the period saw the emergence of the Bangladesh Jamaat-e-Islami (BJI) under the leadership of Ghulam Azam who was a leading collaborator of the 1971 Genocide and a key accused of committing war crimes. With Ghulam Azam's return to Bangladesh in 1978, the BJI started rebuilding itself and in a convention held in the precincts of the Eden Hotel in Dhaka on 25–27 May 1979, the BJI formally re-emerged as a political party. Since then they have been spreading their deep tentacles in the countryside by setting up madrassas for children and Shariat courts. Flush with funds from Pakistan and the Middle East, they increasingly became a formidable cadre based political force – propagating Islamist world views – who wielded significant manoeuvring power over the Bangladeshi polity and society.[36]

As parliamentary democracy was formally restored during the 1990s (post Zia and Ershad's regime), vocal resistance against Islamist onslaughts were staged by the Awami League (AL) in association with secular leftist forces and civil society groups. On 29 December 1991 as Ghulam Azam was elected the *Ameer* of the BJI, the "*Ekattorer Ghatak Dalal Nirmul Committee*" (Committee to Uproot the Killers and Collaborators of Seventy-one)[37] started building up public support for Azam's trial[38]. The Nirmul Committee raised the issue of the trial of the war criminals, for the first time, in a People's Court given the government's inability to try them. They further sought the cooperation of all the political, social, and cultural organizations that had supported the Liberation War in order to massify and popularize its demands for the trials. Subsequently, 13 political parties including the Awami League (AL), the Communist Party of Bangladesh (CPB), the Workers' Party, the Jatiya Samajtantrik Dal (JSD), the National Awami Party (NAP), and the Ganatantri Dal supported the programme of trying Azam at the People's Court. A concomitant citizens' movement was organized under the leadership of Shahid Janani Jahanara Imam, who on 11 February 1992 formed the "*Muktijuddher Chetana Bastabayan o Ekattorer Ghatak Dalal Nirmuljatiya Samanyaya Committee*" (National Coordination Committee to Realise the Consciousness of the Liberation War and Uproot the Killers Collaborators of Seventy-one) to integrate all the supporting forces under one single platform. However, regrettably such attempts of staging integrated protest movements failed. This was partly due to the reluctance showed by the major political parties to marshal the country's anti-war crime movement and partly due to the lack of unity and cohesion at the level of the civil society[39].

It was not until 2008 that the issue of the trial of the war criminals of 1971 was revived. The AL government assumed the holding of trials as one of its primary agendas to win the electoral mandate in 2009; and after winning the same, the AL government continued with its promise to hold the war crimes trials with a significant vim. As most of the leaders of the Jamaat fell into the category of convicts of war crimes, the BJI entered into a tacit alliance with the Bangladesh Nationalist Party (BNP) – the strongest rival of the AL – to oppose the trials. The AL government also kept no stones unturned to roll the national and social agenda (the trials) into a political one in view of the impending 10th Jatiya Sangsad elections in 2014. For instance, the landmark decision of de-registering the BJI – the largest Islamist political party of Bangladesh – from the national electoral roll by the Bangladesh High Court on 1 August 2013 was considered a calculated measure by the AL government to increase its political clout prior to elections. Similarly, the BNP's open support for the fanatic radicals – the Jamaat and Hefazat-e-Islam – that organized violence against the protesting masses, was evidently a strategy to retain its Islamist vote-bank in the upcoming general elections.

This underscores the way narrow "politicking" by the competing political parties has always (and still continues to) undermined the true agenda of the trials, which is to render social justice to the victims and their family members. Even though the Shahbag Movement aimed to buttress the need for the same, using essentially peaceful, apolitical, and popular means of protest, it could not save itself from getting dragged into the vicious politics of polarization, intolerance, and deadlock, which in turn led to the definite escalation of societal violence. Accordingly, Bangladesh experienced reprehensible political violence during the year 2013–2014, wherein as per the Annual Human Rights Reports of *Odhikar*, 506 people were killed and some 24,176 were injured in 2013; while in 2014 an estimated 190 people were killed, 9,429 injured, and 1,321 arrested[40]. The nation also saw some of the most gruesome murders of bloggers, secular activists, religious associates, and foreign nationals taking place with concomitant rise in the activities of religious fundamentalists.[41] Thus, the Shahbag Movement – which is considerably a significant flashpoint in the history of democracy and social movements in Bangladesh – through both its successes and failures speaks loudly of the vicious political practice in Bangladesh. This unscrupulous political history of Bangladesh therefore reasonably explains what prevents the polity from realizing its most cherished ideals.

Conclusion: lessons from a re-constructed history of genocide

The dominant and widely professed historiography of Bangladesh stemming from the history of its Liberation War of Independence and the Genocide of 1971 is therefore a "constructed" one. It is both rooted in as well as precursory to further "violence" – be it a covert form of violence upon the "silenced" rape victims of the genocide or systemic ethnic violence upon the marginalized hill people of CHT; or a form of obscured psychological violence upon the war victims and their family members who are deprived of social justice through the much encumbered trials of the war criminals; or overt corporal violence upon the common masses who are often victims of "street-violence" that is caused due to the socio-political viscosity of the indignant polity. It is, therefore, imperative to carefully de-construct and subsequently re-construct such a history with inherent biases (gender, ethnic, and political biases) and impregnated violence.

For polities that are fundamentally dichotomous and rift with intricate challenges, such as that of the Bangladeshi polity, it is therefore important to: first, diligently advocate a "reasonable" lesson rather than an encompassing lesson for practicing ultimate intolerance. For instance, a case specific approach might prove to be more useful than an overly theoretical exposition on universal moral principles like justice, equality, fraternity, or tolerance. Second, as history is recollected through multifarious ways leaving ample scope for fallacious constructions, it will be necessary to keep a critical check on every possible shift in the blasé recollection of such memories. It is only through the same that a plausible re-construction of the history will be possible. For instance, recognizable shifts in the form of biases (gender, ethnic, and political) can be identified during the course of recollection of the memories of the 1971 Genocide in Bangladesh. Lastly, but most importantly, a mere recount of the brutal memories of genocide is not enough. It is essential to keep a responsible check on such memories, as it leaves scope for harnessing a negative outlook, which in turn may cause immensurable harm to the human society. For instance, smitten by brutal reality, instances of following a radical path and yielding to the course of hyper-nationalism is an example not unknown or difficult to understand. Therefore, significant attention given in these directions is likely to help draw a reasonable lesson from a marked history of genocide.

However, in conclusion, I choose to hint at a fundamental dilemma that may leave one with much disquiet: while any re-construction of history is presumably set to challenge the dominant construction of history, will it be prudent to render the very base of the perceptible history unstable by challenging it? Maybe "Yes" or maybe "No". I leave this question intentionally unanswered, to leave scope for speculation among scholars of History and Genocide Studies, who should best determine the most plausible ways to "re-construct" history keeping factual accuracies and societal conventions in mind.

Notes

1 These haunting words are inscribed above the museum entrance at Dachau, which is the site of the former Nazi concentration camp. Israel W. Charny, ed., in *Encyclopedia of Genocide*, vol. 1 (Santa Barbara: ABC-CLIO Inc., 1999), lvii.

2 During the post-World War II period, Raphael Lemkin, a Polish-Jewish lawyer, coined this new term "genocide" (Geno = Species, Cide = Murder of) meaning "the murder of a people". He used this new term to describe the Nazi policies of systematic murder of the Jewish people, and thanks to his efforts, the United Nations Convention of Genocide, which is the world's major legal statement to date on genocide, was passed on 20 January 1951.

3 On several instances, scholars have argued that actions such as torching of villages, killing of men, and even wiping out communities in large numbers are often done without an "intent" to eliminate an entire human race, and hence should not be counted as genocide on the basis of sheer resemblance, but only as mass murder, massacre or slaughter, human rights abuses, annihilation, pogroms, or anything likewise. While, in other extreme instances, scholars have even considered cases of euthanasia killings as an act of genocide for being "precursory" to mass killings, although, in actual practice, they might not seem to be so. These examples affirm the subjective relativity in defining an act of genocide based on the measure of "intent."

4 On a vast array of instances, an act of genocide through its resultant social and economic changes in the society is known to bring about psychological and cultural harm upon its victims (individuals or groups) who tend to lose their mental cohesion and social identity, if not their lives.

5 The concept "politicide" or "political mass murder" needs to be understood in this context to explain cases where groups of victims are defined by their political positions or actions and when one of the perpetrators is the State or its agents.

6 This encompasses situations in which at least one party to a civil war systematically uses deadly force to destroy the civilian support base of its opponent.

7 Barbara Harff, "No Lessons Learned from the Holocaust? Assessing Risks of Genocide and Political Mass Murder since 1955," *The American Political Science Review* 97, no. 1 (2003): 58, www.jstor.org/stable/3118221.

8 Rudolph J. Rummel, "Power, Genocide and Mass Murder," *Journal of Peace Research. Sage Publications Ltd* 31, no. 1 (1994): 1–10.

9 The term "semitic" has been used to mean "racial" here, skipping its formal lexical usage to mean racial discrimination specifically during the holocaust.

10 According to *New York Times* (28 March 1971) 10,000 people were killed; *New York Times* (29 March 1971) 5,000–7,000 people were killed in Dhaka; *The Sydney Morning Herald* (29 March 1971) 10,000–100,000 was killed; *New York Times* (1 April 1971) 35,000 was killed in Dhaka during the Operation Searchlight. www. genocidebangladesh.org/ (accessed on 10 July 2017).

11 I hereby draw upon my field trip experiences in Bangladesh commenced between 2013 and 2016. My personal visits to the Bangladesh National Museum, Liberation War Museum, Museum of Independence, Bangabandhu Memorial Museum at 32 Dhanmondi, the Central Language Martyrs' Memorial (Shaheed Minar) monument at Dhaka University, and the National Martyrs' Memorial at Savar have helped in shaping my views significantly.

12 "Operation Searchlight" was a planned military action carried out by the Pakistani Army to curb the Bengali nationalist movement in erstwhile East Pakistan (present Bangladesh). The operation was launched on 25 March 1971 with the aim of taking control of all the major cities of East Pakistan and then eliminating all opposition, political or military, within one month.

13 Amena Mohsin, "Gendered Nation, Gendered Peace: A Study of Bangladesh," in *Peace Process and Peace Accords*, ed. Ed Samir Kumar Das, vol. 2 (New Delhi: Sage Publications Ltd., South Asian Peace Studies, 2005), 223–25.

14 As rightly pointed out by Claudia Card, "social death" which lay at the centre of genocide takes ones focus off the body counts or loss of talents; and instead, directs one to mourn losses of relationships that create community and give meaning to the development of talents. Claudia Card, "Genocide and Social Death", *Feminist Philosophy and the Problem of Evil* 18, no. 1 (2003): 63–79.

15 Mookherjee, Nayanika. "Remembering to Forget: Public Secrecy and Memory of Sexual Violence in the BangladeshWar of 1971." *The Journal of the Royal Anthropological Institute*. 12, no. 2 (2006): 433–450. Nayanika Mookherjee, "Remembering to Forget: Public Secrecy and Memory of Sexual Violence in the Bangladesh War of 1971," *The Journal of the Royal Anthropological Institute* 12, no. 2 (2006): 433–450.

16 Ibid., 433.
17 Ibid., 434.
18 Susan Brownmiller, *"In Against Our Will: Men, Women and Rape,"* (New York: Bantam Books, 1975), 1–541.
19 Meghna Guhathakurta explains how the program of rehabilitation of the victimized women into the society turned into a tragic "marry them off" campaign. See in Mohsin, Amena. "Gendered Nation, Gendered Peace: A Study of Bangladesh." *Peace Process and Peace Accords.* Ed. Samir Kumar Das. (New Delhi: Sage Publications Ltd, South Asian Peace Studies: Vol. 2, 2005), 223–225.
20 Mohsin, Amena. "Gendered Nation, Gendered Peace: A Study of Bangladesh." *Peace Process and Peace Accords.* Ed. Samir Kumar Das. (New Delhi: Sage Publications Ltd., South Asian Peace Studies: Vol. 2, 2005), 223.
21 Hasan Hafizur Rahman, ed., *"Bangladesher Swadhinata Juddho: Dalilpatra"* (Government of Bangladesh, n.d.).
22 Willem Van Schendel, "The Invention of the 'Jummas': State Formation and Ethnicity in Southeastern Bangladesh," *Modern Asian Studies. Cambridge University Press* 26, no. 1 (February 1992): 95–128.
23 T.H. Lewin, *Wild Races of the Eastern Frontier of India* (Delhi: Mittal Publications, n.d.); T.H. Lewin, *The Hill Tracts of Chittagong and the Dwellers Therein: With Comparative Vocabularies of the Hill Dialects* (Calcutta: Bengal Printing Company Ltd, n.d.); R.H. Sneyd Hutchinson, *An Account of the Chittagong Hill Tracts* (Calcutta: Bengal Secretariat Book Depot, n.d.); J.P. Mills, "'Notes on a Tour in the Chittagong Hill Tracts in 1926,'" in *Census of India, 1931, Volume V: Bengal & Sikkim, Appendix II*, n.d., 514–21.
24 See the travel account by M.D. Francis Buchanan, *"'An Account of a Journey Undertaken by Order of the Board of Trade through the Provinces of Chittagong and Tiperah in Order to Look out for the Places Most Proper for the Cultivation of Spices'"* (British Library, Manuscript: 798).
25 The lone elected member to the Bangladesh parliament from CHT and one of the ardent champions of the Hill people's cause.
26 Siddharta Chakma, *Proshongo Parbattya Chattagram* (Calcutta, 1986), 5.
27 The concept of "state-nation" accepts that political boundaries do not and need not coincide with cultural boundaries and that a political community can be imagined across deep diversities. Yadav, Yogendra. India is a state-nation, not a nation-state. News18.com. August 27, 2013. www.news18.com/news/india/india-is-a-state-nation-not-a-nation-state-yogendra-yadav-634632.html (accessed on July 10, 2017).
28 Mohsin, "Gendered Nation, Gendered Peace: A Study of Bangladesh," 225–229.
29 Ethnicity is one of the most elusive and mysterious concepts that defines a social structure. It may be simplistically defined as a state of belonging to a social group that has a common national or cultural tradition. But again, for a "social group" to be termed as an "ethnic group" permits no simple answer. It is rather a complex and overlapping category including various racial, religious, linguistic, or other such groupings. Furthermore, it is a kind of consciousness that may give rise to a conflict situation, which in turn, can depend entirely upon the context in which people form their consciousness, and particularly, regarding the other ethnic group which they recognize as existing at that very context.
30 The term *"Rajakar"* is used to denote the auxiliary forces who worked for the (West) Pakistani Army from within Bangladesh during the Liberation War of Independence. They are widely accused of corroborating the genocide of 1971 in alliance with the (West) Pakistani Armed forces.
31 Srimanti Sarkar, "The Shahbag Fizzle: Significance of the Upheaval in Bangladesh", *The Sunday Statesman* [Op-Ed Article]. February 14 (2016).
32 The Constitution (Fifteenth Amendment) Act, 2011 (Act XIV of 2011), Section 3 substituted the second paragraph of the amended constitution under the military regime to state that: "Pledging that the high ideals of nationalism, socialism, democracy

and secularism, which inspired our heroic people to dedicate themselves to, and our brave martyrs to sacrifice their lives in, the national liberation struggle, shall be the fundamental principles of the Constitution". *The Constitution of the Republic of Bangladesh*, Legislative and Parliamentary Affairs Division, Ministry of Law, Justice and 2010, http://bdlaws.minlaw.gov.bd/sections_detail.php?id=367&sections_id=24556 (accessed on April 3, 2014).

33 Hiranmay Karlekar, *Bangladesh: The Next Afghanistan?* (New Delhi: Sage Publications, 2005), 49.
34 He not only invoked *"Bismillah-ir-Rahman-ir-Rahim"* (In the name of Allah, the Beneficent, the Merciful) above the Preamble of the constitution but also amended the same to remove the clause of "secularism" from among the principles of state policy together with many other changes.
35 M. Rafique Islam, "Constitutionalism and Governance in Bangladesh," in *Development Governance and the Environment in South Asia: A Focus on Bangladesh*, ed. Ed Mohammad Alauddin and Samiul Hasan (New York: Macmillan Press Ltd., 1999), 169–73.
36 Karlekar, *Bangladesh: The Next Afghanistan?*, 51.
37 The Committee to Uproot the Killers and Collaborators of Seventy-one was set up on 19 January 1992 by 101 widely respected citizens of Bangladesh comprising of civil activists, veteran academicians, writers, journalists, freedom fighters, and various other professionals.
38 Karlekar, *Bangladesh: The Next Afghanistan?*, 54.
39 Mohammad Tanzimuddin Khan, "The Politics of Deception and The Spirit of Shahbag," *New Age. , February* 24 (2013).
40 Sarkar, "The Shahbag Fizzle: Significance of the Upheaval in Bangladesh."
41 Cops link major killings of blogger-activists [like Ahmed Rajiv Haider (15 February 2013), Avijit Roy (26 February 2015), Oyasiqur Rhaman (30 March 2015), Ananta Bijoy Das (12 May 2015), Niloy Neel (7 August 2015), and Faisal Arefin Dipan (31 October 2015)]; foreign nationals [like Italian national, Cesare Tavella (28 September 2015) and Japanese national, Hoshi Kunio (3 October 2015)]; religious associates (like PDB ex-chairman Muhammad Khizir Khan (5 October 2015), ASI Ibrahim Mollah (22 October 2015, Hindu-priest Jogeshwar Dasadhikary (21 February 2016), Abdur Razzak (14 March 2016), Christian-convert Hussain Ali (22 March 2016)]; secular activists [Nizamudiin Samad (6 April 2016), Prof. AFM Rezaul Karim Siddiquee (23 April 2016)] and others [like police constable, Mukul Hossain (4 November 2015)] to the hanging of the war criminals as the national consensus alarmingly got divided between the secularists and the fundamentalists. "Cops Link Major Killings to Hanging of War Criminals", *The Daily Star*, 16 May 2016.

7 Holocaust denial and minimization in the Indian Urdu press

Md. Muddassir Quamar

Violent conflicts are painful, especially for communities that face organized violence, genocide, or riots, and leave deep scars upon sufferers, both individuals and societies. Some of the major incidents of organized violence or genocides became a matter of global shame when the extent of brutality and violence becomes known. The last century has been witness to many such incidents including the genocide of Armenians in Ottoman Turkey, violence against Kurds and Shias in Iraq during Saddam Hussein's regime, the mass killings in Bosnia, the Rwandan genocide, the Cultural Revolution in China, and so on. One such incident was the Holocaust against Jews in Europe resulting in more than 6 million victims under Nazi Germany during World War II.

Jews had faced discrimination and violence in Europe since the time they were forced to migrate and become a diaspora after the destruction of the Second Temple in AD 70 but the extent of violence and brutalities incurred on them by Nazi Germany has been unprecedented, not just in Jewish but in human history. The Holocaust, as it came to be known, was a racist attempt to exterminate the Jews in Germany and all places that came under German occupation during the World War II. The incident shook the conscience of humanity and was responsible for mass migration of Jews to Western Europe and the US. It further fuelled the demand for a Jewish national home that eventually led to the creation of Israel in 1948 and the migration of a significant number of Jews to the newly formed state.

India has its own history of suffering from violence as well as discrimination against sections of society on the basis of birth, engrained in the caste system. The religious divide during the Indian freedom struggle led to frequent bouts of violence between Hindus and Muslims. The divide eventually led to the partition of India at the end of the British colonial rule but this caused large-scale violence on both sides of the newly formed border. Estimates suggest that nearly 2 million people were killed during the violence that ensued and approximately 14 million were displaced. However, the level of awareness and academic study of the causes and consequences of genocides or mass killings remains minimal in India. Hence it is not surprising that the level of awareness of the Holocaust is nearly absent in the Indian context and there is a dearth of academic and media discussions on the issue.

This chapter deals with the issue of Holocaust from a perspective of creating academic debate on the subject, especially in India and generating a wider awareness against genocide and mass killings. It looks into the way the issue of the Holocaust against Jews is covered and portrayed in the Indian Urdu press. It highlights the lack of awareness among significant section of Indians about the Holocaust and emphasizes the need to create awareness and debate on the issue that should underscore the travails of mass killings and genocides. The chapter articulates a lack of awareness and understanding of the issue among a majority in the Indian Urdu press. It concludes that Holocaust denial and minimization is not a frequent phenomenon in the Indian Urdu press, but it nevertheless is present. Further, it argues that this denial or minimization emanates due to historical ignorance of Holocaust, insensitivity towards the victims and a biased understanding of the Israeli–Palestinian conflict.

Urdu press in India

Before coming to the analysis of Holocaust coverage in the Urdu press, it is important to map the popularity of Urdu language and press in India and contextualize it within the larger Indian media scenario. Urdu is widely spoken and even more widely understood in various parts of India. In popular culture, especially Hindi cinema, one finds significant use of the Urdu language. This is more so in the case of songs, where the Urdu *ghazal* has gained significant popularity. In fact, spoken Urdu and Hindi are not much different from each other and those claiming either of the two as their mother tongue can easily understand each other without putting much stress on their vocabularies. Scholars articulate the similar origin of the two languages and the forced linguistic division is largely a product of a political trajectory that has its roots in the pre-independence national movement[1].

As per official figures, nearly 60 million Indians comprising 5.1 per cent of the population are Urdu speakers[2]. They are largely concentrated in the Indo-Gangetic belt, that is, in the northern plains from Punjab in the west to Bihar and West Bengal in the east. Nevertheless, a small number of Urdu speakers can also be found in other parts including the central, southern, and western states of Madhya Pradesh, Telangana, Andhra Pradesh, and Maharashtra. It is one of the 22 scheduled languages in India, meaning it is recognized as one of the official languages of the state. In addition, Urdu has the status of official language in many Indian states including Jammu and Kashmir, Uttar Pradesh, Bihar, Telangana, West Bengal, and the national capital region of Delhi.

An important dimension of Urdu in India is its association with Muslims. This has more to do with the historical evolution of Indian national movement and the Hindu–Muslim divide that ensued in the process. The trajectory of this religious divide in the Indian national movement was also reflected in the linguistic division between Urdu and Hindi and gradually the two languages became identified with the two communities[3]. The phenomenon continued in post-independence India, leading to Urdu becoming confined to the language of Muslims.

In reality, however, Urdu is not the *lingua franca* of all South Asian Muslim but of a significant section of them, making it possible for them to transcend ethnic and geographical boundaries by communicating in it.

According to the 2011 census, India has nearly 172 million Muslims (Census 2001)[4] that is, 14 per cent of the total population and which according to estimates is the second largest in the world after Indonesia[5]. It also means that less than a third of Indian Muslims are Urdu speakers and even fewer are readers of the Urdu press.

Notwithstanding the population figures and Urdu being largely confined to Muslims, India has a vibrant and widespread Urdu press. According to the *Registrar of Newspapers for India* as of 2014–2015 there were 1,661 Urdu newspapers including 1,121 dailies with a total daily circulation of 33.25 million[6]. Hence, it is the third largest press in India after Hindi and English, so far as the print medium is concerned, both in terms of number of publications and daily circulation[7]. Since the Indian Urdu press largely caters to the Muslim population, it would not be wrong to assume that the way Urdu press covers the Holocaust reflects the perceptions of a significant section of the Indian Muslims.

Note on methodology

The chapter is based on content analysis of nearly 15 Urdu newspapers published in different cities in India based on four to five years of monitoring of their editorial content and coverage. Newspapers include *Rashtriya Sahara* (Delhi edition), which is one of the largest circulated Urdu dailies in India and has nine editions; *Dawat* (Delhi), which is mouthpiece of Jamat-e-Islami Hind, an Islamist organization founded by Abul Ala' Maududi; *Sahafat* (Lucknow edition), which is a pro-Iran daily; *Urdu Times* (Mumbai); *Etemaad, Siasat, Munsif* (all Hyderabad); *Akhbare-e-Mashriq* (Kolkata), which has socialist leanings; *Qaumi Tanzim* (Patna); *Qaumi Raftar* (Lucknow); *Hamara Samaj* (Delhi); *Daily Roshni* (Srinagar); *Inquilab* (Mumbai); *Hindustan Express* (Delhi); and *Nai Duniya*, a popular tabloid. These newspapers are chosen on the basis of their popularity reflected in circulation numbers and at least one newspaper from different parts of India is taken for analysis so as to have a pan-India view. Hence, it is not only newspapers from Delhi or Mumbai but many other cities including from southern and eastern India that have been included for analysis.

At the same time, diversity in terms of various schools of thought and political inclinations is kept in mind while choosing the newspapers to reflect the diversity among Indian Muslims. Though there are Urdu television news channels and even the state-owned *Doordarshan* has Urdu language broadcasts, this paper is confined to newspapers because of the small reach of the Urdu broadcast media in comparison to the print media. Urdu television news channels are not included, hence it is only print media, but digital medium was used for monitoring the content, that is, web-based content is used.

The Holocaust in the Urdu press

Looking into the coverage of Urdu newspapers, one finds ample discussions on conflicts, violence, genocide, and issues related to victims of violence, but the references are largely confined to violence against Indian Muslims or Muslims in the global context. One rarely comes across news coverage, commentaries, or editorials on the Holocaust. Hence, there is little or almost no exclusive discussion on the Holocaust. It shows that the issue is not considered important as neither the victims nor the perpetrators are the direct audience of the Indian Urdu press. This absence of coverage and discussion highlights a lack of awareness among the Indian Urdu press in particular and the Indian Muslims in general about the Holocaust. It also means that there is a less emphasis on Holocaust denial and this is important because one finds rampant media campaigns to either deny the occurrence of Holocaust or minimize its extent to a small number of victims in the Arab media sphere, in Pakistani Urdu media, or even in the Iranian political sphere[8].

While exclusive coverage of the Holocaust is rare, it does not mean the issue is never discussed. Generally, discussion of the Holocaust comes in the context of the Israeli–Palestinian conflict. In fact, not just Holocaust, discussions on Jews are largely contextualized within the debate on the Israeli–Palestinian conflict. Portrayal of Jews in the Urdu press is often prejudiced and at times even abusive, exhibiting the extent to which conflicts can affect perceptions about "enemy" groups or communities. Urdu newspapers are often found using instigative language against Israel and Jews. For example, at the peak of Israel's military action in the Gaza Strip in 2014, an editorial in *Rashtriya Sahara* (21 July) argued that the time has come for Palestinians and their supporters all over the world to start attacking Israeli installations and interests across the globe in response to the killings in Gaza[9]. Interestingly, the same editorial condemned similar revengeful utterances from Israeli politicians after the kidnapping and murder of three Jewish teens.

This has happened despite evidence to suggest cordial Muslim-Jewish relations in undivided India[10]. The situation started to change with the deterioration of Jewish-Muslim relations over Palestine and the intensification of the conflict after the formation of Israel and the subsequent Arab-Israeli wars. The conflict affected Indian Muslim perceptions of Jews and antagonized their views of the Jewish people and Israel. Historically, this was evident from their opposition to pro-Jewish British policies in mandate Palestine[11] and this continues in contemporary times with Muslim community leaders opposing close relations between India and Israel[12]. It is argued that one of the reasons for India to delay establishing diplomatic relations with Israel was consideration for the sentiments of the Indian Muslim community[13].

It is important to contextualize the sense of anger among a section of Indian Muslims and the Urdu press towards Israel and Jews because of the continued failure of the Palestinians' struggle for statehood. Regular bouts of violence between the Israeli and Palestinian sides have not helped the matter either. Though the deteriorating security situation and the emergence of many other problems in the Middle East have pushed the Israeli–Palestinian conflict on the back burner, the issue continues to evoke emotional and passionate reactions in support of the Palestinians. Urdu newspapers are found to be at the forefront in covering issues pertaining to the Middle East including the Israeli–Palestinian conflict and more or less suffer from a biased understanding of the conflict.

In fact, one can identify a number of features when it comes to the coverage of issues related to the Middle East in the Indian Urdu press. Similarly, some of the common issues can be found that remain in recurring focus. For example, the status of Jerusalem and the issue of the Muslim claim to the Al-Aqsa mosque, the refugee problem, the lack of statehood of Palestine, the question of settlements in occupied territories, and the wars in Gaza Strip are issues that find regular discussions in the Urdu press.

Some of the features in the coverage of the Middle East in the Indian Urdu press are also persistent. One of the most common features is to harp on the conspiracy theories. Predominantly, these newspapers are not the source of such theories, rather they are mostly picked from Western authors who find conspiracy in one or the other major global event. Urdu newspapers and columnists are fond of picking such explanations and disseminate it through their writings. Hence, the narrative of the Western-Jewish-Zionist conspiracy against Islam and Muslims is a predominant feature in the Indian Urdu press. For example, while the Urdu press recognizes the perils of Jihadi terror, it refuses to believe that Muslims are the actual perpetrators of such activities or they are involved on their own and keeps trying to find means and ways to link the origin of terrorist groups such as the Islamic State to the US or Israel[14]. There are condemnations of violence perpetuated by Jihadist organizations but time and again there are references to "Zionist conspiracy to divide or weaken Arabs and Muslims"[15].

While it is understandable to be critical of Israel on occasions where it violates international laws and human rights, it is risible to see Israel and Jewish/Zionist conspiracies being blamed even in instances where it has been a target of attack or violence. For example, the coverage of the attack on an Israeli diplomat in New Delhi on 13 February 2012, was indicative that it is a Jewish conspiracy to indict Iran. It was argued that Israel wants India to break its ties with Iran and plans to invade the Islamic Republic and thus has staged a "mild" attack on its own diplomats "where nobody died" to create a case for the coming attack on Iran[16]. When investigations suggested involvement of Iranian citizens and a senior Urdu journalist Syed Ahmed Kazmi was arrested on suspicions of his involvement (he was later acquitted) many newspapers started a campaign to save him and used abusive language against Jews and Israel[17].

Frequently, major and minor incidents or developments in the region are blamed on a Jewish conspiracy, sometimes without any direct involvement of Israel such as the Arab Spring. When the protests broke out in Tunisia after the self-immolation of Mohamed Bouazizi in December 2010 and spread to other Arab countries, Urdu newspapers were almost sure or, at least, suspected that the protests and demonstrations and the subsequent civil wars and bloodshed were results of Western and Zionist conspiracies[18]. Although, as the situation became more complex many opinions and editorials did some rational analyses, the narrative of "Zionist conspiracy" did not completely disappear amidst a continuously deteriorating situation and the rise of the monstrous Islamic State.

The Arab Spring and the rise of Islamic State are not isolated instances where the Urdu press was looking for conspiracies. In fact, one finds a fetish for conspiracy theories in the Indian Urdu press. Incidents, such as the 9/11, where the involvement of al-Qaeda was proved were also blamed on a Zionist conspiracy to defame and implicate global Muslims and wage a war against Muslim countries. The idea that Israel or Zionist agents were involved in the 9/11 attack to incite the US to go for war against Muslim nations was promoted mainly by Jeff Rense, a well-known American conspiracy theorist, and was picked by many in the Indian Urdu press. Undoubtedly, the Urdu press was not the original source of these conspiracy theories but played a role in disseminating them among Indian Muslims.

While the tendency to blame Israel and a Zionist conspiracy in the Urdu press is nauseating; there are also instances when one sees the Urdu press evoking the idea that Israeli society is degenerating and that its majority Jewish population is disenchanted not just with the leadership but the country itself and are leaving in hordes to countries in Europe and the US. It is argued that the young Israelis do not care about the Holocaust and do not relate with the sentiments of the older generation that came to mandate Palestine to save themselves from Nazi atrocities. Implicitly, it is suggested that somehow the Holocaust was just an excuse to migrate to Palestine and establish Israel[19]. On the other hand, one also sees speculations that Israel is losing its sheen within the international community and that its supporters are abandoning it because of its inhumane and oppressive behaviour against the Palestinians. For example, *Dawat*, which is the mouthpiece of Jamat-e-Islami Hind,[20] in an editorial on 4 February 2013 argues that,

> its [Israel's] supporters and friends have also undergone change. They have now become less powerful, making Israel extremely nervous. Security concerns have reached extreme levels. The existential crisis to the state of Israel has become deeper ... its non-Jewish friends have started to question its strategies while divisions have also erupted among the Jewish population.[21]

Subtle denials of the Holocaust

Importantly, as noted above, one rarely finds any direct articles or editorials questioning the validity of the Holocaust but there are subtle denials. Largely, the debate gets convoluted with other issues, especially the Israeli–Palestinian conflict. In fact, not just the Holocaust but discussions on Jews are also contextualized within the debate on the Israeli–Palestinian conflict. One finds portrayal of Jews in the Indian Urdu press to be prejudiced that at times exhibits abuse and instigative language[22]. Hatred of Jews as a community though has some religious connotations, the continued non-resolution of the Israeli-Palestinian conflict, Palestinian statelessness, and the perceived excesses of Israeli actions against Palestinians has complicated the matter to the worse.

Though one rarely finds any direct articles or editorials questioning the Holocaust, there are subtle denials. Broadly, one finds three themes around which the subtle denials revolve. First, it is suggested that the Jews used the Holocaust to claim a homeland in Palestine, that is, they used persecution at the hands of Nazis in Europe to claim Palestine as their National Home. Second, it is argued that the number of victims in the Holocaust was utterly exaggerated by influential Jewish individuals and organizations to gain international sympathy. Third, one often finds reference to the "so called" Holocaust in the Urdu press while discussing issues related and at time even unrelated to the Israeli–Palestinian conflict.

One finds a number of examples of suggestions that Jews claimed persecution at the hands of Nazi Germany to leverage their claim for a National Home in Palestine. For example, while discussing the freedom flotilla incident (May 2010), an editorial in *Roznama Munsif*, a Hyderabad based daily, argued that,

> The worst incident in history of the world was the creation of the Zionist state of Israel in 1948, a slap on the face of Islamic world. *The story of the so-called Holocaust against Jews* at the hands of Nazis was made an excuse to establish Israel. The cursed nation in turn has made the life of Palestinians a hell and has pushed them out of their homes forcing them to live in refugee camps (emphasis added).[23]

Similarly, *Roznama Sahafat* in its editorial on 3 June 2010 on the flotilla raid incident argued that Israel will face global ire for its brutalities against the civilian population in Gaza. One sees antisemitic remarks and use of abusive language against Jews[24]. References to the Holocaust point out that the global sympathy for the Jews was evoked due to Nazi brutality but this has not prevented Israel from doing the same against Palestinians. For example, in an *Urdu Times* column on 27 June 2010 the author argued that younger Jews do not care about the Holocaust and are migrating out of Israel because they do not relate to such an incident, suggesting doubts about the Holocaust[25]. One can clearly see the suggestion that the Holocaust is perhaps either a myth or at least much exaggerated in its magnitude to gain global sympathy for the creation of the State of Israel.

One can find similar examples in other newspapers too. For example, *Rashtriya Sahara* on 20 October 2012, while discussing the Iran nuclear issue and Israeli opposition to any deal argued that Israel is trying to evoke controversy and wishes to play the victim like it has always used the issue of the Holocaust to gain the sympathys of the international community. It said:

> Israel has made it an issue [Iranian nuclear program] of existential threat and the Jewish lobby has started to put pressure on American Senate to act against Iran because protection of Israel is a constitutional duty of the US. Obama is well aware of the situation but cannot go against the Senate. Even then he has refused to declare a "red line" against Iranian nuclear program. However, Obama under pressure had to issue pro-Israel statements. The point is that Israel wants to use the Iranian nuclear program to gain international support, just the way it has always used the Holocaust. The problem is it is not working in Israeli favor because most of the countries do not see Iranian nuclear program as a threat.[26]

The context

The problem lies in the lack of resolution of the Israeli–Palestinian conflict and the unwillingness on both sides to find a solution. It is within this context of animosity towards Israel and Jews that the coverage of the Holocaust in the Urdu press can be located. The continued occupation of Palestinian territories, settlements, wars in Gaza, and the perception of the oppression of Palestinians fuels many in the Urdu press to join the bandwagon of Holocaust denial or minimization. Though marginal, there is another angle to the portrayal of the Holocaust, that is, the justification of the mass killings of Jews at the hands of Nazi Germany as a deserved "divine punishment". It is argued that Jews are a "cursed" community and God keeps punishing them because they are "disobedient" of his injunctions, and hence they deserved to be killed; in other words, the Holocaust was justified.

One can understand a religious or ideological affinity with the Palestinian cause, and hence, a legitimate and rational criticism of Israeli actions or policies against Palestinians or in the occupied territories. The portrayal of Jews as extremely "violent", "inhuman" and "lunatic" people, however, seems to emanate from religious zeal, especially because many cite Islamic sacred scriptures (Quran and Hadith) to condemn Jews and argue that they are the people who have been "condemned" for their non-obedience to the wills of Allah. This leads Urdu newspapers to often use a diabolical language and religious and historical symbolism to condemn Israel in justification of the idea that the *Bani Israel* (Quranic term for Jews) are indeed a "cursed" people and divine intervention will lead to the end of Jewish occupation of Palestine and the holy city of Jerusalem. For example, *Urdu Times* in an opinion piece on 6 February 2013, writes:

> Israel has termed Iran as "an international threat." There cannot be a bigger joke than this as a country perceived to be an international threat by people of its own race, is terming a country that has never attacked any other country, as an international threat. A recent survey in Europe had brought startling results; 22 per cent of the European population thought that Israel was an international threat. Anyone studying the psychology and characteristics of Jews could come to the same conclusion.[27]

The editorial goes on to argue that if the land of Palestine is restored to the Palestinians, the world will immediately become peaceful and the only solution to this "cancer on earth [Israel]" is a surgical operation to remove this cancer, meaning "to wipe Israel off the map of earth". The kind of language used by Mahmoud Ahmedinejad as president of Iran that invited international condemnation is actually not uncommon in the Urdu press. Use of religious and historical symbolism is also a recurring phenomenon. The same editorial ends with a wish that "the world awaits the coming of another Salahuddin"[28].

Conclusion

The Holocaust is an important issue, but awareness of it is minimal in India. This is despite good relations with Israel and historically being home to a small Jewish community. Moreover, India despite suffering from problems of mass killings, does not have academic or research institutions focusing on the study of causes, consequences, or prevention of mass killings, and, hence, there are no institutions that focus on Holocaust education either. As far as the Indian Urdu press is concerned, one finds serious lack of awareness of the Holocaust. Urdu being associated with Muslims and the Israeli–Palestinian conflict being intertwined with the Jewish–Muslim problem, the coverage of the Holocaust in the Indian Urdu press becomes more complex and problematic. There is hardly any coverage and when it appears it is as a mere passing reference while discussing issues related to the conflict. It is usually considered as the primary reason for the current state of affairs of the Palestinian people. It can be argued that the instances of Holocaust denial and minimization in the Indian Urdu press are not as frequent as in the Pakistani Urdu press or for that matter as in the Arab public sphere. The Holocaust denial or/and minimization in the Indian Urdu press also does not attain the high-pitched noise Iranian politics, but it, nevertheless, is present.

Notes

1 Paul R. Brass, *Language, Religion and Politics in North India* (London: Cambridge University Press, 1974); Abdul Jamil, *The Politics of Language Urdu/Hindi: An Artificial Divide: African Heritage, Mesopotamian Roots, Indian Culture and British Colonialism* (New York: Algora Publishing, 2006).
2 Office of the Registrar General and Census Commissioner, Ministry of Home Affairs, Government of India, "Abstract of speakers' strength of languages and mother tongues – 2001". Available from: www.censusindia.gov.in/Census_Data_2001/Census_Data_Online/Language/Statement1.aspx (Accessed 3 June 2016).
3 Paul R. Brass, *Language, Religion and Politics in North India* (London: Cambridge University Press, 1974).
4 Office of the Registrar General and Census Commissioner, Ministry of Home Affairs, Government of India, "C-01 Population by Religious Community (India & State/UTs/District/Sub-Distt/Town Level)", *Population Enumeration Data, Data on Religion.* Available from: www.censusindia.gov.in/2011census/population_enumeration.html (Accessed 3 June 2016).
5 "10 Countries with the Largest Muslim Populations, 2010 and 2050", *Pew Research Center* 2 (April 2015), www.pewforum.org/2015/04/02/muslims/pf_15-04-02_projectionstables74/.
6 Registrar of Newspapers for India, Ministry of Information and Broadcasting, Government of India, *59th Annual Report: Press in India, 2014–15*, p. 12.
7 Ibid.
8 Stephen Wicken, "Views of the Holocaust in Arab Media and Public", *Discourse. Yale Journal of International Affairs*, 2006, 103–15.
9 *Insaniyat Ke Liye Almiya (A Tragedy for Humanity* (Rashtriya Sahara, Delhi, 2014), 7.
10 Navras Aafreedi, "Jewish-Muslim Relations in South Asia: Where Antipathy Lives without Jews. Asian Jewish Life", *October*, no. ue 15 (2014): 14–16.
11 P.R. Kumaraswamy, "Indian Muslims and the Three Js: Jews, Jerusalem and the Jewish State", in *Ma'oz, Moshe (Ed.)Muslim Attitudes to Jews and Israel: The Ambivalences of Rejection, Antagonism, Tolerance and Cooperation* (Brighton and Portland: Sussex Academy Press, 2010), 215–29.
12 For example, a Press Statement signed by five prominent Indian Muslim leaders urged India to scale down its ties with Israel after the 2012 visit of External Affairs Minister S. M. Krishna to Israel; see: Anonymous (2012) Indian Muslim leaders urge India to scale down ties with Israel. *The Milli Gazette*, January 17. Available from: (Accessed 2 June 2016).
13 P.R. Kumaraswamy, *India's Israel Policy* (New York: Columbia University Press, 2010).

14 *Daesh ka Tashiri Harba (Propaganda Tactics of Daesh)* (Siasat, Hyderabad, April 28), 6.; *Arab Mamalik Me Hukumat Ka Masla (Governance in Arab Countries)* (Munsif, Hyderabad, 2011), 6.

15 *Arab Mamalik Me Hukumat Ka Masla (Governance in Arab Countries)*, 6.

16 *Israeli Hukmaran Bokhlagaye Hain (Israeli Leaders Are Baffled)* (Rashtriya Sahara, Delhi, 2012), 7.; "Iran Ko Badnam Karne Ki Sazish? (Is It a Conspiracy to Defame Iran?)", in *February*, vol. 17 (Etemaad, Hyderabad, 2012), 4.

17 "Kazmi Ki Giraftari Nihayat Badbakhtana Fe'l (Kazmi's Arrest Is a Sinister Action", *Sahafat*, Lucknow, March 12 (2012): 5.

18 "Misrke Halat Se Israel Ko Pareshani (Israel Worried about Developments in Egypt", *Sahafat, Lucknow, February* 2 (2011): 5.

19 "Yahudi Israel Chorkar Ja Rahe Hain (Jews running away from Israel)", *Urdu Times*, Mumbai, June 27 (2010): 5.

20 Jamat-e-Islami Hind is the Indian chapter of an Islamist organization founded in undivided India in 1941 by well-known South Asian Muslim figure Abul Ala' Maududi. The group has presence in Pakistan and Bangladesh as well, where it is a political-religious organization. In India, it refrains partaking in politics and confines its activities to community services.

21 "Israeli Karwai (Israel's Actions)", in *February*, vol. 4 (Dawat, Delhi, 2013), 3.

22 Quamar, Md. Muddassir (2016) "Jews in Indian Urdu Press", *Café Dissensus*, 7 January. Available from: https://cafedissensus.com/2016/01/07/jews-in-indian-urdu-press/ (Accessed on 15 May 2016).

23 *Israeli Barbariat (Israeli Barbarism)* (Munsif, Hyderabad, 2010), 5.

24 "Yahudion Ke Khilaf Aalmi Tahreek Hogi (There Would Be International Movement against Jews", in *Roznama Sahafat*, Lucknow, June, vol. 2 (Roznama Sahafat, Lucknow, 2010), 5.

25 "Yahudi Israel Chorkar Ja Rahe Hain (Jews running away from Israel)", 7.

26 *Amrika-Israel-Iran EkMusallas (The US-Israel-Iran Triangle* (Rashtriya Sahara, Delhi, 2012), 7.

27 "AalmiKhatraKaun? (Who Is an International Threat?)", *Urdu Times*, Mumbai 6 (February 2013): 3.

28 Ibid.

Part 3
Education

8 Holocaust education and remembrance in Australia

Moving from family and community remembrance to human rights education

Suzanne D. Rutland and Suzanne Hampel

Introduction

The twentieth century has been recognized as a century of genocide. From the tragedy of the Armenians during World War I into the twenty-first century, millions of people, men, women, and children, have been murdered in the name of racial, religious, or tribal purity. This included the 6 million Jews murdered during the Holocaust, constituting two thirds of European Jewry. Since the 1980s, approaches have been implemented so that the human tragedy of the Holocaust can be used for education against racism and human rights abuses. As a result, this particularistic tragedy has taken on a more universal connotation, representing the ultimate evil (Gross and Stevick, 2015; Gross, 2018). In recent years, the Australian government has become part of this global trend, with Holocaust education being introduced into school curricula and government support for other key developments.

The Holocaust, universal messages, and human rights

The concepts of universal human rights were a product of the French Revolution and modernization but the need for a clear definition of human rights only emerged after the Holocaust and in response to decolonization. In 1948 the United Nations issued its Universal Declaration of Human Rights, which set the benchmark for the definition of the key elements relating to human rights. Subsequently, the United Nations has held various conventions dealing with human rights, which have led to further fine tuning and conceptualization. Currently, human rights are seen to incorporate the areas of civil and political rights; economic, social, and cultural rights; and humanitarian rights (Burridge et al., 2014).

In the early post-war era, approaches to Holocaust education focused on the particularistic nature of the Holocaust, with survivors strongly opposing any comparisons – for them, the Holocaust was "unique". Gradually, especially since 1980, attitudes began to change, including among the survivor generation and their descendants. This change was fostered with the opening of Holocaust museums in the 1990s (including the United States Holocaust Museum in Washington and The House of the Wannsee Conference, Berlin) and the ongoing instances of genocide. These events provided the basis for the significant changes that occurred in the late 1990s (Alba, 2015). As well, a number of scholars began to explore the role Holocaust education could play in combatting racism and bigotry, reinforcing this issue (Short, 1997; Carrington and Short, 1997; Brown and Davies, 1998; Hector, 2000; Supple, 1998).

In 1998, the prime minister of Sweden convened a special commission to create an international force, marking the beginnings of the International Holocaust Remembrance Alliance (IHRA). In January 2000, the Stockholm International Forum on the Holocaust was held, with 45 countries in attendance, representing historians, politicians, and heads of state. The Forum issued the Stockholm Declaration, which states:

> With humanity still scarred by genocide, ethnic cleansing, racism, antisemitism and xenophobia, the international community shares a solemn responsibility to fight those evils. Together we must uphold the terrible truth of the Holocaust against those who deny it. We must strengthen the moral commitment of our peoples, and the political commitment of our governments, to ensure that future generations can understand the causes of the Holocaust and reflect upon its consequences.
>
>   (www.holocaustremembrance.com/about-us/stockholm-declaration)

With these developments, the issue of the universal messages of the Holocaust and human rights education has become the focus of a number of key scholars writing in the field of Holocaust education. The introduction of 27 January, the date when Auschwitz was liberated, as the International Holocaust Memorial Day has also increased awareness of Holocaust education as a universal tool against racism and bigotry (Burtonwood, 2002).

Israeli historian Yehuda Bauer, who provided the inspiration for the founding of the IHRA as well as the International Holocaust Memorial Day, has remained deeply involved with promoting the universal messages of the Holocaust. He wrote about these messages in his seminal and controversial book, *Rethinking the Holocaust* (2001). Until the 1980s, Bauer had stressed the uniqueness of the Holocaust, taking a particularistic approach and opposing comparison of other events of mass destruction with the Holocaust. He rethought these positions in the 1990s as he witnessed the genocides in Serbia, Bosnia, and Rwanda. He argued that once something happens in human history it can be repeated, and that the Holocaust should be recognized as the "paradigm" of genocide. Through Bauer's advocacy, there has been a move from using the word "Holocaust" as a particularistic concept to using the word "genocide," which is a universal concept (Gross, 2018).

This has led to a significant expansion of the literature on this issue, reinforced by the problems of ongoing genocides, globalization, post-liberalism, and the passing of the Holocaust survivor generation. As Gross and Stevick (2015) argued in their book, *As the Witnesses Fall Silent*, with the passing of the survivor generation, developing a broader approach to Holocaust education is imperative. In a subsequent article Gross (2018) has argued that "the universal lessons of the Holocaust, as the example of ultimate evil through the consequences of racism, can be an important part of teaching global citizenship and human rights. This guarantees the future and meaning of Holocaust education" (Gross, 2018, 6). In this study, Gross outlines in detail the various stages of Holocaust historiography and educational approaches, as they moved from the particular to the universal.

Similarly, in his book *Lessons of the Holocaust*, Michael R. Marrus (2015) stresses that there is value in the work of Holocaust historians, as it "not only deepens understanding of a great watershed in the history of our times but also enlarges our knowledge of the human condition" (162). He argues that studying history is akin to traveling back in time, but the hope is that one can return enriched by the experience. The Holocaust reveals a new level of man's inhumanity to man and, for this reason, it has become the symbol of ultimate evil and "a major reference point for our time, constantly kept in view for one's judgment about the state of the world" (169). It is against this international background that the Australian experience will be examined.

Australian background

The Australian Jewish community and Holocaust memory

Around 35,000 Jewish refugees and Holocaust survivors found a safe haven in Australia before and after the war. Thus, Australian Jewry is largely a post-Holocaust community, with Melbourne having the highest percentage of survivors on a pro-rata population basis. In the period from 1936 to 1941 around 9,000 pre-war Jewish refugees, including German and Austria Jewish internees sent out by the British, settled in Australia. The Australian Jewish community was reinforced in the period 1945–1954 with 17,000 post-war survivor migrants, supplemented by a further 8,000 survivors between 1954 and 1961, with some Polish 'Jews' being permitted to leave by the communists in the late 1950s and Jewish Hungarian survivor escapees, who managed to flee Hungary from 1956 to 1957 during the Hungarian revolution (Rutland et al., 2001). By 1961, Australia's Jewish population had almost trebled to 59,343, of whom around 26,000 were not from a refugee or survivor background (Figure 8.1).

Today, Australian Jewry is a vibrant community of c.115,000–120,000 people, mainly concentrated in the two major cities, Melbourne and Sydney, on Australia's Eastern coastline.

Most survivors embraced their new homeland, but they were reluctant to speak about their experiences. The past was too painful to talk about. Australian Jewish writer and survivor of the Lodz ghetto, Jacob G. Rosenberg (1994), expressed this anguish in a poem entitled, "No Exit":

How do you describe it?
    What alphabet do you employ?
    What words?
    What language?
    What silence, what scream?

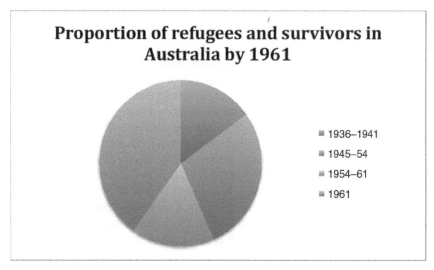

Proportion of refugees and survivors in Australia by 1961

- 1936–1941
- 1945–54
- 1954–61
- 1961

1936–1941 pre-war refugees and internees (9,000)
1945–54 post-war survivor migration (17,000)
1954–61 Polish and Hungarian survivor escapees (8,000)
1961 non-survivor Jewish population (26,000)

Figure 8.1 Proportion of refugees and survivors in Australia by 1961. Statistics from Appendix I. Rutland S.D., *Edge of the Diaspora: Two Centuries of Jewish Settlement in Australia*, New York: Holmes & Meier, 2001, 405.

As in other parts of the world, there were a number of reasons for this silence. For many, their terrible wartime lives were "unspeakable" (Rutland et al., 2017). People often responded inappropriately or with disbelief. Many survivors believed that the best way to secure continuity of Jewish life was by having children to replace those who had died and they wished to shelter their children from the horrors they had experienced. They felt that they should focus on rebuilding their lives in Australia, and to do this, they needed to put the past behind them.

Jewish novelist, Mark Baker, son of Polish Jewish survivor and author of *The Fiftieth Gate*, described the "wall of silence" as follows:

> I grew up in a household where there was silence – silence about my parents' stories. I didn't ask, so my parents never answered me. We didn't talk "about that". My parents never spoke, but their dreams – their night-mares – are my dreams. These dreams were inarticulate, they were com-municated in silence. I carried their dreams, their pain … With my book, I wanted to know. I wanted us to talk about those dreams. I wanted to break the silence.
>
> (quoted in Rutland and Caplan, 1998, 318)

Another child of survivors, Ruth Wajnryb (2001, 6), further explored the topic in great depth in her book, *The Silence: How Tragedy Shapes Talk*. She wrote:

> It was as if we'd arrived from another planet, with no records or recollections, no memory. We lived in the present and for the future. We were busy. We had plans. We had ambitions. We had this space in time that was now. And we were working hard toward what we could imagine ahead of us. But there was no past. The past was cordoned off, sealed out. There was a complete severance with what went before.

Early memorialization in Australia was largely within the family. Parents named children after lost ones. Particularly in Melbourne, where 60 per cent of survivors settled, there were reunions of *landsmannschaften* (organizations of people from the same town or village). One group that commemorated their survival and migration to Australia as a group was the "Buchenwald boys." They celebrated their liberation on 11 April 1945 with an annual ball, with music, dancing, drinking, and stories. There were also annual Jewish community events commemorating the Warsaw Ghetto Uprising of April/May 1943, when a remnant of Jewish fighters held out against the Germans for three weeks. However, it took over three decades before Holocaust memorialization and education took on a broader compass (Berman, 2001; Rutland and Caplan, 1998).

The breaking of the silence

As in other parts of the world, the breaking of the "silence" began in Australia in the late 1970s. In Sydney, the New South Wales Jewish Board of Deputies formed a Holocaust Remembrance Committee in November 1979 and began to organize the annual community commemorations for Holocaust Memorial Day, which later extended into a week of events. Then, in 1981, the first World Gathering of Holocaust survivors took place at Yad Vashem with the participation of an Australian delegation. In the same year, the Jewish service organization, B'nai B'rith (Sons of the Covenant), held the first Australian Holocaust exhibition in Sydney and Melbourne. In 1982, The Australian Holocaust Survivors' Association was formed, holding its first function in 1983. Another key milestone was the International Gathering of Holocaust Survivors held in Sydney in 1985, with survivors from both major centres participating.

Following on from the B'nai B'rith 1981 travelling exhibition, the community realized that more permanent exhibitions were needed. In 1984, the Jewish Holocaust and Research Centre was opened in Elsternwick, Melbourne – an early development for the establishment of Holocaust museums (Cooke and Lee-Frieze, 2015). Sydney took longer, with two rival projects being proposed, but in 1992 the Sydney Jewish Museum opened, combining both Australian Jewish History and the Holocaust. These museums were largely funded by local Jewish survivors and their focus was particularistic, as they argued that the Holocaust was a unique event in human history, and that it should not be compared with other genocides (Alba, 2016).

In 1988 when "March of the Living," a program of Jewish youth visiting Poland and Auschwitz started, the Australian Jewish community opposed participation. One thousand survivors signed a petition opposing the program. As Sam Lipski, a Melbourne Jewish journalist wrote: "For many in our community, Poland is a painful memory … a graveyard for millions of European Jews during the Holocaust" (Sam Lipski, *AJN*, 2 February 1989). It was only in 2001, with a major generational shift, that the Australian Jewish community formally joined the program. Since then over 1,000 Australian Jewish students have participated in the program (Rutland et al., 2015b).

Moving from the particular to the universal

The Jewish survivor community realized that they needed to educate the next generation, both Jewish and non-Jewish, and they wanted to create a platform for their education efforts. This led to the establishment of Holocaust museums in Melbourne and Sydney. Survivors began speaking to school groups, mainly not Jewish, in the museums. These education programs have expanded, with the Sydney Jewish community hosting 27,000 school students and Melbourne 23,000 school students in 2019.

As well, both government and non-government schools began introducing the Holocaust within the History syllabus and there have been programs of professional development for History teachers, most important of which has been an Australian Educators' program started at Yad Vashem, Jerusalem's Holocaust Museum in 1987. Over 450 Australian schoolteachers, again mainly non-Jews, have been sponsored to study at Yad Vashem. At the 9th International Conference on Holocaust Education at Yad Vashem's International School for Holocaust Studies in July 2014, seven Australian educators from Perth, Melbourne, Sydney, and Brisbane participated, sponsored by the Gandel Holocaust Studies Program for Australian Educators (Gandel Holocaust Studies Program for Australian Educators, n.d.).

As mentioned, the Holocaust museums in Melbourne and Sydney were funded and run from within the Jewish survivor community, later followed by a shift to the museums gaining broader support from across the Jewish community but with fairly minimal government assistance. A key federal government initiative was the opening of a witnesses and survivors' exhibition at the Australian War Memorial Museum in Canberra in November 2016 (Hector, 2016). This was done in consultation with the Melbourne Jewish Holocaust Centre.

In tandem with these various developments, the Australian government decided to apply to join the International Holocaust Remembrance Alliance (IHRA, n.d.). Gaining full membership of the IHRA is a three-stage process. After a period at observer nation status from July 2015, Australian progressed to be a liaison nation in November 2017 and in June 2019 was accepted as a full IHRA member. As such, Australia officially became the 33rd member of the IHRA and the first Pacific nation to join this organization. The Australian delegation's head of mission, Ambassador Lynette Wood, remarked: "We look forward to the enhanced opportunities to learn from IHRA members and to share our unique perspective on Holocaust education, research and remembrance" (IHRA Press Release, 10 June 2019).

In order to gain full membership, the Australian IHRA expert delegation actively observed and participated in working groups and project committees at plenaries and in the work done between each plenary; prepared the required reports outlining all the activities relating to Holocaust memory, memorialization, and education in Australia; and developed two pilot projects, one on Holocaust education/ commemoration (Holocaust Memorial Week) and the second relating to the monitoring of online hate. This work is now ongoing and Australian IHRA delegates will now have full participation in their respective working groups and committees due to full membership status. The members of the delegation will be deeply involved in fostering Holocaust education and memory and advocating against racism, antisemitism, and on-line hate. Australia's full membership does mean that the government has committed to maintaining and increasing Holocaust education initiatives in Australia but how this will be actualized still needs to be clarified.

The place of the Holocaust in Australian State History Syllabi, Years 7–10

Former Education Minister (and first female PM), Julia Gillard introduced the concept of a National History Curriculum in 2010, but this still has not been fully implemented. Whilst Holocaust education has been made mandatory at the national level, since this policy has not been fully implemented, the approach is different in each state, because education is still largely state-based. The national history syllabus also provides very little direction about pedagogic approaches.

In theory, History is compulsory for all Australian students from Years 7–10, with the average hours that history is taught in Australian secondary schools being between 40 and 50 hours per year, for four years, but there are significant variations from state to state. These variations are evident in Table 8.1:

As this table illustrates, in the last few years, the Holocaust is one very small component of the syllabus and teaching it in any detail is not compulsory. It is likely to receive between 1 and 3 hours in Year 10. However, the determinant is based on teacher choice in terms of hours allocated and content taught with some teachers choosing to give a much greater focus on teaching the Holocaust, resulting in a very wide spectrum of approaches.

In 2019, two antisemitic incidents in Melbourne, one involving a five-year old boy and the other a 12-year old boy in secondary school raised significant concerns. In the first instance, the five-year old was repeatedly called a "cockroach" and "dirty Jew," as well as being tormented in the toilets because he was circumcised. In the second case, a gang of boys, led by a bully of Anglo-Celtic background, invited a Jewish boy to play soccer with them in the park, but when they arrived there they started physically threatening him and forced him to kiss the shoe of another boy, a Muslim boy, who was pressured into the situation. One student filmed the act, which was then shared on social media. In this case, the student who was the victim was forced to leave the school and was threatened by the gang with further abuse if he attended any other local public school.

These two cases led the Victorian government's Minister of Education, James Merlino, to announce a review of the incidents and commit to a number of recommendations to support students, families, and schools in responding to

Table 8.1 Government curricula determined at state level: the place of the Holocaust in state history syllabi, 2016

State	Mandated	Hours	Topics
Victoria	No mandated hours for school subjects	History F average 50 hours taught in Year 10 World War II F20 hours Holocaust – under 'significant turning points in World War II.' Actual number of teaching hours: difficult to determine 30 minutes – 3 hours	• investigating the scale and significance of the Holocaust, using primary sources • Key events in the European theatre of war, for example, Germany's invasion of Poland in 1939, the Holocaust from 1942–45 and the Russians reaching Berlin in 1945.
NSW	Yes – schools must teach history F50 hours	Actual number of Holocaust teaching hours: teacher choice	• Outline and sequence the changing scope and nature of warfare from trenches in World War I to the Holocaust and the use of the atomic bombs to end World War II
Queensland	Yes – minimum teaching hours approx. 45 hours for history	Qld follows the Australian National Curriculum Old history curriculum currently under review Actual number of Holocaust teaching hours: teacher choice	• Examination of significant events of World War II, including the Holocaust and use of the atomic bomb
South Australia/ Western Australia Tasmania	No mandated hours for history	SA/WA/Tasmania follow the Australian National Curriculum Actual number of Holocaust teaching hours: teacher choice	• Examination of significant events of World War II, including the Holocaust and use of the atomic bomb
Northern Territory	Yes – minimum teaching hours approx.. 50 hours for history	NT follows the Australian National Curriculum Actual numbers of Holocaust teaching hours: teacher choice	

antisemitism and racist bullying. One of the key recommendations was to ensure that Holocaust education is mandated in every Victorian secondary school for Years 9 and 10, starting in 2020. Following this review, a committee of Holocaust education experts was established to develop and implement updated teaching and learning resources for the Victorian history curriculum.

Different approaches to human rights education

In 2012, the Sydney Jewish Museum began a major renovation of its Holocaust exhibition on the upper floors of its building. The final approach marked a major generational shift, moving for the first time to a more universalistic framework from its longstanding inward focus. Throughout the exhibition, opened officially in March 2017, the experience of other persecuted groups, including the homosexuals, gypsies, and disabled is incorporated. As well, the final top floor of the museum incorporates an additional permanent exhibition, the *Holocaust and Human Rights*, focusing on other human rights issues, including Indigenous Australians. Thus, "the universal aspects of the survivors' legacy, a legacy once focused on the "the personal, private and Jewish origins", has been firmly established" (Alba, 2016). In this way, Holocaust memory has taken on a broader connotation, with the message of the need to fight against racism and genocide for universal human rights being a central motif, as seen in the recent generational changes that have occurred in Australia (Gross and Rutland, 2014).

In a presentation at a recent conference, Breann Fallon (2019) discussed how the museum seeks to achieve this aim of teaching about human rights from the universal lessons of the Holocaust through its recently renovated exhibition. Since the *Holocaust and Human Rights* exhibition is positioned at the highest level of the museum, it is the final station that the students come to after undertaking a tour of the museum and then hearing a survivor story. The Human Rights Centre comprises three main sections. The first presents a timeline that outlines the major developments relating to human rights with an Australian focus. The main section in the middle of the display consists of four separate tables, each dealing with a different current Australian issue associated with human rights. These are refugees and asylum seekers; people with disabilities, both mental and physical; the LGBTQI community; and the indigenous Australians. The concept here is for the students to "come to the table" for different conversations. The guide or teacher can allow students to focus on one issue, or to find commonalities across the issues. Finally, on the third wall, students can write post-it notes with their thoughts about this exhibition. Their responses show how the messages of their study of the Holocaust has helped them to reflect on the broader topic of human rights. The exhibition is relevant to a number of different areas in the government curriculum, including History and Legal Studies. The museum also runs different programs aiming to reach out to the relevant age groups, from Year 6 to Year 12. The focus is on teaching the students how to think, rather than just providing content. The exhibition also seeks to take a conceptual approach, such as examining the issue of power and authority, rather than taking a purely chronological, historical approach.

Bringing human rights education into practical curricular frameworks is challenging, as is teaching the Holocaust. The concept of the *Holocaust and Human Rights* exhibition is to challenge each individual student to question critically his or her stand towards the key issues under discussion. In order to achieve this aim, the most effective pedagogic approaches to engage the students and to sensitize them to cruelty and abuse need to be identified.

Current literature on such pedagogy stresses the need for education to be reciprocal. In her presentation, Fallon referred to the research of Al-Daraweesh and Snauwaert (2013) who advocate for a hermeneutic understanding in a pedagogical approach that takes human rights away from its own construct and considers equivalent of similarities in order to refocus on the relationship between the individual and society. Once the equivalents/similarities have been considered, their human rights reciprocals can be brought into the discussion (Al-Daraweesh and Snauwaert 2013, 396–397). They stress that it is necessary to ensure that the sharing of the information is not just a lecture but a discussion, involving analysis. It is isomorphic because the fact that one human right is taken away during the Holocaust as illustrated through an individual survivor story, can encourage the students consider those who face the same situation today. As they explain:

> All traditions value human life, and respect it, in a manner that organizes the relation between individuals in different social groups. The isomorphic equivalents of human rights constitute the overlapping principle between the conceptualization of human rights in Western traditions and the conceptualization of human rights in non-Western traditions. This differentiation calls for naming the latter the "isomorphic equivalents of human rights". The differences and similarities between both traditions, Western and non-Western, necessitates not only the typological naming of rights, but also the hermeneutical grounding of rights conceptualization.
>
> (Al-Daraweesh and Snauwaert 2013, 400)

In this way, human rights education can "enable each individual to question critically his or her own stand" (Al-Daraweesh and Snauwaert 2013, 396), forcing them to think about people outside own community thereby encouraging active citizenship. Through doing this, it makes the discussion around the events of the Holocaust real for the students.

The strong impact of this section of the museum using the Holocaust as the primary example of the abuse of human rights is seen in the comments written on the post-it notes pinned on the wall in the museum. These include comments such as: "Don't stay silent; fight back," "Language is Power! Speak up," "Why do people refuse to love one another, and instead decide to kill and hurt?" There are also comments such as this has happened again so how has the world changed? In this respect, many of the survivor guides end their personal stories with the message, as one survivor expressed it, that there is only one race – the human race – and that what the students see around them is a mosaic with different faces, different colours, and different cuisines. Speaking at the recent conference as part of Fallon's presentation, this Sydney survivor explained that he draws the students' attention to nature "where one sees many different species of trees, different flowers and other vegetation, yet they do not try to destroy each other. They do complete for sunshine or moisture, but they never destroy or don't accept their neighbour." In 2020, the new Adelaide Holocaust Museum and Steiner Education Centre opened with its education program planning to draw on lessons from the Holocaust with a focus on human rights and other genocides as it develops (www.ahmsec.org.au/).

Thus, the new approach in both Sydney and Adelaide is to stress that learning about the Holocaust can help to teach students how racism and bigotry can lead to the emergence of the ultimate evil in human society and the right way to behave in the acceptance of the "Other" for the sake of humanity. There is a realization that as the Holocaust moves further and further away from the present, it is the messages of human rights education that makes its study still relevant and that without that connection the story could be lost. At the same time, two thirds of its museum tour still focus on the particulars of the Holocaust and it is only the last third of the tour that introduces the broader, human rights story of other groups and situations.

In contrast to this approach, the Jewish Holocaust Centre in Melbourne, which is currently constructing a totally new building and museum, has taken a different approach. Its curators and designers decided not to dedicate a specific section to human rights education in its exhibition, but rather to just focus on integrating the issue of human rights into its pedagogic approaches. With Melbourne Jewry absorbing more Jewish survivors than Sydney, and the fact that on a pro-rata population basis it has the highest proportion of survivors outside of Israel, this continued focus on the more particularistic aspects in their actual display is understandable. At the same time, they are moving to the more universalistic approach of human rights education in their pedagogy.

Another key non-government organization that focuses on Holocaust education is Courage to Care. In 1998, B'nai B'rith, a Jewish service organization in Australia, introduced Courage to Care, a student-centred program totally focused on the Holocaust, in New South Wales and Victoria. It focuses on the rescuers, those who had the "courage to care" and who risked their lives to save victims of the Nazis. Its aim is to convey the message of community tolerance and living in harmony, emphasizing the importance of standing up against persecution, especially against minority groups (Cohen 2005). The Courage to Care, New South Wales, website (2009) describes the program as follows:

Really caring for your fellow human beings sometimes takes courage.

* Communal tolerance and living in harmony come from better understanding other cultures and backgrounds.
* Standing up against racism and persecution takes courage but improves world harmony and peace.
* Just one individual can make a difference – action against apathy – a sense of empathy.

Each year, the project targets two or three communities and schools to visit the exhibition in each state, in both metropolitan and rural areas. Between 1998, when it started, and 2005 it attracted 155,000 participants, of whom 55,000 were school children (Cohen, 2005, 121). In a study of the Sydney organization, Sharon Kangisser-Cohen (2005, 122) analysed 40 evaluation forms from Year 10 students (aged 15) from one public school and observed several schools where the program was offered over an intensive three-day period. She found that hearing a survivor's story had the greatest impact on the students, because hearing from an historical witness was very moving and made the story real. As one student wrote, "It was amazing; it is so different to hear the story from someone who actually experienced it" (Cohen, 2005, 124). In Melbourne, a total of 140,000 school children have participated in the program since its inception, and the organizers have received ongoing positive feedback.

Although these NGOs have focused on school education, they have increased their reach, especially with a focus on police education. In this way, both the Sydney Jewish Museum and Courage to Care in Melbourne seek to take a more universalistic approach, providing the police with the opportunity to be witnesses to the direct involvement of police units in the Nazi program killing fields of mass murder, but also showing the direct roles played by the Polish Blue Police and the Jewish Police. They then use these examples for discussion relating to ethical decisions which police need to make and parallel between hate crimes and authority. The Melbourne program stresses the importance of diversity and inclusion in the police, the need to focus on helping the victim and also provide ideas on how to be an "upstander" rather than a "bystander."

There is a slight difference in focus between the Sydney and Melbourne programs. The Sydney Jewish Museum has aimed at targeting senior officers, but they have found that these officers often return with all the members of their unit, and the ultimate goal is to have all police officers in New South Wales undertake this program. In contrast, in Melbourne, Courage to Care focuses its attention on trainee police officers. Evaluations are undertaken by the police and not by the education providers, who do not know the names of the participants for reasons of privacy, but the feedback has been very positive.

For the Sydney Jewish Museum, this is only one of a number of programs; they also have programs for army officers relating to ethical decision-making for the army and others such as an empathy program for health workers.

Another unique Australian program, which has taken on the concept of "Upstander" in its title, focuses on one of the key songs from the Holocaust, *Zov Nit Keynmol* (Never say this is the end of the road for you), known as the "Partisans' Song," which traditionally has been sung at Holocaust commemoration ceremonies. The lyrics of the song were written by Hirsh Glick in the Vilna Ghetto in 1943, and put to music by his friend Rachel Margolis, who was a partisan and survived the Holocaust, although Glick himself perished. Perth-based Eli Rabinowitz, decided to use the song as an educational tool, and this approach has developed into an international project supported by World (Organisation for Rehabilitation through Training) with the students learning it in Hebrew, Yiddish, and their native language. It has become a symbol of hope showing how an individual can make a difference and as an example of defiance and protest, conveying the messages of resistance against evil to school children across the world.

Rabinowitz has encouraged schools of all different religions and backgrounds to introduce the song as a means of bridge building across the different groups. The song has been translated into 24 languages, including most recently into Noongar, the aboriginal language spoken in the Perth region. Rabinowitz uses his website, blogs, and social media to "make a world of difference and a different world!"

These different examples illustrate how human rights education is becoming a central element of Holocaust education in Australia. They have all emerged with the turn of the twenty-first century and are indicative of the major change from the personal, family commemorations of the early years after the Holocaust, with a particularistic focus on the uniqueness of the Holocaust, to conveying the broader, human rights messages, which are universal. As discussed, many scholars argue that this transition is essential if Holocaust education is to remain relevant to future generations.

Conclusions and challenges

Within the Jewish community there has been a major shift from a more parochial approach to Holocaust education to a more universalistic approach, focusing on human rights and genocide. As well, Holocaust education is considered important in Australia, as seen with its introduction into the various state History curricula. Whilst there are a number of university Holocaust programs, these are not compulsory for History teachers. This gap in knowledge creates the challenge of the need to introduce more professional development for History teachers who choose to focus on teaching the Holocaust, and its concomitant universal message. As well, there is the challenge of involving groups for whom the Holocaust has less relevance, in particular Muslim school children, as demonstrated by recent research (Afridi, 2017; Rutland et al., 2001, 2015a; Mendes, 2008; Shoham et al., 2003). Philipp Schorch has argued that "the research findings suggest that the life worlds of students, their personal backgrounds and schools, are intertwined with their interpretive engagements with the exhibition and need to be considered for museum practices and further research" (Schorch, 2015, 47). Taking into account the universal message of human rights needs to be incorporated into this approach.

References

Afridi, Mehnaz M. *Shoah Through Muslim Eyes*. Brighton, MA: Academic Studies Press, 2017.

Alba, A. "Transmitting the Survivor's Voice: Redeveloping the Sydney Jewish Museum." *Dapim: Studies on the Holocaust* 30, no. 3 (2016): 243–257.

Alba, Avril. *The Holocaust Memorial Museum: Sacred Secular Space*. London: Palgrave Macmillan, 2015.

Al-Daraweesh, F., and D.T. Snauwaert. "Toward a Hermeneutical Theory of International Human Rights Education." *Educational Theory* 63, no. 4 (2013): 389–411.

Bauer, Y. *Rethinking the Holocaust*. New Haven and London: Yale University Press, 2001.

Berman, J.E. *Remembrance in Australian Jewish Communities, 1945–2000*. Perth: University of Western Australia Press, 2001.

Brown, M., and I. Davies. "The Holocaust and Education for Citizenship: The Teaching of History, Religion and Human Rights in England." *Educational Review* 50, no. 1 (1998): 75–83.

Burridge, N., J. Buchanan and A. Chodkiewicz. "Human Rights Education in the Australian Curriculum: An Australian Study." *Australian Journal of Teacher Education* 39, no. 3 (2014): 18–36. doi:10.14221/ajte.2014v39n3.7.

Burtonwood, N. "Holocaust Memorial Day in Schools – Context, Process and Content: A Review of Research into Holocaust Education." *Educational Research* 44, no. 1 (2002): 69–82. https://doi.org/10.1080/00131880110107360.

Carrington, B., and G. Short. "Holocaust Education, Anti-Racism and Citizenship." *Educational Review* 49, no. 3 (1997): 271–282.

Cohen, S.K. "'Courage to Care': A first encounter between the Holocaust and Australian school students." *Australian Journal of Jewish Studies*, 19 (2005): 121–133.

Cooke, S., and D. Lee-Frieze. *The Interior of Our Memories: A History of Melbourne's Jewish Holocaust Centre*. Melbourne: Hybrid Publishers, 2015.

Fallon, B. *"Expanding Holocaust Education by Incorporating Human Rights."* In *Unpublished Presentation, Second Conference of the Australian Association of Holocaust Organisations*. Sydney, 2019.

"Gandel Holocaust Studies Program for Australian Educators, The International School of Holocaust Studies, Yad Vashem." *Jerusalem*, n.d. www.yadvashem.org/yv/en/education/international_projects/australian_educators/index.asp.

Gross, Z. "Process of the Universalization of Holocaust Education: Problems and Challenges." *Contemporary Jewry* 38 (2018): 5–20. https://doi.org/10.1007/s12397-017-9237-2.

Gross, Z. and S. D. Rutland. "Intergenerational Challenges in Australian Jewish School Education." *Religious Education* 109, no. 2 (2014): 143–161.

Gross, Z., and E.D. Stevick "Holocaust Education in the 21st Century: Curriculum, Policy and Practice." *As the Witnesses Fall Silent: 21st Century Holocaust Education in Curriculum, Policy and Practice*. Geneva: Springer, 2015, 3–15.

Hector, S. "Teaching the Holocaust in England." In *Teaching the Holocaust*, edited by I. Davies. London: Continuum, 2000.

"Holocaust Exhibition Telling Stories of Survivors Opens at the Australian War Memorial'." *ABC News*, November 30, 2016. www.abc.net.au/news/2016-11-30/holocaust-exhibition-opens-at-awm/8079682.

International Holocaust Remembrance Alliance, www.holocaustremembrance.com/about-us/stockholm-declaration n.d.

Marrus, M.R. *Lessons from the Holocaust*. Toronto, Buffalo, London: University of Toronto Press, 2015.

Mendes, P. "Antisemitism Among Muslim Youth: A Sydney Teacher's Perspective." *ADC Special Report*, no. 37 (2008).

Rosenberg, J. *My Father's Silence*. Melbourne, Victoria: Focus Publishing Pty Ltd, 1994.

Rutland, S.D. *Edge of the Diaspora: Two Centuries of Jewish Settlement in Australia*. New York: Holmes & Meier, 2001.

Rutland, S.D.. "Genocide or Holocaust Education: Exploring Different Australian Approaches for Muslim School Children." In *As the Witnesses Fall Silent: 21st Century Holocaust Education in Curriculum, Policy and Practice*, edited by Z. Gross and Stevick, 225–243. Geneva: Springer, 2015a.

Rutland, S.D.. *Legacies of Violence: Rendering the Unspeakable Past in Modern Australia*. Edited by R. Mason. New York: Berghahn, 2017.

Rutland, S.D.. "'Returning to a Graveyard': Australian Debates about March of the Living to Poland." In *Aftermath: Genocide, Memory and History*, edited by K. Auerbach, 141–165. Melbourne: Monash University Publishing, 2015b.

Rutland, S.D., and S.A. Caplan. *With One Voice: The History of the New South Wales Jewish Board of Deputies*. Sydney: Australian Jewish Historical Society, 1998.

Schorch, P. "Experiencing Differences and Negotiating Prejudices at the Immigration Museum Melbourne." *International Journal of Heritage Studies* 21, no. 1 (2015): 46–64.

Shoham, E., N. Shiloah, and R. Kalisman. "Arab Teachers and Holocaust Education: Arab Teachers Study Holocaust Education in Israel." *Teaching and Teacher Education* 19 (2003): 609–625.

Short, G. "Role of the Holocaust in Antiracist Education: A View from the United Kingdom." *New Community* 23, no. 1 (1997): 75–88.

Supple, C. *From Prejudice to Genocide: Learning about the Holocaust*. Revised Edition. Stoke-On-Trent: Trentham Books, 1998.

Wajnryb, R. *The Silence: How Tragedy Shapes Talk*. Sydney: Allen & Unwin, 2001.

9 New developments in Holocaust and genocide education in South Africa

The case study of the Johannesburg Holocaust & Genocide Centre

Tali Nates

Introduction

South Africa's Minister of Basic Education, Mrs Angie Motshekga, put forward strongly the case for history education saying: "History encourages civic responsibility and critical thinking – these are key values needed in a democratic society. The study of History creates a platform for constructive and informed debates about peace, human rights, and democratic values."[1]

In 2007, the study of 'Nazi Germany and the Holocaust' was included in the new national social sciences and history curriculum for Grade 9 and Grade 11 (15 and 17 years old) in South Africa, the only African country that included it at that time. The National Department of Education decided to implement a curriculum that emphasizes human rights, based on the Constitution and Bill of Rights of South Africa (Act 108 of 1996). These documents were directly influenced by the Universal Declaration of Human Rights (UDHR). One of the aims of this curriculum is that students will learn about equality, human dignity, and social justice and act in the interests of a society that respects democratic values. Dr André Keet, who at that time was part of the South African Human Rights Commission (SAHRC), said about this inclusion:

> It is widely accepted that the events of the Holocaust represented one of the most extreme human rights violations in the history of humankind. The lessons drawn from this crime against humanity played a defining role in the construction and development of contemporary human rights. Therefore, and alongside the many historical and present-day human rights atrocities across the world and our continent, the inclusion of the Holocaust in the curriculum was never disputed.[2]

The new curriculum's intention was to assist learners in understanding that during the 1930s and early 1940s human rights, racism, and discrimination were not given much political or legal attention. Only after World War II and the Holocaust, with the establishment of the United Nations, was there an acknowledgement of the importance of human rights. In December 1948, the world witnessed both the passing of the Universal Declaration of Human Rights, as well as the birth of the Convention on the Prevention and Punishment of the Crime of Genocide.

However, despite these encouraging developments, 1948 was also the year in which the discriminatory system of Apartheid was legalized in South Africa. It would take another 50 years for South Africa to sign the Universal Declaration of Human Rights on 10 December 1998.

The inclusion of the Holocaust in the national curriculum represents this commitment to protecting and educating about human rights. Social sciences educators are required to teach this history across the country for a recommended 15 hours in the first term of the Grade 9 year. Topics included among others: Hitler and the Nazis, Nuremberg Laws, Second World War, Death camps and genocide, the Holocaust, the "Final Solution", resistance such as the Warsaw Ghetto Uprising and more.[3] In the second term, it is followed by the study of Apartheid. Learners who choose History as one of their elected Matriculation examination subjects explore in the second term of Grade 11 the topic of "Ideas of Race in the 19th and 20th Centuries". This covers topics such as Nazi racial ideology, the creation of a racial state in Germany, groups targeted by the Nazis, the "Final Solution", and the Nuremberg Trials.[4]

Through learning about the Holocaust first and then Apartheid, the curriculum aim is that learners will be better equipped to make connections to current issues, including human rights abuses in South Africa and throughout the African continent.

Holocaust memory and education in South Africa

Archbishop Emeritus Desmond Tutu, talking at the opening of the Cape Town Holocaust Centre in August 1999 about the importance of Holocaust memory and education, said:

> We learn about the Holocaust so that we can become more human, more gentle, more caring, more compassionate, valuing every person as being of infinite worth, so precious that we know such atrocities will never happen again and the world will be a more humane place.[5]

Speaking in the southern tip of Africa, he places Holocaust memory and education at the heart of a cry to the world to learn from this universal traumatic past. However, Holocaust and genocide education is a relatively new field of education and memory in South Africa. Until 1994, interest in Holocaust memory was mainly confined to the small Jewish community of the country.[6] Only in the post-Apartheid years has there been a growing interest and development in Holocaust and genocide research, memorialization, and education in the broader society.

The majority of Jews living in South Africa today are descendants of Jewish immigrants from Lithuania and Latvia who came to the country between 1880 and 1930 (until the implementation of the 1930 Quota Act) seeking refuge from poverty and discrimination. Between 1933 and 1936, 3,621 German Jews escaping Hitler's oppression came to South Africa.[7] However, this immigration was stopped with the introduction of the 1937 Aliens Act and, during World War II, only 220

Jewish immigrants were able to enter the country. After the war, approximately 300 Holocaust survivors moved to South Africa. They established a survivors' organization named Sh'erit ha-Pletah (שארית הפליטה, "the surviving remnants"), which played a significant role in commemorating and educating the community about the Holocaust. They also assisted the South African Jewish Board of Deputies (SAJBD) to organize yearly commemoration ceremonies for the Holocaust around the country.

The first Holocaust memorials were established in different Jewish cemeteries in South Africa a few years after the end of World War II. South African sculptor Herman Wald's 1959 Johannesburg memorial to the six million with its six symbolic ram's horns (Shofar) is evocative and emotional. Wald said: "Through the ram's horns the dead are blasting out the Sixth Commandment: 'Though shalt not kill'."[8] Most Jewish cemeteries in the larger cities of South Africa have their own memorials to the victims of the Holocaust, where they hold yearly commemorations on Yom Ha'Shoah (Holocaust Remembrance Day; on the Hebrew date of 27th of Nisan – the start of the Warsaw Ghetto Uprising).

Travelling exhibitions played an important role in the early development of education and remembrance of the Holocaust in South Africa. Most were also aimed at the small Jewish community. The most impactful exhibition aimed at the broader society was the "Anne Frank in Our World" exhibition that travelled throughout South Africa and Namibia in 1994–1995. For the first time in South African history, the country's own history of human rights abuse (the Apartheid period) was also included alongside the story of Anne Frank and the Holocaust. This exhibition was seen by thousands of visitors, including learners and educators. The exhibition highlighted the role Holocaust education could play in post-Apartheid South Africa by raising issues of prejudice and abuse of power. In the context of the painful history of racism in South Africa, the realization that "white" people could also suffer, and at the hand of other "whites" – allowed for new learning processes. Because of the country's painful Apartheid past, South Africans tend to see all human rights violations through the prism of "white vs. black". Learning about the Holocaust and later about the 1994 genocide in Rwanda shattered this defined prism by exploring "whites vs. whites" in the Holocaust and "blacks vs. blacks" in the Rwandan case study. This allowed for a new perspective in discussing and learning about oppression and discrimination.

Following the success of the Anne Frank exhibition, the first South African Holocaust Centre was opened in 1999 in Cape Town, a first of its kind in Africa. Founded by Myra Osrin, the Cape Town Holocaust Centre's (from 2017 it changed its name to the Cape Town Holocaust and Genocide Centre) mission is to serve as a memorial to the six million Jews who were killed in the Holocaust and all victims of Nazi Germany. It opened as an educational centre with a permanent exhibition that included an introduction to race, racism, and Apartheid in South Africa alongside the history of the Holocaust. A revamped permanent exhibition, opened in January 2016, included a brief introduction to the history of genocide in the twentieth century.

In 2008 a second education and memory centre was opened in Durban, South Africa. Founded by Mary Kluk, the Durban Holocaust Centre (in 2017 it also changed its name to the Durban Holocaust and Genocide Centre) looks at the Holocaust with a specific focus on the story of Anne Frank. Its permanent exhibition concludes with an exploration of the role of rescuers in different genocides in the twentieth century.

The Johannesburg Holocaust & Genocide Centre (JHGC), the third centre to be established in South Africa, started operating from a temporary office with a small team in 2008. In 2016, the team moved to a ground-breaking symbolic building in the heart of the city. The landmark institution was built in partnership with the City of Johannesburg. Its official opening took place in March 2019.

In 2008 a national association encompassing the three independent Centres in the country, the South African Holocaust & Genocide Foundation (SAHGF), was established to create better coordination and cohesion nationally in the field of Holocaust and genocide education.[9]

The three independent Centres are the main organizations that support Holocaust education throughout South Africa. Educators' training workshops are held every year in all nine provinces of the country for a minimum of eight hours. Each educator who attends a training workshop receives a set of classroom support materials developed by the SAHGF called The *Holocaust: Lessons for Humanity* (generously supported by the Claims Conference, The Conference on Jewish Material Claims Against Germany). It comprises a learner's workbook, educator's manual, DVD (including a Holocaust history film and a compilation of survivors' testimonies film), and each school receives a teaching poster set. South Africa is a vast country with a growing population. Most schools have no access to the three Centres' permanent exhibitions, thus the SAHGF's classroom posters and a portable travelling exhibition support the teaching of the Holocaust in schools across the country. The Johannesburg Holocaust & Genocide Centre developed a new Holocaust and Genocide travelling exhibition used around South Africa as well as in a few other countries in Africa including Mozambique, Nigeria, and the Gambia.

When it comes to the history of the Holocaust, many South African educators have little to no knowledge of its content. There have been many social sciences and history textbooks published since 2007, yet the way in which they deal with the Holocaust is varied and, in some cases, even inaccurate. For example, some textbooks mention the Holocaust as a footnote to World War II, while others use information that is inaccurate or historically incorrect. Through the educators' training workshops, the SAHGF encourages the educators and subsequently their learners to use the resources developed by the Foundation rather than those inaccurate textbooks when possible.

The SAHGF conducted a few evaluation processes in the past years. One of the more comprehensive, held in 2012, was done by an independent research and consulting company who conducted a longitudinal study on the national educator training programmes of the SAHGF from 2007 to 2011.[10] The evaluators met with three focus groups and conducted quantitative surveys with a random sample of 1,388 workshop participants across the country. They found that over 98 per cent agreed that the training programme increased their knowledge of Holocaust history. A similar percentage stated that the history of the Holocaust and the issues it raises can be used to build a culture that respects human dignity and human rights and enabled them to connect the human rights abuse of the past with the present. When asked about their change in attitudes, over 97 per cent stated that the programme motivated them to become a change agent who can affect positive change. The evaluation findings confirmed that it is easier to learn values and moral lessons from a history removed from one's own experience yet have some parallels to the country's narrative.

The three Centres also conduct ongoing learners' evaluations showing that Holocaust and genocide education allows learners to make a connection between history and current issues of today, and these lessons often translate into social activism. It indicates that teaching the history of the Holocaust and genocide can create opportunities for learners to reflect on the consequences of choices. Looking into the future, the hope is that learners will be able to move from knowing what they "should do", to actually doing it. There are very few other opportunities in the national curriculum where learners can make such connections. Understanding the role of bystanders and activists and choosing to act is important especially in a young democracy such as South Africa. As can be seen later in the chapter, this is also an ongoing challenge.

There are tens of thousands of visitors coming to the three Centres in South Africa every year. Learners and educators are taking part in the ongoing educational workshops the Centres offer; other special interest groups, such as the South African Defense Force and the Police Force, also take part in special educational programmes. In addition, many temporary exhibitions, lectures, plays, film screenings, commemorations, and other special public events are held regularly at the Centres, all of which attract a large and diverse audiences.

Educators and learners comment that teaching the history of the Holocaust serves as an excellent entry point to look at issues of human rights. Many feels that this history is removed from the local experience – it happened over 70 years ago in a different continent – it is also a less emotionally charged topic for South Africans. For these reasons, it allows us to make connections to discussions on discrimination and prejudice, such as racism and xenophobia, which otherwise are not addressed easily.

Development of the new Johannesburg Holocaust & Genocide Centre

When the Johannesburg Holocaust & Genocide Centre (JHGC) was founded in 2008, it chose to focus on the history of the Holocaust and the 1994 genocide in Rwanda. Its core exhibition covers genocides in the twentieth century, starting in 1904 with the Herero and Nama genocide in today's Namibia and the Armenian Genocide of 1915. It also looks at the development of the word genocide through the history of Raphael Lemkin and explores the Convention for the Prevention and Punishment of Genocide and its aftermath. The exhibition also looks at racism in South Africa and the implementation of Apartheid in the same year when the Universal Declaration of Human Rights was passed in the United Nations. Lastly, the exhibition looks at the rise of hate and "othering" of

African refugees and migrants in South Africa and the outbreak of xenophobic attacks since 2008.

The Centre serves as a memorial to the victims of the Holocaust and genocide with a particular attention to the 6 million Jews who were killed in the Holocaust, all victims of Nazi Germany, and the more than 800,000 Tutsi victims of the genocide in Rwanda. It raises awareness of genocide and teaches about the consequences of prejudice, racism, antisemitism, xenophobia, and homophobia, and the dangers of indifference, apathy, and silence to freedom and democracy.[11] The JHGC is a centre of memory, education, and where lessons for humanity can be learned from the darkest of chapters in human history.[12] It is one of the largest such centres in Africa, built over more than 3600 square metres. It includes among other things seminar rooms, temporary exhibition spaces, a resource centre, and a core exhibition. Other spaces such as a memorial garden and plaza, as well as a coffee and gift shop, are also an integral part of the Centre.

The development of the Centre was a public–private partnership between a not-for-profit institution (JHGC) and the City of Johannesburg. The iconic building is full of symbolism – from its railway line facade to the trees around it, the English Bond brickwork resembling that brickwork of Auschwitz, the voids and unfinished indentations representing the loss of life and potential, and the placement of windows in the permanent exhibition space, inviting a discussion with the visitors about witnessing genocide in the past and what is happening in the world today that we witness ourselves.

The Centre's decision to focus on the genocide in Rwanda, came because of the belief that South Africans need to learn from this history. In April 1994, South Africans were celebrating their freedom from Apartheid, standing proudly in queues for hours to vote in the country's first democratic elections; only a mere three and a half hours' flight away, in the same continent and time, in Rwanda, hundreds of thousands of Tutsi and some politically moderate Hutu were murdered during a period of three months. Two countries in Africa made very different choices. All our education programmes link to lessons for humanity that are relevant to South Africa – a country still struggling with the legacy of Apartheid. Through the history of Rwanda and stories of individuals, communities, and governments – we teach about moral choices and their consequences.

The core exhibition and subsequently the education programmes focus on stories and artefacts of survivors who settled in South Africa. The Centre collected for many years photographs, objects, and documents from survivors of the Holocaust and the genocide in Rwanda. Some of the collections are rare and exceptional. The Lichtenstein collection, donated to the Centre by the family of Berlin-born Jewish refugee Herbert Lichtenstein, who came to South Africa in 1936, contains photographs, letters, and artefacts from Berlin, the journey to South Africa, and military service in the South African Army during World War II. Among the artefacts, there are letters signed by Berlin Rabbi Leo Beck and an army "dog tag" that includes the letter J for Jewish.

Another rare collection is the Wellisch collection, a comprehensive collection of more than 100 letters that tell the story of Walter Wellisch, a Viennese Jewish refugee who came to South Africa. Letters from his family continued to arrive from Vienna and later from the ghetto of Theresienstadt. The letters describe the death of his twin brother, Paul, in Theresienstadt and the deportation of his parents to Auschwitz-Birkenau. The letters continued until November 1944. The only one of the family to survive the Holocaust was Walter's sister-in-law Bella (Paul's wife) who was not Jewish but chose to go to Theresienstadt with her husband and his parents.

Holocaust survivors donated different personal belongings such as a childhood doll kept by Hungarian survivor Veronica Phillips. The doll stayed in the ghetto in Budapest with her mother while Veronica was deported first to Ravensbrück concentration camp and then to Penig and Johanngeorgenstadt Concentration Camps and was liberated after taking part in a "death march". When she returned to Budapest, her mother gave her back the doll. Veronica donated it to the JHGC during a moving dedication ceremony in September 2015.[13]

Survivor of the genocide in Rwanda Xavier Ngabo donated a key to his parents' house and a rosary belonging to his murdered mother, Beatrice. After giving his testimony in one of the schools in Johannesburg, learners who heard his story, sponsored his return to Rwanda in 2010 to find the remains of his parents and to bury them. During this emotional trip, he uncovered the artefacts and donated them to the Centre.

An extensive archive of artefacts from Europe and Rwanda was also collected. The JHGC partner with organizations and institutions around the world to showcase artefacts from Holocaust-period Europe and 1994 Rwanda. A partnership with Father Patrick Desbois' organization, Yahad-in-Unum,[14] allowed for very meaningful artefacts from the mass killing sites in the Ukraine to be displayed at the JHGC. These include a house key, a child's dreidel,[15] and empty shells taken from the killing pits. Working with the National Commission for the Fight Against Genocide (CNLG)[16] in Rwanda, moving artefacts of victims from the Catholic Churches of Nyamata and Ntarama[17] are on display at the JHGC. Victims' clothes, shoes, notebooks, and schoolbooks tell the story of thousands of men, women, and children murdered in what they perceived to be a place of safety. Artefacts belonging to the perpetrators such as machetes are also on display.

In addition to the artefacts, hours of testimonies by Holocaust and Rwandan survivors were recorded and 24 films were created especially for the exhibition and are also used in the education programmes. The films focus on the voices of survivors, but also those of bystanders, resisters, rescuers, and perpetrators. For many of the Rwandan survivors, when filmed, it was the first time they told their story, more than 20 years after the genocide. The films made for the genocide in Rwanda section also cover themes of resistance and the world's response and inaction.

The Johannesburg Holocaust & Genocide Centre runs Holocaust Survivors' group activities and survivors are among the Centre's volunteers. Rwandan genocide survivors also meet regularly and they, too, volunteer at the Centre. Holocaust and Rwanda genocide survivors are offering their testimonies at schools and to other groups. South Africa has a great oral tradition and the use of storytelling to acquire knowledge, values, ethics, and morals is highly appreciated and encouraged. Using testimonies of survivors, perpetrators, bystanders, resisters, or rescuers have the potential to bring both the content of the Holocaust and the Rwanda genocide as well as its lessons, to life. When the learners sponsored the trip of Rwandan survivor Xavier Ngabo to Rwanda to bury his parents, it was an example where they made the connection between the history they learned about in the classroom and the role they can play as activists in the present. They definitely changed his life!

The education team at the JHGC offers many programmes in Holocaust, genocide, and human rights education. The programmes vary in focus, length, and the age group they are offered to and when possible, uses the core exhibition in an interactive and meaningful way. The focus of all the programmes is on critical thinking and when possible, connects to examining a range of moral choices that people took during the Holocaust and the 1994 genocide in Rwanda. It looks at the choices made by various role players – perpetrators, bystanders, collaborators, and rescuers – and examines the range of actions of these players through historical examples. Mostly, the focus is on bystander and activist, rescuer, or resister's behaviour. Looking at bystanders – people who witnessed atrocities but did not act or speak out – we often quote Primo Levi who said: "In spite of the varied possibilities for information, most Germans didn't know because they didn't want to know. Because, indeed, they wanted not to know."[18] This rings especially true to South Africans who lived next to the prisons and torture chambers of the Apartheid regime.

We also look at the choices of rescuers and resisters. For example, Jaap van Proosdij who lived in Pretoria, South Africa, was a Dutch rescuer who saved dozens of Jews in the Netherlands during the Holocaust. When asked: "Why did you do it"? he answered with a question of his own: "If you see a drowning man, won't you save him?" For him, it was a rhetorical question. But sadly, for many, the answer is not so clear-cut. Most people would not save the drowning man, be it out of fear for their own lives or just the thought that someone else swims better and would do it instead. Stories such as Jaap's encourage learners to use critical thinking and develop tools for dealing with these difficult dilemmas.

The programmes also look at what Lawrence Langer[19] termed, "choiceless choices", by, for example, sharing the story of Abba Kovner who called on Jews in the Vilna ghetto to resist the Nazis in January 1942. He was regarded as one of the leaders of the resistance (United Partisan Organisation, "Fareynigte Partizaner Organizatsye", or FPO) and was perceived as a hero, but when asked about it after the war he reflected on the time when he was about to leave the ghetto to the forests to fight the Nazis. His old mother begged him not to leave her – she told him that she was afraid and needed him. But he chose to leave. "Was I the hero of the resistance or was I the coward that abandoned his mother when she needed me most?" he reflected.[20]

Irene Klass, a Holocaust survivor who survived the Warsaw ghetto and lives in Johannesburg, said to Rwandan genocide survivor Sylvestre Sendacyeye: "I thought that when the world learned what had happened to us, it could never happen again. But it did ...[21]" Despite the passing of the Genocide Convention in 1948, and the commitment of the world to uphold "Never Again", genocide happens again and again. Through the education work of the Johannesburg Holocaust & Genocide Centre, the hope is that learners will be encouraged to speak out in the face of injustice; that they will have the courage to move from bystander to activist behaviour. In so doing the aim is to create a more caring and just society in which human rights and diversity are respected and valued and to empower the youth to safeguard democracy, to prevent mass violence and "othering".

Finally, the Johannesburg team also offer support to one of the newest regional Holocaust Centres in Africa, "The Beau Bassin Jewish Detainees Memorial & Information Centre" on the island of Mauritius, which opened in the end of 2014. The Centre and its adjoining Jewish cemetery tell the little-known story of the almost 1,600 deported Jewish refugees, who fled Nazi-occupied Europe and whom Britain deported to the island in December 1940. The refugees were held for almost five years in a prison complex in Mauritius and 126 of them died and were buried in the Jewish Cemetery at St Martin near Port Louis. This chapter in history is now also featured in the JHGC core exhibition.

Some of the challenges in Holocaust education in South Africa

South Africa is a large country with a population of over 55 million, including many asylum seekers, refugees, and migrants from around Africa. There are 11 official languages spoken in the country but learners and educators are supposed to teach and learn in English and write their exams in that language. For most, English is not their mother tongue and at times is only their third or fourth language. In many schools, class size is also a huge problem, with up to 50–60 learners in one class. There are also many infrastructure problems with not enough classrooms, toilets, and even desks and chairs. There are still many schools without electricity, while others don't have equipment for audio-visual teaching or access to the Internet. There are also places where classes are still held outside. Learners also encounter many problems with the delivery of textbooks in some of the country's provinces.[22] This severely impact the learner's ability to learn.

In a country where simple infrastructure is still such a challenge and where many of the schools are in deep rural areas, training the educators on how to teach the Holocaust is very important but also increasingly challenging. Graeme Bloch, an education policy analyst at the Development Bank of Southern Africa, wrote about the state of schools in the country:

> the vast majority of schools are dysfunctional in that they are not producing the meaningful outcomes that are their primary goal … vast inequalities are produced and reproduced in schools, so that a small band of at most 20% produces the great majority of graduates and success stories in the system.[23]

When it comes to Holocaust education, despite it being a compulsory part of the curriculum, most schools have no access to the Holocaust exhibitions and educational resources in the three Centres in Johannesburg, Durban, and Cape Town. With more than 430,000 educators in South Africa,[24] educators' training remains an enormous challenge. Educators have little to no prior knowledge of the Holocaust. This history was never included as a module in the national curriculum before 2007, and there were no local textbooks dealing with its content.

In addition, for the majority of South Africans, modern European history is approached with a degree of scepticism, as it is often viewed through the devastating impact of colonialism.

This year the country celebrates 27 years of democracy and 25 years since the "Truth and Reconciliation Commission". Yet there is huge concern about South Africa's still unresolved issues and continued difficulty in facing its own past. In South Africa, educators at times "compare suffering" between the Holocaust, other genocides, and Apartheid. Some feel that Apartheid was not "as bad as the Holocaust" or as one educator commented: "you think that Apartheid was a walk in the park". On the other hand, there is lack of understanding of what genocide is and one often hears declarations such as "Apartheid was also genocide".[25]

A constant challenge is the difficulty of making a connection between learning the history of the Holocaust and its lessons, and actually implementing that lesson in the reality of South Africa. In March 2008, just two months before the eruption of the horrific violence against foreigners in South Africa, the SAHGF held a workshop for 60 Grade 9 educators in Johannesburg. Working in small groups, the educators were given an exercise in which they had to analyse a story where "their colleagues had complained that the foreigners came to South Africa and took South African jobs". A substantial number of participants agreed that this was, in fact, true. They became angry and emotional and even added to the complaints against foreigners. It was as if all barriers had come down as the participants raged about foreigners in South Africa.[26] It was a disturbing precursor to the violence ahead. It was clear that many of the educators had bought into the values and moral lessons of history only insofar as they did not affect them personally. It was easier to be "politically correct" when learning about history, much harder to translate that history and make it relevant to their lives today. In May 2008, 62 mainly African, foreigners were killed by angry mobs around South Africa. Sadly, xenophobic attacks continue to plague the country with sporadic attacks happening again and again, the latest in September 2019 with 12 people losing their lives in the violence.

In conclusion

Holocaust and genocide education programmes offered in South Africa are taught with the hope that learners and educators can make a connection between past and the present and translate it into social activism. Teaching the history of the Holocaust and genocide creates an opportunity for learners and educators to reflect on the consequences of choices. The hope is that they will be able to move from knowing what they "should do", to actually doing it. There are very few other opportunities in the national curriculum where learners can make such connections.

Understanding the role of bystanders and activists and choosing to act is important especially in a young democracy such as South Africa. Realizing that there is a choice is critical. During the xenophobic attacks of May 2008, one of the educators who went through extensive Holocaust training created an opportunity for her learners to make their own posters and banners and demonstrate outside the school against those attacks. The learners translated the lessons of the Holocaust to actively becoming activists for change themselves.

As South Africa continues to struggle with many issues relating to racism and xenophobia, the national curriculum aims to assist with the promotion of human rights and peace by challenging prejudices involving race, class, gender, ethnicity, and "othering". The words of Auschwitz survivor and writer Primo Levi, in the entrance to the Johannesburg Holocaust & Genocide Centre should serve as a warning to us all: "It happened therefore it can happen again; this is the core of what we have to say. It can happen, and it can happen everywhere."[27]

Notes

1 Minister of Basic Education, Mrs Angie Motshekga (2015). 1st History Round-Table Discussion, *DBE Conference Centre*, Pretoria, 3 December 2015.
2 Richard Freedman, "Teaching the Holocaust to Non-Traditional Audiences: The South African Experience," in *Yad Vashem International Conference* (Jerusalem, 2008). In Yad Vashem International Conference. Jerusalem, 7–10 July.
3 Education.gov.za. (2016), [Accessed 3 October 2016], Available at: www.education.gov.za/Portals/0/CD/National%20Curriculum%20Statements%20and%20Vocational/CAPS%20SP%20%20SOCIAL%20SCIENCE%20GR%207-9%20%20.pdf?ver=2015-01-27-160206-107
4 Education.gov.za (2016), [Accessed 21 December 2016], Available at: www.education.gov.za/Portals/0/CD/National%20Curriculum%20Statements%20and%20Vocational/CAPS%20FET%20%20HISTORY%20GR%2010-12%20%20WeB.pdf?ver=2015-01-27-154219-397
5 *The Holocaust, Lessons for Humanity, Learner's Interactive Resource Book*, 2004, 44.
6 At its height in 1980, the Jewish community numbered 117,963 Jews; G. Shimoni and G. Shimoni, *Community and Conscience* (Hanover: Brandeis University Press published by University Press of, 2003).
7 The Immigration of Jews into the Union, 1926–1936: An Analysis of Official Statistics, South African Jewish Board of Deputies (1937), p. 6.
8 Hermanwald.com (2016) [online] Available at: www.hermanwald.com/pages/FormViewAdd.aspx?id=187
9 To read more about the SAHGF go to the website: https://jhbholocaust.co.za/foundation/
10 An Evaluation of the South African Holocaust and Genocide Foundation's Teacher Training Programme from 2007 to 2011. (2012) Mthente Research and Consulting Services (Pty) Ltd.
11 This falls in line with the vision and mission of the umbrella organization, the South African Holocaust & Genocide Foundation but expand it further.
12 To read more about the JHGC go to their website on: www.jhbholocaust.co.za
13 timeslive.co.za. 2015. *The Times*. [ONLINE] Available at: www.timeslive.co.za/the-times/2015/09/02/Little-items-tell-their-harrowing-stories1 [Accessed 23 December 2016].
14 To read more about Yahad-in-Unum go to their website on: www.yahadinunum.org
15 A child's game for the Jewish festival of Hanukkah.
16 To read more about CNLG go to their website on: www.cnlg.gov.rw/home
17 In Nyamata, on 10–11 April, the Interaham murdered 10,000 Tutsi. In Ntarama, more than 5 000 Tutsi were murdered; very few survived.
18 Primo Levi, *The Reawakening* (New York: Touchstone published by Simon & Schuster, 1995), 251.

19 L. Langer, *Admitting the Holocaust: Collected Essays* (New York: Oxford University Press, 1995), 231.
20 yadvashem.org (2016). [online] Available at: www.yadvashem.org/yv/en/education/newsletter/30/dilemma_revolt.asp#!prettyPhoto [Accessed 21 December 2016].
21 Conversation with Irene Klass. JHGC collection.
22 Hsrc.ac.za (2016). [online] Available at: www.hsrc.ac.za/en/review/hsrc-review-september-2013/understanding-the-limpopo-textbook-saga [Accessed 21 December 2016].
23 Graeme Bloch, *The Toxic Mix, What's Wrong with South Africa's Schools and How to Fix It.* (Cape Town: Tafelberg, 2009), 59.
24 Cde.org.za (2016). [online] Available at: www.cde.org.za/wp-content/uploads/2015/03/Final-Revised-ES-TeacherSupplyandDemand2025.pdf [Accessed 21 December 2016].
25 Tali Nates, "'But, Apartheid Was Also Genocide … What about Our Suffering?' Teaching the Holocaust in South Africa–Opportunities and Challenges," *Intercultural Education* 21, no. S1 (2010): secs. 17–26.
26 Michelle Friedman, "Report on Follow-up Workshop: Understanding Apartheid and the Holocaust," in *Presented to the Gauteng Department of Education*, 2008.
27 Primo Levi, *Survival in Auschwitz and the Reawakening: Two Memoirs* (New York: Summit Books, 1986).

10 A case of naive normalization?

India's misbeliefs about Hitler and schooling on the Holocaust

Anubhav Roy

Introduction

Writing for the *Daily Beast*, journalist Dilip D'Souza narrates a personal incident due to its salient indication of a worrisome trend. When his wife, teaching French to adolescents at a high-brow school in metropolitan Mumbai, asked her class "to complete the sentence '*J'admire* … (I admire …)' with the name of the historical figure they most admired," nine out of 25 respondents submitted "*J'admire Adolf Hitler.*" Perturbed, when the teacher probed why only one respondent admitted to admiring Mahatma Gandhi, most of her students alleged that "he was a coward." The discomfort only grew when the class of adolescents – hardly naive for their age – who professed to "admire" one of the most loathed figures of modern history unrepentantly justified their choice by arguing how Hitler was "a fantastic orator [and] a great patriot [who] gave back to Germany a sense of pride that they had lost after the Treaty of Versailles." For the "millions he murdered," there was a pre-meditated partial acquittal: "some of them [the victims] were traitors" (D'Souza 2012).

Rewinding further into the past or forwarding closer to the present only reveals the ghost of the Nazi totalitarian to be nested as cosily in the minds of those of India's youth who struggle to negotiate their nation's diverse ethnic heterogeneity. A *Times of India* survey had revealed in December 2002 that nearly a fifth of the students polled at the most elite colleges of Delhi, Mumbai, Kolkata, and Bangalore "favoured Adolf Hitler as the kind of leader India ought to have." The report had, thus, questioned India's "moral compass" (M. Joshi 2002). Likewise, a 2017 survey by the *Pew Research Center* across 16 Indian states found 55 per cent of respondents in favour of "a strong leader [who] can make decisions without interference from parliament or the courts," which is the highest of the 38 countries surveyed. Additionally, 53 per cent of respondents prescribed military rule. India was labelled an "exceptional case" in both respects (Wike et al. 2017). The case is worsened by the observation that *Mein Kampf* – Hitler's incendiary, imperialist, and antisemitic manifesto from 1925, banned across most of the West while its copyright lasted – is a bestseller amongst India's elite and common readers alike, who buy its bootlegged English and vernacular copies openly from grey and up-market vendors.

The most known local rendition of the *Mein Kampf* reached its 55th edition and 100,000 copies within 12 years of its inaugural release by the Delhi-based Jaico Publishing House in 1998. Bahri Sons, the city's posh bookstore, called it a "classic [they] have to sell" (Scheinert 2014). Crossword, a book-mart with a pan-India presence, admitted that across their outlets in Mumbai, Hitler's auto-biography outsells Gandhi's, with about "70 per cent [of its buyers being] male, […] mostly [in] the age group of 18–35" (NDTV 2010). A casual online search shows that of the 11 country-specific websites of *Amazon.com*, only the Indian portal features the *Mein Kampf* amongst its list of top ten bestselling biographies. Worse, for those on the peripheries of metropolitan cores, there exist vernacular, locally penned biographies of Hitler, which tend to rely on dubious references for their sketchy portrayals of his life, ideas, and policies in suspiciously bright light. Since its first edition released in the 1960s, reprints of V. G. Kanitkar's *Nazi Bhas-masurachaya Udayasta* (The Rise and Fall of the Nazi Demon) have sold in Maha-rashtra as a seminal Marathi chronicle of the Second World War. Between the lines, it considerably aggrandizes Hitler's rise. Similarly, free electronic copies of the *Mein Kampf* translated into Hindi (as *Mera Sangharsh*), Bengali (as *Mein Kampf Onubaad*), and Tamil (as *Enathu Porattam*) are usually a Web-browse away. In 2018, Pegasus For Kids, a niche Indian publisher of books for children, sent the associate dean of the Simon Wisenthal Center for Jewish human rights into a tizzy by featuring Hitler on the cover of a volume titled *Great Leaders* (Schultz 2018).

India's peddling of Nazi-styled iconography and branding is not restricted only to literature. In recent years, the nation has witnessed a café near Mumbai, an apparel store in Ahmedabad, a pool parlour along a national highway, and an ice-cream marque in Meerut themed on Nazi iconography or even named after Hitler, only to embarrassingly draw flak from international media watchdogs and India's microscopic but well-voiced Jewish community. It is also not difficult to find the Nazi replication of the Hindu *Swastika* – the *Hakenkreuz* – stamped on "t-shirts, key-rings, bags, home furnishings" and other such purchasables for sale at India's street-side *bazaars*. Suman Gupta spots unhindered "Hitler references" peppered in India's cinema and television, which allude to the "ultimately good protagonists" (S. Gupta 2015b, Ch. 4, Sec. 2).

Therefore, Zubair Ahmed of the BBC fairly estimates the "business around […] Adolf Hitler [to be] a small-scale industry in India" (Ahmed 2010). While the com-monplace fetishizing of the Nazis and their spearhead by Indians is quite evident, its underlying reasons are not. Why does Hitler, the archetype of ruthless despot-ism and the architect of one of history's worst genocides, continue to command a worrisome degree of idolatry from most sections of India? Despite several jour-nalistic and academic attempts to solve this puzzle, the explanations have largely remained deficient or reductionist, failing to establish enough reasonable causality.

A troubling legacy

Through his elaborate chronicle, Kris Manjapra shows how the relation-ship between Indians and Germans – initially restricted to esoteric intellec-tual exchanges fuelled by mutual cultural curiosity – eventually turned deeply political, when ambitious and often militant nationalists from both nations began envisioning a bilateral "collaboration [...] to destroy the nineteenth-century world order organized by British power" (Manjapra 2014, 1). Attempts to fructify this vision, or the so-called "Hindu-German conspiracies," surfaced most prominently during the First World War, usually in pursuit of one or more of three broad agendas. First, contraband aid from German proxies to diasporic or domestic Indian nationalists, as witnessed in the two bungled arms-trafficking plots of 1915, namely, the Annie-Larsen Affair involving the US-based *Ghadar* Party and the Christmas Day Affair to equip Bengal's *Jugantar* Party. Second, covert German-backed schemes for sabotage or subversion, as epitomized by the ostentatious *Ghadar* Conspiracy to stoke mutinies amongst British Indian Army units between Punjab and Singapore onwards from 1915. Third, formal political endorsement, as garnered from Kaiser Wilhelm II by India's first provisional government-in-exile under Mahendra Pratap at Kabul.

Such anti-British cooperation instilled a favourable impression of Germany on many in India – who suffered a renewed wave of colonial repression after the British volte-face on its brief war-time concessions towards the supportive native political elite – which continued through the interwar years and peaked during the Second World War. Despite the Treaty of Versailles crippling the German economy, noted Indian revolutionary activists such as Chempakaraman Pillai and Bhikaji Cama retained their German contacts. Even with the rise of Hitler, who had ridiculed Indians as *"fakirs"* in *Mein Kampf* and compelled Leftist Indian nationalists like ACN Nambiar to flee Berlin, a number of diasporic Indians stayed on in German cities. In the meantime, in India, Vinayak D. Savarkar – the founder of the militant *Hindu Mahasabha* – published his controversial imperialist manifesto, *Hindu-Pad-Padshahi* (The Hindu Empire), in 1925, nearly coinciding with the German release of the *Mein Kampf* that very year. During a 1938 rally, Savarkar went on to contend that "in Germany, the movement of the Germans is the national movement, but that of the Jews is a communal one." A year thereafter, Madhav S. Golwalkar, a stalwart of the Hindu nationalist *Rashtriya Swayamsevak Sangh* (RSS) and a Marathi peer of Savarkar, hailed the Nazi torment of Jews as "a good lesson for us [Hindus]" (Casolari 2000, 212–228).

In Bengal, the spread of Nazism in Europe inspired Benoy Kumar Sarkar's aspiration for "a Greater Bengali ethnic nationalism," just as it spurred Asit Krishna Mukherji's *New Mercury* faction to "champion Aryanism and [the] anti-British sentiment in India." Mukherji married Maximiani Portas, a noted French collaborator of the RSS, who famously rechristened herself as Savitri Devi and went on to remain a fierce Nazi apologist even after the Second World War (Manjapra 2014, 117–119). Militant ethno-nationalist outfits – some with Brownshirt-like volunteer corps – were hardly peculiar to Hindus. Inayatullah Khan Mashriqi became known for marching his anti-colonial Muslim *Khaksar* paramilitary cadres, donning *khakis* and armed with spades, across Lahore by the 1940s. His efforts even earned him, quite famously, a 1942 Renault-Benz sedan as a gift from his "friend," Hitler (Sheikh 2011).

The politically driven anti-British Indo-German alliance reached its peak when, in the refuge of the Third Reich, the provisional *Azad Hind* (Free India) government-in-exile and the first *Azad Hind Fauj* (Free India Legion, later reconstituted as the Indian National Army) were set up amidst the Second World War by Subhas Chandra Bose, a former president of the Indian National Congress (INC) who escaped to Berlin with disgruntlement against the Gandhian pacifist resistance guiding the INC-led mainstream of India's anti-colonial crusade (Manjapra 2014, 104–05). While no German-endorsed alternative political campaign – with the arguable exception of the brief invasion of northeast India by Bose's Japan-aided *Azad Hind Fauj* – could cause lasting damage to the colonial control over India, the Nazi brand of reactionary nationalism had found ample Indian admirers by the time peace arrived in 1945.

While it may be claimed, as do Subhadra Joshi (1971) and Marzia Casolari (2000), that the seeds of sympathy towards Hitler were sown in India by such Germanophile ideologues and alternative nationalist efforts, there are certain caveats that must be heeded to avert the risk of reductionism. First, the Left-of-Centre INC (present-day Congress Party) – which, in spite of alternatives, was the most legitimate and influential agent of India's anti-colonial movement under Mahatma Gandhi's *de facto* leadership – maintained and propagated a staunchly anti-Nazi worldview, which was unsurprisingly echoed in local press and public attitudes at the time. Second, admiration for fascist or Nazi figures, though conducive for them, was not typical of India's ethno-nationalists. Benito Mussolini, for instance, did not just meet Balakrishna S. Moonje of the RSS, but also Bose, and most notably, Gandhi, who reportedly "hailed" Italy's fascist supremo as "one of the great statesmen of [their] time" (Ghosh 2012).

Third, the stances of India's ethno-nationalists were neither consistent nor homogenous and appeared opportunistic instead. Mashriqi, despite his acquaintance with Hitler, preached liberal-progressive philosophies. While praising the Nazi persecution of Jews, Golwalkar also lauded Jewish Zionists for upholding their "religion [and] culture" in his 1939 thesis, *We* (Golwalkar 1939, 30). Likewise, in late 1947, Savarkar advocated that "the whole of Palestine [was] the National Home of the Jewish people" as part of his bitter condemnation of India's official negation of the UN Partition Plan for Israel as a ploy to appease the "petty Moslem States of Asia" (Quraiza 2004, 11–12). Evidently, the fandom for Nazi idealism among Indian ethno-nationalists was not rooted in antisemitism. In fact, the majoritarian right of India – densely populated by RSS – and *Mahasabha*-tutored hardliners – now champions Indo-Israeli bilateral amity and the territorial claims of Israel. Fourth, ethno-nationalistic parties were hardly in a position to determine India's mainstream political discourses until recently. For decades after its independence, India remained immersed in Nehruvian ethos and pursued socialist nation-building aspirations. Meanwhile, the majoritarian right – the last vestige of Hitler's earliest Indian advocates – stayed marginalized and attained little electoral mileage until the communal *Ram Mandir* (temple) movement of the 1990s.

A contextualizing conundrum

Due to the aforementioned points of scepticism from the perspective of sheer practicality, any attempt to squarely and solely blame early ethno-nationalists for etching the Indian mind with Naziphilia may not be logically tenable. The fallacy is further strengthened by the fact that several political figures who do not subscribe to ethno-nationalist or majoritarian right-wing ideologies in India seem to be as misplaced in their usage of Nazi and Hitler references. Soon after the Telegu Desam Party (TDP) broke its alliance with the federally incumbent – right-of-centre and RSS-affiliated – Bharatiya Janata Party (BJP) in 2018, the former party's actor-turned MP, Naramalli Sivaprasad, entered parliament dressed in Hitler's garb, complete with a *Hakenkreuz* armband and the idiosyncratic moustache. His admitted intention was to "grab attention quickly" and take a jibe at India's Prime Minister and BJP stalwart, Narendra Modi (BBC 2018). Months after Modi was sworn into office in 2014, K. Chandrasekhar Rao (or "KCR"), the firebrand chief minister of the Indian state (or province) of Telangana, grumbled that "he gets described as 'Hitler whenever he called a spade a spade' (PTI 2014)." For such detractors, he reserved a strange retort:

> One says KCR is Hitler, another says KCR is [a] dictator; KCR is definitely Hitler for thieves. I want to be Hitler for the corrupt. I don't feel shy. KCR is Hitler to stop injustice.
>
> (Singh 2014)

Rao is no school-dropout politician. He earned a postgraduate degree in English literature at a reputed urban Indian university before veering towards electoral politics. He well understands that the equating of his policy determinism to Hitler's is no public relations' profit. However, he exhibited little sensitivity. Those possessing a conception of Nazi atrocities, especially the Holocaust – the industrial-scale genocide of six million European Jews – or even the ruthless racial supremacism characteristic of Nazism would refrain from such casual normalization of Hitler. Is such sensitivity common in India? What context does the lay Indian place Hitler in?

Writing on India's awkward affinity for Nazi symbols, *NPR* ascribed the phenomenon to the claim that only a "small percentage of India's vast population [is aware of] European history" (NPR 2012). While naivety cannot be alleged through conjectures, the banal exoneration of divisive historical figures by societies is often fed by poor contextualization and misplaced memorialization. It is, thus, unsurprising that Hitler is revered as a "military genius" in India's neighbour, Pakistan, just as much (Kazim 2010). Zubair Ahmed, quoting local respondents, underlines that "Hitler, [remembered] as a committed patriot [...] who can solve problems," inspires India's youth, who are "faced with a lot of problems" themselves (Ahmed 2010). It is perhaps what explains some of the most consistent Indian consumers of the *Mein Kampf* being students of business management (Gupta 2015a, Ch. 4, Sec. 2). In 2011, a Hindi soap opera airing at a prime-time slot on a widely viewed Indian television channels was titled, *Hitler Didi* (Aunt Hitler), featuring a young woman fighting prejudice ironically nick-named "Hitler," owing to her unyielding attitude. By 2013, it surpassed 400 episodes in its maiden season, despite a strongly worded appeal from New York's Jewish Anti-Defamation League – labelling it as a "terrible trivialization" – to the producers (Haaretz 2011). Similarly, a song from the successful 2009 Tamil action film, *Kanthaswamy*, has nearly half a million views on its official YouTube video despite labelling the male protagonist as "Hitler" for his temper.

At the risk of superficiality, the aforementioned instances outline a pattern of characterization and association. To the average memory in India, Adolf Hitler is recalled as the embodiment of unrelenting absolutism and unsparing ferocity. For many, he merely typifies patriotism, valour, strategic genius, leadership, and, ultimately, inspiration. Given that such attributes did constitute his persona and politics, Machiavellian worldviews accommodative of ruthlessness may consequently find little to complain about on his legacy. The potential for misplaced portrayals cementing along the memories of generations into relatable narratives of history is arguably enunciated best in Pierre Nora's notion of *lieux de mémoire* or memory spaces.

Memory spaces are elements that have grown symbolic of common heritage, where "the past finds articulation" and which enable a "residual sense of continuity" between the fleeting past and the present in the absence of a *"milieu de mémoire"* or consistent reminders (Rothberg 2010, 3–4). For instance, among the many cases that Nora investigates as the *lieux* of populist French history, he observes that nineteenth-century grammarian Pierre Larousse is a prominent memory space representative of that nation's literary zenith. Yet, he "has become a common noun, the origin of which [...] the user has all but forgotten" (Nora 2010, x). Likewise, for the average Indian divorced from the epoch by decades, the history of the Second World War – more so, of Nazi occupation of Europe – may well have crystallized not into a verified and panoramic conception, but into a loose compilation of cherry-picked *lieux* that help propel a convenient, half-baked memorialization of those fragile years. In other words, the uninitiated Indian mind is most likely to be selectively amnesic towards Nazism's history, remembering only the palatable points from Hitler's political resume.

Yet, one may ask why the Holocaust, the event most associated with Nazism in the West, is not a *lieu* in the average Indian's memory of Hitler. Does India know – or get to know – enough about the racially vindicated genocide of Jews by the Nazis? The roots of questionable public preferences and opinions are often traced to structural gaps. In India, a minority of students pursues college degrees and ever fewer continue studying the humanities – especially history – beyond school. Bollywood even has a satirical song from the film *Anpadh* (Illiterate, 1962) questioning the practical utility of learning history (Gupta 2015a). The nation continues to botch its schooling priorities, with reports of textbook controversies, poor teaching methods, and politicization of curricula often grabbing headlines. India's schooling curricula continues to be based on textbooks updated once or twice a decade, some of which even carry shoddily drafted content. Is the Indian commoner's lack of hindsight on Hitler rooted in impoverished rudimentary education on the Holocaust? The answer to this may become clear via a content analysis of a few state-approved high school history textbooks in circulation across India.

A foundational flaw

Since succeeding India's Central Bureau of Textbook Research (CBTR) in 1961, the National Council of Education Research and Training (NCERT) has served as the nation's apex body for the production and prescription of textbooks for schools. For uniformity, circulation of the NCERT's textbooks is mandated for all schools affiliated to the Central Board of Secondary Education (CBSE), a top schooling regulator (India Today 2014). The NCERT's materials are also reproduced by several state (or provincial) education boards like those of Assam, Mizoram, Rajasthan, and Uttarakhand. For the CBSE's history syllabus, the staple NCERT textbook for class (or grade) IX provides an engaging, elaborate, and critically intuitive chapter of Nazism and the Second World War. In it, the Holocaust commands a dedicated sub-section, titled "Knowledge about the Holocaust," and is defined as the extermination of "six million Jews, 200,000 gypsies, one million Polish civilians [...]," among others. The chapter allows the impressionable mind to revisit the tragedy through stimulating images and text-boxes like an image from the Warsaw ghetto or the confession of an Auschwitz survivor. The contents also explain key objects and events associated with the Holocaust, such as Martin Niemoeller's "First They Came," Charlotte Beradt's diary, antisemitic propaganda, supremacist theories, concentration camps (KZs) conditions, and the Nuremburg trials (NCERT 2014, 61–72). The NCERT's textbook for the curious adolescent sets an encouraging benchmark.

Of the 130,000 schools recognized nationwide in 2013, however, 85 per cent were classified as suburban or rural (Dhawan and TNN 2013). The 18,000 high schools that adhere to the CBSE's norms and mandate the NCERT's textbooks are mostly urban (CBSE n.d.). The consumption of the NCERT's mature narrative on Nazism, thus, remains quite esoteric. A vast number of the 85 per cent of schools off city limits are affiliated to provincial boards of education. To promote regional histories and federal autonomy, India allows its states (or provinces) to regulate their own curricula and design their own textbooks. Though state governments also have the option to simply circulate the NCERT's textbooks, few choose to do so. While internal migration in India has slackened, it has long been the norm for children to finish their schooling at rural or suburban schools before opting to shift to metropolitans for college education (Munshi and Rosenzweig 2016). It is at the provincial levels where textbook quality plunges worryingly.

Provincially circulated textbooks drafted by state education boards are prone to errors, poor grades of narration, and even politicization. Resultantly, their reference materials for history are often centres of ignominious controversies, and whimsical omissions and commissions. Of such shortcomings, the poor contextualization of past events and figures – by accident or design – is commonplace. In Punjab, for instance, the state's history textbook for students of class IX tells a concerning tale. Its crudely composed, under-sized section on the Third Reich claims the "Nazis were atheists" and the "Nazi Party [...] agreed on the equality of citizens." Such partial facts are contrasted with the disproportionate extolling of Hitler's industry and agriculture, without enough corresponding reprimand. It overlooks the Holocaust, suggesting that the Nazis merely "wanted to extermi-nate" (Singh and Bhatia 2016, 91–93).

While Punjab's textbook was last revised in 2016, the edition active in the state board schools of Maharashtra have been in circulation since 2013, when the Congress Party was incumbent. Yet, Maharashtra does a shoddier job of educating its class X adolescents about Hitler. Their history textbook shockingly claims that "Hitler […] form [ed] the Nazi Party" and "taught [German] citizens a lesson of sacrifice for the sake of the nation." Without counter-balancing commentary on his atrocities and authoritarianism, such a claim makes Hitler seem a saint. A mere sentence on the "lakhs of Jews killed" is disdainfully tucked between praises for Nazi German agriculture and technology. The laundry-list of the fall-outs of the Second World War that follows includes "moral degradation," but not the Holocaust (Humpe et al. 2014, 26–27).

There are, of course, provincially prepared high school history textbooks that display credible quality in their factual discretion. However, these, too, have gaps when exposing readers to the Nazi crimes against humanity. The Tamil Nadu Board of Secondary Education's most advanced history textbook, intended for near adults about to finish school, dedicates a chapter each to the rise of fascism in Europe and the Second World War, which bring to the fore Hitler's pronounced antisemitism and even note the *Dolchstosslegende* – the perpetuated blaming of the German loss of the First World War on communists, pacifists, and Jews – as one of the drivers of the Nazi ascent. Yet, neither chapter mentions the Holocaust, as the texts only grant a passing reference to the "repressive measures for the economic and cultural boycott of the Jews" within a paragraph-long sub-section titled, "Anti-Jew Policy." The sizeable section on the consequences of the war, too, throws no light on the genocide (TNTESC 2015, 321).

The Higher Secondary Education Board of Kerala – a Leftist bastion politi-cally – teaches the Second World War and the Cold War to 16-year-olds through a single, unified chapter in its history textbook for class X. Its chapter on Nazism is illustrated and interactive enough for the reader's attention. The segment's prime focus, however, is restricted to the geopolitical and military contests of both eras. Consequently, and quite bizarrely, the "annihilation of the Jews" garners a mere sentence concealed within a text-box on Operation Barbarossa (State Council of Education Research and Training 2011, 80). On the other end of the political spectrum, Gujarat, a right-wing fortress for years, educates its school-goers on Nazism at class IX through a couple of paragraphs, one of which suggests that "Nazi soldiers wore blue military uniforms," which is irrelevant and inaccurate. Yet, to its credit, the brief section manages to mention the term "Holocaust," explaining it as the "genocide [of] innumerable European Jews." Alongside, and significantly, it submits that Nazi "policies were targeted at exterminating Jews […] in the name of purification of the German race" (Qureshi et al. 2016, 15).

It must be borne in mind, regardless, that Gujarat's history of history text-books has not been too clean. The state has been in the news more than once for breeding textbook politicization in the recent past. Nandini Manjrekar et al. note an ideological and socio-political impetus behind right-wing Gujarat's tinkering with textbooks in *Textbook Regimes* (Manjrekar et al. 2010). A controversy broke in 2004 when the state's class X history textbook glorified Hitler as a "Supremo" and painted a "frighteningly uncritical picture of fascism and Nazism." The book had to be revised after a human rights activist litigated against it (Mehtal 2004). Thus, detractors see Gujarat as a fertile ground for the politicizing of education (Kumar 2014).

Josh Scheinert observes that the Second World War and its impacts receive stark apathy in India's high school classrooms, where narratives of local and national histories, isolated from international events, tend to dominate. Thus, the memorialization of the Holocaust gets lost in translations of the conflict's broader consequences, leaving "Hitler's legacy removed from the traumas [of] the Holocaust" in India (Scheinert 2014). Also, how tender minds are taught the complex past depends on the quality of instructors. To add to the flawed textbooks, India's school teachers – the translators of the text – often fall short in terms of qualifications and skills. Cut-throat scores attained by rote continue to be encouraged in classrooms, as reports of school teachers failing to satisfy tutoring benchmarks are not rare. As per a 2014 UNESCO survey, teachers' absenteeism varied from 15 per cent to 42 per cent in India (Ullas and TNN 2014). An investigation by the *Bangalore Mirror* and *First Post* revealed that of the 425,000 rural, suburban, and urban teachers sampled in the state of Karnataka, almost 50 per cent were not even graduates. As a sample, it revealed that at a government-run school in urban Bangalore, high school-going adolescents required extra hours of coaching to learn elementary English (Murali 2016). Amidst such persistent systemic ills, even the most engaging history textbook may fail to avert myth from prevailing over fact and Hitler's populism over Gandhi's.

Conclusion

In the Internet age, where the free-flow of opinions and counter-opinions threaten even the most obstinate and ancient of myths, it may be hard to accept that the technology-trained and educated youth shouldering a rising economy's future are unaware about the villainy of a figure they see as a hero. There is no denying the fact that the memorial fogginess on Hitler in India can be traced to his celebration by the ideologues of alternative nationalisms. However, the emboldening and not erosion of such attitudes decades after the fall of Nazi Germany begs an inquiry into underlying structural concerns. His individual traits, more than his politics and policies, inspire Hitler's imagining as a model leader amongst India's young careerists. However, given the lack of importance that the discipline of history gets in India in general, it is unsurprising to find *Mein Kampf* fans even amidst the most educated of Indians.

For students who never return to academic forays into history after school, the lessons learnt at adolescence contribute to their worldviews considerably by remaining with them for a long time. Amongst them, the semantic *lieux* that dominate their memories matter even more. However, in contextualizing Nazism, how much of a student's memory space is devoted to internalizing the Holocaust, which is a warning sign against the normalization of Hitler? India's provincial textbooks, which reach a majority of its students, are a mixed bag in terms of content. In some states, they seem tampered with for political gains. In others, they appear to be victims of designing or regulatory incompetence. Kerala, a state with excellent literacy levels, punches below its weight when teaching about Nazism at its schools. On the flipside, Gujarat, a state tainted by textbook controversies and dominated by the right-wing, manages to mention the Holocaust in its revised textbooks. In most cases, the study materials valid for states show a worrisome lack of sensitivity for the Holocaust, sparing only passing mentions. Though setting the benchmark for school-level Holocaust education, the NCERT's textbooks mostly reach elites. Unqualified instructors and archaic pedagogy only make matters worse. If India wishes to avert international flak for its embarrassing normalization of Nazism well into the twenty-first century, it ought to mould the adolescent school-goer's mind better in order to avoid deformities in its ability to memorialize and contextualize history.

References

Ahmed, Zubair. "Hitler Memoribilia 'Attracts Young Indians.'" *BBC South Asia*, 15 June 2010. http://news.bbc.co.uk/2/hi/south_asia/8660064.stm.

BBC. "India MP Shocks with Hitler Costume Protest in Parliament." *BBC*, 10 August 2018. www.bbc.com/news/world-asia-india-45140801.

Casolari, Marzia. "Hindutva's Foreign Tie-up in the 1930s: Archival Evidence." *Economic & Political Weekly*, January 2000.

CBSE. "E-Affiliation System and Database." CBSE e-Affiliation, n.d. http://cbseaff.nic.in/cbse_aff/schdir_Report/userview.aspx.

Dhawan, Himanshi, and TNN "Enrolment in Schools Rises 14% to 23 Crore." *Times of India*, 22 January 2013. http://timesofindia.indiatimes.com/home/education/news/Enrolment-in-schools-rises-14-to-23-crore/articleshow/18123554.cms#.

D'Souza, Dilip. "Hitler's Strange Afterlife in India." *The Daily Beast*, 30 November 2012. www.thedailybeast.com/articles/2012/11/30/hitler-s-strange-afterlife-in-india.html.

Gaikwad, Rahi. "Gujarat Textbooks Never Far from Controversy." *The Hindu*, 30 July 2014. www.thehindu.com/news/national/gujarat-textbooks-never-far-from-controversy/article6261520.ece.

Ghosh, Palash. "Mussolini and Gandhi: Strange Bedfellows." *IB Times*, 3 March 2012. www.ibtimes.com/mussolini-gandhi-strange-bedfellows-214200.

Golwalkar, Madhav S. *We or Our Nationhood Defined*. Nagpur: Bharat Publications, 1939.

Gupta, Shekhar. "Why We Should Let Aurangzeb Road Be." *Outlook*, 14 September 2015a. www.outlookindia.com/magazine/story/why-we-should-let-aurangzeb-road-be/295248.

Gupta, Suman. *Consumable Texts in Contemporary India: Uncultured Books and Bibliographical Sociology*. New Delhi: Springer, 2015b.

Haaretz. "ADL Calls on Indian Channel to Remove 'Hitler' From Show Title." *Haaretz*, November 22, 2011. www.haaretz.com/jewish/adl-calls-on-indian-channel-to-remove-hitler-from-show-title-1.397120.

Humpe, Santosh S., V.L. Kadam, R.S. Chavan, and P.B. Hingmire. *Social Science I: History and Political Science*. Pune: Maharashtra State Board of Secondary and Higher Secondary Education, 2014.

India Today. "CBSE Schools to Use Only NCERT Books: Minister of State School Education." *India Today*, 19 May 2014. http://indiatoday.intoday.in/education/story/cbse-schools-to-use-ncert-only/1/362572.html.

Joshi, Manoj. "Hitler a Hero: Society without a Moral Compass." *Times of India*, December 26, 2002. http://timesofindia.indiatimes.com/edit-page/LEADER-ARTICLEBRHitler-as-Hero-Society-Without-a-Moral-Compass/articleshow/32382342.cms.

Joshi, Subhadra R.S.S. *Hitler's Heirs: An Exposition of the Para-Military Fascist Character of RSS*. New Delhi: Sampradayikta Virodhi Committee, 1971.

Kazim, Hasnain. "The Fuehrer Cult: Germans Cringe at Hitler's Popularity in Pakistan." *Speigel*, March 17, 2010. www.spiegel.de/international/zeitgeist/the-fuehrer-cult-germans-cringe-at-hitler-s-popularity-in-pakistan-a-683966.html.

Kumar, Raksha. "Hindu Right Rewriting Indian Textbooks." *Al Jazeera*, November 4, 2014. www.aljazeera.com/indepth/features/2014/11/hindu-right-ideology-indian-textbooks-gujarat-20141147028501733.html.

Manjapra, Kris. *Age of Entanglement: German and Indian Intellectuals across Empires*. Cambridge: Harvard University Press, 2014.

Manjrekar, Nandini, T. Shah, J. Lokhande, and N. Chaudhury. *Textbook Regimes: A Feminist Critique of Nation and Identity*. Vadodara: Nirantar, 2010.

Mehtal, Harit. "In Modi's Gujarat, Hitler is a textbook hero." *Times of India*, September 30, 2004. http://timesofindia.indiatimes.com/india/In-Modis-Gujarat-Hitler-is-a-textbook-hero/articleshow/868469.cms.

Munshi, Kaivan, and Mark Rosenzweig. "Rural to Urban Migration in India: Why Labour Mobility Bucks Global Trend." *Indian Express*, March 26, 2016. http://indianexpress.com/article/india/india-news-india/rural-to-urban-migration-in-india-why-labour-mobility-bucks-global-trend/.

Murali, Janaki. "Govt Schools Struggle with Poor Facilities, Unskilled Teachers and High Dropout Rates." *FirstPost*. June, 2016. www.firstpost.com/india/govt-schools-struggle-with-poor-facilities-unskilled-teachers-and-high-dropout-rates-2848972.html.

NCERT. *India and the Contemporary World I*. New Delhi: NCERT, 2014.

NDTV. "Hitler Usurps Mahatma." *NDTV*, October 2, 2010. www.ndtv.com/india-news/hitler-usurps-mahatma-434090.

NPR. "Hitler's Hot in India." *NPR*, December 23, 2012. www.npr.org/2012/12/23/167911062/hitlers-hot-in-india.

Nora, Pierre. *Rethinking France: Les Lieux de Memoire*. Vol. 4. Chicago: University of Chicago Press, 2010.

PTI. "Telangana to Take Tough Steps to Ensure Safety of Women: K Chandrasekhar Rao." *NDTV. October* 6 (2014). www.ndtv.com/south/telangana-to-take-tough-steps-to-ensure-safety-of-women-k-chandrasekhar-rao-675208.

Quraiza, Jai Banu. *Hindu Pro-Zionism & Philo-Semitism*. London: NHSF, 2004.

Qureshi, Salim S., B.S. Bhavsar, D.R. Desai, O.K. Vaghela, and J.H. Joshi. *Social Science (Standard 9)*. Gandhinagar: Gujarat State Board of School Textbooks, 2016.

Rothberg, Michael. "Between Memory and Memory: From Lieux de Mémoire to Noeuds de Mémoire." *Yale French Studies*, no. 118/119 (2010): 3–12.

Saha, Abhishek. "Tasteless but True: Made in India Hitler Ice-Cream, Cafe." *Hindustan Times*, June 2, 2015. www.hindustantimes.com/india/tasteless-but-true-made-in-india-hitler-ice-cream-cafe/story-C6usCqTUqv4zAeU30b0GVM.html.

Scheinert, Josh. "Why Is Adolf Hitler Popular in India?" *Jerusalem Post*, September 29, 2014. www.jpost.com/Opinion/Why-is-Adolf-Hitler-popular-in-India-376622#.

Schultz, Kai. "Indian Children's Book Lists Hitler as Leader 'Who Will Inspire You.'" *New York Times*, March 17, 2018. www.nytimes.com/2018/03/17/world/asia/india-hitler-childrens-book.html.

Sheikh, Majid. "A Nation Forgetting Its History Tends to Lose Its Geography." *Allama Mashriqi Blogspot*. April 5 (2011). http://allama-mashriqi.blogspot.in/2011/04/nation-forgetting-its-history-tends-to.html.

Singh, Siddharth. "The 'Hitler' of the South." *HT Live Mint*, August 18, 2014. www.live-mint.com/Opinion/LoWG57G5tz5CLWGoTfJVSK/The-Hitler-of-the-South.html.

Singh, Sulakhan, and Amar Singh Bhatia. *Social Studies (Part II)*. Jalandhar: Punjab State Education Board, 2016.

State Council of Education Research and Training. *Social Science I (Standard X)*. Thiruananthapuram, Kerala: State Council of Education Research and Training, 2011.

TNTESC. *History (Higher Secondary: Second Year)*. Chennai: Tamil Nadu Textbook and Educational Services Corporation, 2015.

Ullas, S.S., and TNN. "What India Needs: Trained, Motivated Teachers." *Times of India. February* 3 (2014). http://timesofindia.indiatimes.com/city/bengaluru/What-India-needs-Trained-motivated-teachers/articleshow/29796050.cms.

Wike, Richard, Katie Simmons, Bruce Stokes, and Janell Fetterolf. "Spring 2017 Global Attitudes Survey." *Pew Research*. 16 (October 2017). www.pewresearch.org/global/2017/10/16/democracy-widely-supported-little-backing-for-rule-by-strong-leader-or-military/.

11 Holocaust education in India and its challenges

Navras J. Aafreedi

The general perception is that India was neither directly nor indirectly affected by the Holocaust. Although there is nothing else more relevant to India, neither its remembrance nor its study finds any place in the Indian academia. At both secondary and tertiary levels of education it is generally never more than a mere passing reference. The relevance of Holocaust remembrance and studies for India lies in the fact that the Holocaust is the ideal case study for mass violence studies for Indians as they can draw lessons from it while retaining their objectivity as it did not involve any section of their own society. If any episode of mass violence from Indian history is taught it could flare up passions, as whichever community emerges as the perpetrator would object to it. There are many other instances of mass violence in history with no connection to India, but the Holocaust stands out because of its scale and magnitude. Perhaps no democracy without being in a state of war, neither interstate nor civil, has experienced mob violence of the scale and at the frequency that India has. Recurring low-intensity cyclic riots have become a structural feature of Indian society.[1] In spite of this, it has not introduced Mass Violence Studies or Genocide Studies as an academic discipline in its institutions of higher education.

India's refusal to be a member of Holocaust Remembrance Organizations

India refuses to be member of any international organization dedicated to raising Holocaust awareness and promoting its education, for instance the Task Force for International Cooperation on Holocaust Education, Remembrance and Research, established in the wake of the Stockholm Forum in 2000 and which now has thirty-four countries as its members. This organization funds the training of teachers in member countries for the launching or enhancing of Holocaust education.[2] Another such organization is the International Holocaust Remembrance Alliance (IHRA). Both organizations include several countries not affected by the Holocaust, including a number of countries from Asia, yet India refrains from participating in them officially, although IHRA has had Indian scholars participating in its annual conferences.

Absence of Holocaust education in India

It has been observed that the countries that have introduced Holocaust education in their curriculum have been considerably successful in the prevention of mass violence. The absence of Mass Violence or Genocide Studies in Indian academia is explained by the fact that most of the universities in India are either fully or partially funded by the state, whose record in preventing mass violence and bringing the guilty to justice has been dismal. In fact, many of the accused have gone on to enjoy ministerial positions. So, there is always this fear that the introduction of Mass Violence Studies might put it in a tight spot. Another prerequisite to curriculum development in Genocide Studies in India is not to include cases of mass violence from India, lest the course gets dragged into unnecessary controversy and dirty politics.

Even if the Holocaust did not have any fallout for India, its ignorance has certainly led to Hitler gaining immense popularity among Indians. Even if Hitler's popularity in India cannot be attributed to Nazism in the country yet, it cannot be dismissed simply as an obsession with and a craving for strong leadership. It is certainly alarming if the world's most populous democracy, home to one-sixth of mankind, with the largest diaspora in the world, admires Hitler more than any other non-Indian leader and is hardly aware of the Holocaust. And even the tiny section of its population that is not ignorant of it either believes it to have been a necessary collateral damage for the greater good of the German nation or underplays it as the only wrongdoing by Hitler, hence pardonable. It is a paradox that in a country that has never really known antisemitism, and where it remains largely unknown even today except for certain sections of its Muslims[3] and Christians, Hitler is gaining popularity. Hitler's autobiography has increased in sales to the tune of 15 per cent in just a decade. The phenomenon can also be seen in the release of films in various Indian languages with the eponymous protagonist as the namesake of Hitler. Similarly, the name Aryan has recently become popular as a first name among Indians and there is a growing demand for Hitler memorabilia.[4] There is no paucity of such Indians who have the name Hitler for their Facebook profile.

Considering this, it is not hard to understand how in several cases people facing charges of inciting mobs to violence leading to pogroms have gone on to enjoy ministerial positions in successive Indian governments, as pointed out above. It also hints at why the state's record in preventing the occurrence of mass violence and bringing the guilty to justice has been so dismal in India.

Reluctance of the state to introduce Holocaust/Genocide Studies

It seems that the state on its part would always be reluctant to introduce Genocide or Mass Violence Studies in academia as a discipline for it would have the potential of opening Pandora's box. It can be well explained with an example from Israel:

> In 1953, Yad Vashem was established as Israel's official memorial for the commemoration of the Holocaust through education, research, documentation,

and remembrance. But while the Holocaust was commemorated publicly, in reality the difficulties of the 1950s obscured the survivors' suffering, they were encouraged to adopt the national ethos and forget the past. Little historical material or literary fiction was written about the Holocaust, survivors were minor characters in the nascent film industry, and psychological services were minimal. This changed in 1960 when Mossad agents in Argentina captured Adolph Eichmann (1906–1962) and brought him back to Israel to stand trial. Though he would be found guilty and sentenced to be hanged (Israel's only death sentence), the significance of his trial extended far beyond the discussion of his complicity. Rather, it opened the way for public conversations about survivor suffering, the Zionist leadership's activities during the Holocaust, and the treatment of survivors in post-war Israel.[5]

India has never witnessed any figure as prominent in Indian politics as Eichmann was in Nazi Germany being found guilty of perpetrating mass violence and being sentenced to any rigorous punishment, let alone life imprisonment or death. Hence, cases of mass violence, mob violence, and pogroms do not last long in national memory.

The challenges to raising Holocaust awareness: Holocaust denial and trivialization

Muslim Holocaust deniers apparently believe, according to Meir Litvak, "that the memory of the Holocaust was the foundation of Western support for the establishment of the State of Israel. Therefore, refuting it would severely undermine Israel's legitimacy in the West and help in its eradication".[6] For them, "it never happened or else was hugely exaggerated".[7] As the eminent scholar of antisemitism, the late Robert Wistrich pointed out: "The denial of the Holocaust – whether in Britain, France (where it first originated), America or other Western countries – has become an integral part of the revamped antisemitic mythology of a world Jewish conspiracy."[8]

The fact is that it was not the Holocaust but the *Yishuv* that founded the State of Israel. Had there not been a thriving self-governing community or 600,000-strong *Yishuv* (the Zionist Jewish entity residing in pre-State Israel) built over years since the first settlement in 1860, the 360,000 survivors would not have found a shelter. "And the UN November 1947 partition resolution, voting for the establishment of a Jewish State", as the eminent Holocaust scholar Dina Porat points out,

> came indeed after the Holocaust but not as its direct result. Political considerations, such as the Soviet interest in replacing Britain in the Middle East and in preventing American future influence in the area, were much more instrumental than belated empathy.[9]

She reports:

> Since early 2005, a working definition of antisemitism, agreed upon by the twenty-seven EU countries, states clearly that "denying the fact, scope,

mechanisms (e.g., gas chambers) or intentionality of the genocide of the Jewish people at the hands of National Socialist Germany and its supporters and accomplices during WW-II (the Holocaust), [and that] accusing the Jews as a people, or Israel as a state, of inventing or exaggerating the Holocaust" are considered acts of antisemitism. A more recent working definition of Holocaust denial, reached by the ITF member states in 2010, which draws on the EU decision, also defines denial as a form of antisemitism. Antisemitism is by now punishable by laws and other forms of regulations in some twenty countries.[10]

Alan Johnson has identified four forms of Holocaust inversion that emanate out of "the unhinged portrayal of Israel as a genocidist state":

> First, the depiction of Israelis as the new Nazis and the Palestinians as the new Jews; an inversion of reality. … Second, the Zionist ideology and movement is made to appear in the Anti-Zionist Ideology as akin to Nazism, or is considered alongside of, or in comparison to, or even collaborating with Nazism. … Third, the Holocaust is turned into "moral lesson" for, or a "moral indictment" of the Jews – an inversion of morality. … Fourth, Holocaust memory appears within the Anti-Zionist ideology only as a politicized and manipulated thing, a club wielded instrumentally, with malice aforethought, by bullying Jews, for Jewish ends.[11]

Overcoming the ignorance of history

No matter how big a commercial hit Steven Spielberg's Academy Award winning film *Schindler's List* (1993) may have been across the world, it was a big flop in India, a country with the largest cinema audience and the fifth biggest box office market worth 1.7 billion US dollars, according to Theatrical Market Statistics.[12] Its total gross earning to date stands at merely US$129,292.[13] In sharp contrast, the film *Jurassic Park* (1993), released the same year by the same filmmaker, has earned US$7,001,330 to date in the same country, India. It is important to pay attention to this considering how significant a pedagogical tool cinema is now. In spite of being described as "by far the finest, fullest dramatic film ever made about the Holocaust" (Terrence Rafferty),[14] it failed to impress the Indian audience who could not relate to the suffering of the Jews in the film perhaps because of their own ignorance of them and not because of any shortcoming of the film. One naturally feels more for those one is familiar with than for those who are complete strangers. Also, the fact that they had no historical background of the Holocaust aggravated the situation.

Two thousand Jews managed to find refuge in India during the Holocaust. In response to the arrival of Holocaust refugees, the Indian Jews founded the Jewish Relief Association (JRA) in 1934 to help them. The JRA got the Central Council for Refugees in London to guarantee maintenance to the government of India for every refugee admitted to India. In addition to this, they also managed to attract support from the Council for German Jewry, which enabled them to financially support every Jewish refugee for the initial five years in India. According to the figure published by JRA, there were 1,080 European Jews in India in 1943. The figure certainly does not include all Jewish refugees in India at that time, as not everybody went through JRA. As immigrants with valid passports were not asked if they were Jewish, the number of Jews who fled to India is believed to be much more. The Indian Jews learnt about the Holocaust largely from these Jews, because the press in India at that time was focused on reporting the struggle for national independence from the British and gave little space to news of the then ongoing Holocaust.[15]

But in spite of this, today even the Jews among Indians like most of their fellow countrymen, know fairly little about the Holocaust, let alone comprehend the scale and the magnitude of the colossal tragedy, as indicated by the Indian Jewish novelist Esther David in an anecdote she narrates in her auto-ethnographic novel (actually a collection of intertwined short stories) *Shalom India Housing Society* (2007) in which a Jewish character mistakes Yom HaShoah for a joyous Jewish festival meant to be celebrated and organizes a party to do so. Holocaust commemoration events even in Mumbai (Bombay), which has the highest concentration of Jews in India, register the participation of Jews in very small numbers. English language national daily newspaper *Hindustan Times* reported in 2011 that only 20 people turned up for a Holocaust commemoration event, jointly organized by the Israeli and German consuls in Mumbai.[16] This testifies to the widespread ignorance of the Holocaust among Indians and also their lack of interest in learning about it.

With the exception of those who happen to be neighbours to Jews in cities like Mumbai, Thane, Ahmedabad, and Kolkata, most Indians never come into any direct contact with them because of their miniscule numbers. They know them only through secondary sources, often not reliable. As a numerically insignificant religious community, Jews fall in the category of "Others" in the Indian Census, making up 0.7 per cent of the total population of India, which was estimated to be 1.25 billion in 2011. With estimates of the Jewish population varying from 3,000 to 10,000 (5,000 being the most reliable) their proportion in the total population of India is a mere 0.0004 per cent of the total population.[17]

The fact that we not only require Holocaust education but also education in Jewish history to make the students completely understand why the colossal tragedy took place is well illustrated by what the eminent Holocaust scholar Dina Porat writes:

> It is becoming increasingly clear that the Holocaust, which was to have been a source of empathy and compassion for the Jews, more and more enhances a negative image of the "Jew" and of the Jewish State and fosters post-Holocaust antisemitism. The pre-Holocaust image of the Jew as an all-powerful, avaricious manipulator of power was a crucial motive for the mass murder of European Jewry. Nowadays, in the post-Holocaust era the Jew is being portrayed in a no less repulsive way, indicating that the changes in social and political circumstances after the Holocaust have become a new source of antisemitism. Holocaust education has also not yet proved itself to

be barrier against antisemitism, for youngsters, whose ignorance is coupled by naivete, often raise questions such as these: Why the Jews? Why all the Jews? What's wrong with them? Was their murder really initiated without any logical reason, or other good motive? Six million – how indeed did so many Jews, who do not seem to be helpless today, allow this to be done to them.[18]

These are questions that can be answered only through education in Jewish history. "The ignorance about Judaism and Jewish history is, of course, a particularly fertile breeding-ground for antisemitism" as Robert Wistrich cautioned us.[19] And "the rise of antisemitism anywhere is a threat to people everywhere. Thus, in fighting antisemitism we fight for the future of all humanity", as the former United Nations Secretary General Kofi Annan said in 2004.

It is because of this widespread ignorance of the Holocaust and of the Jewish history that people easily fall for the antisemitic propaganda aimed at denying, minimizing, or trivializing the Holocaust. Conscious of this and committed to its resolution of being two hundred years ahead, made on the occasion of it bicentenary in 2017, Presidency University, Kolkata, emerged as the only university in Asia outside of China and Israel to have an undergraduate course in Global Jewish History.

India's response to the Holocaust

India was largely indifferent towards the Jewish problem and was primarily concerned with the plight of the Arabs in mandated Palestine.

M.K. Gandhi called the Jews "Untouchables of Christianity" and advised them to adopt the method of Satyagraha in the belief that it would eventually soften even Hitler's "heart of stone". He calls Hitler's deeds "the actions of a crazy but brave young man":

> Can the Jews resist this organized and shameless persecution? Is there a way to preserve their self-respect, and not to feel helpless neglected and forlorn? I submit there is ... I would refuse to be expelled or to submit to discriminating treatment. And for doing this, I should not wait for the fellow Jews to join me in civil resistance but would have confidence that in the end the rest are bound to follow my example. If one Jew or all the Jews were to accept the prescription here offered, he or they cannot be worse off than now ... The calculated violence of Hitler may even result in a general massacre of the Jews by way of his first answer to the declaration of such hostilities. But if the Jewish mind could be prepared for voluntary suffering, even the massacre I have imagined could be turned into a day of thanksgiving and joy that Jehovah had wrought deliverance of the race even at the hands of the tyrant.[20]

Gandhi also wrote:

> But the German persecution of the Jews seems to have no parallel in history. The tyrants of old never went so mad as Hitler seems to have gone. And he

is doing it with religious zeal … If there ever could be justifiable war in the name of and for humanity, a war against Germany to prevent the wanton persecution of a whole race, would be completely justified. But I do not believe in any war. A discussion of the pros and cons of such war is therefore outside my horizon or province.[21]

Gandhi's proclamations on the eve of World War II betrayed his lack of understanding of the Nazi evil and also that of political realism. Gandhi's words evoked great resentment in the Jewish world. Some of the most significant responses appeared in Yehuda Leon Magnes' and Martin Buber's famous letters to Gandhi and also in letters written by Hayim Greenberg, the editor of the American Zionist Socialist newspaper *The Jewish Frontier* and by Avraham Sohet, the editor of the Indian Jewish newspaper from Bombay *The Jewish Advocate*.[22]

Driven by his profound belief in non-violence and the principles of Satyagraha, according to which one must do everything possible to be considerate of one's enemy and make a genuine attempt to understand him in situations of conflict, Gandhi wrote a couple of letters to Hitler. The first one was written on 23 July 1939. In this letter, which Gandhi sent with great hesitation, and was concealed by the British censorship, he wrote:

> Dear Friend,
> Friends have been urging me to write to you for the sake of humanity. But I have resisted their request, because of the feeling that any letter from me would be impertinence. Something tells me that I must not calculate and that I must make my appeal for whatever it may be worth. It is quite clear that you are today the one person in the world who can prevent a war which may reduce humanity to the savage state. Must you pay that price for an object however worthy it may appear to you to be? Will you listen to the appeal of one who has deliberately shunned the method of war not without considerable success? Anyway, I anticipate your forgiveness, if I have erred in writing to you. I remain, your sincere friend.[23]

Gandhi's second letter to Hitler, a public one, appeared in the press on Christmas Eve, 1940, when the German forces were at the zenith of their success and when the Britain stood isolated in the battle against Hitler. Gandhi explains right at the beginning of the letter why he calls him "Dear friend", but also ensures to makes it clear that he does not approve of his deeds and he is defiantly more critical:

> Dear Friend,
> That I address you as a friend is no formality. I own no foes. My business in life has been for the past 33 years to enlist the friendship of the whole of humanity by befriending mankind, irrespective of race, colour or creed. We

have no doubt about your bravery or devotion to your fatherland, nor do we believe that you are the monster described by your opponents. But your own writings and pronouncements and those of your friends and admirers leave no room for doubt that many of your acts are monstrous and unbecoming of human dignity, especially in the estimation of men like me who believe in universal friendliness.[24]

Jawaharlal Nehru called the Jews "People without a home or nation" and sponsored a resolution in the Congress Working Committee. Although the exact date is not known, yet it can be said that it probably happened in December 1938 at the Wardha session, the one that took place shortly after Nehru returned from Europe. The draft resolution read:

> The Committee sees no objection to the employment in India of such Jewish refugees as are experts and specialists and who can fit in with the new order in India and accept Indian standards.[25]

It was, however, rejected by the then Congress President Subhas Chandra Bose, who four years later, in 1942, was reported by the *Jewish Chronicle* of London as having published an article in *Angriff*, a journal of Goebbels, saying that "anti-Semitism should become part of the Indian liberation movement because the Jews had helped the British to exploit Indians (21 August 1942)". Although by then Bose had left the Congress, he continued to command a strong influence in the party.[26] Commenting on the pro-Nazi influences of Subhas Chandra Bose, especially while he was Congress President during 1937–1939, Nehru remarked:

> He (that is, Congress President Bose) did not approve of any step being taken by the Congress which was anti-Japanese or anti-German or anti-Italian. And yet such was the feeling in Congress and the country that he did not oppose this or many other manifestations of Congress sympathy for China and the victims of Fascist and Nazi aggression.[27]

Nehru's proposal was opposed by the Hindu right. The fact that Bose met Hitler and tried to win his support in raising an army against the British in India often deludes Indians into believing that Hitler actually made a significant contribution to India's struggle for freedom.

The Indian National Congress' response was that of an unusually subdued silence. It adopted a formal resolution neither on the Jewish problem nor on the Holocaust. It only made a passing reference to the Holocaust in its foreign policy resolution adopted in the 1939 annual session, which declared:

> International morality has sunk so low in Central and South Western Europe that the world has witnessed with horror, the organized terrorism of the Nazi government against the people of the Jewish race ... The Congress disassociates itself entirely from British policy which has consistently aided the

Fascist powers and helped in the destruction of the democratic countries. The Congress is opposed to imperialism and fascism alike and is convinced that world peace and progress required the ending of both of these.[28]

Earlier the Congress Party mentioned "the plight of Jews in Europe" for the first time in December 1938. The Congress Working Committee (CWC) resolution on Palestine, declared inter alia: "While sympathizing with the plight of Jews in Europe and elsewhere, the Committee deplores that in Palestine the Jews have relied on British armed forces to advance their special claims and thus aligned themselves on the side of British imperialism."[29]

Kumaraswamy finds the response of the Congress Party mild and muted considering the colossal scale of the catastrophe. Even if one takes into account that the "normal functioning of the party was seriously hampered" as a result of the "severe restrictions" "imposed by the British" leading to the incarceration of all the top leaders, like Gandhi and Nehru, it fails to explain the position of the Congress Party. The Indian National Congress adopted as many as six resolutions since early 1920 on Palestine and expressed its sympathy and support, but comes across as indifferent towards the Nazi gas chambers.[30]

In sharp contrast to the Muslims and Congress Party's arch rival, the Muslim League, which actively lobbied for their co-religionists in Palestine, the Jews had no constituency that could lobby the Congress party to be more vocal on the issue of the Holocaust.[31] Kumaraswamy states that even Gandhi "never made any direct reference to the Holocaust even after the end of the Second World War; he recognised that the Jews were 'a persecuted people worthy of world sympathy'."[32]

Courses on the Holocaust taught in India

Taking this into account, in 2016 Presidency University in Kolkata launched a postgraduate course, titled "A History of Mass Violence: Twentieth Century to the Present". It has attracted much attention from the press and stories on it have appeared in some of the most prominent English language daily newspapers in India, such as *The Times of India*[33] and *The Indian Express*,[34] and in the prominent magazine *The Business Standard*.[35] Just a few institutions in South-Asia have the academic discipline Peace and Conflict Studies, but hardly any has the discipline Genocide Studies, let alone Holocaust Studies. However, with the launch of this postgraduate course at Presidency University, Kolkata, Holocaust and its related topics are gradually getting some attention.

The course at Presidency University, Kolkata, instead of being focused on different genocides, pogroms, and episodes of mass violence, draws attention to 19 different aspects of mass violence. While discussing those aspects it takes different genocides for case studies. The 19 aspects are the following: challenges of definition and nomenclature, causes, warning signs, propaganda, hateful or inflammatory speech, state's connivance or inaction, mass atrocities, complicity, bystanders, rescuers, resistance, displacement, responses (state's response, judicial response, national response, international response, literary and cinematic response, response of the press), role of academia, trauma, rehabilitation, reconciliation, conflicting narratives, denial or minimization, remembrance, and memorialization.

Efforts and the way ahead

There is a huge scarcity of educational resources in India on the Holocaust. The only scholarly books on the Holocaust are those that are available in the libraries of a few premier universities or big bookshops, read or accessed by only a tiny section of scholars in India interested in the study of political violence.

Efforts have been made to change this in the past few years.[36] Given the high rate of illiteracy and the low rate of education in India, cinema can be the most effective means of raising awareness of the Holocaust. Love for cinema is one of the few things that unite all Indians. There are a number of movie channels in India that can be approached for the telecast of films on the Holocaust dubbed in Hindi and other Indian languages on the national television. Such films, dubbed in Indian languages, could be distributed among NGOs working in India for the promotion of communal harmony for public screenings. In 2009, a Holocaust films retrospective was organized at the two major universities in Lucknow (a major centre of Muslim scholarship), the University of Lucknow and the Ambedkar University there. It happened to be the first ever in South Asia, during which 46 films were screened over 14 days.[37] The first ever Holocaust-themed Hindi language play was staged by students in 2015 at Gautam Buddha University in Greater Noida.[38] Both the Holocaust films retrospective in Lucknow and the play at Gautam Buddha University were accompanied by Holocaust poster exhibitions. In 2016, a genocide and Holocaust-themed conference was held at the Jindal Centre for Israel Studies (JCIS), O.P. Jindal Global University in association with Middle East Institute New Delhi, Society for Social Regeneration & Equity (SSRE) and the United States Holocaust Memorial Museum (USHMM). The very next year, that is 2017, the Department of History at Presidency University in Kolkata held a Holocaust-focused conference. Presidency University, Kolkata, began the commemoration of its bicentenary in January 2017 with a Holocaust exhibition on Anne Frank. In October–November 2017, the department of History, Presidency University, hosted Alvin Rosenfeld, Director of the Institute for the Study of Contemporary Antisemitism, Indiana University, as Scholar-in-Residence. Rosenfeld gave a series of lectures on the Holocaust and antisemitism during his residency there.

As far as the textbooks are concerned, Holocaust is rarely ever mentioned by name. The Nazi genocide against Jews is generally nothing more than a passing reference. The only literature on the Holocaust available in Hindi, the *lingua franca* of almost all north Indians and the fourth most widely spoken language in the world (UNESCO), are the following[39]:

• Pandey, Ajay Shankar, *Hitler kā Yātnā Grah: Concentration Camp méin Tīn Ghanté* (Hitler's Torture Centre: Three Hours in a Concentration Camp) Radhakrishna Paperbacks, Delhi, 2002, (First Paperback Edition 2004)

- Milgram, Avraham and Robert Rozett, eds, *Holocaust: Bahudhā Pūchhé Jāné Vālé Prashna* (Holocaust: Frequently Asked Questions) Translated by Sheba Jeremiah Nagaokar, Yad Vashem and the Israeli Parliamentary Association for Holocaust Remembrance and Aid to Survivors, Jerusalem, 2005
- Borowski, Tadeausz, *Gas Chamber ke liyekripya is taraf: Nazi Yātana Shivir ki Kahāniyaṅ* (This Way for the Gas, Ladies and Gentlemen), translator, Yogendra Krishna, Samvad Prakashan, Mumbai and Meerut, 2006
- Hindi translation of *The Diary of Anne Frank*
- Hindi translation of Vikram Seth's *Two Lives*

The following steps, if taken could go a long way in creating awareness of the Holocaust in India, so badly needed:

1. Launch of a Teacher Training Programme through the National Council for Teacher Education (NCTE)
2. Introduction of Holocaust and Mass Violence Studies at the secondary level of education through the incorporation of the subject in the syllabi of the various national boards of education, like the Central Board for Secondary Education (CBSE), Indian Council for Secondary Education (ICSE) as well as in the syllabi of all state boards.
3. Publication of books on the Holocaust and Mass Violence by National Council for Educational Research and Training (NCERT), suitable for secondary level education in all major languages of India.
4. Introduction of Holocaust and Mass Violence Studies through the involvement of National Assessment and Accreditation Council (NAAC) and the University Grants Commission (UGC) at the tertiary level of education.
5. Establishment of academic positions in Mass Violence Studies in premier institutions.

Conclusion

There are lessons to be learned from the study of the Holocaust. A number of countries, like Australia, South Africa, and the United States, geographically far away from Europe where the Holocaust took place, have introduced Holocaust education in their curriculum. It is high time India followed suit.

Notes

1 Graff, Violette and Juliette Galonnier, "Hindu-Muslim Communal Riots in India – I (1947–1986)", *Encyclopédiedes violences de masse*, 15 July 2013. www.sciencespo. fr/mass-violence-war-massacre-resistance/en/document/hindu-muslim-communal-riots-india-i-1947-1986.html (Accessed on November 15, 2019).
2 Porat, Dina, "Holocaust Denial and the Image of the Jew, or: 'They Boycott Auschwitz as an Israeli Product', in Alvin H. Rosenfeld, ed., *Resurgent Antisemitism: Global Perspectives* (Bloomington and Indianapolis: Indiana University Press, 2013), p. 469.
3 Aafreedi, Navras Jaat, "Jewish-Muslim Relations in South Asia: Where antipathy lives without Jews", *Asian Jewish Life*, Issue 15, October 2014, pp. 13–16.

Aafreedi, Navras Jaat, "Muslim-Jewish Relations in South Asia", Blog of the Woolf Institute, Cambridge, UK, 28 November 2016: www.woolf.cam.ac.uk/blog/muslim-jewish-relations-in-south-asia (Accessed on February 17, 2018).

Aafreedi, Navras Jaat, "Jewish-Muslim Relations in South Asia: An Introduction", *Café Dissensus*, Issue 21, January 2016: https://cafedissensus.com/2016/01/07/guest-editorial-jewish-muslim-relations-in-south-asia-an-introduction/ (Accessed on 17 February 2018).

4 See the special issue of the online magazine *Café Dissensus* guest edited by Navras J. Aafreedi on the theme, "India's Response to the Holocaust and its Perception of Hitler", *Café Dissensus*, Issue 31 (January 2017): https://cafedissensus.com/2017/01/20/contents-indias-response-to-the-holocaust-and-its-perception-of-hitler-issue-31/

Aafreedi, Navras Jaat, "The Paradox of the Popularity of Hitler in India", *Asian Jewish Life*, Issue 14, April 2014, pp. 14–16.

5 Nelson, Cary, Rachel S. Harris, and Kenneth W. Stein, "The History of Israel", in Cary Nelson and Gabriel Brahm, eds., *The Case Against Academic Boycotts of Israel* (Chicago and New York: MLA Members for Scholars Rights, Distributed by Wayne State University Press, 2015), pp. 413–414.

6 Litvak, Meir, "The Islamic Republic of Iran and the Holocaust: Anti-Semitism and Anti-Zionism", in Jeffrey Herf, ed., *Anti-Semitism and Anti-Zionism in Historical Perspective: Convergence and Divergence* (New York: Routledge, 2006), p. 251.

7 Wistrich, Robert S., "Anti-Zionist Connections: Communism, Radical Islam, and the Left" in Alvin H Rosenfeld, ed., *Resurgent Antisemitism: Global Perspectives* (Bloomington and Indianapolis: Indiana University Press, 2013), p. 407.

8 Wistrich, Robert S., *Antisemitism: The Longest Hatred* (New York: Pantheon Books, 1991), p. 112.

9 Porat, *Op. Cit.*, p. 477.

10 *Ibid.*, p. 473.

11 Johnson, Alan, "Intellectual Incitement: The Anti-Zionist Ideology and the Anti-Zionist Subject", in Cary Nelson and Gabriel Brahm, eds., *The Case Against Academic Boycotts of Israel* (Chicago and New York: MLA Members for Scholars Rights, Distributed by Wayne State University Press, 2015), pp. 267–268.

12 Theatrical Market Statistics, p. 5: www.mpaa.org/wp-content/uploads/2015/03/MPAA-Theatrical-Market-Statistics-2014.pdf (Accessed on March 26, 2017).

13 Data: Box Office Mojo: www.boxofficemojo.com/movies/?page=intl&id=schindlerslist.htm (Accessed on 26 March 2017).

14 Quoted in Rosenfeld, Alvin H., *The End of the Holocaust* (Bloomington and Indianapolis: Indiana University Press, 2011), p. 82.

15 Weil, Shalva, "From Persecution to Freedom: Central European Jewish Refugees and their Host Communities in India", in Anil Bhatti and Johannes H. Voigt, eds, *Jewish Exile in India: 1933–1945* (New Delhi: Manohar in association with Max Mueller Bhavan, 2005), pp. 64–84.

Also see Cronin, Joseph and Indra Sengupta, *The City as Refuge: Jewish Calcutta and refugees from Hitler's Europe* (New Delhi: Max Weber Stiftung India Branch Office, 2018).

16 "Jews Pay Homage to Holocaust Martyrs", *Hindustan Times*, Mumbai, 3 May 2011, Appendix 1, p. 2.

17 Guttman, Anna, *Writing Indians and Jews: Metaphorics of Jewishness in South Asian Literature* (New York: Palgrave Macmillan, 2013), p. 1.

18 Porat, Dina, "Holocaust Denial and the Image of the Jew, or 'They Boycott Auschwitz as an Israeli Product'", in Alvin H. Rosenfeld, ed., *Resurgent Antisemitism: Global Perspectives* (Bloomington and Indianapolis: Indiana University Press, 2013), p. 472.

19 Wistrich, Robert S., *Antisemitism: The Longest Hatred* (New York: Pantheon Books, 1991), p. 166.

20 *Harijan*, 26 November 1938, as cited in Lev, Shimon, "'Can the Jews resist this organised and shameless persecution?' – Gandhi's Attitude to the Holocaust", *Gandhi*

Marg, Vol. 35, Number 3, October–December 2013, pp. 347–373, and Lev, Shimon, "Melting Hitler's Heart of Stone: Gandhi's Attitude to the Holocaust", *The Journal of Indo-Judaic Studies*, Vol. 13, Fall 2013, pp. 37–55.

21 *Ibid.*

22 *Ibid.*

23 Complete Works of Mahatma Gandhi, Vol. 76, 23 July 1939, p. 156. www.gandhiashramsevagram.org/gandhi-literature/mahatma-gandhi-collected-works-volume-76.pdf (Accessed on 4 November 2019).

24 *ibid.*

25 Cited in Kumaraswamy, P. R., *India's Israel Policy* (New York: Columbia University Press, 2010), p. 51.

26 Egorova, Yulia, *Jews and India: Perceptions and Image* (Routledge, London and New York, 2006), p. 39.

27 Kumaraswamy, P. R., "India and the Holocaust: Perceptions of the Indian National Congress", *The Journal of Indo-Judaic Studies*, Vol. 3, 2000, p. 122.

28 *Ibid.*, p. 118.

29 *Ibid.*

30 *Ibid.*, p. 120.

31 *Ibid.*, p. 121.

32 Kumaraswamy, P.R., *Squaring the Circle: Mahatma Gandhi and the Jewish National Home* (KW Publishers & ICWA, 2018), p.52.

33 Basu, Somdatta, "Mass Violence in Presi History Book", *The Times of India*, Kolkata, 27 February 2017, p. 1: http://timesofindia.indiatimes.com/city/kolkata/mass-violence-in-presi-history-book/articleshow/57366155.cms (Accessed on 26 March 2017).

34 Express News Service, "Presidency University Introduces Paper on Mass Killings for Postgraduate History Students", *The Indian Express*, 28 February 2017: http://indianexpress.com/article/india/violence-students-presidency-university-introduces-paper-on-mass-killings-for-postgraduate-history-students/ (Accessed on March 26, 2017).

35 IANS, "First for India: Presidency's Holocaust-focused course on history of mass violence", *Business Standard*, 21 March 2017: www.business-standard.com/article/news-ians/first-for-india-presidency-s-holocaust-focused-course-on-history-of-mass-violence-117032100275_1.html (Accessed on 26 March 2017).

36 Navras J. Aafreedi spearheaded the initiatives in Lucknow, Gautam Buddha University in Greater Noida, and Presidency University in Kolkata. See the following: Egorova, Yulia, *Jews and Muslims in South Asia: Reflections on Difference, Religion and Race* (New York: Oxford University Press, 2018), p. 57; Guttman, Anna, *Writing Indians and Jews: Metaphorics of Jewishness in South Asian Literature* (New York: Palgrave Macmillan, 2013), pp. 169–170; Wald, Shalom Salomon and Arielle Kandel, *India, Israel and the Jewish People: Looking Ahead, Looking Back 25 Years after Normalization* (Jerusalem: The Jewish People Policy Institute, 2017), pp. 138–139.

37 Aafreedi, Navras Jaat, "The First Ever Holocaust Films Retrospective in South Asia", *Journal of Indo-Judaic Studies*, Vol. XI, 2010, pp. 149–152.

38 Aafreedi, Navras Jaat, "First known Hindi play on Holocaust presented", *San Diego Jewish World*, January 16, 2015: www.sdjewishworld.com/2015/01/16/first-known-hindi-play-holocaust-presented/ (Accessed on 17 February 2018).

    Anonymous, "Indian Students Put On First-Ever Play on Holocaust", United with Israel, 20 January 2015: https://unitedwithisrael.org/indian-students-put-on-first-ever-play-on-holocaust/ (Accessed on 17 February 2018).

39 Aafreedi, Navras Jaat, "Holocaust and Hitler in Hindi", in *Café Dissensus*, Issue 31, January 2017: https://cafedissensus.com/2017/01/20/holocaust-and-hitler-in-hindi/ (Accessed on 17 February 2018).

Part 4
Reflections

12 Sonderkommando Photo 4 and the portrayal of the invisible[1]

David Patterson

The Sonderkommando of Birkenau ranged from 400 in 1942 to about 1,000 in 1944; the detail consisted of mostly Jewish inmates who were forced to do the mind-bending and back-breaking labour in the gas chambers and ovens of the crematoria. Collecting the material remains of human beings reduced to mere matter, they collected clothing and jewellery, hair and gold teeth, skin, and bones from the dead. On occasion, a worker would find members of his own family among the bodies that he dragged naked from the gas chambers and shoved into the ovens of the crematoria; so it happened with Béla Katz in Elie Wiesel's *Night*, who fed his own father into the ovens (Wiesel 1956). Every three months or so the men of the Sonderkommando were themselves gassed and burned, as they were considered *Geheimnisträger* or "bearers of secrets" (Greif 2005). We know this from the few survivors of the Sonderkommando, such as Filip Müller and Shlomo Venezia, who were almost without exception part of the last Sonderkommando unit, the men who staged the Birkenau Uprising of 7 October 1944 (Müller 1979; Venezia 2009). In that uprising 451 Jews were killed; dozens of others were rounded up, tortured, and executed for their complicity in the rebellion. One month later, on 7 November, the Nazis destroyed the crematoria and left them in ruins.

The irony of the designation of *Geheimnisträger* is striking, since the Nazis regarded all Jewish people as *Geheimnisträger*, the bearers of the secret truth that sanctifies every human life, the secret of Torah that would undermine the entire totalitarian project of National Socialism. In the photographs shown below we glimpse the non-representable secret for which the Jews and the Sonderkommando members were murdered; indeed, gazing into these images, we ourselves are transformed into *Geheimnisträger*. Here, as Emil Fackenheim has said, "we touch upon an Ultimate" (Fackenheim 1989). Given the time and place of their making, it is nothing short of a miracle that we hold these photographs in our trembling hands. And yet we have these images before our eyes. They are photographs of the transcendent trace of what Auschwitz was. In their transcendence lies a trace of the secret borne by the *Geheimnisträger*.

Taking up an examination of the photographs, we inch our way toward the thin periphery of the unreality of Birkenau, a non-place inhabited by the non-men of the Sonderkommando. In doing so, we tread a metaphysical minefield. The eye of the viewer merges with the unblinking eye of a camera, unable to turn away.

The blood chills. The heart turns to stone. Thus, we have the collisions with the non-representable – non-representable because the images illustrate the truth that in Birkenau reality exceeded imagination. Yes, these are among the photographs taken under pain of death, like the diaries written in the darkness and dead of night in the gullet of the anti-world, the diaries unearthed in the late 1950s and early 1960s (Bezwinska 1973). More than that, however, they are photographs of the earthquake that shook the soul of the photographer whose eyes saw the body and soul of Israel, the God of the Covenant, and all of humanity's truth and meaning and sanctity consigned to the pit. One must ease into these photographs, like easing into a lake of fire, into a realm devoid of truth, humanity, and divinity at a time when the living were indistinguishable from the dead.

The four photographs, numbered 280 – 283, were taken in August 1944 at Crematorium V by Alberto Israel Errera (1913 – August 1944), an officer in the Greek Navy known simply as Alex. Errera joined the partisans upon the Nazis' occupation of Greece in April 1941. He was arrested on 25 March 1944 and deported from Athens to Auschwitz on 2 April (Greif 2005). Alter Fajnzylberg, Shlomo and Josel Dragon, and David Szmulewski assisted Errera in the clandestine task of taking the photographs. Helena Dantón, who worked in the SS canteen, smuggled photos out of the camp in a tube of toothpaste (Didi-Huberman 2003).

On 4 September 1944 Helena handed over the film to Polish political prisoners Jósef Cyrankiewicz and Stanislaw Klodzinski, who in turn added a note to be sent with the film to the Polish resistance in Kraków: "Urgent … Sending you photos of Birkenau showing prisoners sent to gas chambers. One photo shows one of the stakes at which bodies were burned when the crematorium could not manage to burn all the bodies" (Didi-Huberman 2003). Cropped images of the photographs were first published in 1945. (The matter of cropping the photographs will prove to be crucial.) In 1947 one of the photographs was exhibited at Auschwitz. The others appeared in 1958 in Warsaw in the book *1939–1945: We Have Not Forgotten* edited by Stanisław Wrzos-Glinka, Tadeusz Mazur, and Jerzy Tomaszewski. "If we look at the four photographs of Birkenau as *tear-images* rather than *veil-images*", writes Didi-Huberman, "as the exception rather than the rule, we find ourselves perceiving a *naked horror*, a horror that leaves us all the more devastated as it ceases to bear the hyperbolic mark of the 'unimaginable'"(Didi-Huberman 2003). And so we realize that the task of one transformed into a witness through these photographic images is not about imagination. Indeed, the Nazi evil was not unimaginable – it was everything imaginable. The task at hand, rather, is to testify to the absolute sanctity of the other human being that in those days of death and destruction came under a most radical assault.

Photo 1 is photograph number 280, the first of the four smuggled out of the camp. "The *mass of black* that surrounds the sight of the cadavers and the pits", Didi-Huberman observes, "is the space of the gas chamber: the *dark room* into which one had to retreat … to give light to the work of the *Sonderkommando* … That mass of black gives us the situation itself … the condition of existence of the photographs themselves" (Didi-Huberman 2003). In the mass of blackness we behold the depths of the darkness from which the bodies of Jewish men, women, and children were dragged from the gas chamber into the pits. It is a darkness

Figure 12.1 Photo 1 "Sonderkommando" Photographs. https://en.wikipedia.org/wiki/
Sonderkommando_photographs, permission granted by the Auschwitz-
Birkenau State Museum

that reeks of body fluids and the soul-searing screams of the dead that reverberate
in the chamber. For the viewer, the black frame forms not a border but a barrier,
like "Arbeit Macht Frei", that cannot be traversed. From this dark edge we peer
into the abyss of the Shoah. The mass of black is the oppressive mass of the anti-
world, a black hole from which no light can emanate. What Didi-Huberman calls

"the situation itself" is unlike any situation on Planet Earth: it is the non-situation, the uncondition, of Planet Auschwitz. The black mass in the photograph is the dark matter that dominates the concentrationary universe. To be sure, it *is* the *concentrationary* universe: there is nothing ontological about "the condition of existence of the photographs themselves".

Nicholas Chare elaborates: "The black frame forms part of the noise of the photographs. These images are edged by horror: the blackness is the boundary that permits the photograph to be. To remove this ambiguous edge is to avoid confronting the origin of the horrors portrayed in the pictures" (Chare 2011). Yes, the *noise* of the photographs. It is the deafening noise of the gas chamber, the gullet from which Alex takes the photograph, even as it threatens to swallow him up. It is the chamber's echoing noise of the boundary that erases all boundaries between life and death, between good and evil. The burning of the bodies is not Auschwitz; no, the mass of black is Auschwitz, if anything can be said to be Auschwitz. Chare continues:

> These pictures can be given the appearance of coherence ... Yet a part of the darkness will always resist this desire to contour it. It remains rather that out of which contour arises, bordering all interpretations yet resisting being delimited by them. Shape momentarily disappears in this darkness.
>
> (Chare 2011)

As shape disappears in this darkness, so does the word disappear in the rumbling silence of the photograph. Here the photographic image is precisely *not* a representation of anything one can name: what you see in this photograph *is not* how it was, and yet here it is. That is the purpose of the edge of black. To remove the edge, then, is to remove the invisible, non-representable aspect of the event.

Longing to take away the horror, we take away the darkness. Thus, attempting to restore something to which one might give voice, we display a cropped version of this image. Absent the darkness, the image can be appropriated, known, and thematized; it can be offered as evidence of a crime committed, evidence of mass murder even where the term *murder* falls short of the unreality. Behold the cropped image:

The trees stand in the background, mute and indifferent. The sky is a blank, grey, silent canopy of indifference, emptied of the sun. There are no birds overhead; indeed, there is no "overhead", no dimension of height, for the heavens themselves are occluded by the cloud of smoke made of the ashes of the Jewish people. Look at the man trying to make his way through the bodies, struggling not to stumble: it is as though he were walking through a minefield or over an abyss that threatens to devour his dead soul, as though he were about to fall into the growing gulf of the dead, as though the ashen earth piled knee-deep with bodies whose dead hands grab at him might at any moment open up and swallow him. His arms are stretched outward: he is trying to keep his balance. Or is he trying to fly away to join the other Jews launched skyward on the column of smoke and ash?

We see a man with his hands on his hips, as though he were out on a routine job, perhaps the man in charge of the labour crew. Images from our own past

Figure 12.2 Photo 1 Cropped, "Sonderkommando" Photographs. https://en.wikipedia. org/wiki/Sonderkommando_photographs, permission granted by the Auschwitz-Birkenau State Museum

come to mind: we who have had summer jobs as laborers have seen this image. We have seen our boss assume this pose, as if to say, "Get to work!" For the men on this Sonderkommando – who knew nothing of winter, since the winter Sonder-kommando had long since been gassed and burned – this was their summer job. Hands on his hips, the foreman takes a breather and breathes in the remains of the burning bodies of Jews, seeking a moment of respite from the exhausting toil in the heat of August 1944. But there is no respite. Not from this. Next to him another man scratches his head, as though working out some mundane matter regarding the task at hand. "Do we need more kerosene and timber? When are we going to finish burning this batch? How shall we divide up the goods taken from these Jews? How many more will they send us? When do we break for lunch?" Perhaps he gazes upon the cadavers surrounding him and sees himself among them. For he knows he will never leave this place alive.

Yes, the cadavers: look more closely. You peer into the image and ask, both knowing and afraid to know: "Are those human *bodies*?! Are they *human* bod-ies?!" This is not how human beings bury the bodies of dead human beings. The smoke rises from what is precisely *not* a funeral pyre; it occludes nature herself in this most unnatural scene. Neither a funeral nor a burial of bodies, this is at best a disposal of refuse. Here we have the radical opposite of bodies prepared by the *Cheverah Kadishah*, the company assembled to prepare one who is created in the image and likeness of the Holy One for a return to the Holy One. Members of

Figure 12.3 Photo 2 "Sonderkommando" Photographs. https://en.wikipedia.org/wiki/
Sonderkommando_photographs, permission granted by the Auschwitz-
Birkenau State Museum

the *Cheverah Kadishah* speak to the departed and comfort them as they prepare them, assuring them that their passage to the upper worlds will be a smooth one, careful to observe modesty, and apologizing for any discomfort that might have been caused to the one who has passed. Here we have none of that. What, indeed, could these men say to these dead? Perhaps they cursed the bodies of the murdered Jews lying all around them, cursed the burial that was not a blessing but a

Figure 12.4 Photo 2 Cropped, "Sonderkommando" Photographs. https://en.wikipedia.org/ wiki/Sonderkommando_photographs, permission granted by the Auschwitz- Birkenau State Museum

burden, the burial that was not a burial. This, then, is a death that is not death, a death that is an assault on death, a death that drives away the Angel of Death, the Angel of a Thousand Eyes, whose eyes gaze back at us through the camera lens.

This is photograph number 281, the second in the series of four. Alex withdraws into the depths of the gas chamber for fear of being seen – or out of fear of what he sees. Withdrawing into this darkness, Alex becomes part of the darkness, clambering to become invisible in his attempt to photograph the invisible – to photograph not just the burning of bodies but the invisible evil that is Auschwitz-Birkenau. His testimony is not limited to a field of vision: his withdrawal into the gas chamber, occluding the field of vision, is itself part of his vision and his testimony. It is a testimony haunted by screams and prayers and outcries to a God grown deaf, steeped in the dying guttural praying of the Shema, with hands raised to the heavens, clawing at the walls, and clinging to loved ones. It is as though one of those who were gassed were clicking the camera's shutter, hoping that no one outside, friend or foe, would hear the click, praying that everyone on the outside, friend, and foe, would behold the image snatched from this piece of Planet Auschwitz.

This is a photograph of the obliteration of the millennial teaching and testimony of the Jewish people. It is an image of the total reversal of the "cloud of smoke by day" and the "pillar of fire by night" that guided the Jewish people from their exile to the Land of the Covenant (Exodus 13:21). Is there any way for *this* cloud of smoke to guide us out of our own exile? Here the confusion of values and reality is so radical that there is no day or night, no good or evil, no life or death, but only the cloud of smoke, of flame and ash – not to guide the Jewish people but to consume them. That is the meaning of the black mass, a meaning from which we struggle to flee, as we crop the black mass from the photograph.

Once again we see men hard at work at their summer job. They tug and they pull; they grunt and they groan, pronouncing imprecations upon the heat of August and the heat of the flames. The fence in the background announces the infinite distance between world and anti-world, between the world of trees and the world of corpses. And yet, like the column of smoke riding the winds, the world of corpses spills over the fence and into the world of trees, as we discover in Photograph 282.

This is a photograph not only of a horrific scene of Jews being prepared for mass murder but also of Alex's mad desperation, as if the photographer were himself photographed rushing through this haunted wood, trying to capture an image of the Nazi's radical evil, desperately struggling to deliver a message that he cannot deliver. He cannot deliver it, even with this image, because the evil is ineffable. He runs not only to avoid getting caught but perhaps also to flee the scene, as if he and all of humanity were implicated by what comes into the field of the camera lens. Indeed, there is no innocent viewing of this image: to look is to be implicated. The lens looks upward to the trees and the sky, like an outcry or a curse hurled to the heavens. Aimed at the smoky grey expanse, the camera photographs a sky transformed into a Jewish cemetery. With its viewfinder turned heavenward, the camera captures the dimension of height from which the Most High is absent. The heavens are as vast as they are silent, dwarfing the

Figure 12.5 Photo 3 "Sonderkommando" Photographs. https://en.wikipedia.org/wiki/
Sonderkommando_photographs, permission granted by the Auschwitz-
Birkenau State Museum

naked humanoid figures on the lower left, so small that these human beings seem
to be insignificant to the "composition" of photograph itself. And yet they are
precisely the subject of the photograph, a subject that can be viewed only by
looking askance, like looking slightly away in order to behold a star that eludes
direct vision. This is where the corpses piled next to the pit of flames had been
just hours before they were photographed, before they were herded into the gas
chamber. This is what they looked like, naked yet radically unnatural.

In an act of voyeurism that exceeds obscenity, certain individuals have produced a cropped version of Photograph 282:

Much of the sky and most of the trees are left out of the cropped photograph. It
zeros in on a humanity inhumanly laid bare, ascending to the left, about to ascend
to their invisible graves on high. Among the naked women are clothed men with
no apparent interest in the women's nakedness, grim guides herding these helpless women to their destruction, performing their designated duty of processing
units. They are the Sonderkommando members in this Sonderkommando photograph, men exposed far more than their naked victims are exposed. How do
these doomed women register what is happening all around them? They smell

Figure 12.6 Photo 3 Cropped, "Sonderkommando" Photographs. https://en.wikipedia.org/
wiki/Sonderkommando_photographs, permission granted by the Auschwitz-
Birkenau State Museum

the stench of burning flesh. They hear the roar of the flames. They see the smoke
rising above the trees. Are they going insane? Or is the Shema rising to their lips?

The ostensible purpose of cropping the first three Sonderkommando photographs is to get a close-up of their subject matter, so that it may be "used" as proof
of this episode in the history of the Third Germany. And yet, the subject matter is
lost in the cropping: in the cropped photographs the transcendent, non-representable, invisible Auschwitz has itself been cropped out. Auschwitz has been cropped
out. The Jews have been cropped out. The metaphysical, transcendent truth of this
evil has been cropped out. Just as Photo 4 has always been cropped out.

There is no cropped version of the fourth photograph, number 283. There is
nothing to zoom in on, no photographic subject, nothing to *see*, nothing to serve as
evidence, nothing of the ontological or the representable, because it *shows* nothing. The first three images are displayed on the website of the Auschwitz-Birkenau State Museum, but not the fourth. It has been cropped from the other three.
The same is the case in the British Imperial War Museum. And in his *History of
the Holocaust* Yehuda Bauer notes that "three photographs of the crematoria compounds" were smuggled out; he makes no mention of the fourth, probably assuming that the fourth photograph is not a photograph of anything (Bauer 1982). For
purposes of history, memory, and Jewish testimony, it is as though there were no
fourth photograph. Therefore, Bauer perhaps concluded, it is useless, because it
could never be entered as evidence of anything. Evidence belongs to the representable, to what can be *shown*. But just as we have been implicated by what the
other three photographs have shown, so must we find the courage to confront
what is shown in this fourth image, the image cropped from the other three.

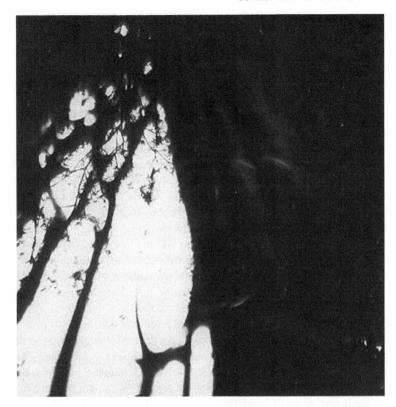

Figure 12.7 Photo 4 "Sonderkommando" Photographs. https://en.wikipedia.org/wiki/
Sonderkommando_photographs, permission granted by the Auschwitz-
Birkenau State Museum

At first glance, this appears to be a photograph of nothing discernible. It is,
indeed, made of what was cropped from the others, made of the darkness of the
black mass and the immensity of the grey sky. But it *shows* nothing. And yet, for
that reason alone, Photo 4 is a photograph of the anti-world of Auschwitz-Birkenau, a world in which nothing was hidden, hence there was nothing to *show*.
Didi-Huberman insists that to say it is useless because it shows nothing "is to
forget all that it tells us phenomenologically about the photographer: the impossibility of aiming the camera, the risk undergone, the urgency, the fact that he may
have been running, the awkwardness, the sun in his eyes, and perhaps breath-
lessness too" (Didi-Huberman 2003). Doubling back on itself, it is a photograph
of the desperate effort to take the photograph. It bears witness to the erasure of
boundaries, when more was real than was possible, where there were no criminals
and no madmen: there lies the horror conveyed in Sonderkommando Photo 4.

"The final *Sonderkommando* photograph", Chare emphasizes, "gestures
towards such a dissolution of boundaries. It shows the dissolution of shape. It
shows the spectator the horror of a world without boundaries" (Chare 2011). This
is the world in which the horror is that there is no horror. The subject of the fourth

photograph, in other words, is the invisible; it is the *anti-* in the anti-world. The term *invisible* here refers to nothing that might be shown or made manifest; it refers, rather, to the elusive essence of Auschwitz. That is why there is nothing to crop. The point of cropping the first three photographs was to show more, to make more visible; and yet the very act of cropping them veiled what they might otherwise have shown.

Significantly, the photograph is made more of darkness than of light; it has just enough light to show the grotesquely contorted images of darkness, the darkness of a mad desperation and a desperate madness. If we did not know that Alex was frantically running through the trees of a haunted wood, we would not take those dark forms to be trees. Rising up in a world that is not a world, they are trees that are not trees, trees of the Knowledge of Good and Evil in a realm devoid of all knowledge, of all good, and of all evil, edged not by flaming swords but by pits of flames – no Tree of Life here. Nor is there any Tree of Knowledge. There is no tree of anything. This is a photo of the anti-Garden of the anti-Eden: Sonderkommando Photo 4, then, is the most graphic of the Sonderkommando photographs, depicting a horror that surpasses depiction. It does not show nothing – it shows nothingness, what Chare calls the "horror of a world without boundaries", which is not only the anti-world of Auschwitz but is also the world that now lives in the shadow of Auschwitz. If, moreover, it is a photograph of a soul gone insane, it is also a mirror. That is why, like Perseus, we must hold up a reflective shield to avoid gazing directly upon it. That is why we leave it out of history books and museum exhibits.

Here before our eyes, through the eye of the Sonderkommando's *camera lucida*, we see the haunted wood in which we are lost. We might suppose that the photographic testimony of Sonderkommando Photo 4 could help us find our way out of the wood and into the light. But the opposite is the case. Indeed, taking the photographs was no help to Alex Errera: three days after he risked his life to convey the image of the ineffable horror of the anti-world he was captured and beaten to death (Bowman 2009).

So, what exactly is the point of examining Sonderkommando Photo 4? Above all, it is not to try to imagine "what it was like", an exercise as futile as it is obscene. This is not a photograph of "what it was like". It is an image of what Auschwitz was *about*, of what Auschwitz *meant* (if anything), of what Auschwitz *was*. Worse than vanity, the question of "what it was like" is a diversion, a flight from the stark truth that we human beings created Auschwitz, an escape into the moral safety of solipsistic sympathy. Much more urgent than imagining what it was like is confronting how it implicates us. Pretending to imagine what it was like, we pretend to control it. Then we can complacently "work through it" and thus "get over it" (LaCapra 2001); we can take possession of the event and thus control it, like holding a viper by the head. Calling us to a reckoning, however, Sonderkommando Photo 4 comprehends, apprehends, and lays claim to us in order to put to us the first question put to the first human being: Where are you? That is why we leave it out.

In all of the images we have encountered, but most profoundly in Sonderkommando Photo 4, this question singles us out. We look for murderers and victims and never look to ourselves: to speak of murderers and victims is to speak the language of a world that can be represented in language. But that language is undone in the anti-world, so that all we have left is this image that "shows nothing". Human beings murder and are murdered – hence the prohibition: Thou shalt no murder. In the inhuman, non-human, anti-human realm of Auschwitz these words, like all words, collapse into the ashes that cover the ground and clog the air. They too are lost in the woods of Sonderkommando Photo 4. Indeed, the haunted wood in which we remain lost is the one thing, the single thread, that appears in in all four of the Sonderkommando photographs. This is no accident.

What, then, is to be done? If Alex Errera had the courage to venture into the gas chambers and then to run through these woods, out of breath, for his very life, in order to take these photographs, even at the cost of his life, then we must summon the courage to gaze upon these images and offer up a reckoning of our own lives – without excuses. Sonderkommando Photo 4 robs us of all our excuses. That too is a reason for excluding it.

As Fackenheim has said,

> The Nazi logic of destruction was irresistible: *it was, nevertheless, being resisted.* This logic is a *novum* in human history, the source of an unprecedented, abiding horror: but resistance to it on the part of the most radically exposed, too, is a *novum* in history, and it is the source of an unprecedented, abiding wonder. *To hear and obey the commanding Voice of Auschwitz is an 'ontological' possibility, here and now, because the hearing and obeying was already an 'ontic' reality, then and there.*
>
> (Fackenheim 1989)

Sonderkommando Photo 4 is a photograph of the ontic reality of a resistance that should not have been there: there should be no such photograph. And yet Photo 4 *speaks*. It speaks in the imperative. It speaks in an absolute imperative from on high, revealing as it does an occluded dimension of height. What Fackenheim calls "the commanding Voice of Auschwitz" is the Voice of the transcendent, the Voice that reverberates throughout the contours of Sonderkommando Photo 4. It is the ineffable Voice of the invisible revealed in the photographic transcendence of the Holocaust that we have seen in these images. And so, we realize that transcendence happens not in a swoon but in a summons: shall we answer for what we have seen here? If so, let us prepare to stand, each and every one, along the road from Auschwitz to Jerusalem, and speak what was done.

Note

1 The photographs in this article are available at "*Sonderkommando* Photographs", Wikipedia, https://en.wikipedia.org/wiki/Sonderkommando_photographs. The photographs are in the public domain, because, according to Article 3 of the copyright law of March 29, 1926, of the Republic of Poland and Article 2 of the copyright law of 10 July 1952, of the People's Republic of Poland, all photographs by Polish photographers (or published for the first time in Poland or simultaneously in Poland and abroad) published without a clear copyright notice before the law was changed on 23 May 1994, are assumed public domain in Poland. Permission has been granted by the Auschwitz-Birkenau State Museum to publish these photographs.

References

Auden, W.H. "September 1, 1939." *W.H. Auden, Selected Poems*. New York: Random House, n.d.

Bauer, Y. *A History of the Holocaust*. New York: Franklin Watts, 1982.

Bezwinska, J., ed. *Amidst a Nightmare of Crime: Manuscripts of Members of Sonderkommando*. Oswiecim: State Museum, 1973.

Bowman, S.B. *The Agony of Greek Jews, 1940–1945*. Stanford: Stanford University Press, 2009.

Chare, N. *Auschwitz and Afterimages: Abjection, Witnessing and Representation, I*. London: B. Tauris, 2011.

Didi-Huberman, G. *Images in Spite of All: Fours Photographs from Auschwitz*. Translated by B. Shane. Chicago: Lillis, University of Chicago Press, 2003.

Fackenheim, E.L. *To Mend the World: Foundations of Post-Holocaust Jewish Thought*. New York: Schocken Books, 1989.

Greif, G. *We Wept without Tears: Testimonies of the Jewish Sonderkommando from Auschwitz*. Coral Gables: University of Miami Press, 2005.

LaCapra, D. *Writing History, Writing Trauma*. Baltimore: Johns Hopkins University Press, 2001.

Müller, F. *Auschwitz Inferno: The Testimony of a Sonderkommando*. Translated by Susanna Flatauer. London: Routledge & Kegan Paul, 1979.

Venezia, S. *Inside the Gas Chambers: Eight Months inside the Sonderkommando of Auschwitz*. Malden, Mass: Polity Press, 2009.

Wiesel, E. *Night*. New York: Hill & Wang, 1956.

13 Overcoming "intimate hatreds"

Reflections on violence against Yezidis

Tutku Ayhan and Güneş Murat Tezcür

Introduction

The self-styled Islamic State (IS), which itself was a product of years of a vicious civil war in Iraq, left a long trail of blood and tears when it occupied Syria and Iraq from 2013 to 2019. Both the IS campaigns and military actions taken against the IS by various local and international actors involved high levels of human rights violations and civilian victimization.[1] At the same time, the ordeal of Yezidis, a religious group concentrated in northern Iraq, at the hands of the IS was unprecedented in its scope. On the morning of 3 August 2014, the IS executed a coordinated attack against the Yezidi towns and villages surrounding Mt Sinjar, located in the north-western corner of Iraq. As the Kurdish forces in control of the area withdrew without putting up any resistance, tens of thousands of Yezidis made a desperate attempt to seek refuge on top of Mt Sinjar. The IS swiftly executed men and older boys who were unable to do so. The captured women and children were enslaved. A large number of Yezidis who managed to reach Mt Sinjar died because of thirst, hunger, and exhaustion. Overall, more than 3,000 Yezidis were killed and around 6,500 of them were enslaved.[2] While many other groups including Christians, Shiite Arabs and Turkomans, Sunni Arabs, and Sunni Kurds were targets of the IS, the violence against Yezidis was exceptional given its intensity and repertoire.

Why did the IS target Yezidis so viciously? We address this question by adopting a historical perspective and comparing the IS campaign with previous episodes of anti-Yezidi violence. The dominant contemporary Yezidi self-perception is a community that has been persecuted by local and imperial Muslim rules throughout the centuries. From this perspective that has a cyclical view of violence, there was nothing unprecedented and exceptional about the IS actions. In fact, the IS campaign of 2014 is labelled as the "74th *firman*" targeting Yezidis *qua* Yezidis, a label that signifies a strong pattern of historical continuity in victimization of Yezidis because of their religious beliefs.[3] All these campaigns were informed and justified by orthodox Islamic perspectives that characterized Yezidis as "apostates", "polytheists", or "heretics". Since the group was located outside of the moral order of a society, discriminatory and violent practices targeting its members were easily justifiable on Islamic grounds.

We argue that historical patterns characterizing the relations between Yezidis and their mostly Sunni Muslim neighbours have exhibited complexity and countervailing tendencies that could not be accurately captured by a prism of minority victimhood. While religiously inspired demonization of Yezidis has a well-documented and widespread record, it rarely led to violent campaigns. Most campaigns taken by Ottoman rulers against Yezidis on Mt Sinjar were motivated by matters of governance aims such as securing major transportation and communication routes, collecting taxes, and conscripting recruits. Moreover, Yezidis were not simply passive victims but engaged in various political alliances with non-Yezidi forces throughout history.[4] There is also a long pattern of repeated interactions between Yezidi and their Muslim neighbours (mostly Sunni but also Shiites) involving mutual visits and commercial exchanges.[5]

At the same time, we also show that religious prejudices and biases played a necessary role in fomenting anti-Yezidi violence and providing justifications for practices that would not have been feasible in the absence of such justifications. Yezidis' perceived status as religious outsiders was used as a tool of legitimation in military campaigns leading to aggravated patterns of violence involving mass executions and enslavement. Furthermore, the absence of any notable Islamic discourse (at least until very recently) that explicitly challenged and refuted widespread pejorative views of Yezidis left the community particularly vulnerable to campaigns inspired by religious hatred. As a marginalized minority lacking no orthodox religiosity and with very limited public presence and recognition until 2014, Yezidis were subject of wild rumours and gross misconceptions about the very nature of their beliefs. From a more optimistic view, a paradoxical consequence of the IS attacks in 2014 could be the growing international and Muslim awareness of Yezidis and acceptance of them as a group entitled to rights and protections. Our discussion is informed by a survey of secondary literature about Yezidi political history, more than a hundred in-depth interviews conducted in Dohuk province of Iraqi Kurdistan in 2018 and 2019, and original documents in primary languages including Kurdish and Turkish.

A brief note about Yezidism

Yezidis, whose religion originated in northern Iraq, had been living in geographical landscape that is now today shared between Iraq, Syria, Turkey, and Iran. A significant number of them migrated to Russia (currently Armenia and Georgia) in the aftermath of the Russo-Ottoman wars during the nineteenth and twentieth centuries. With the second half of the twentieth century, they also moved to Western European countries such as Germany, France, and the Netherlands. Their faith, which has its own distinctive characteristics, evolved in interaction with Islam, Christianity, and Zoroastrianism. They were for a long time labelled as "devil-worshippers" by outsiders who mistook the image of the holiest of angels in Yezidi theology, Tawus-i Melek, as Satan.

There is still a lack of consensus among scholars on the historical origins of Yezidism. It is widely accepted that Sheik Adi, who has a very central place in Yezidi religious teachings, was actually the Muslim mystic and Sufi Adi b. Musafir

(b. in Lebanon in 1075) who settled in the Hakkari mountains (the border zone between contemporary Turkey and Iraq) by 1111. His tomb in Lalish valley (currently located in Iraqi Kurdistan) gradually became the holiest place of Yezidism. His followers would be soon called the "Adawiya" order (Kreyenbroek 1995, 27–31). In the subsequent centuries, Yezidism, which is now quite different from the Sufi teachings of Adi b. Musafir, became popular among Kurds inhabiting the mountainous area. According to a historical interpretation, Yezidism became a distinct religion through Kurdish syncretism of Islamic and Christian beliefs during the thirteenth and fourteenth centuries. An alternative historical reading, which is favoured by most Yezidis, suggests that Yezidism has ancient roots preceding both Islam and Christianity but adopted some of their traditions for survival purposes (Guest 1993, 29). Kreyenbroek (1995) acknowledges the development of the faith based on a mystic interpretation of Islam, yet he thinks of the influence of Sufism on the Yezidi religion as limited. He traces the origins of Yezidism to an interaction of Islam, Zoroastrianism, and pre-Zoroastrian beliefs in Iran. The lack of a written body of teachings has, without doubt, hampered the development of an official, monolithic Yezidi theology that, in turn, contributed to Muslim perceptions of Yezidi identity as a "liminal minority" whose core beliefs remained ill-defined and ambivalent. Accordingly, Yezidis were not given the status of "People of the Book", which entails certain tolerance and protections for minority groups living under Islamic rule.[6]

Yezidis under the Ottomans

The experience of Yezidis under the Ottoman Empire (r. early sixteenth to early twentieth centuries) can be summarized in terms of their relations with the local Kurds and Ottoman authorities. The Yezidi-Sunni Kurdish relations have evolved throughout history. There were long periods of time where they lived together as members of the same tribe, or under a confederation of Kurdish tribes. They sometimes formed alliances; at other times fought each other. There are also times when shared tribal networks prevailed over opposing religious identities. For instance, the Ottoman campaign led by Firari Mustafa Pasha against the Yezidis of Sinjar – described by the illustrious Ottoman traveller Evliya Celebi in his *Seyahatname* (written in the seventeenth century) – was related to the revolt of Abdal Khan of Bitlis who was allied with Yezidis (Guest 1993, 50). In the early nineteenth century, a Yezidi leader called "Mirza Agha ruled over a mixed population of Yezidis, Muslims and Christians" until his defeat by the Ottomans in 1837 (Fuccaro 1999, 63).

Going back to the sixteenth to seventeenth centuries, we see certain Yezidi leaders appointed as governors by the Ottoman rulers. For example, Sultan Suleyman appointed Daseni chiefs as rulers of Soran in the 1530s. Mir Mirza of the Daseni tribe fought with Murad IV in the conquest of Baghdad in 1638. In 1649, he was appointed as Governor of Mosul and kept this post for a year before traveling to Istanbul. On his way back, he was intercepted and executed on the orders of Melek Ahmed Pasha, the Grand Vizier (Guest 1993, 49). This shows how a Yezidi chieftain occupied a governor position, albeit briefly, under the Ottomans.

Mt Sinjar, which was home to several prominent Yezidi tribes, had command-ing views of the caravan routes linking Ottoman cities in Mesopotamia and Anatolia. Sheref Khan, the author of *Sherafname* chronicling Kurdish dynasties (1596–1599) (Alsancakli 2017), describes Yezidis as "pundits who live off from agriculture and robbery" (Allison 2001, 33). As a matter of fact, Ottoman expe-ditions to Mt Sinjar until the nineteenth century was primarily motivated by lim-iting Yezidi raids targeting caravans. Actually, local rulers conducted a series of expeditions against Sinjar to contain Yezidi raids during the eighteenth century (Longrigg 1925, 126; Guest 2010, 60). At the same time, violence against Yezidis on Mt Sinjar was often justified in religious terms. For instance, in an expedition against Mt Sinjar in 1795, the official justification for violence against Yezidis mentions them as infidels and heretical – legitimizing their punishment including the enslavement of women and children by Islamic law (Gölbaşı 2013, 3–4).

Violence against Yezidis of Sheikhan, where Lalish is located, and Sinjar esca-lated throughout the nineteenth century. In fact, one of the oldest persecutions ordinary Yezidis mention when asked about previous *firmans* in history is the massacre by the Kurdish Mir of Rawanduz, Mir Muhammad Kor, who killed the Yezidi Mir Eli Beg who refused to convert to Islam and massacred Yezidis of Sheikhan on the eastern bank of the Tigris overlooking Mosul (Layard 1850, 276–277). Yet, tribal conflicts rather than pure religious hatred appear to be the motivating force behind the slaughters, which is also called the Soran Massacre. Soran Kurds were long-time enemies of the Daseni Yezidis and in 1832, Yezidi Mir of Sheikhan, Ali Beg, invited Ali Aga, a Kurdish chieftain, to his home and had him murdered. An eminent Kurdish mullah appealed to Mir Mohammad to take revenge. However, it is also true that religious prejudices deeply affect the form the violence directed against Yezidis take. During the Bedirxan revolts in 1844, Yezidis, together with Nestorians and Jacobites, were enslaved and sold in the slave markets. Christians were liberated after the British intervention, but Yezidis, who lacked such protection, were not. Moreover, the government could not order the return of "converted slaves or of those female slaves who had had children by their masters" (Erdem 1996, 46).

During the early centralization efforts, campaigns to establish direct Ottoman control against Mt. Sinjar were intensified (Guest 1993, 89; Forbes 1839, 411; Layard 1850, 314). Sinjar's geopolitical importance directed the central govern-ment's attention on controlling the trade routes and eliminating the risk of bandit attacks. In 1837, Hafiz Pasha attacked Sinjar as part of a larger campaign against Kurdis emirates, aimed at securing the line of communication between Diyarbakir and Mosul (Guest 2010, 74–75). He made Yezidis a tribute of the Sultan – Yezidi female captives were sold in the Mardin slave market – but he let them keep their religion (Forbes 1839, 409; Guest 2010, 74).[7] From 1849 on, Ottomans estab-lished a regular presence in northern Sinjar whereas they had no permanent access to the area before 1837 (Fuccaro 1999, 4).

Erdem observes that the centralization reforms during the Tanzimat prevented the large-scale kidnapping and enslavement of Yezidis, Nestorians, and Jews (1996, 59–60). He also writes that such government protection was not extended to Yezidis before Tanzimat (1996, 46). The Tanzimat period also changed the official discourse on the community. Before Tanzimat, even though mass killings of Yezidis were mostly driven by geopolitical concerns, the attacks were justified on a religious basis where Yezidis were labelled as "apostates" whose killings and enslavement were permissible. However, as the Tanzimat era abolished the distinction between Muslim and non-Muslim, the official discourse when referring to Yezidis changed to one that described them as "heretics" whose identity and beliefs needed to be corrected, either by advice, coercion, or violence (Gölbaşı 2013, 4–5).

During this period, Yezidi demands for exemption from conscription was a primary source of conflict and interaction between the Ottoman administration and Yezidi tribes (Allison 2001). The Yezidi delegation visiting Istanbul in 1849 obtained exemption from conscription with British help (Guest 1993, 104–108). The Yezidi leaders also wrote a petition arguing their exemption from conscription on religious grounds in 1872. However, the Ottoman government concluded in 1885 that Yezidis, just like Muslims, had to be recruited in the army.

The Ottoman policy towards Yezidis gained a new dimension with the ascendancy of Abdulhamid II (r. 1876–1909). During his reign, Muslim identity increasingly became central to the Sultan's perceptions of loyalty among his subjects. During a time when nationalism and missionary activity among non-Muslim groups of the Empire was on the increase, the conversion of Yezidis and other heterodox groups such as Alevis and Druzes into Islam to ensure their political loyalty appeared imperative in the eyes of the Abdulhamid regime (Gölbaşı 2013). Their conscription was a crucial step in their eventual conversion.

In 1892, the Ottoman authorities requested Yezidi leaders to convert to Islam. The latter refused this request order claiming that their religion is older than Islam. Some of the leaders were sent to exile. Yezidis were told that they could keep their religion as long as they paid their tax debts. Soon after, however, came the massacres of Omer Wehbi Pasha, which occupy a central place in the collective memory of Yezidis. He was sent to Mosul in 1892 by the Sultan. His mission involved institutionalizing a system of conscription, collection of taxes, and resettlement of tribes. He seemed to take the initiative to achieve these goals with violence in the face of lack of Yezidi cooperation (Guest 2010, 134–140; Deringil 1998, 71–5).[8] Around 500 Yezidis were killed in the Sinjar campaign in November–December 1892 (Gölbaşı 2009, 131). The Lalish temple was converted into a madrasa, sacred Yezidi objects were confiscated, and mosques were built in Yezidi villages. Following the events, Yezidis brought seven decapitated bodies to Mosul and presented them to an investigative commission sent by Istanbul – leading to moral outrage (Gölbaşı 2009, 134). It appears that the Ottoman authorities was not fond of Pasha's bloody methods aiming for forced conversion and recalled him. However, Lalish was returned to Yezidis only in 1904, and looted sacred objects in 1914. This episode suggests that while Ottomans employed indiscriminate violence against Yezidis who were perceived to be a heretical group, the Ottoman-Yezidi relations had multiple dimensions, which complicates the Yezidi victimhood discourse.

After Omer Wehbi Pasha's campaigns, though the attempts to conscript Yezidis continued, they no longer involved direct violence. For the remaining years of the Empire, there is no record of massive Ottoman violence targeting Yezidis. During

World War I, some Armenians fleeing from genocidal Ottoman attacks took refuge on Mt Sinjar. In February 1918, the Ottomans sent a small expedition to Sinjar as Yezidis threatened Ottoman lines of communication with Iraq. Ismail Beg was already in touch with British. After the attack, he brought a British officer to Sinjar in July. The last punitive Ottoman expedition took place in September (Guest 2010, 178–180).

Yezidis under the Iraqi state

According to the Commission charged in 1925 with informing the League of Nations about the demography of ethnic groups in Mosul and their will for the future of the province, Yezidis preferred an Iraq with a European mandate to a Turkish rule but preferred a Turkish rule to Iraq without a mandate (League of Nations 1925). However, they continued to have a marginalized status during and after the British mandate rule. The reports written by British Consulate staff in Mosul in the 1940s demonstrate the continuing nature of earlier Yezidi concerns under the new nation-state without much change: Yezidis are reported to have crossed the border to Syria to avoid conscription to the Iraqi army (Gökçen 2012, 431–434). The letters addressed to British officials by Yezidi leaders asked for their intervention and protection on issues related to the conflicts with Arab authorities, compulsory enrolment, and the complaints about the Shammar tribe, which they accuse of confiscating Yezidi lands (Gökçen 2012, 438). Yezidi chieftains also indicated not recognizing the Iraqi state's legitimacy but that they were ready to recognize British authority.

Although Yezidis' conflicts with the central government seem to be mostly related to the latter's concerns over the control of a semi-autonomous tribe, the religious aspect is also dominant in its treatment of Yezidi settlements. Since the beginning of the British Mandate, the community asked for a Christian district governor in Sinjar but their appeal to the authorities remained unanswered and the position was always occupied by a Muslim. Also, the Arab Shammar tribe's interests seem to be taken much more seriously by the Iraqi government who supported them over Yezidis (Gökçen 2012, 482).

The Rise of the Kurdish National Movement – 1960s–1970s

The Umayyad origins of Adi b. Musafir (Kreyenbroek 1995) has led, historically, to debated claims on the ancestry of Yezidis which trace their genealogy back to the Umayyad caliph Merwan b. el-Hakam (Guest 2010, 15)[9] or even to the first Umayyad caliph, Mu'awiya I (Fuccaro 1999, 174). During the 1960s, the Iraqi regime also propagated the Umayyad ancestry of Yezidis, declaring them Arabs and forcing them to register as such. On the Kurdish side, the idea of Zoroastrian origins of Yezidis gained popularity among Kurdish nationalists in the 1970s (Fuccaro 1999, 15). With the rise of the Kurdish nationalist movement in Iraq, some Yezidis in Sinjar joined peshmerga and fought for the Kurdish independence movement while others supported the regime and enrolled in the Iraqi army. In Sheikhan, the royal mir's (Prince) family also had opposing political alignments; Mir Hayri supported Mustafa Barzani whereas Mir Tahsin showed loyalty to Saddam.

After the collapse of the Kurdish nationalist revolt in 1975, Yezidis were resettled in collective towns surrounding the Sinjar mountain, losing all their lands to Arabs. Saddam used this resettlement and Arabization policy to cut Yezidi support to Kurdish fighters and to have a better control on the population of Sinjar.

> During Saddam's time, in the 1960s ... many people in Sinjar established connections with the September revolution. The Ba'ath leadership under Saddam Hussein and Ahmet Hasan al-Bakr made a declaration on 11 March 1970. They granted autonomy to Kurdistan. When the autonomy of Kurdistan increased, Sinjar got in contact with the revolution. Several local committees and offices were established in the south and north of Sinjar. Peshmerga put up many headquarters. Forces and arms were brought to Sinjar.
>
> What did the Ba'ath government do after 1970s? The district governor of Sinjar was killed on July 3, 1972. Ba'ath Party arrested anyone who was in contact with the (Barzani's) Party. They exiled women and children. People fled to Syria, Kurdistan, Iran. They captured my uncle and his relatives and executed him on the grounds of killing the district governor. He had nothing to do with the killing. But that's what they accused him for. They brought all these Arabs from Sinjar's surroundings, they settled them near Yezidi lands and villages. They brought them from (Jezeera) Til Azer
>
> They demolished 145 Yezidi and Kurdish villages in 1975 and built 11 collective towns. In the summer of 1975. They gave Arabic names to these compounds. Then they registered Yezidis as Arabs. They took away their Kurdish IDs.
>
> (Personal interview, 26 May 2018)

We had two field visits to Duhok, Iraqi Kurdistan (in the summer of 2018 and 2019), and we conducted more than a hundred in-depth interviews with displaced Sinjari Yezidis and non-displaced Yezidis, as well as activists, politicians, and professionals working on the Yezidi case since the 2014 IS attacks. When asked about their lives under the Saddam regime, our respondents described the period as being difficult but at the same time safe and free of religious persecution.

> During Saddam, they wouldn't dare to do anything to Yezidis. Everybody was under his control. Nobody would dare. We would go to Rabia (to do farming on Arab lands). We weren't scared of anything. From the beginning, they were bad people (these kirivs), but they couldn't do anything back then.
>
> (Personal interview, 11 May 2019)

At the societal level, Muslim (both Arab and Kurd) attitudes towards Yezidis seem to always have been distant and occupied with prejudice.

> For religious reasons, they (Sunni Arabs) were not eating Yezidis' yogurt or lamb, they didn't drink their water. If a Yezidi opened a bakery shop,

they would not buy bread from there. If a Yezidi butcher cut an animal's meat, they would not buy that meat … Sunni Kurds of Sinjar were actually Yezidis centuries ago. But they were worse than Arabs. Arabs learned these bad behaviors towards Yezidis from Kurds. They were the ones to tell Arabs not to eat Yezidi food. Some of those Kurds in Sinjar were with the regime, they seized Yezidi lands.

(Personal interview, 23 May 2018)

Up until 2014, Yezidis and their Muslim neighbours practised a tradition where a Muslim/Yezidi adult man would hold a Yezidi/Muslim boy on his lap during his circumcision. These men would become *kirivs* (godfather) to these children and the two families would be considered as bonded by blood. *Kirivs* are responsible for helping the boy and his family whenever they are in need. In many testimonies, Muslim *kirivs* were told to be one of the first to attack Yezidis when the IS seized Sinjar. According to our informants, Yezidis no longer choose their *kirivs* among Muslims. From a functionalist point of view, the institution itself can be considered as a protection mechanism for Yezidi families.

We would become each other's *kirivs*, for cultural reasons but also for reasons related to fear. We were being repressed, and we became *kirivs* so that they don't repress us.

(Personal interview, 23 May 2018)

To sum up, Yezidis' existence in contemporary Iraq (especially in Sinjar) appears as both socially (religiously) and economically marginalized. They were denied land tenure in the collective villages they were forcibly resettled by the regime and their claims for land are still not resolved (UNHABITAT 2015). As they are not considered "People-of-the-book" by the Orthodox Islam, they lacked recognition and religious protection in Iraq. They were for a long time forced to register as either Arab or Kurd on their ID cards. A survey by UNDP in 2006 describes the overall deprivation in Sinjar as "very extreme" with very limited water sources and basic infrastructure and high levels of poverty and illiteracy (UNAMI 2009). Moreover, Yezidis did not only face religious discrimination by Sunni Arabs and Kurds, but several Shia clergies also referred to them as "unbelievers" and "infidels" before 2014.[10] Even Christians were reported to describe Yezidis as "devil-worshippers" (Allison 2001, 37). Nevertheless, it would not be accurate to consider the Yezidi condition as in total isolation. Throughout history, Yezidis engaged in tribal and socio-religious relations with their Kurdish and Arab neighbours. Even though they lacked the power to emerge as an independent political group, they were still part of the political scenery since the foundation of the Iraqi state and they formed diverse alliances with different actors.

Yezidis in the post-2003 order

In the environment of chaos and sectarian violence in Iraq following the fall of the regime in 2003, discriminatory attitudes and discourses against Yezidis came to light once again, turning soon into open violence. In time, there was an increase in the kidnapping and killing of Yezidis in Baghdad, Mosul, and Sinjar. In 2006, al Qaeda was distributing pamphlets calling Muslims to kill Yezidis whom they accused as being infidels. From 2003 to 2014, the Mosul, Ba'aj, and Tal Afar areas, which became a hub for Sunni insurgency (Holocaust Museum 2015), gradually turned into no-go areas for Yezidis.[11] According to a UNAMI report, the Islamic State of Iraq imposed a siege on Sinjar as early as 2006, calling its Yezidi inhabitants unbelievers (UNAMI 2009).

Our respondents interpreted their post-2003 condition as the eruption of deep-seated hatreds against themselves once the dictator who kept everything under his repressive control was gone:

> It has been 20 years it has been this way between Yezidis and Muslims. Since the fall of Saddam, it has been this way.
>
> (Personal interview, 11 May 2019)

As Sunni extremists started targeting Yezidis along with other religious minority groups, the Kurdish government that aimed to increase its control over disputed areas since the beginning of the war, especially over Nineveh and Sinjar, once again declared Yezidi people, hence Sinjar, as being part of Kurdistan. Duhok became the provincial centre of Sinjar in 2006. The Kurdistan Democratic Party (KDP) set up party offices and the peshmerga boosted its presence in Sinjar. For Yezidis who were already isolated from Mosul and the rest of Iraq and who felt threatened by the growing Sunni extremism in the region, welcoming KDP and its investments and services – as well as its relatively secular ideology – stands out as a necessity rather than a deliberate political choice. In 2007, two large trucks carrying explosives were detonated in the Yezidi villages of Siba Sex Xidir and Til Azer. Yezidis consider this massacre, which killed over 300 people and marked the biggest suicide attack in Iraq since 2003, as the 73rd *firman*. The KRG presence in Sinjar became permanent after the attack with several checkpoints established throughout Sinjar.

> Arabs did it (the bombings in 2007). Arabs around us. Why did they do this to us? Because we are Yezidi. The second reason is because we supported KDP. But the main reason is our Yezidiness. These each are a *firman*.
>
> (Personal interview, 26 May 2018)

However, the KDP support for Sinjar was more in the form of creating patronage networks.[12] Anyone who was not registered to the party could not receive any public employment opportunity. Some respondents accused local members of the party of using the funds sent to Sinjar for investment for their own personal use (Personal interview, 30 May 2018). In the meantime, the Sunni tribal leaders in Sinjar seem to develop resentment not only against Kurds who increased their political leverage on the ground but also against Yezidis that they perceived as collaborators of Kurdish parties with Mir Tahsin Beg and the Baba Sheikh declaring their support for the KRG. As a matter of fact, a Yezidi political party called Yezidi Movement for Progress and Reform, which promotes an independent movement and identity, was formed in Sinjar in 2005. However, from 2005 to 2014, it lost its votes to Kurdish parties that probably seemed more convincing for ordinary Yezidis who seek security more than anything else.[13]

While more and more Yezidis joined the peshmerga forces after 2003, others continued to serve in the Iraqi army. There were also those who worked for the US army as interpreters. The income opportunities in working for the armed forces led to improvements in the economic conditions of Sinjari Yezidis in the post-2003 era.[14] Local Arabs, who were already uncomfortable with Yezidis' seeming collaboration with Kurdish parties, appear to feel even more resentment against the changing socioeconomic dynamics. On top of that, Peshmerga makes it harder for Arab tribes to visit villages in Sinjar, which further increases Arab-Yezidi tensions.

> Peshmerga did not let Arabs cross the borders. They made us lots of enemies.
>
> (Dinç 2017, 211)

> Between 2004 and 2014, Yezidis got more political power. Arab leaders I met back then (who did not know that I was Yezidi) used to tell me "How come a Yezidi becomes my mayor?" They could not accept that.
>
> (Personal interview, 5 May 2019)

The August 2014 attacks

> Muslims did not like Yezidis since the beginning, but they could not do anything about it. Now [with the IS attacks] they found the opportunity.
>
> (Personal interview, 30 April 2019)

The Islamic State's genocidal campaign against the Yezidis seem to give local Sunni tribes the opportunity to act on their growing anti-Yezidi feelings. In many cases, foreign fighters of the IS could locate and seize Yezidi villages with the complicity of members of local Arab and Kurdish tribes such as the Tat, Khatuni, Mitewta, Khawatina and Mutaywit. The group began its campaign on Sinjar by attacking the Yezidi villages in the south and south-west, the towns of Gerzerik and Siba Sex Xidir, on the night of 3 August 2014. The attacks continued through the morning with assaults on the villages in the north and the east of Sinjar. Some fighters were from Syria; others were Sunni Turkmen from Tel Afar. According to our own informants and Yezidi accounts in other sources, members of local Muslim tribes who had long been neighbours of Yezidis, including their *kirivs*, joined the IS and preyed on Yezidis.

> Very few of them were foreigners. The rest were the locals of the region. There were few Chechen, Afghan, Algerian and Tunisian but the rest was all from surrounding villages. It was Arabs around us; but Sunnis from Tel Afar and some Kurds from Sinjar were also with them. There were also Kurds from Halabja and Zakho. Kurds from many regions were also with them.
>
> (Personal interview, 26 May 2018)

Looking at the vicious treatment of Yezidis, the role of Salafi-jihadist ideology of IS manifest itself as the decisive factor: when the group seized Mosul in June 2014, one of its first targets was Shia religious sites. It then massacred around 600 Shia prisoners in the Badush prison (Holocaust Museum 2015). Christians in the city were offered three options: they had to convert to Islam, stay as Christians but pay the *jizre* tax, or leave the city. Even though there is reporting about the execution of some Christians (and even the kidnapping of Christian women), IS does not seem to have engaged in a systematic persecution of Christians or to follow a policy of enslavement for Christian women. Shias were usually executed on the spot.[15] Yezidis, on the other hand, had only one option besides execution, which was to convert to Islam.[16] The aftermath of the taking of Yezidi captives was also well coordinated: captives were taken to pre-designated places and they were usually moved from one location to another. Yezidi women were registered and sold on the slave markets according to the regulations put up by the group (UNAMI/OHCRC 2016).

We were telling them "Yezidis also know of God; they are cognizant of Angels". They were saying "That may be true, but you are committing shirk.[17] You don't have a book." We were responding "In truth, we know God better than you do. We do everything in his name." They would say "No" (Personal interview, 26 May 2018).

Obviously, not all Muslim tribes of Sinjar took part in the genocide. Some respondents indicated getting help from their Muslim neighbours, especially from Kurdish families, while fleeing the IS. These neighbours let Yezidis know of the IS advance to give them enough time to get out of Sinjar or run to the mountain. Others brought food and water to those trapped on the mountain or they gave them their own cars to help them escape. Yet still, if peshmerga's retreat from Sinjar just before the attacks, leaving Yezidis defenceless is one reason for the heavy loss in the massacres; the complicity of local Sunni tribes to the terrorist group appears as another.

As stated in other sources, during our field research we also came across several Yezidi narratives where Muslims were telling their Yezidi neighbours "We were waiting for this day, for this opportunity". We heard from different informants the story of a Muslim *kiriv* who had once, after a Yezidi boy's circumcision, held the hand of the Yezidi mother who was giving him back the piece of clothing used during the ceremony before letting her go. Apparently, he recognized the same woman among IS captives and took her by force saying, "I have been waiting for this moment since the time I held your hand on that day". Overall, after the last *firman,* the Yezidi self-perceptions of their communal history as a history of persecutions is clearly reinforced. According to the dominant discourses in our data, the Yezidi genocide was driven primarily by religious motivations. Yezidis are a harmless, peaceful, and disempowered community, yet Muslims would never allow their existence in Iraq and they would persecute Yezidis again as soon as they have the chance.

They are bad people. Yezidis didn't have any support. Since creation, Muslims and Yezidis are each other's enemy.

(Personal interview, 11 May 2019)

Religious coexistence in perilous times?

From orthodox Islam perspectives, Yezidis are a liminal minority lacking a legitimate status. Throughout history, they have been targets of persecution by both local rulers and the Ottoman government. The contemporary Yezidi discourse centres around the notion of religious victimization. However, the historical perspective developed in this chapter complicates this picture and suggests that geopolitical and governance concerns including tax collection, conscription, and security of transportation routes played important roles in anti-Yezidi violence.

Then, does the IS campaign against Yezidis present a novel development without any historical precedent? The IS violence had some unique characteristics as it was exclusively justified on religious grounds (i.e. Yezidis not being People of the Book and their religion lacking any legitimacy). There were no strong non-religious reasons for the IS to engage in mass killing and enslavement of Yezidis, who presented no threat to the growing power of Salafi jihadists by the summer of 2014. Compared to other groups targeted by the IS, only Yezidis were subjected to systematic and sustained sexual violence in large numbers. Several previous campaigns targeting Yezidis before the twentieth century also involved such practices that were justified on religious grounds. Yet, in those campaigns, geopolitical goals and religious motives were more intertwined. For instance, the forced conversion campaign of Omer Wehbi Pasha in 1892–1893 officially aimed to ensure Yezidi's loyalty to the Sultan rather than their physical extermination. It was also abandoned shortly after the news of massacres reached the Ottoman capital. In this regard, the IS represents an aberration in terms of its explicit religious justifications and systematic pursuit of violence against Yezidis. At the same time, same religious sources used by the IS were also utilized in previous episodes of anti-Yezidi violence suggesting a pattern of historical continuity.

What do all these bring in terms of religious coexistence in Iraq involving Yezidis? While the impunity of local tribes who participated in the attacks and the overall insecurity in Sinjar pose challenges for intercommunal reconciliation, as a paradoxical consequence of the genocide, Yezidis increased their visibility and international profile. More willing than ever, Kurdish nationalists attempt to treat Yezidism as the original Kurdish religion. The growing Yezidi diaspora provides reference information to the outside world who knew very little about their religion before 2014 and challenges the discriminatory orthodox Islam perspectives. Displacement from Sinjar and mass immigration surely bring considerable risks for the survival and practice of their religious identity, but their increased visibility and acceptance as a minority group entitled to rights and protection gives hope for the future of intercommunal relations.

Notes

1 The IS engaged in widespread and intentional targeting of civilians. The US-led international coalition operations also resulted in the deaths and displacements of large number of civilians, especially as a result of airstrikes and artillery bombardments of IS held population centres. For a granular documentation of the effects of the coalition attacks in Raqqa, the major city held by the IS, see Amnesty International, "War in Raqqa: Rhetoric versus Reality." https://raqqa.amnesty.org.

2 Five years after the attacks, a majority of the captives were liberated, typically via ransom payments.

3 For instance, the Yezidi Human Rights Organization chronologically lists 33 of the 72 *firmans* in Yezidi history on their website (from 637 to 1914): www.yezidihuman-rights.org/yezidi-genocide.php.

4 Yezidi oral traditions provide some insights into the complicated dynamics of Yezidi–Muslim relations. For instance, a well-known *stran* is about Silemane Miste, a Kurdish bandit from the tribe of Doski, who killed a Western missionary in Duhok in the 1950s. It "opens with a wish that God should destroy the house of the missionary who was trying to harm Islam" (Allison 2001, 45).

5 For example, the Shiite Babawat group visits the Yezidi Hababat tribe in Balad, offering gifts to the sacred image of Melek Tawus. According to (Fuccaro 1999, 53), they also attended Yezidi religious event.

6 Yezidis are thought to have two sacred books whose origins go back to the times of Sheik Adi and his follower Sheik Hasan. However, these books, whose original copies are perceived to be lost, play a role in neither the transmission of Yezidi religion nor its practice.

7 The Habbabat tribe, which converted to Islam after the Hafiz Pasha attack, returned to Yezidism by the 1850s (Fuccaro 1999, 16).

8 For details of the violent campaign, see Gölbaşı 2009, 117–126 and 129–130. Parry also talks about the ambush of the Ottoman expedition in Sinjar and slaying of 500 Yezidis and enslavement of their women and girls in Sheikhan area (1895, 253–254, 257–258).

9 While these claims remain mythical, some Yezidi traditions refer to Yazid ibn Mu'awiya, the second Umayyad caliph, son of Mu'awiya I, in reverence and as a divine being (Kreyenbroek 1995, 27).

10 www.youtube.com/watch?v=6xGe-b8dXD4

11 Yezidis began to travel to Kurdish cities instead of Mosul to get medical help (UNAMI, 2009).

12 According to the ICG 2009 Report, compared to Sinjar, KDP engages in bigger investments in Sheikhan area where Yezidi religious and political leaders reside.

13 The Kurdish Alliance had 60 per cent of the votes in Sinjar in the 2005 Provincial elections while the Yezidi Movement for Progress and Reform got 20 per cent of the votes. In 2009, the Kurdish parties' alliance scored 77 per cent of the votes whereas Yezidi parties' vote share dropped to 6 per cent (UNAMI 2009).

14 During the interviews, many respondents told us about the nice houses Yezidis were constructing in their villages.

15 There is a need for further investigation on the number and treatment of enslaved Shia women of Tel Afar. The question of whether the IS treatment of Shias constitute genocide is also still not properly answered.

16 In some cases, those who accepted conversion were also executed (Otten 2017).

17 In Islam, the concept of "shirk" refers to the sin of associating partners to God, usually in the form of attributing divine powers to a subject or to religious scholars. Those who are believed to commit the sin are considered "polytheist."

References

Allison, C. *The Yezidi Oral Tradition in Iraqi Kurdistan*. Richmond: Curzon Press, 2001.

Alsancakli, S. "Matrimonial Alliances and the Transmission of Dynastic Power in Kurdistan: The Case of the Diyadinids of Bidlis in the Fifteenth to Seventeenth Centuries." *Eurasian Studies* 15, no. 2 (2017): 222–249.

Deringil, S. *The Well-Protected Domains: Ideology and the Legitimation of Power in the Ottoman Empire, 1876–1909*. London: Tauris Academic Studies, 1998.

Dinç, N.K. *Ezidilerin 73. Fermanı: ŞengalSoykırımı*. İstanbul: Zan Vakfı, 2017.

Erdem, Y. *Slavery in the Ottoman Empire and its Demise: 1800–1909.* New York: Springer, 1996.

Forbes, F. "A Visit to the Sinjar Hills in 1838, with Some Account of the Sect of Yezidis, and of Various Places in the Mesopotamian Desert, between the Rivers Tigris and Khabur." *Journal of the Royal Geographical Society of London,* 1839.

Fuccaro, N. *The Other Kurds: Yazidis in Colonial Iraq.* London: IB Tauris, 1999.

Gökçen, A. *Osmanlı ve İngiliz Arşiv Belgelerinde Yezidiler.* Istanbul: Bilgi University, 2012.

Gölbaşı, E. "Heretik' Aşiretlerve II." *Abdülhamid Rejimi: Zorunlu Askerlik Meselesive İhtida Siyaseti Odağında Yezidiler ve Osmanlı İdaresi. Tarih ve Toplum* 9 (2009): 87–156.

Gölbaşı, E.. "Turning the 'Heretics' into Loyal Muslim Subjects: Imperial Anxieties, the Politics of Religious Conversion, and the Yezidis in the H Amidian Era." *The Muslim World* 103, no. 1 (2013): 3–23.

Guest, J.S. *Survival among the Kurds: A History of the Yezidis.* London: Routledge, 1993.

Kreyenbroek, P.G. *Yezidism–Its Background, Observances, and Textual Tradition.* New York: Edwin Mellen Press, 1995.

Layard, A.H. *Nineveh and Its Remains: With an Account of a Visit to the Chaldean Christians of Kurdistan, and the Yesidis, or Devil Worshippers; and an Inquiry into the Manners and Arts of the Ancient Assyrians.* London: A. and W. Galignani and Company, Baudry's European Library, 1850.

Longrigg, S.H. *Four Centuries of Modern Iraq.* Oxford: Clarendon Press, 1925.

Nations, League. *Question of the Frontier Between Turkey and Iraq.* Geneva: Published by League of Nations, 1925.

Otten, C. *With Ash on Their Faces: Yezidi Women and the Islamic State.* New York: OR Books, 2017.

Report, Holocaust Museum Bearing Witness. *Our Generation Is Gone: The Islamic State's Targeting of Iraqi Minorities in Ninewa,* 2015.

UNAMI. *District Analysis Summary. Sinjar District and Qahtaniya Sub-District,* Baghdad: UNAMI (United Nations Assistance Mission for Iraq), 2009.

UNAMI/OHCHR. *A Call for Accountability and Protection: Yezidi Survivors of Atrocities Committed by ISIL,* Baghdad: UNAMI (United Nations Assistance Mission for Iraq), 2016.

UNHABITAT. *Emerging Land Tenure Issues Among Displaced Yazidis from Sinjar, Iraq,* 2015.

14 The state and its margins

Changing notions of marginality in Turkey

Anita Sengupta

Nazan Ustundag in an article entitled "Praise for the Marginal Groups" reasoned that Gezi Park became a revolt against marginalization. He argued that the 50 per cent vote that the AKP administration received in the elections advanced a new phase, the 100-year-old "marginalize the ones who do not resemble you" in Turkey.[1] Therefore, precisely because the AKP aimed at marginalizing each and every one of the 50 per cent of Turkey that did not resemble its constituents, they revolted against it on grounds of Gezi Park.

> All the groups labelled as "marginal" by the city governor and the prime minister is legal. Most of these groups are, in fact, leftists and revolutionary organizations. And precisely because they routinely come under attack by the state, harassed in their assemblies and protests, taken into detention without charge and choked by gas despite being legal and legitimate social organizations, they know state violence well and know even better how to resist it. Those groups labelled as "marginal" have always carried their flags and banners through which they claimed their existence in the squares of Turkey. For example, the Kurdish "Yurtsever" youth have always carried and still carry the banners of Abdullah Ocalan, their choice of a leader, demanding his liberation. Another example is the anarchists who carry a black flag and struggle for a society without the imposition of a state ... Although they all operate on legal grounds and subsequently partake in the formation named as the "Taksim Solidarity Platform" they have been continuously, systematically, and in every space imaginable, rendered as convicts of a grey place. Because they struggle, in this grey space in social life, whereby the line between legality and illegality is being blurred by state violence itself, the conventional adjective that comes to mind to label them in Turkey is indeed no other than "marginal."[2]

According to Ustundag, groups identified as marginal in Istanbul and elsewhere mainly hailed from the secular and liberal middle class. However, religious conservatives, the AKP's main voter base, were equally uneasy with the events and with state responses. The government lost ground with both religious communities like the Gulen who had traditionally been their main ally against the Kemalist state establishment as well as the more secular conservatives due to imposition of new restrictions like the one on the consumption of alcohol. Faced with an outpouring of criticism in the aftermath of the imposition, President Erdogan retorted "go and drink at home", suggesting that there is no place in the public space for those who have preferences other than those prescribed by the government.

New definitions of the "margin" have therefore been created with state recognition of a sharp differentiation between supporters of the AKP and those who have opposed its policies in the course of the recent protests throughout Turkey. A number of writings in the immediate post Gezi Park period stressed that what the protesters wanted was a guarantee that the Turkish government would respect differences among its citizens and there would be no AKP-inspired behavioural norms imposed on Turkish citizens. President Erdogan claims to govern for 50 per cent of the population who have repeatedly voted for the party thereby marginalizing the rest who have been frustrated about the government's stand on issues ranging from property development and media rights to the role of religion and access to alcohol, all of which is viewed as attempts to impose conservative values on a secular society. Being "marginal" has thereby acquired political overtones that define belonging in terms of ideological convergence. This therefore is also a heterogeneous "margin" that would be subject to change depending on electoral performance. As the definition of the "margin" is transformed in Turkey, this chapter will be an attempt to examine how the Turkish state continues to exclude certain groups from its definition of who constitutes its "relevant" citizen and thereby creates new notions of marginality. The chapter begins by looking into the more cosmopolitan experience of Ottomanism that is gradually transformed as "boundaries" are created in Republican Turkey.³

Cosmopolitan Ottomanism

The Ottomans created a strong state where political power was centralized in the hands of the Sultan. The Ottoman Empire was a cosmopolitan, multi-ethnic, multi religious society in which non-Muslim communities – Greeks, Armenians, and Jews – played very important economic and administrative roles but were not permitted to exercise political power. Power was centralized in the hands of the Sultan and a small clique totally loyal to him and the state intervened in order to exploit all sectors of society without favouring anyone of them. Consequently, the social and economic sectors tended to remain stable and stagnant since no sector of the economy, agrarian, commercial, or industrial, was permitted to become dominant and upset the balance. However, with the expansion of the world economy the Ottomans had to adjust to trends outside their control. Anachronistic political and socio-economic structures led to what is described as Ottoman decline vis-à-vis Europe. The "decline of the Ottoman state" was followed by the emergence of a new state. The French Revolution led to further changes and underlined the need for institutional reforms. The most significant among them was the replacement of the Janissaries by a new style army and the creation of a new bureaucratic class. This class though loyal to the Ottoman dynasty possessed a higher sense of loyalty to the state and launched a programme of reform and reorganization known as *Tanzimat*. The state that began to take shape after the

Gulhane reforms of 1839 was different. It began to move away from patrimony and its interventions were selective.

Although the founders of the Ottoman Empire had consisted of tribal groups, merchant craftsmen and Sufis, mostly Turkish in origin, the state did not display conscious awareness of its ethnicity. Eventually, the Empire also included several major ethnic communities among them Greeks, Serbians, Bulgarians, and Arabs and a collective myth of common ancestry, historical memories of statehood, and elements of common culture, an idea of a specific homeland and a sense of group solidarity developed. The Turkic groups of Kazan, Crimea, and Azerbaijan likewise constituted ethnic communities not very different from those of the non-Turks in the Ottoman Empire. The Muslims of Russia subsequently played an important role in defining the developing ethno-national identity and nationalist ideology of the Ottoman Turks, just as they, in turn, were profoundly influenced by the modernization movement and the education system of the Ottoman Empire. In fact, Kemal Karpat argues that the concept of some sort of Muslim union emerged mainly as a reaction to Russia's occupation of Central Asia.[4]

The imperial Ottoman system, therefore, had been open to outsiders and had refashioned multi-linguistic and multi-religious populations into Ottomanist provincial societies during the last centuries of the Ottoman Empire. Under the Ottoman Empire, nationalities were defined in terms of religious affiliation rather than ethnicity. Diverse peoples of Turkic, Lazi, Kurdish, Greek, and Armenian backgrounds came to form an entirely new kind of society as they participated in Ottoman military and religious institutions. It was only in the late nineteenth and early twentieth centuries when the non-Muslims as well as non-Turkish Muslims began clamouring for independence and the Ottoman Empire became a hotbed of nationalist uprisings, that the notion of Turkishness assumed political relevance. The transformation of various groups who constituted the Ottoman world into ethno-national communities developed through different stages of development among the Turkic groups themselves and finally culminated in the emergence of "Turkishness" and Turkism in the Ottoman Empire.

The linear reduction of the Ottoman multi-lingual, multi-ethnic and multi-religious society into a secular "Turkic people" has now been brought into question. Recent historiography has modified this view by tracing institutional, economic, and educational continuities between the late Ottoman and early Republican periods. There have also been attempts to explain the resurgence of Islamic populism in late twentieth century Turkey by tracing its roots to identity formation in the nineteenth century.[5] In the course of his study of the transformation of the Ottoman state in the nineteenth century, Karpat challenges the dominant narrative of Turkish history that draws a clear distinction between religious forms of identity and the modern secular national identity that developed in the Republican era. Karpat argues that the nineteenth century saw the secularization of religious identity in ways that allowed for the clear marriage between Islam and Turkish nationalism. He emphasizes that in the classical Ottoman state ethnic identity coincided with religious identity among both Muslims and Christians and in the age of modernity the blend of faith and ethnicity and the change in the order of their priority gave each major ethnic group in the Ottoman state its specific "national" characteristics. The emergence of the Turks as an ethnic community (and eventually as a nation) was the consequence both of the blend of faith and ethnicity and also of the drive towards modernity.

Further, both the Ottoman state and the Ottoman landed middle classes created a modern public space that allowed for the dissemination of a kind of Islamic "populism" distinctly different from the kind of religious practice that had existed in the preceding century. Rather than relegate religion to the sphere of private life Ottomans, rulers and the public chose to politicize Islam, marrying it to ethnic identity. The opening up of Islamic societies to Western capitalism led to the rise of a landed middle class that espoused a form of revivalist and populist Islam inimical to Western/Russian expansion. These revivalist movements were open to indigenous forms of political reform and particularly adept at mobilizing at the grass roots level. In the Ottoman case the state was able to co-opt the populist impulse and harness it to its own needs. Here, the rise of the new middle class, as a result of the rise of capitalism and market forces, institutional and educational reforms, the expansion of communication networks, and the almost continuous threat to the survival of the state, created an alliance between the middle classes and the state bureaucrats. The policy of co-optation culminated in the Hamidian period with progressive secularization of religion as a category of thought and identity. Ottoman intellectuals and bureaucrats recast religion as a "civilization" and turned Islam into an instrument of foreign policy under the guise of Pan Islamism.

Karpat argues that the genesis of Turkish nationalism was a multifaceted process occurring in several stages of identity accretion proceeding from universal Ottomanism and Islamism to specific ethnic Turkishness and Turkism. The modernization process undertaken by the state coupled with Ottoman territorial losses to Europe and Russia disrupted the lives of Muslims and was the catalyst for the development of new identities. The reforming Sultans of the nineteenth century introduced the notion of allegiance to a territorial state independent of loyalty to the house of Osman. The tension between what Karpat vaguely describes as the "community nation" that owed allegiance to a universal Islamic umma and the notion of territorial state remained unresolved for much of the Hamidian era. Abdul Hamid's pan Islamic and populist policy succeeded only partially in resolving this tension for his subjects. Karpat argues that the Ottoman losses to Europe and Russia brought a large and mostly educated community of Caucasians, Turks, and Muslim Slavs to the capital and Anatolian cities. These groups played a large part in the articulation of Turkish and Ottoman identity. The Russian Turks were the precursors of the ethnic nationalism of Ziya Gokalp but their legacy was only evident after the Young Turk revolution of 1908. Their victory in shaping the Turkishness of Ottoman identity was not inevitable as it was highly contested. During the last decades of the nineteenth century, Ottomanism played a much larger role in defining the identity of the subjects of the Empire than ethnic Turkishness. Muslims from the Balkans played an important part in articulating "Ottomaness," a belief in equal citizenship for all, in constitutional rights and an allegiance to the Ottoman state. Under Abdul Hamid's rule, the Ottomanists and the Constitutionalists went into exile. After heavy losses in the Balkans Abdul Hamid was not averse to encouraging a kind of Ottomanism defined by Islam rather than constitutional rights, with Turkish Anatolians and Arabs as its main proponents.

A variety of economic, cultural, and social forces, both domestic and international, forced the traditional Ottoman corporatist states, first to create a common Ottoman political identity for all its citizens, regardless of faith and language, and then to realign itself religiously, culturally and politically with the most numerous of these citizens, the Muslims. This process of "Ottomanization" sought to remould all existing ancient identities, well preserved under the old system, into something new, which could be referred to as "re-Islamization" "Turkification," "Arabization" or the like, which involved a cultural and political transformation and identity change without parallel in earlier Islamic history. This transformation was a result of change, class differentiation, education, the discovery of ethno-regional history, and so on and of geographical factors that produced a certain homogenization at one level and promoted diversity and differentiation at another.

For the Ottomans, the encounter with modernity was one where the state already existed as did its bureaucracy and social organization. It was a multi-ethnic and multi-religious state with a long tradition in state craft and assimilation. Nationalism for such a state structure would mean disintegration and loss of power. The primary concern of the elite was therefore an answer as to how to save this state structure from the military and ideological threats emanating from Europe. Three solutions were suggested; Ottomanism, Islamism, and Turkish nationalism. Ottomanism sought to unite different ethnic and religious groups under one political structure. Islamism was suggested as a tool for integration for the Muslim population, with the breakaway of the non-Muslims in the Balkans. Turkish nationalism was suggested as the last solution in case the non-Turkish constituents of the Empire also broke off. However, the modernizing elite itself was not a uniform group. Debates within the Young Turk movement, identified as the focal context in which the early conception of Turkish nationalism was developed, show a significant distinction between Tatar migrants and the indigenous Ottoman intelligentsia. The former was more ethnically oriented while the latter were more concerned with the future of the state rather than the nation.[6] There was also a distinction between the elites of the periphery (*tasrali*) and those of the centre (*Istanbullu*). The elites at the periphery were more apt to stress populist policies and ideas, which in turn create a more suitable framework for the development of nationalist ideas. On the other hand, the elites at the centre were more concerned about the preservation of existing power structures. Cevdet Yilmaz and Mustafa Sahin argue that the Ottoman experience shows a combination of these two types of state and stateless elites. The first group favoured a civic, though elitist and statist conception of nationality whereas the second group placed more emphasis on ethnicity and descent from a common ancestor.[7]

Boundaries

A plethora of debates exists on the viability of the Kemalist project, that focus on how the transformation of the traditional Ottoman cosmopolitan ethos in the course of a project of creating a "modern" Turkey lead to denial of diversity within the state and subsequent attempts at neutralizing heterogeneity. Critical rethinking of this project of modernity in recent times has sought to come to terms with the cultural plurality of a society that had traditionally imbibed within itself varied groups with multiple religious and ethnic identities. Sponsored by a government whose own "Islamic" background remains an anathema to the Kemalists, it has brought to the forefront policies of assimilation that fell short of transforming a majority of Kurds into "Turks." It has been suggested that just as the first modernizers of the Ottoman Empire, the *Tanzimat* reformers, attempted to forestall the collapse of the state by incorporating Christian minorities as equal citizens the AKP government is planning an "opening" that seeks to bring to an end the Kurdish question by setting the stage for the assertion of societal auton-omy.[8] It has been noted that the conflict between the "old Turkey" represented by the Kemalist establishment and the "new Turkey" represented by civil society has to be resolved through the establishment of a more inclusive social contract that addresses the cultural diversity of Turkish society. Here, it has been argued that a neo-Ottoman ethos would be more pluralistic and cosmopolitan. It is undeniable that compared to the Ottoman system Kemalism was essentially exclusivist and attempted to create a uniform Turkish citizen, which resulted in the denial of Turkey's "true" cosmopolitan identity.

In fact, it was the creation of a "Turkish" identity and the non-recognition or "denial" of the existence of other communities/identities along with a denial of the "pre-modern"/Ottoman past of Turkey that led to the creation of the "other" within society. This is reflected in its policies towards its minorities fallout of which has been what is now identified the Kurdish question or *Kurt Sorunu*. The Kemalist modernity project was oriented towards a particular vision of a "modern" Turkish state, which had attempted the transformation of a multicul-tural multilingual society into a nation "happy to call itself Turkish." The aim of "Turkish" modernity was to create a Turkey that conformed to the principles of "advanced civilization" where attachment to "traditional" issues like religios-ity and ethnicity were perceived as irrational. The attempt was to transcend the monarchical and imperial structures of the Ottoman society and replace them with rational bureaucratic institutions under the rule of law within a nation-state. However, it has been argued, the insistence on modernization proved to be an ideological handicap both from a conceptual as well as a pragmatic point of view. And one of the fallouts of this has been the Kurdish issue. Similarly, the dis-satisfaction of the Alawite minority appears as a potential cause for crisis. The inability of the state to recognize the Alawites as a separate group within the state has led to the comment that the Turkish "Model" has not matured over the years.[9]

The period between 1919 and 1923 witnessed the first formulations of defini-tive boundary producing discourses of Turkish political life, such as the supreme political objective of political unity based on territorial integrity, the Muslim majority as an organic totality, terms of ethnic and religious differentiation, the unity-disruptive minority rights, threats to national security and the cultural and political meanings of Turkishness in foreign policy texts of the nationalist govern-ment. Ahmet Icduygu and Ozlem Kasygusuz argue that these discourses shaped the formation of the domestic public sphere and featured a new citizenship identity different from the Imperial model of membership and political community.[10] Subsequent debates on identity within the Republic often echoed these early conceptualizations about the nature of the state and its political culture. The question "who is a Turk?" involved both official identification in terms of all inhabitants of Turkey but also self-identification of groups who claimed a separate national community. Turkish "nationalism" emerged in an era of political disaster for the Empire that increased perceptions of vulnerability among the Turkish-Muslim community particularly since it was accompanied by mass scale violence and deportations of people to Anatolia. It has been argued, that as a result three overlapping but inexact categories of "Turkishness" were identified. The first was territorial, and the most inclusive. The second was religious and embedded in the *millet* system. The third and most non-inclusive was ethno-religious.[11] The debate on what constitutes "Turkishness" continues and has, in fact, assumed significance in recent times with an attempt to reconnect both within the Ottoman realm as well as with historical roots in Central Asia.

With the declaration of the Republic the newly born state took an increasingly modernist and secularist character, which was accompanied by a series of social and political reforms. This process included a redefinition of the national identity with an emphasis on territoriality rather than religion. For the founders of the Turkish Republic the European and in particular the French experience of the past century was central to their project. The 1924 Constitution defined a "Turk" as anyone living within the boundaries of Turkey and attached to Turkey by bonds of citizenship. Legally, the state would be indifferent to a citizen's religious or ethnic identity. Yet, from the very beginning it was clear that in practice matters would evolve differently. The indication of this divergence appeared during the assembly debates on citizenship when a member of the Assembly remarked with striking frankness that the legal definition was fine, but the "real" citizens of Turkey were the Hanafi Muslims who spoke Turkish. Such a definition risked leaving out not only the Kurds, who did not speak any Turkish and belonged to the Shafi branch of Sunni Islam, outside the definition of "real" citizenship in the new Turkish republic but also Arabs and Alevis who constitute the second largest religious community in Turkey. The portrayal of Kurds as an ethnic community with the right to self-rule changed in 1924 when a new Constitution replaced the 1921 Constitution. Article 88 of the 1924 Constitution states

> The people of Turkey regardless of their religion and race would, in terms of citizenship, be called Turkish.[12]

As Mesut Yegen notes, a first reading of this text seems to suggest that "Turkishness" designed by Turkish citizenship is defined in political terms. It refers also to those who do not have a Turkish ethnic origin yet reside on Turkish territory.[13] This has prompted the position that Turkish citizenship has nothing to do with real or assumed ethnic descent and that it is expansionist and inclusive rather than exclusivist and differentialist. However, Yegen argues that the wording itself indicates that there is a more authentic Turkishness considered by the state, which is not based just on citizenship but on ethnic terms. While the 1924 Constitution still recognized the existence of various ethnic groups in Turkey, it also stated that no special rights of any kind would be granted to these communities. This was spelled out in the new Constitution and continues to be a matter of debate even today.

> Our state is a nation state. It is not a multi-national state. The state does not recognize any nation other than the Turks. There are other people who come from different races (ethnic groups) and who should have equal rights within the country. Yet it is not possible to give rights to these people according to their racial (ethnic) status.[14]

While a number of groups who could not be confined within the official definition of "Turk" were affected by the changes, the case of the Alevis continue to be problematic. Sufism has played a significant role in the history of Islam and in Turkey the Nakshbandis, the Mevlevis and the Alevi-Bektashi developed close relations with the state at various times. Though the vast majority of the Alevis are ethnic and linguistic Turks Alevi' is a blanket term for a large number of different heterodox communities whose actual beliefs and rituals differ significantly. Linguistically, four groups may be distinguished and about 20 per cent of them are ethnic Kurds. In the late Ottoman times Bektashism became synonymous with non-conformism in religious matters.[15] During the nineteenth century after the collapse of the Janissaries the non-conformist Bektashis became free thinkers and in the twentieth century was progressive.

As discussions concerning the question of Turkish nationality intensified at the beginning of the twentieth century, the Young Turks turned to the Alevi-Bektashis for support. Their stress on Turkish identity appealed to the new ideological currents. Many of them saw modern nationalism under Kemal as a chance for better relationships between themselves and the state authorities. The prohibition against all *tarikats*, including those of the Bektashis therefore marked a setback. By tradition, common people had been more closely attached to the Sufi *tarikats* than to the *ulema*. The secularizing reforms, in the fields of law and education through which the power of the *ulema* was reduced, therefore, did not concern ordinary people too much. Changes carried out with the aim of secularizing the state did not arouse strong feelings among the masses. It was different with the reforms aiming to secularize daily life. Prohibition of the *tarikats* and closing of the *tekkes* (lodges) and *turbes* (shrines of saints) meant that places of popular worship were closed, and this caused resentment. For most of the people loyalty to the nation did not prevent strong religious feeling. However, as modernization progressed the contradiction between republicanism and Islam posed questions which itself led to a new phase of development in the relationship between popular Islam and official secularism. At the time of the establishment of the Turkish Republic in 1923 and the implementation of its secular reforms, the Alevis welcomed the formation of the new state and supported the Ataturk's leadership in the hope that with the new state would come new acceptance of the Alevis and greater roles for them within society. During the first great Kurdish rebellion in 1925, which had a strong religious colouring, Kurdish Alevi tribes actually fought against the rebels. Many Kurdish Alevis voluntarily assimilated to Turkish culture and came to identify themselves as Turks rather than Kurds.

The Alevis' gradual integration into the wider society – migration to towns, education, careers in public service – brought them into closer contact and sometimes direct competition with strict Sunnis, from whom they had remained socially separated for centuries. This caused growing tensions, which was exacerbated during the political polarization that began in the 1970s. The radical left, defining the Alevi rebellions of the past as proto-communist movements, considered the Alevis as its natural allies. The extreme right, on the other hand, concentrated their recruitment efforts on the conservative Sunni Muslims of mixed regions by fanning their fear of the Alevis and provoking violent incidents. This was followed by a series of Sunni-Alevi clashes resulting in increasing alienation of Turkey's Alevis from the state. The military takeover of 1980 claimed that the aim of the takeover was to reverse the divisive trends and political violence in Turkey. The military actively fostered a version of Sunni Islam. This became a major factor contributing to Alevi revival.

When in 1989 the ban on associations was somewhat relaxed, Alevi voluntary associations emerged. Under the sponsorship of these associations, Alevi rituals were publicly performed and houses of worship were opened. There was a sudden wave of publications by Alevi intellectuals seeking to explain Alevi history and doctrine. These developments marked an important departure in the nature of Alevism, the transition from a secret, initiatory, locally anchored, and orally transmitted religion to a public religion with formalized doctrine and ritual. This revival received encouragement from secular elements in the political establishment who considered the Alevis as their natural allies against the rise of political Islam. The growing influence of the PKK among Turkey's Kurds by the late 1980s increasingly also among the Alevi Kurds, gave the authorities another incentive to allow and even stimulate the development of Alevism as an alternative "ethnic" identity. In the 1990s the state began to publicly support Alevism by sponsoring the annual festival commemorating the Alevi saint Haji-Bektash. Many Alevis were happy with the degree of cooptation within the political establishment and there was an attempt to transform Haji Bektash into a symbol for loyalty to the Turkish state. However, there remained sections of the authority who were suspicious of the Alevis because of their previous inclination towards left-wing politics. The events in Sivas and the clashes between the police and Alevi demonstrators in the Gazi neighbourhood of Istanbul in March 1995, radicalized the Alevi revival and showed the rift between the government and the community. It also demonstrated the deep-rooted divisions within Turkish society.[16]

The emergence of a new margin

Events in Turkey unfolded when a call went out on 28 May 2013 for people to defend the Taksim Gezi Park against bulldozers that had appeared overnight to uproot trees as a first step towards replacing the park with a reconstruction of the historic Taksim Military Barracks demolished in 1940. The initial alert came from Taksim Solidarity, an umbrella platform that had been organized to spearhead movements against urban transformation projects that characterize the ruling AKP's (*Adalet ve Kalkinma Partisi* or Justice and Development Party) urban policy. This included environmentally destructive infrastructural projects like the third Bosporus Bridge and the Istanbul Canal and the privatization of formerly public spaces like the Gezi Park. What began with a small group of people keeping watch over the trees rapidly grew into round-the-clock occupation of the park with the number of people increasing every day. When police used tear-gas and water cannons on the occupants and set up barricades to keep them out, there was a wave of protest that was replicated in 67 cities from Ankara to Izmir, Adana and Hatay.

The makeup and content of the protests varied widely from city to city with different slogans and symbols. The millions of people who joined in the movement were, however, united by two broad concerns; a sense of frustration with the then prime minister and present Turkish President Recep Tayyip Erdogan and his party's approach to governance on a range of issues and anger at the violent response of the police and failure of mainstream Turkish media to cover it. The protests involved the participation of people from every ideological position in Turkish politics except for the supporters of the AKP themselves. The majority were middle class and secular, but the participation of working-class people, practising Muslims, and ethnic and religious minorities belies any attempt to characterize this movement as "being organized by extremist elements" and lacking public support as claimed by Erdogan. The positions and goals of the people participating in the demonstrations were diverse and sometimes incompatible, but the common spirit of resistance was undeniable. The significance of the movement to "take back" the public space, the alignment of dissent, and the slogans built around the threatened trees were extensively debated in the social media.

It is difficult to predict the impact of the events various ongoing political processes. The March 2014 local elections, following the Gezi Protests of 2013, in fact gave the AKP around 45 per cent of the votes, up from the 39 per cent that the AKP received in the last local elections in 2009, indicating a huge victory for Erdogan. This has been interpreted to mean that Erdogan's policies and response to the popular unrest has not had an impact on the voting pattern and a number of reasons have been cited for this.[17] Experts therefore noted that comparison of the Gezi Park protests with the Arab Spring was wrong as Erdogan is a democratically elected leader. However, they also argued that Erdogan's understanding of democracy seemed to be restricted to the ballot box.

> He thinks that by getting 50% of the votes in the last election, he can act as he wants to. But there are still 50% who did not elect him. This section of the Turkish society demands to be heard.[18]

Most people who commented on the character of the movement stressed the fact that the movement was very heterogeneous. It has also been stressed that the groups who gathered in Taksim and elsewhere were pressing for different demands. Many were protesting against the style of governance, others found Turkey's staunch Kemalist identity to have diminished, there were environmentalist groups seeking protection of plants and trees against urbanization, also included were groups aiming to get more labour rights from the country's expanding holding companies and corporations.

Erdogan, however, argued that the unrest was not reflective of the legitimate grievances of the Turks:

> The protests were nothing more than the minority's attempt to dominate the majority ... We could not have allowed this, and we will not allow it.[19]

Erdogan described the protestors as looters, a small minority of marginal characters and extremists while seriously undermining the number of people involved.[20] In fact, a neologism *chapulling* was introduced into Turkish political lexicon when the Erdogan referred to the demonstrators at the Gezi Park and elsewhere as *chapulcu*. He emphasized

> We cannot watch some capulcu inciting our people ... Yes, we will also build a mosque. I do not need permission for this; neither from the head of the Republican Peoples' Party (CHP) nor from a few *chapulcu*. I got permission from the fifty percent of the citizens who elected us as the governing party.[21]

The term, which in Turkish means looters, was later appropriated by the protestors to mean fighting for your rights. However, the events did not mark a turning point in domestic politics. Noteworthy as the demonstrators were for their resilience, Erdogan had a point when he said, "I would gather 200,000 where they gather 20 and where they gather 100,000, I would gather 1 million party supporters".[22] The protests have had deeper implications that cannot be washed away by crude headcounts. This celebration of the majority has been matched by those who have indicated clearly that 'democracy is not just what the majority wants. It is also about what the minority wants. Democracy is not just about elections'.[23]

While there have been attempts at a democratic opening certain actions of the government have been problematic. Among them is the naming of the proposed third bridge over the Bosporus in Istanbul after Yavuz Sultan Selim, an Ottoman Sultan. Some of Turkey's Alevis claim that the Sultan was responsible for the brutal massacre of the Alevis in the early part of the sixteenth century. Historians, however, dispute these claims saying that many killings happened on both sides as a result of the war between Persians and Turks at the time. The spirit of Sultan Selim "the Grim" reverberated from foreign policy into domestic politics. Naming the prospective third Bosphorous Bridge after the Sultan was a message not only to the Alevis but also to Iran and Syria. Even though Erdogan keeps repeating that "we should cast out those fermenting sectarianism" naming the bridge after Selim fuelled the anger of the Alevis, already irked by the way that Turkey had intervened in Syria. The Alevi wound had been previously reopened amid a series of incidents such as the marking of Alevi homes in Adiyaman, Izmir, and Gaziantep and wall graffiti in Erzincan threatening to "burn all infidel Alevis". Istanbul's Alevi majority Gazi neighbourhood was already in a state of low intensity revolt on 14 June 2013, when Erdogan rubbed salt in the wound. In a speech at a party function he said that the 11 May bombings in Reyhanli had "martyred 53 Sunni citizens of ours" – the first time that the Sunni majority had been highlighted.

Similarly, the decision of the government to implement urban transformation through sudden top-down decisions that do not sufficiently account for environmental protection or consultation with citizens has been criticized as making the emergence of a consensus on the pace and nature of economic development difficult. The period of economic growth following the 2002 general elections led to major advances in Turkey's public services and infrastructure including airports, roads and highways, high speed railroads, utilities, hospitals, universities, and museums. In parallel, the vast process of urban transformation and renewal has taken place in many Turkish cities. Boosted by economic success and unchallenged political predominance the AKP government launched a number of initiatives the most emblematic of which were in or around Istanbul. Some were presented as indispensable for Turkey's economic growth like the third bridge over the Bosphorus and a third airport for Istanbul. In undertaking these mega projects, the government would not only have to take note of issues of sustainable development but also address legal considerations. This urban transformation was criticized both for the excessive centralization of the decision-making and the lack of consultation with citizens before projects were started.[24] In a number of instances there have been substantial amendments to legislative, regulatory, and administrative frameworks for these projects. Attempts by civil societies to introduce local consultation mechanisms for urban transformation projects have been overlooked.

It is not surprising that the issue of urban transformation has morphed into a nationwide political problem in Turkey. It is now the symbol of the country's disputed style of democratic management. The Taksim renovation project has become the symbol of the AKP's majoritarian concept of democracy. As Prime Minister Erdogan pointed out on 7 June 2013:

> We have said that we are going to demolish the AKM (the Ataturk Cultural Centre) on Taksim Square and build a huge opera house there. Participants of this vandalism immediately responded, "we won't let you demolish it". Excuse me, but we made this decision before elections and the majority of the people said "yes" for us in the elections. People supported us because they supported these projects.[25]

These statements have posed fundamental questions about the nature of democracy put forward by the AKP in terms of the ways in which the opinions, beliefs, and lifestyles of half of the population who did not vote for the AKP have been disregarded.

Conclusions: In the aftermath of Gezi

Much like Gezi, which was essentially a spontaneous gathering challenging state control of public and private space, the 450 kilometres "Justice March" from

Ankara to Istanbul in 2017 mobilized people from different backgrounds and political affiliations. Led by a quest for "Justice," its aim was to infuse a sense of confidence in the opposition rather than anticipate a halt to the slide to authoritarianism. In Turkey, the post Gezi years have seen indiscriminate nationwide arrests particularly since the failed June 2016 coup, the removal of 1,100 academics for signing a petition to cease armed conflict in Kurdish-dominated areas, state control of media houses, intolerance of any voices of dissent and most significantly a future where executive, legislative, and judicial power will be concentrated in a single authoritarian hand. While the immediate catalyst for the march was the arrest of Republican Peoples Party (CHP) MP Enis Berberoglu and his indictment for 25 years the basic drivers for the march and its success was a due to a combination of the above-mentioned factors. The probability of a transformation of the Turkish political landscape as an upshot of the march reflects expectations that similar mass movements in the region had anticipated. It is nearly nine years since the self-immolation of a street vendor in Tunisia initiated a revolutionary year that saw protestors voice their complaints against inequality, injustice, and a lack of dignity. However, apart from Tunisia, a reversal of the democratic trend soon became evident in the other states and the basic issues that had led to the first spurt of protests were never addressed. This raises the fundamental question of what happened to the crowds that led the "first spring" and why did a search for democracy lead to renewed repression, anarchy, and devastation across the region? More importantly, it seeks to inquire whether a "second spring" is in the offing as Kemal Kilicdaroglu, leader of CHP seemed to imply when he noted "Nobody should think that this march has ended; this march is a beginning" at the concluding rally in Istanbul.

Notes

1 Nazan Ustundag, "Praise for the Marginal Groups", *Jadaliyya*, June 13, 2013, www.jadaliyya.com/Details/28777 (Accessed 17 August 2013).
2 Ustundag, "Praise for the Marginal Groups."
3 For a detailed discussion of the two following subsections see Anita Sengupta, *Symbols and the Image of the State in Eurasia* (New Delhi, Heidelberg, New York, Dordrecht, London Springer, 2016).
4 Kemal Karpat, *The Politicization of Islam: Reconstructing Identity, State, Faith and Community in the Late Ottoman State* (Oxford: Oxford University Press, 2001).
5 Kemal Karpat, *The Politicization of Islam.*
6 Cevdet Tilmaz and Mustafa Sahin, "Modernity and Economic Nationalism in the Formation of Turkish Nationalism", *Mediterranean Quarterly* 17, no. 2 (2006), 53–71.
7 Tilmaz and Sahin, "Modernity and Economic Nationalism in the Formation of Turkish Nationalism."
8 Halil M. Karaveli, "Could Turkey's Glasnost Establish Equality As The Founding Principle Of The State?" *Turkey Analyst* 2, no. 23 (2009).
9 Idris Bal, *Turkey's Relations With the West and Turkic Republics, The Rise and Fall of the Turkish Model* (Burlington: Ashgate, 2000).
10 Ahmet Icduygu and Ozlem Kaygusuz, "The Politics of Citizenship by Drawing Borders: Foreign Policy and the Construction of National Citizenship Identity in Turkey", *Middle Eastern Studies* 40, no. 6 (2004), 26–50.

11 Soner Cagaptay and Islam, *Secularism and Nationalism in Modern Turkey, Who Is a Turk?* (London and New York: Routledge, 2006).

12 Mesut Yegen, "Citizenship and Ethnicity in Turkey", in *The Politics of Modern Turkey*, ed. Ali Carkoglu and William Hale, vol. IV (London and New York: Routledge, 2008), 254.

13 Yegen, " Citizenship and Ethnicity in Turkey", p 254.

14 *Records of the Assembly on 1924 Constitution* cited from Mesut Yegen, "Prospective Turks or Pseudo Citizens: Kurds in Turkey", p 599 *Middle East Journal* 63, no. 4 (2009): 597–615.

15 Martin Bruinessen, *Kurds, Turks and the Alevi Revival in Turkey*, n.d., www.let.ruu.nl/oriental_studies/mvbalevi.html.

16 Ayfer Karakaya-Stump, "The AKP, Sectarianism and the Alevi's Struggle for Equal Rights in Turkey", *National Identities*, January 2017, 53–67.

17 For a detailed analysis see Bayram Balci, "Turkey: Local Elections Gave Huge Victory to Erdogan", *Foreign Policy Journal, Op Ed April* 3 (2014).

18 Safak Bas, an analyst at the European Stability Initiative, Berlin, cited from "Turkey's Protests Indicate Growing Independence of Civil Society", *Eurasiareview, News and Analysis*, 15 June 2013.

19 Cited from "Turkey Unrest: Unions Call Strike Over Crackdown", *BBC News Europe*, 17 June 2013.

20 Ufuk Adak, "Ottomanaglia and the Protests in Turkey", *Jadaliyya*, 15 June 2013.

21 Recep Tayyip Erdogan during a speech on 2 June 2013 from *Chapulling* en.wikipedia.org/wiki/Chapulling

22 "Judy Asks: "Is Erdogan Finished?" *Carnegie Europe*, 5 June2013.

23 Cited from a conversation reported in Thomas Friedman L., "Postcard from Turkey", *New York Times, The Opinion Pages*, 18 June 2013.

24 Marc Pierini, "Urban Transformation in Turkey", *Carnegie Europe*, 20 June 2013.

25 Cited from Pierini, "Urban Transformation in Turkey."

Part 5

Trauma

15 Pinochet's dictatorship and reflections on trauma in Chile

How much have we learned in terms of human rights?

Nancy Nicholls Lopeandía

Thinking about trauma

The French neurologist and psychiatrist Boris Cyrulnik, who has developed the concept of resilience extensively, writes with respect to trauma:

> We can only speak of a traumatic situation if there has been a fracture, that is, only if a surprise with cataclysmic proportions – or sometimes insidious character – submerges the subject, shakes him and sends him into a torrent, in a direction he would have preferred not to take.
>
> (Cyrulnik, 2003, 33)

The author, therefore, emphasizes that the event that disrupts the life of an individual possesses the virulence of an extreme phenomenon of nature that produces a radical break in its previous conformation.

When speaking of trauma experienced by Chileans between 1973 and 1990 and which even has a current dimension, the "fracture with cataclysmic proportions" of which Cyrulnik speaks, was carried in actions based on the political power emanating from the state, which is why, unlike other traumatic situations caused, for example, by events in nature, in this case there is a socio-political dimension that cannot be underestimated. This is why several authors, when speaking of Chilean trauma, incorporate social and political variables, arguing that what is disturbed is the individual in his "biopsychosocial conformation" (Madariaga, 2018). Thus, in order to measure the trauma caused in individuals by their submission to the forms of coercion of the dictatorial regime, the individual cannot be separated from society, and it is society, and not only the individual, that is affected to the point of entering a process of extreme destructuring. Along these same lines, Carlos Madariaga understands trauma as a "total social fact," a concept he borrows from the anthropologist E. Menéndez, to allude to the overlaps between the psychic structure of individuals and the societal structure (Madariaga, 2018). In the 1980s, when repression had intensified in the context of massive national protests against the regime, the Latin American Institute of Mental Health and Human Rights (ILAS) adopted the following definition, by psychologist and psychoanalyst María Isabel Castillo, to refer to the trauma experienced by thousands of Chileans:

Extreme traumatization is a process that accounts for a specific type of traumatization, which is dependent on socio-political events. It is characterized by its intensity, permanence in time and by the interdependence that occurs between the social and the psychological. It is a specific type of traumatization, which exceeds the capacity of the psychic structure of the subjects and of society to respond adequately to this process. Its aim is the destruction of the individual, his interpersonal relationships and his belonging to society. Extreme traumatization is marked by a way of exercising power in society, where the socio-political structure is based on destructuring and extermination. The process of traumatization is not limited in time and develops sequentially.

(ILAS, 2019, 12)

Trauma in Chile: the breakdown of individual lives and societal dynamics

The coup d'état has been interpreted by most of the academic literature on the period as a profound break in the Chilean political tradition of the twentieth century that affected all areas of national life, modifying the lives of Chileans. Collier and Sater describe it as the "worst political break in the history of the Republic" (Collier and Sater, 1999, 307). For Lechner and Güell, based on other studies,

September 11, 1973 is lived by Chileans as a rupture – that in both personal and national life – and is a sharp incision between before and after. The interpretation (justifying or opposing) of the coup varies, but tends to understand it as an event that disrupts everything. Suddenly, extreme situations that seemed impossible become part of everyday life. The rupture is lived as something "unspeakable," finally inexplicable. It represents a social trauma.

(Lechner and Güell, 2005, 30)

The rupture would have been expressed in the first place as the end of the continuity of the democratic political system that had been developing throughout most of the twentieth century. However, it affected and disrupted life at various levels and in diverse spheres, even reaching the level of coexistence among Chileans, social practices, and private life. The rupture cannot be fully understood without incorporating the meaning that the deposed government had for thousands of Chileans, especially those from working class backgrounds who had supported it from the beginning. The Popular Unity government came to power following the triumph in the presidential elections of its candidate Salvador Allende, who assumed the presidency of the Republic in November 1970 and put into practice a Marxist transition to socialism. This was done peacefully and democratically, and was the first elected Marxist government in the world.

For the supporters of the socialist experiment, Allende's thousand days in power were lived as a unique, unprecedented historical moment, which materialized long-held aspirations, projects and dreams in the socio-political sphere.

Behind these dreams and projects was the imaginary of a more egalitarian and just society that would give space to the workers, inahbitants of poorer neighbourhoods, and subsistence farmers (*campesinos*) in national economic wealth and political decision-making. For what some people was the materialization of a long-dreamed-of political project, for others was the threat of the end of democracy and freedom, at the hands of a government that declared itself Marxist and which, a few months after being in power, had nationalized the country's industries, services and strategic banks. The coup d'état abruptly put an end to these interpretations, signifying relief and joy for the opponents of Allende and deep disappointment and sadness for his supporters.

One of the purposes of the new political regime was the destruction of all traces of the government of the Popular Unity, which was blamed for the state of generalized crisis experienced in the country. The military Junta that took power after the coup d'état promptly initiated a discourse in which the Armed Forces and Security Forces were presented as the salvation of the country in the face of the threat, and potential threat, of Marxism. For that reason, the persecution of the political and social leaders of the Popular Unity, who were arrested, imprisoned, executed, and disappeared, also tortured in the great majority of cases, became a state policy. The struggle against Marxist communism – based on a narrative of war – was the basis on which the use of violence and repression was established, and which was maintained, with different levels of intensity throughout the almost 17 years of the regime. According to the "Truth Reports," between 11 September 1973 and 11 March 1990, there were 3,216 victims of serious human rights violations, i.e. detained, disappeared, executed, and tortured to death, and 38,254 victims of political imprisonment and torture (Valech Report II, 2011).

The systematic violation of the human rights of thousands of people generated trauma, which must be understood both in its personal dimension, that is, in those directly affected by the repressive measures, and in its social dimension, involving society as a whole. The individual trauma manifested itself as soon as the human rights violations began to take place; the dehumanizing and perverse nature of the repression caused profound damage to the victims and their direct relatives, not only on a physical level but also an emotional one. The nature and forms of the repression – summary executions, deaths in alleged clashes, disappearances, physical and psychological torture, intimidation of family members, among many others – took by surprise not only those affected, but civil society as a whole.

Unlike what happened in other dictatorial contexts, in Chile, the churches played a predominant role in the defence of human rights. Priests, nuns, and lay people linked to the churches, but also key ecclesiastical figures such as Cardinal Raúl Silva Henríquez, Archbishop of Santiago, acted with surprising speed in defence of those being persecuted. The articulation of these actions were possible since, even before the coup, international ecumenical organizations such as the World Council of Churches were following events in Chile closely. In the ecumenical community in Latin America and in other countries, the voice of alert had been given to the possibility of a new coup d'état in the region, and the World Council of Churches called for the formation of ecumenical organizations that could act on behalf of the persecuted if this happened (Nicholls, 2019). On the other hand, some of the deaths carried out by the military were witnessed by the civilian population and reached the ears of the priests, who did not doubt the veracity of the accounts because they came from people they trusted. It was the confirmation of those deaths and of the persecution of foreigners and Chileans connected to the Popular Unity, which moved the world of churches to act early. On 3 October 1973, representatives of the Catholic and Protestant churches created the National Committee for Aid to Refugees (CONAR) and on October, the Catholic Church created the Pro Peace Committee, to support Chileans who were being persecuted. Both organizations had to be dissolved for different reasons but were reconfigured, the first one giving birth to the Social Support Foundation of the Christian Churches (FASIC) in 1975 and the second to the Vicarage of Solidarity in 1976, Both, through diverse material and legal assistance, and medical and psychiatric resources, gave support to the victims and their direct relatives during the whole period of dictatorship (Garcés and Nicholls, 2005). In 1980, the Corporation for the Rights of the People joined in this work (Lira, 2010).

The mental health teams of these institutions had professional training in psychology and psychiatry; however, the nature of the damage caused in those who suffered the coercive measures of the dictatorship, required new approaches that were different from traditional ones since, on the one hand there was extreme dehumanizing aggression, while on the other it was essential to integrate the political factor. This was related to the fact that it was left-wing militancy or adherence to Allende's government that had provoked the arrests, followed by actions of opposition to the dictatorship once the new regime was installed in power. It was also necessary to consider that the coercion was applied by the state itself, which under legitimate and democratic circumstances should protect the lives and integrity of its citizens. The teams were sought out new literature and exchanged ideas among themselves and with professionals abroad. Among the range of authors consulted were those who had written and reflected on the Holocaust, including those based on their own experiences in the Nazi concentration camps. Despite the differences in context and nature of the actions perpetrated against the victims, these reflections were key to understanding the repression in Chile (Lira, 2010). This literary corpus, nurtured by exchanges of ideas with other professionals, created the platform for the teams in Chile to generate their own approach that would provide the most effective possible responses to the systematic, unprecedented aggression by a Chilean totalitarian state.

Those who arrived at the doors of the human rights organizations were people who had passed through the concentration camps, through prison and torture, relatives of disappeared and executed detainees, those who had been sent to remote locations under observation ("relegated"), and later the exiles who began to return to the country. Torture in particular produced trauma that was difficult to conceptualize based on the term commonly used in psychology and psychiatry. Post-war writings on the extreme experiences of Holocaust survivors generated understanding that what was being experienced in Chile was an extreme traumatic situation. Bruno Bettelheim was relevant in this conceptualization since, writing about his time in the Nazi concentration camps, he spoke of the unpredictable nature of the events, the constant threat to life, and the impossibility of safeguarding it. Besides all the contextual differences, what was happening in Chile was echoed in the horror of the Nazi camps (ILAS, 2019).

As noted above, the trauma caused by the dictatorship in Chile cannot be understood only by its impact on a personal level, since the social dimension is a constitutive part of it. Primarily, because the trauma slips from the personal experience – in the body and in the psyche – to the set of social relations that involve the family and different collectivities or groups to which the affected individual belongs (Madariaga, 2018). Second, because the trauma was produced by the actions that the authoritarian power exercised – acting as exemplary punishment – on the bodies and minds of those who adhered to a certain political ideology and acted in accordance with it. In this sense, trauma is a product of the experience of political violence, and therefore of the conscious decisions and acts of some human beings toward others (ILAS, 2019).

To this must be added the notion that society as a whole was affected by the repressive measures imposed by the regime. Throughout much of the almost 17 years of the dictatorship, Pinochet decreed a "state of siege" in national territory, which gave him broad powers to limit the exercise of personal freedoms. In practice, this meant that any violation of the rules of the state of siege was the jurisdiction of military rather than civil courts (Rettig Report, 2007). The raids on homes, not necessarily those of militants or political opponents, especially in the peripheral neighbourhoods, were carried out at different times not only after the coup d'état, but also in the context of national protests against the regime. This under-analysed form of repression had effects on the family group, not only parents and other adults but also children, some of them only a few years old. Faced with the violence with which the police or military forces acted, the sensation of impotence due to the arbitrary nature of the situation, and their total defenceless-ness, these children experienced grave disruptive events that left traces in their memories. Many of the detentions and humiliating acts perpetrated by the police or military forces towards the population were done in public, on the streets in plain sight of passers-by. It is true that the repression in Chile had a secret face, applied in the camps for detainees and above all in the clandestine centres of prison, torture, and extermination. However, the regime was keen that some of the repression practised against its opponents would reach the eyes and ears of the wider population, so that it would act as a warning of what could happen to anyone who chose a path of active opposition.

Daily life was disrupted and fear took hold of the citizens, who understood that any behaviour contrary to the regime could be interpreted as a subversive or terrorist action with consequences for their physical and psychological integrity and could ultimately even lead to death. Fear was not experienced with the same intensity, nor was it the result of the same events. Except for the regime's supporters, it affected all citizens. The repression was practised indiscriminately and with extreme brutality in the working class neighbourhoods of the urban peripheries, in the massive demonstrations against the regime that took place between 1983 and 1986 on a monthly basis, and among young students who had organized themselves politically in the 1980s in secret, among many others. Fear was also installed among Chileans who were concerned of being denounced by their neighbours if their thoughts about the regime were known. A tacit silence reigned as social behaviour, except in circles of trust, as people avoided being handed over to the forces of repression. This silence could be interpreted as self-censorship, and it was often accompanied with a certain conformity in the population (Padilla and Comas-Díaz, 1987).

The entire coercive policy of the regime, of intimidation and terror, was guided from the beginning by the conception of the internal enemy that justified the military being in power, fed by the doctrine of National Security. Based on this doctrine, not all Chileans were regarded as citizens, as a division was established between "them" and "us." They, the "enemies of the fatherland" were "subversives," "terrorists," "Marxist-Leninists," who by virtue of their ideological-political options, and above all their political conduct, were degraded to a subhuman condition. One prominent member of the Military Junta called them "humanoids," another "Marxist cancer." As Lira and Castillo point out, by attributing to them a condition of otherness marked by their malignant identity, the exercise of dehumanization became possible (Lira and Castillo, 1993). Stripped of their human condition, as happened in other historical circumstances, it became easier for the security forces to eliminate them.

It is important to point out that on a scale of intensity and prevalence of fear, those who experienced it most intensely were the militants of the left, supporters of the Popular Unity at the outset, and later, political opponents of the Pinochet regime. As Lira and Castillo explain, fear is conceived as a specific reaction to a concrete situation of threat; however, in the context of the dictatorship, fear became chronic, in that it was a permanent state, since the threat was also a permanent state. This chronic fear was experienced not only by those who were directly affected, but by the entire society (Lira and Castillo, 1993), which understood its vulnerability in the face of a totalitarian and arbitrary regime that applied a systematic policy of repression to the civilian population. As Timmermann points out, society had to incorporate the violation of human rights as a fact of daily life (Timmermann, 2005).

Transition to democracy: confronting traumatic memory

Chile began its transition to democracy in March 1990, when the first democratic president since 1973 was elected by popular vote. The transition, which followed the path of the 1980 constitution dictated by Pinochet himself, had to face diverse challenges: overcoming the authoritarian enclaves left by Pinochet, the poverty that in 1990 included 11.6 per cent of households as indigent and 34.6 per cent as poor (CASEN, 1990), and the grave human rights violations committed by agents of the state under the dictatorship.

In 1990, Chile was a deeply divided country in which the scars of the dictatorship's crimes were far from healed. The regime had made an enormous effort to cover up the most serious crimes, such as those resulting in death and disappearances, but also torture. It had even created storylines to deny the existence of detention and disappearance when pressure from international bodies such as the

UN General Assembly began to be felt strongly in the country. Consequently, a first challenge was the search for the truth. It should not be forgotten that in the 1988 plebiscite, which decided whether or not Pinochet would continue in power (the "Yes" option, meant the continuity of the dictatorship), received 43 per cent of the vote (García, 2006). This is not an insignificant percentage of population that continued to interpret the coup as an event that had saved the country from Marxism, valuing the order imposed by the dictator and his "economic miracle." This narrative was generally accompanied by a denial, relativization or justification of the crimes against humanity that had been perpetrated.

Faced with this scenario, the transition governments of the victorious centre-left coalition – called the Concertación de Partidos por la Democracia – created truth commissions. The first of these, the National Commission for Truth and Reconciliation, was convened by the President of the Republic in 1990 and resulted in the so-called Rettig Report. This report provided people with reliable and exhaustive information on the victims, as well as on the functioning of the repressive apparatus, including the identification of clandestine centres of torture and extermination throughout the country, the divisions of the Armed Forces and Security Forces that were involved, the bodies specifically created by the military to direct and execute repressive activities, and the collaboration of civil society in these tasks, among other aspects. The report also, in a complete and explicit way, provided descriptions of the atrocious forms of human rights violations, including torture. Although it is impossible for a report to cover all cases of human rights violations, the Rettig Report became the official truth about what happened in the field of human rights during the dictatorship and was regarded as such by civil society more broadly. Later, in 2004, the Valech Commission investigated the cases of imprisonment and torture that had not been included in the first report, since the Rettig Commission had focused exclusively on the victims that had died. Finally, the Valech Commission II, which operated from the beginning of 2010 to mid-2011, provided a list of new cases of victims not covered in the previous reports.

The reports contributed to the clarification of the truth, which was one of the primary demands of the victims and their families since the beginning of the dictatorship. Little by little, the way was opened for the widespread acceptance in public opinion of the unquestionable veracity of the crimes against humanity committed by Pinochet's agents. The emblematic memory as salvation, which placed the military as saviours of what it understood as the catastrophe of the Popular Unity (Stern, 2000), lost followers, and this was spurred by other events such as the Riggs case – which exposed the millions of dollars held in secret accounts that Pinochet kept in the United States – and the memories of the victims' sufferings and their struggles, which gained space in the public gaze. At the same time, and from the beginning of the transition, various projects aimed at memorializing the victims of the dictatorship began to materialize. This path coincided with an international context, predominantly in the West, in which the figure of the victim, especially through the memory of the Holocaust, achieved unquestionable visibility and recognition in the public space, becoming the vector of memory par excellence and the icon of the twentieth century (Traverso, 2018).

Relatives of the victims and survivors organized themselves to convert the clandestine detention and extermination centres into sites of memory for the remembrance of the victims, for pedagogical work mainly focused on the new generations, and in more general terms for the fight against "forgetting," especially when the State tried to encourage this. Throughout Chile, civil society has been raising memorials that evoke the fallen during the regime. The memory of the horrific events of the dictatorship gradually received the attention of artists, writers, journalists, and academics from different disciplines who, after years of silence, narrated the crimes against humanity committed by Pinochet in different representational devices. If the 1990s had been characterized by a silencing of civil society around the controversial issues of the recent past, especially that of human rights violations, the new millennium was characterized by an explosion of memory.

Commemorations of the anniversary of the coup d'état were particularly prolific. For the 40-year commemoration of the coup there was a significant production of plays, documentaries and journalistic programs that were shown on open television channels, and academic seminars with the presence of outstanding intellectuals at the national and international level, while commemorative and symbolic events proliferated in the sites of memory, in the working class neighbourhoods, and in the former National Congress. Little by little, the memory of what happened was exposed; what at first was unmentionable in the public space was appearing, for example, on national television screens, e.g. in 2011, "The Cardinal's Archives" series. Although the series is fictional, it is based on real events of human rights violations, all linked to the protective actions carried out by the Vicarage of Solidarity created by Cardinal Raúl Silva Enríquez. For the first time on open television, the torture of dictatorship was shown. This is something that at first was not wanted to be seen, and was much less recognized, by the right-wing and Pinochet's supporters.

The testimonies of the victims and their direct relatives, which in the 1990s had remained in the background, made their triumphal entry into the public space, and were used for staging, films, and documentaries. Survivors and their families were invited to news programs on television and radio, and their testimonies became sources for numerous academic studies that linked the history and memory of the dictatorship. Several human rights organizations created during the dictatorship turned the documentation produced by years of defence of the victims into archives for public use, and were joined by the oral testimony archives created in the 1990s by several former clandestine detention centres that became sites of memory, such as Villa Grimaldi, Londres 38, and Estadio Nacional. In 2010, the State inaugurated the Museum of Memory and Human Rights, a modern building that houses an exhibition in various formats on human rights violations under the dictatorship, based on the narrative of the Truth Reports.

The set of actions aimed at uncovering the truth and producing memory about human rights violations, carried out on the initiative of civil society and the State, have enabled a process of dealing with extreme trauma. However, this process, due to its limitations and inadequacies, has reached an impasse, in which it is impossible to advance as a society in order to overcome this trauma. This impasse is related to a very important issue that the transition to democracy could not adequately resolve and that even today appears as a significant, pending debt. This is transitional justice, or the process of resolving the large-scale conflicts and abuses of the past, which includes holding those responsible for the crimes accountable and ensuring justice (OHCHR, 2014). From the beginning of the transition, it was clear to wider society that the State would not open the channels to allow for broad condemnation of the military involved in the crimes. None of the Truth Reports revealed the identity of the criminals, and the State's attempts to get the military to provide information about the fate and destiny of the disappeared detainees through a Dialogue Roundtable excluded recognition of those responsible for the human rights violations (Zalaquett, 2000).

For many years, the courts of justice were unable to move forward with the complaints filed by the victims and their families because they were bound by the Amnesty Law passed by Pinochet in 1978, which prevented the prosecution of those responsible for crimes committed prior to that date, and which has been considered a self-amnesty. However, two events removed the judiciary from this limitation and tipped the balance in favour of the victims. One was the judicial reform that came into force in the mid-90s and distanced the most overtly pro-Pinochet judges from the Supreme Court. The other was the arrest of Pinochet in London in October 1998, which was very significant on a symbolic level. Both converged in a revival of human rights causes, leading to the imprisonment of some of the military personnel responsible (Collins, 2013). However, today the greatest obstacle facing the human rights cases is the age of those who were responsible. This group is an ageing population that is dying without having spent a day behind bars. The phenomenon known as "biological impunity," in addition to implying an absence of punishment, has meant that the possibility of knowing the truth and the whereabouts of the victims who have not yet been located, is increasingly remote (UDP Human Rights Report, 2016).

The scant justice achieved under the post-dictatorship governments has remained an indelible stain on the transition process, even after the transition was considered complete. This situation has accentuated a widespread sense of impunity with respect to the dark and convulsed period of the dictatorship. For the victims and their families, it has been especially frustrating and painful. The most extreme case of impunity is that related to the disappeared detainees, since very few family members have known the fate of their loved ones (the truth about their whereabouts has not been revealed) and their remains have not been found either. According to information collected by the Human Rights Observatory of the Diego Portales University in 2019, the location and fate of 1,000 disappeared detainees are still unknown (Collins and UDP Observatory, 2019).

Impunity has unleashed a process of retraumatization in the victims and their families who, upon seeing that there is no punishment for the perpetrators, feel an accentuated sense of helplessness, impotence, and lack of protection. Diverse symptoms – depression, panic attacks, physical ailments, among others – are reactivated in the face of the unfolding of concrete political events, such as the most complex moments of Pinochet's detention in London or the results of the Dialogue Roundtable created to advance the search for disappeared detainees. All were ultimately characterized by the triumph of impunity (Madariaga, 2001).

Furthermore, the trauma has been perpetuated in the present through transgenerational transmission (Cerutti, 2015). The children of disappeared detainees, even when they were very young when one of their parents was arrested and later disappeared, have lived with a burden that has accompanied them throughout their lives, impacting their place in the world, their conception of life and their social relations. Many other children of victims of the repression lived extreme traumatic experiences that were inscribed in their bodies at an early age, but in the absence of suitable language they could not be symbolized or were not communicated due to the magnitude of the damage, thus remaining encapsulated within the individual. These children, now adults, require treatment for various psychosomatic illnesses (ILAS, 2019).

We are clearly in the presence of a trauma that does not recede and is perpetuated through time, affecting not only the victims and their descendants but society as a whole. In the words of Carlos Madariaga, it is a trauma that: "travels through time constantly transforming itself while preserving, in its intimate and genetic foundations, a nucleus of identity, an elemental particularity that makes it recognizable" (Madariga, 2018, 76).

Social uprising and uses of traumatic memory from the recent past

A few days before the largest social mobilizations in Chile since the end of the dictatorship, the President of the Republic – Sebastián Piñera – declared that the country was an oasis in the Latin American context, characterized by political stability and economic growth (*Cooperativa*, 9 October 2019). No judgement could have been more mistaken; the so-called "social explosion" that began on 18 October 2019 demonstrated that a deep malaise and discontent had been brewing among Chileans for decades, and this exploded with fury. The citizen's movement was maintained for months and was only interrupted by the coronavirus pandemic, which forced people off the streets and into a prolonged quarantine.

This social movement was not a surprise, although for the government and a political class detached from the needs and acute social and economic problems of society, it seemed to be an otherworldly phenomenon. Over the last decade, various social movements, led by secondary school students, teachers, environmentalists, indigenous groups, pensioners, and women had taken to the streets to demand solutions to their problems. These demands included, in the vast majority of cases, social justice, equity and non-discriminatory treatment, whether social, ethnic or by gender. All of these movements had something in common: they were protesting against the inequalities and injustices generated by the extreme neoliberal model that has governed not only the economy but also the areas of social security, health, and education since the Chicago Boys installed the model in Chile in the 1970s. The detonator of the explosion was the rise in the cost of public transport that led young high school students to demonstrate their opposition and take part in massive events of civil disobedience in the Santiago subway. From that point on, the movement spread massively. In the most emblematic moment of the movement, on 25 October 2019 in Santiago, the epicentre of the events, 1,200,000 people (of a national population of 17 million) demonstrated against structural injustices.

It was a mobilization that combined peaceful strategies with forms of manifestation of unusual violence. In Santiago, the Plaza Baquedano, located in the centre of the city, became the focal point and for months was the scene of demonstrations, which included the destruction and burning of private property and public infrastructure in the surrounding area. The greatest damage to public infrastructure occurred in the Santiago metro system, which suffered losses of US$300 million, leaving 79 stations damaged, of which 10 were vandalized, set on fire, and totally destroyed (Urquieta, 2019).

The government of Sebastián Piñera faced the social crisis with very little political skill, privileging repression and confrontational language over negotiation and the willingness to respond to the economic and social demands that were at the centre of the outbreak. In this context, the President decreed a state of emergency in the metropolitan region and called the military onto the streets, a measure that later extended to other regions of the country. Both the Security Forces and the Army Forces deployed indiscriminate violence towards the civilian population without distinguishing between peaceful and violent demonstrations, which raised the alarm of human rights organizations as well as social and political opposition leaders and public opinion in general. The Human Rights Institute and the Children's Ombudsman denounced the use of indiscriminate and exacerbated violence by these forces. One of the most dramatic consequences of the repression were the eye traumas (some of them with total or partial loss of vision) that 359 people suffered due to the action of the special forces and their use of "rubber bullets" in the context of the mobilizations (INDH, 2019). To this must be added the reports of sexual assault in the police precincts where detained demonstrators were taken.

In this context, Chile was visited by several international human rights organizations, including Amnesty International, Human Rights Watch, the Inter-American Commission on Human Rights, and the United Nations High Commissioner for Human Rights. The latter's report, released in November 2019, concluded that both the Security Forces and the Army had failed to respect international human rights norms and standards, specifically in the management of crowds and the use of force. They had also used non-lethal force in peaceful demonstrations and failed to comply with the gradual and progressive use of instruments of dispersion in violent demonstrations, had not practiced dialogue or used dissuasive methods, and had made disproportionate use of riot guns in peaceful demonstrations, leading to a large number of injured people. As of 19 November 2019, there were ongoing investigations into 19 people who died in the context of the demonstrations, some involving agents of the state. The High Commissioner also found that there were around 350 people with eye or facial injuries, some of which were severe eye trauma with partial or total loss of sight in the context of the use of non-lethal weapons by the *Carabineros* (OHCHR, 2019).

In historical perspective, it is surprising and worrying that a country that experienced a prolonged military dictatorship with a systematic policy of human rights violations, and therefore experienced extreme social trauma, is once again the scene of serious human rights violations. What has gone wrong? It is clear that it is not enough to know the historical facts or to keep the memory of what happened alive to ensure that the State and society respect human rights. Incorporating them as values that guide individual conduct, but also public policies and the practices of the institutions that sustain democracy, requires profound changes that involve broad human rights education. This should include not only knowledge of historical events of a traumatic nature, but also an honest and in-depth discussion of their causes and main effects, so as to shed light on the present situation in which it is necessary to value others and respect their lives and integrity.

On the other hand, a society whose political institutions have not been able to carry out a successful transitional justice process is not contributing to making human rights a priority on its political agenda. The signal from the political class in power, although not sought or explicit, was to favour impunity in the early 1990s rather than to generate conflicts that threatened weak democratic stability. The unresolved tensions of the recent past have therefore continued into subsequent decades, reappearing and expressing conflicts, tensions and traumas of the dictatorial period, albeit dressed in new clothes and revitalized with new actors. For example, can the repudiation and hostility of large sectors of civil society towards the Security Forces and the Army be explained only by their violation of human rights today, or is it also nourished by the memory and impunity of their crimes under the dictatorship?

It is also relevant to consider that, in Chile, democracy has been built on the basis of inequality and inequity – caused by the unrestricted continuation of the neoliberal model imposed by Pinochet – and discrimination and mistreatment – anchored in a traditional classism and machismo – that does not respect a basic principle of human rights: dignity. Inequity has historical roots; however, it is necessary to indicate that during the dictatorship it was exacerbated through regressive measures in the areas of labour, social security, health, and education. Post-dictatorial governments have not carried out structural reforms to modify this state of affairs, consequently economic and social rights have been relegated and dormant (UDP Human Rights Report, 2019). The social uprising woke them up, showing that what was violated under the dictatorship was not only the right to life and physical and psychological integrity, but also the economic, social, and cultural rights of thousands of citizens, who after 1990, sadly realized that there would be no profound changes in these areas.

Chile has not yet overcome the trauma caused by the dictatorship. The effects of this trauma are slipping through the interstices left by the fractures in justice, and through the gaps in the scaffolding of the truth of what happened, even reaching the second and third generations of victims. This is compounded by the sustained neglect of the social and economic rights of the majority sectors of the population throughout the post-dictatorship governments, which has generated a sense of abuse, exploitation, and lack of dignity.

Following Todorov's reflection on the uses of memory, it would be pertinent to ask whether in Chile, particularly the State, has used the traumatic memory of the coup and the repressive dictatorship to put it at the service of present causes, as occurs in the "exemplary memory." According to the author, this memory does not deny the uniqueness of the historical events that gave rise to it, but it does use them to understand similar situations in the present, so that it becomes the motor for action. A lesson is drawn from the past, Todorov points out, where exemplary use also means moving "from the particular to the universal, that is, to the principle of justice, to the moral norm, to the political ideal" (Todorov, 2013). It is key for contemporary Chilean society to revisit the past, but not as a mere formal and rhetorical exercise, but rather to ask ourselves what elements of the past have been perpetuated, causing division and fractures among Chileans, and what lessons we can learn from the conflict we have lived through, and what uses we can give to memory in order to avoid repetition. Without this critical exercise, we run the risk of failing again and again with respect to human rights, deepening the traumatic wounds and exposing the scars that we carry.

References

Centro de Derechos Humanos, UDP, *Informe Anual sobre Derechos Humanos en Chile*. Santiago: Ediciones UDP, 2016.

Centro de Derechos Humanos UDP [UDP Human Rights Report]. *Informe Anual sobre Derechos Humanos en Chile*. Santiago: Ediciones UDP, 2019.

Cerutti, Amadine. "La desaparición forzada como trauma psicosocial en Chile: herencia, transmisión y memoria de un daño transgeneracional." *Multitemas Campo Grande*, número especial, (2015), 35–47. https://doi.org/10.20435/multi.v0iespecial.157

Cyrulnik, Boris. *El murmullo de los fantasmas. Volver a la vida después de un trauma*. Barcelona: Gedisa, 2003.

Collier, Simon and William F. Sater. *Historia de Chile 1808–1994*. Madrid: Cambridge University Press, 1999.

Collins, Cath. "Chile a más de dos décadas de justicia de transición." *Revista de Ciencia Política* 51, no. 2 (2013), 79–113. doi:10.5354/0716-1077.2013.30316

Comisión Asesora Presidencial para la Calificación de Detenidos Desaparecidos, Ejecutados Políticos y Víctimas de Prisión Política y Tortura [Valech Report II]. (2011). *Informe y Nómina de Personas Reconocidas como Víctimas en la Comisión Asesora Presidencial para la Calificación de Detenidos Desaparecidos, Ejecutados Políticos y Víctimas de Prisión, Política y Tortura (Valech II)*. http://bibliotecadigital.indh.cl/handle/123456789/600

Cooperativa. cl. 9 October 2019. Chile es un verdadero oasis en una América Latina convulsionada. www.cooperativa.cl/noticias/pais/presidente-pinera/presidente-pinera-chile-es-un-verdadero-oasis-en-una-america-latina/2019-10-09/063956.html

Corporación Nacional de Reparación y Reconciliación [Rettig Report]. *Informe de la Comisión Nacional de Verdad y Reconciliación*. Santiago: Salesianos Impresores, 2007.

Garcés, Mario and Nancy Nicholls. *Para una historia de los DDHH en Chile: Historia institucional de la Fundación de Ayuda Social de las Iglesias Cristianas, 1975–1990 FASIC*. Santiago: LOM, 2005.

García, Carolina. "El peso de la memoria en los inicios de la transición a la democracia en Chile (1987–1988)." *Historia* 39 no. 2 (2006), 431–475.

ILAS. *Trauma político y la transmisión transgeneracional del daño*. Santiago: Subsecretaría de Derechos Humanos, 2019.

INDH. *Información constatada por el INDH al 20-12-2019*. 2019. www.indh.cl/bb/wp-content/uploads/2019/12/informe-20-dic.pdf

Lechner, Norbert and Pedro Güell. "Construcción social de las memorias en la transición chilena." En E. Jelin y S. Kaufman (Comps.), *Subjetividad y figuras de la memoria*, 17–46. Buenos Aires: Siglo XXI, 2005.

Lira, E. and Castillo M.I. "Trauma político y memoria social." *Psicología Política* 6 (1993), 95–116.

Lira, E. "Trauma, duelo, reparación y memoria." *Revista de Estudios Sociales* 36 (2010), 14–28.

Madariaga, C. Tortura y trauma psicosocial. Ponencia presentada en la Conferencia Internacional Consecuencias de la Tortura en la Salud de la Población Chilena: Desafíos del Presente, Santiago, Chile, 2001.

Madariaga, C. "El trauma social como problema de salud pública en Chile. ¿Es "reparable" la 'reparación'?" *Temas de actualidad. Revista chilena de salud pública* 22, no. 1 (2018), 75–86.

MIDEPLAN. *Encuesta CASEN 1990.* 1990. www.desarrollosocialyfamilia.gob.cl/btca/txtcompleto/DIGITALIZADOS/Folletos%20Mide/m-15-1991.pdf

Nicholls N. "Defensa de los DDHH en Chile en el contexto transnacional del movimiento de defensa de los derechos humanos, 1973–1990." *Estudos Ibero-Americanos* 45, no. 1 (2019), 43–56.

Oficina del Alto Comisionado de Naciones Unidas para los Derechos Humanos, 2014. *Justicia Transicional y derechos económicos, sociales y culturales.* www.ohchr.org/Documents/Publications/HR-PUB-13-05_sp.pdf

Oficina del Alto Comisionado de Naciones Unidas para los Derechos Humanos. *Informe sobre la misión a Chile*, 30 de octubre-22 de noviembre de 2019. www.ohchr.org/Documents/Countries/CL/Report_Chile_2019_SP.pdf

Padilla, A. and Comas-Díaz L. "Miedo y represión política en Chile." *Revista Latinoamericana de Psicología* 19, no. 2 (1987), 133–146.

Stern, S. "De la memoria suelta a la memoria emblemática: hacia el recordar y el olvidar como proceso histórico (Chile, 1973–1998)." En: M. Garcés et al. (Comp.) *Memoria para un nuevo siglo. Chile, miradas a la segunda mitad del siglo XX* (pp. 11–33). Santiago: LOM, 2000.

Timmermann, F. *El Factor Pinochet. Dispositivos de poder, Legitimación, Elites Chile 1973–1980.* Santiago: UCSH, 2005.

Todorov, T. *Los usos de la memoria.* Santiago: Museo de la Memoria y los Derechos Humanos, 2013.

Traverso, E. *Melancolía de izquierda. Marxismo, historia y memoria.* Buenos Aires: FCE, 2018.

Urquieta, C. 24 October 2019, *Dura pena para el Metro: no tiene seguros para estaciones ni trenes CIPER.* www.ciperchile.cl/2019/10/24/dura-perdida-para-el-metro-no-tiene-seguros-para-estaciones-ni-trenes/

Zalaquett J. "La Mesa de Diálogo sobre Derechos Humanos y el proceso de transición política en Chile." *Estudios Públicos* 79 (2000), 5–30.

Part 6
Memorialization

16 "Grassroots" Holocaust museums

Revealing untold stories

Stephanie Shosh Rotem

Holocaust museums, like other history museums, are established to teach the public about historical events and convey values and ideology through the exhibitions they display. Seeking to be relevant to a diverse audience of visitors, Holocaust museums define their goals as imparting universal humanistic "lessons." This is reflected in the museums' mission statements: the Holocaust Museum Houston (HMH), for example, states that it aims "to teach the dangers of hatred, prejudice and apathy."[1] The mission statement of the Anne Frank House in Amsterdam declares the museum's motivation to "raise awareness of the dangers of anti-Semitism, racism and discrimination and the importance of freedom, equal rights and democracy."[2] The Florida Holocaust Museum in St Petersburg, another example, seeks "to teach members of all races and cultures the inherent worth and dignity of human life in order to prevent future genocides".[3] All of these statements express a belief that disseminating knowledge of the Holocaust and the historical circumstances and events leading up to it to the museum's visitors, especially to "the young generation", "will immunize them against racism, intolerance, bigotry and hate".[4]

Holocaust museums are generally established by powerful organizations – states, municipalities, and nations – and the values they convey serve to enforce good citizenship and patriotism. In many countries, Holocaust education is integrated in the official educational program and a visit to a Holocaust museum is mandatory for high school students. In some states and cities, Holocaust education and museum visits are incorporated into college courses, and even military and police training. Such is the case in Israel, where Holocaust commemoration is inseparable from almost every aspect of society and culture, and the National Holocaust museum, Yad Vashem, is treated as a central, even sacred site.

This article will discuss a recent phenomenon in Israel – the formation of a different type of Holocaust museum, a non-institutional or as I will call it, "grassroots" Holocaust museum, which has sprung up alongside the national museum. They are characterized by being created at the hands of individuals or distinctive communities and that they either narrate forgotten stories or events of the Holocaust and World War II or are designed to address and appeal to a particular rather than a wide audience.

The establishment of Yad Vashem

The first national museum, of any type, to be built in Israel was Yad Vashem, a Holocaust museum founded in 1953 just five years after the declaration of Israel as an independent state. At that time, the Jewish population of Israel numbered 716,000 and comprised people that immigrated before World War II, and others that fled to it straight from the ashes, in which 6 million European Jews were murdered. They arrived from dozens of countries, with different cultures and languages. Israel became a meeting of people from East European countries (mainly Poland, Russia, and Romania), Western Europe (mainly Germany, France, and Great Britain), the United States, South America, the Middle East (Yemen, Syria, Iraq, and Persia), and Africa (Egypt, Morocco, and Tunis). They spoke various languages, ate different foods, dressed differently, and even practised their Jewish religious customs in distinctive manners. The State's main mission in these formative years was to form a cohesive society that would share common ideals and values. The creation of an Israeli national institution of Holocaust commemoration was one of many acts taken towards achieving this goal.

The museum was inspired by the personal vision of political activist Mordechai Shenhavi. According to his account of the events, he first heard of the Jewish Holocaust in Europe in the summer of 1942 and immediately had a dream in which "millions of Jews were walking towards Zion carrying tombstones on their backs... each one of them removed the stone and placed it in order or not, and the monument of their lives was thus founded".[5] He reacted to his dream by writing a detailed plan for a commemorative site that he presented to the Jewish National Fund (JNF). The plan he proposed was monumental by any standard. The institution was to be situated within a 500,000 square metre "Garden of the People", surrounded by what he described as "pavilions of Jewish heroism throughout the ages", a cemetery, a "symbolic cemetery", a sanatorium, a hotel, central archives, sports facilities, a convention hall, offices, and dormitories for "the orphans of Israel and victims of the war".[6]

The JNF did not accept the grandiose plan but did not completely reject it either. Undecided, deliberations were put on hold for two years. After learning that the Hebrew University and the Jewish Agency were planning competing projects of Holocaust commemoration, JNF talks were resumed. In preparation of the committee's renewed activity, Shenhavi rewrote his proposal and named it for the first time – "Yad Vashem". In Hebrew, this means "a place and a name" and it is quoted from the Book of Isaiah, where it eludes to an everlasting memorial: "Even unto them will I give in my house and within my walls a place and a name better than that of sons and of daughters: I will give them an everlasting name that shall not be cut off" (56:5).

The project, however, was still unapproved when Israel's War of Independence broke out in November 1947. The committee did not reconvene until after the war ended and the State of Israel was established. Finally, in March 1953, after years of deliberations, official measures were taken towards Holocaust commemoration, and the "Holocaust and Heroism Remembrance Law – Yad Vashem" was enacted. Under this law, a nationally funded authority would create a memorial to gather into the homeland material regarding all those members of the Jewish people who laid down their lives, who fought and rebelled against the Nazi enemy and his collaborators, and to perpetuate their memory and that of the communities, organizations and institutions which were destroyed because they were Jewish.[7]

The institution would also collect, investigate, and publish testimonies, cooperate with other commemorative institutions and represent Israel at international memorial ventures and ceremonies commemorating the victims of the Nazi regime.

The site chosen for the memorial (which only later included a museum) was in Jerusalem, adjacent to Mount Herzl, the official military cemetery and the burial site of the nation's leaders, including Theodor Herzl, "Prophet" of the Modern State. The land was officially allocated to Yad Vashem in July 1954 and renamed Mount Remembrance. The proximity of the memorial to Mount Herzl is symbolic of the conceptual tie explicitly drawn between the destruction of Jewish Diaspora and resurrection in the form of the State of Israel.[8]

Not only by the chosen site, but also in its architecture and exhibitions, Yad Vashem, the memorial campus and museum, meshes the historical events of the Holocaust with the creation of the State of Israel and writes a metanarrative of "ashes to life". Since its inception, it has become the supreme Israeli authority on Holocaust commemoration: all of the State's Holocaust Remembrance Day ceremonies take place there and Israeli schoolchildren are brought to Yad Vashem on field trips as part of the State's educational curriculum. As part of the diplomatic protocol, official visits to the State of Israel include a tour of Yad Vashem and a ceremonial wreath-laying in *Ohel Yizkor*, its memorial hall.

Until the 1980s, the importance of the Holocaust to the creation of the State of Israel and the stature of Yad Vashem, which represented it, were not questioned. For the young State, metanarratives and collective memories were essential to unify the culturally and socially diverse society. Further, surrounded by enemies, and challenged by endless war and struggle, Israelis, many of whom were first or second generation Holocaust survivors, believed that only a strong nation and army would prevent a second catastrophe.[9] Thus, the Holocaust was indoctrinated into the most basic values of the State and its survival, and Yad Vashem became an undisputed site of pilgrimage.

Fracturing the metanarrative and the creation of "grassroots" Holocaust museums

As the State of Israel solidified and became more tenable, collective identity began to be questioned; hidden voices surfaced and individual experiences became more valued. This change, according to Israeli historian Daniel Gutwein was prompted by "the privatization revolution that Israel went through and it was influenced by the political and moral dilemmas involved in the First Lebanon War and the first Intifada".[10] In this spirit, a new ideological discourse emerged in the 1980s in both academic and public spheres, which began to criticize the utilization of the Holocaust by the State to strengthen its ideology, and questioned the centrality of the Holocaust as the nation's metanarrative.[11]

As a result of the change, Yad Vashem's hegemony as an institution of Israeli social and cultural indoctrination began to decline. The explicit narrative constructed within the museum, which depicted the destruction of Jewish life in Europe as the catalyst to the establishment of an independent Jewish State in the Land of Israel, was newly scrutinized. Did the Holocaust necessarily lead to the advent of the State of Israel? Was that the most valuable lesson to be instilled in the museum? Or are there other, more "universal lessons" to be learned from the historical events?

The events of the Holocaust and World War II were so vast that no museum could be expected to encompass them all. The process of selecting the events to be displayed is extremely complex. The museums' historians and curators need to consider who and what signifies the events, communities, and individuals as worthy of particular mention? Should the museum narrate an exhibition based on the greatness of loss? The ability to generate emotion? Remarkability? As all of these questions cannot be answered within any museum, it was inevitable that in Yad Vashem, too, many events remained latent, in peril of being forever forgotten. As the State's metanarrative began to fracture in the 1980s, questions regarding the exhibition at Yad Vashem, the national museum, surfaced: whose story is narrated there and whose is overlooked?

Eventually, these unanswered questions led to the inception of "grassroots" museums created by individuals or small communities, to counter the State's stance and display alternative, personal and unique, accounts and memories.

Untold stories: forgotten communities

One type of "untold story" found in grassroots Holocaust museums has to do with Jewish communities whose fate in the Holocaust is either unknown to the general public or not fully recognized by it. The "Salonika and Greece Jewry Heritage Center" in Petach Tikva, for example, was founded to expose the largely ignored tragedy of Thessaloniki Jewry. For many years, the history of the Jewish community of Thessaloniki, Greece, was not included in the collective memory of the Holocaust. To this day, its story is not a part of the permanent exhibition at Yad Vashem, the National museum, but is displayed separately, outside the museum halls, in the research institute's corridor.

The Jewish community of Thessaloniki began to form in the second century BC, and on the eve of World War II counted over 50,000 – the largest Jewish community in Greece and one of the most prominent in the Balkans. The Nazis invaded Thessaloniki in 1941 and cast their racial laws on the city's inhabitants in 1943. Between March and August of that year, 19 transports left the city, exiling 48,533 Jews to Auschwitz Concentration Camp where most were murdered in gas chambers. At the end of the War, only two thousand Thessaloniki Jews survived. Approximately half of those immigrated to Israel and the other to the United States, Canada, Australia, and South America.

The small Thessaloniki community that immigrated to Israel settled in cities and villages across the country, learned to speak Hebrew, acquired job skills, and adjusted to their new lives. Like most immigrating communities, a larger emphasis was put on assimilating into new surroundings than on maintaining past culture, language, and traditions. Thus, while the Holocaust was inscribed as a key event in the construction of Israeli identity and citizenship, the particular story of the Thessaloniki tragedy was not brought to light. The metanarrative was built upon the events and experiences of the hegemonic group – East European Jews, mainly of Polish, Romanian, and Russian descent, excluding the stories of lesser-known communities, such as that of Thessaloniki.

A strong desire to bring their story to general awareness began to seethe within the Thessaloniki immigrants in the late 1980s. In addition to the general shift of discourse mentioned before, this surge may also be attributed to a music album published at that time by Israeli singer Yehuda Poliker, himself the son of Thessaloniki survivors. The album, named "Dust and Ashes," sings not only of the community's tragic tale but also of its sad longing and yearning to the beloved hometown of the past. Eventually, the community's desire was translated into the creation of an exhibition at the Ghetto Fighters' House, the second largest Holocaust museum in Israel. The exhibition, funded by the community itself, opened to the public in 1993. It was on display until in 2010, the hosting museum began major renovations and the exhibition panels were removed and stored away.

Concurrently, renewed interest in commemorating Thessaloniki Jewish history was also stirred amongst the residents of the Recanati Home for the Aged. This institution, founded in 1956 in Petah Tikva, houses approximately two hundred descendants of Greek, Turkish, Egyptian, and Bulgarian origin, whose primary language is Ladino. The home was initiated and is largely supported by Leon Recanati, an affluent banker and prominent member of the Thessaloniki community in Israel, as a philanthropic act to provide his community elders with a comfortable retirement home.

The residents of the home decided to create a small exhibition based on their memories and experiences.[12] At first, they collected an eclectic array of artefacts: documents, photographs, costumes, and even kitchen utensils; however, as their exhibition began to take shape they recognized the need to add historical and pedagogical content. They located the Ghetto Fighter's House's stranded exhibition panels and persuaded the museum to donate them to their project. The panels were then transported to the home and are now the core of the small museum.

The museum consists of three exhibitions: (1) "The History of Thessaloniki Jewry"; (2) "The Traditions and Lifestyle of the Thessaloniki Jews"; and (3) "The Holocaust". It also holds a research library and archive, and an informal lounge that contains books and records for public use, run by a local author and storyteller. The museum is an active meeting point and educational site for schoolchildren, soldiers, adults, and senior citizens. It offers lectures and informal encounters with Holocaust survivors residing in the home, arts and crafts workshops, storytelling, and Friday night dinners in the spirit of Thessaloniki Jewish tradition.

Thus, the "Salonika Center" suggests an alternative setting to Yad Vashem, the national museum. Rather than writing a cohesive metanarrative, to accentuate the common experiences of Israeli society, it narrates a particular, overlooked story of one of its communities. Created by a group of non-professional but passionate elderlies rather than an army of historians, curators, and designers – this museum, in contrast to Yad Vashem, is intimate and personal.

The "Salonika and Greece Jewry Heritage Center" is just one example of museums that display the experience of a particular community during the Holocaust. Other examples are the "Museum of Libyan Jewry" in Or Yehuda, which includes an exhibition and memorial space dedicated to Libyan Jews that perished in the Holocaust, and the "Memorial Museum of the Hungarian Speaking Jewry". Established in Safed in 1986, it "depicts the magnificent past of the Jewish communities in Hungary, Transylvania, Slovakia, Carpathian-Russia, Bachka, Banat and Burgenland, and reflects on their contribution to Jewish history and world culture".[13] In the museum's Hebrew website, the importance of the permanent exhibition's chapter dedicated to "Holocaust, Heroism and Rescue Efforts" is explained: "The Holocaust of Hungarian Jewry has not been granted its deserved place within Israel's other [Holocaust] museums."[14]

Untold stories: unique experiences

Generally, Holocaust museums' exhibitions follow a uniform format. They begin with a display of pre-war Jewish life in Europe and continue to narrate a chronological progression of the events: the rise of antisemitism, the rise of the Nazi regime, the enforcement of racial laws, life in the ghetto, deportation, death camps, and finally liberation and salvation. Although this may be the most widespread experience of European Jews in the Holocaust, it was not the only one. As written by historian Doris Bergen:

> The Holocaust was an event of global proportions, involving perpetrators, victims, bystanders, beneficiaries, and rescuers from all over Europe and elsewhere in the world. Any attempt to grasp it in its entirety must begin with recognition of that massive scope.[15]

Thus, any attempt to represent the Holocaust in a single exhibition is futile.

The Israeli National Holocaust museum Yad Vashem, however, has adopted this uniform model. The exhibition begins with "The World that Was," which presents a work of video art created by Michal Rovner depicting the Jewish world before the Holocaust. It continues with "From Equals to Outcasts," which portrays the anti-Jewish policies of Nazi Germany, followed by "The Awful Beginning: World War II and the Beginning of the Destruction of Jewish Life in Poland". The exhibition progresses with "Between Walls and fences"; "Mass Murder. The 'Final Solution' Begins"; "Jewish Uprisings in the Midst of Destruction"; "The Last Jews: The Concentration Camp Universe and the Death Marches"; and "Return to Life". As the exhibition begins with a work of art, so it ends. The final gallery "Epilogue – Facing the Loss," contains a video art display by Uri Tzaig that reflects on the horrors and imminent death during the Holocaust.

Yad Vashem occupies over 4,200 square metres, has more than 1,200 artefacts on display and some one hundred video screens showing survivor testimonies and short documentary films and newsreels – and yet, innumerable stories remain untold and countless experiences unrecognized. Thus, "grassroots" Holocaust museums have been created by individuals or groups motivated to reveal their unique experience that has not been acknowledged there.

One such example is "David's Creation – A Private Museum of Holocaust Education," which was set up in Achva Academic College located in a rural area south of Tel Aviv. The museum displays the entire collection of Holocaust survivor David Nissenbaum's artistic work that expresses his emotions on the fate of the Jewish people in the Holocaust. According to the college's website, the museum's purpose is "not to recount the historical events of the Holocaust, but rather the unique experience of the artist in face of the murder of his people and the loss of his family".[16]

Another museum of distinct character was established in the northern city of Karmiel in 1995. "The Museum of Jewish Soldiers' Heroism" was created by Israel Fillet, a Russian immigrant, who served in the Red Army during World War II. The exhibition is based on material that he collected over 40 years and supplemented with artefacts and documents donated by other local veterans of the Red Army.[17] Veterans who volunteer as mentors and mediators in the museum, enthusiastically recount their own memories and tales to the visitors, mostly local school classes.

Over one million people emigrated from the former USSR to Israel during the 1990s, following perestroika and the collapse of the Communist Regime. Amongst the immigrants were approximately 20,000 elderly veterans of the Red Army that fought in World War II. According to anthropologist Sveta Roberman, in the USSR these veterans were recognized as heroes and were "major agents in centring the war at the heart of the Soviet national identity".[18] However, they found that in their new country the "historical image of the Jewish WWII soldier was almost entirely absent from Israeli arenas of memory and commemoration".[19] In their struggle to assimilate and belong, they challenge the Israeli metanarrative and introduce a new perspective – that of the "Soviet soldier, destroying Nazism … bringing liberation to the world" as playing a crucial role in the creation of the State.[20]

At first, Red Army veterans became present in Israeli society in Victory Parades and social clubs. As they gained strength, museums similar to the one described above were founded across the country, particularly in cities with a large concentration of Russian immigrants: for example, the "Museum of Heroism" in Hadera (1995), and the "Museum of Jewish Heroism in the Holocaust and WWII," in Ashdod (2010).

Holocaust museums and focused audiences

A different group of "grassroots" museums is distinctive not because of the story they tell but due to the messages they seek to convey and the audience they target. These are museums established by and for the ultra-Orthodox Jewish (*Haredi*) communities in Israel.

The ultra-Orthodox Jews in Israel, which in 2010 accounted for 10.8 per cent of the Israeli general population, are not a homogenous group.[21] However, according to Menachem Friedman, they can be identified by shared characteristics that include

> a commitment to Torah study; an absolute commitment to the tradition of East European Jewry; a commitment to strict and meticulous application of the *halakhah* (rabbinical law); and rejection of Zionism – or, at the very least, a view of Zionism as valueless, even if it is acceptable after the fact.[22]

Thus, the State's metanarrative that establishes a connection between the destruction of Jewish life in Europe and its resurrection in the Land of Israel is not generally accepted by the ultra-Orthodox, and the rituals of Holocaust commemoration created to enforce this narrative, including the reverence of Yad Vashem, have therefore been rejected. The Holocaust is mainly commemorated by ultra-Orthodox Jews in prayer and fasting.

In recent years, however, there has been a change and several museums are being developed by the ultra-Orthodox in an attempt to "tell the story" in a way that is both meaningful to their own communities, and disseminates their values and beliefs to the surrounding society.

The Chamber of the Holocaust (*Martef Hashoah*) was established in 1948 (five years before Yad Vashem) by the Israeli Ministry of Religious Affairs on Mt Zion in the Old City of Jerusalem. Its purpose was to serve as a memorial hall and "symbolic burial ground" for the 6 million Jewish Holocaust victims.[23] Rabbi Samuel Zanvil Kahana, who was the driving force towards the establishment of the Chamber of the Holocaust, wrote in its mission statement:

> The Chamber of the Holocaust stands adjacent to the Tomb of King David, tied to it by pangs of the Messiah … within it, traditional commemoration takes place in honour of the martyrs, according to customary rituals: lighting candles, religious study, and saying *Kaddish*.[24]

The main part of the Chamber of the Holocaust is a display of more than one thousand memorial plaques dedicated to perished Jewish European communities. The plaques were prepared and donated to the Chamber of the Holocaust by representatives of the communities, who are also responsible for holding annual ceremonies on the memorial site. It is important to note that all the plaques commemorate communities rather than individuals or particular events. In this way, the Chamber of the Holocaust enunciates the event as a catastrophe of the Jewish people as a whole, rather than the tragedy of the specific victims. The majority of other objects on display are religious objects and books. A large wooden table is situated in the middle of the hall, which is used by the adjacent *yeshiva* for religious readings. The message is clear: Bible study continues despite the attempts of the Nazis to destroy the spirit of the Jewish people, which for ultra-Orthodox Jewry, according to Alex Lavon, is the most meaningful form of commemorating the victims.[25]

It is clear from its setup that the Chamber of the Holocaust was never intended to be a museum but rather a religious memorial space dedicated to prayer and study. This, however, has changed in the past decade. The institution is now called "Chamber of the Holocaust Museum & Memorial". It has employed both historians and curators to redesign the space, and has even begun the painstaking process of applying for recognition as a museum by the Israeli Ministry of Culture. The "musealization" of the Chamber of the Holocaust points on one hand to changing patterns of commemoration within the ultra-Orthodox communities, and on the other, towards their insistence on narrating the events according to their particular values rather than conforming to the national stance.

A similar museum, the "Prager Center," is now under development in Bnei Brak, a satellite city of Tel Aviv, which is populated predominately by ultra-Orthodox Jews. The museum will be an annex of the "Archives of Martyrdom," which was established in 1964 by the author and Holocaust researcher Rabbi Moshe Prager, himself a Holocaust survivor. The archives were founded to collect documents, photographs, and personal testimonies for the benefit of scholars and the public. The addition of the new centre will transform the original character of this religious institution – much like the Chamber of the Holocaust in Jerusalem – from an institution of study and research to a museum.

According to the archive's website, the future museum, similarly to other institutional Holocaust museums, will present a chronological display of the historical events. However, the events will be presented through a particular prism. The unique perspective of the planned exhibition is described as "highlighting the richness and vitality of Jewish values even during this dark era".[26] The motivation for the establishment of the museum is also explained:

> Through these values, which are the core of the Jewish response to the Holocaust, we seek to connect the visitors, the youth in particular, to the strength of the Jewish heritage that has passed from generation to generation, and accorded resistance to the individual and the public.[27]

This short statement contains the incentive for creating a public museum – utilizing Holocaust commemoration to strengthen and disseminate religious Jewish values and beliefs. This can be understood as a way to make Holocaust memory meaningful to the ultra-Orthodox communities; however, it can also be understood as a reaction to most Holocaust museums around the world, which seek to universalize the "lessons of the Holocaust" in order to make them relevant to a wide audience.[28] The debate of universal versus Jewish lessons has become a very heated issue regarding Holocaust commemoration in general, and its manifestation in museums, in particular. Currently, most museums have adopted a universal approach in which the Holocaust of European Jews is utilized to contemplate humanistic values such as racism and tolerance rather than disseminate Jewish history and values. The Prager Center, in contrast, which is founded and funded by the ultra-Orthodox community, seeks to reflect on issues particular to Jewish belief, tradition and faith.

Conclusion

The museums discussed above are different but share a common goal – to challenge the existing Israeli metanarrative of the Holocaust set by the State and inscribed in Yad Vashem, its National museum. Reflecting on these museums in relation to Israeli society raises unanswerable questions. It is assumed that museums reflect the society of their founders and if that is the case, what can the recent eruption of these previously hidden voices teach us? Is this a sign of a permanent and stable society that has established a cohesive metanarrative and collective memory and can now accept the undercurrent of other voices? In contrast, should we view this fragmentation as a sign of fragility? Is the attempt of gathering the exiled Jewish people and rebuilding a consolidated society in the Land of Israel failing?

Perhaps, in the medium, we should acknowledge that citizens of the twenty-first-century are both part of a metanarrative, striving to belong and connect to their nations' history and values – but also connected to their particular community and personal experiences, traditions, and history. Thus, these museums do not necessarily challenge Yad Vashem's prominent position as metanarrator of a shared historical event but rather provide space for more, less dominant, voices to be heard.

Contemplating these sites in the context of twenty-first-century museums raises questions of another type. How can these museums, created and maintained by first and second-generation Holocaust survivors with minimal funding from the government or municipalities, stand up to the sophisticated standards set by contemporary museums? How can they possibly attract visitors or gain recognition surrounded by imposing, technologically advanced, and properly funded museums? As of today, most of these "grassroots" museums rely on volunteers who are generally Holocaust survivors or their offspring – who will take over as they age and pass away? Will these somewhat subversive "grassroots" museums and the contested memories they treasure be revered by subsequent generations or will they be, once again, consigned to oblivion, buried under the weight and burden of collective memory and identity?

Notes

1 www.hmh.org/au_home.shtml (Accessed 1 January 2019).
2 www.annefrank.org/en/Sitewide/Organisation/Annual-Report-2015/Organisation/Mission-and-strategic-objectives/-aims (Accessed 1 January 2019).
3 www.flholocaustmuseum.org/mission (Accessed 1 January 2019).
4 Stephanie Shosh Rotem, "Jewish Empowerment or Universal Values – New Directions for American Holocaust Museums", *Dapim Journal: Studies on the Holocaust* 27, no. 2 (2013), 129–153.
5 Yad Vashem Archives (YVA), Administrative files, Box II, folder 14 [Hebrew]. For a detailed description of Yad Vashem's foundation, see Stephanie S. Rotem, *Constructing Memory. Architectural Narratives of Holocaust Museums*, Bern, 2013, 31–39.
6 Rotem, *Constructing Memory*, 31–37.
7 The "Martyrs' and Heroes Remembrance (Yad Vashem) Law 5713-1953", was signed by Moshe Sharett, Minister of Foreign Affairs and Acting Prime Minister; Ben-Zion Dinur, Minister of Education and Culture; and Yitzchak Ben-Zvi, President of the State, on 19 August 1953. The translation of the law is provided by Yad Vashem.

8 In 2003, the "linking path" was paved between the cemetery and the museum, further emphasizing this connection. The path was inaugurated in April 2003, to mark the 60th anniversary of the Warsaw Ghetto Uprising. The opening ceremony included a march from the cemetery to Yad Vashem that took place on 22 April 2004, midway between Yom Hashoah (Israel's Holocaust Remembrance Day) and Israel Independence Day (see Jackie Feldman, "Between Yad Vashem and Mt. Herzl: Changing Inscriptions of Sacrifice on Jerusalem's 'Mountain of Memory,'" *Anthropological Quarterly* 80, no. 4 (2007), 1155.)

9 Noa Schori-Eyal Yechiel Klar and Yonat Klar, "The 'Never Again' State of Israel: The Emergence of the Holocaust as a Core Feature of Israeli Identity and Its Four Incongruent Voices", *Journal of Social Issues* 69, no. 1 (2013), 125–43.

10 Henry Wasserman, "On the Nationalization of the Memory of the Six Million", *Politika* 8 (1986), 6–7, 55, 37. The "privatization revolution in Israel" refers to political changes that occurred after 1978, when for the first time since the foundation of the State of Israel, the Socialist party lost its power and a right-wing liberal government was formed. In the decade that followed, most of the State-owned assets were turned over to the private sector, creating tremendous upheaval.

11 In academia, see, for example: Henry Wasserman, "On the Nationalization of the Memory of the Six Million", *Politika*, 8, 1986, 6–7, 55 [Hebrew]. For an example in the public sphere, see: Yehuda Elkana, "A Plea for Forgetting", *Ha'aretz*, 2 March 1988.

12 The events leading up to the establishment of the museum were recounted to me by by Roni Arnia, the Director of the Recanati Home for the Aged, in April 2015, at Tel Aviv University. I thank Tal Zur for bringing the museum to my attention and introducing me to Mr. Arnia.

13 www.hjm.org.il/?leftframe=menueng.html&mainframe=/main.aspx/En   (Accessed 1 January 2019).

14 www.hjm.org.il/hol/rescue/, 1 January 2019. [Hebrew]

15 Doris L. Bergen, *The Holocaust: A Concise History*, Lanham, Rowman & Littlefield Publishers, 2009, vii.

16 www.achva.ac.il/sites/default/files/achvafiles/pdf-general/museom_shoa.pdf (Accessed 1 January 2019). [Hebrew]

17 Karmiel has a large population of immigrants, over 16,000, who emigrated from the former Soviet Union in the early 1990s.

18 Sveta Roberman, "Fighting to Belong: Soviet WWII Veterans in Israel", *Ethos. Journal of the Society for Psychological Anthropology* 35, no. 4 (2007), 447–477, 459.

19 Roberman, "Fighting to Belong", 460.

20 Roberman, "Fighting to Belong", 451.

21 Reuven Gal, *The Ultra-Orthodox in Israeli Society: An Update* (Haifa, 2015), 3. [Hebrew]

22 Menachem Friedman, *Ultra-Orthodox Society — Sources, Trends, and Processes*, Jerusalem, 1991, 9. [Hebrew] Translated and quoted in: Michal Shaul, "Testimonies of Ultra-Orthodox Holocaust Survivors", *Between 'Public Memory' and 'Private Memory', Yad Vashem Studies* 35, no. 2 (2007), 143–185, 144.

23 For a detailed account of the Chamber's establishment, see: Doron Bar, *Holocaust Commemoration in Israel in the 1950s: The Holocaust Cellar on Mount Zion*, n.d., 16–38.

24 Alex Lavon, "The Holocaust Cellar on Mt. Zion: Traditional Remembrance and Official Memory", *Israelim. Multidisciplinary Periodical in Israel Studies* 3 (2011), 71–91, 75. [Hebrew]

25 Lavon, "The Holocaust Cellar on Mt. Zion", 78.

26 www.ganzach.org.il/ (Accessed 1 January 2019). [Hebrew]

27 www.ganzach.org.il/ (Accessed 1 January 2019). [Hebrew]

28 On a discussion of 'universalizing' the messages conveyed in Holocaust museums, see Rotem, "Jewish Empowerment or Universal Values – New Directions for American Holocaust Museums", 129–153.

17 Fabric, food, song

The quiet continuities in Bengali life 70 years after partition

Rituparna Roy

Contextualizing continuities in Bengali life

While thinking of the Partition of India in 1947, the first things that come to mind are communal violence, the dislocation of millions on both sides of the border, and the destitution that they faced thereafter.

The history of that rupture has been well documented. In fact, it has inspired two generations of outstanding historical scholarship, with interesting new turns in historiography in the last three decades: the focus of attention shifting from causes to experiences, and from national to regional histories of Partition[1]; exploring experiences of women[2] and Dalits; bringing in de-colonization[3] and migration[4] into the discussion, and the digital archiving of oral histories[5] in the last decade.

The Partition of India has also been immortalized in literature and cinema. The trauma of forced migration and the enormous struggle for survival that was the lot of the refugees have nowhere been more eloquently articulated than in the Partition films of Ritwik Ghatak, an East Bengali refugee himself, who never accepted the fact of Partition.[6]

The human dimension of the Partition and its aftermath in Bengal also found expression in a rich body of literature spanning several decades, right from Narayan Sanyal's *Bakultala P. L. Camp* in 1955 to Mihir Sengupta's *Bishad Briksha* ("Tree of Sorrow") in 2005.[7]

In that entire literary corpus – as indeed in real life – pain, loss, and longing on the one hand, and a resolute re-fashioning of identity on the other, have defined the post-Partition experiences of Bengalis. But there have been other narratives too …

My late mother has left me a wardrobe full of sarees. Among the ones I prize the most is a "Dhakai," a muslin that originates from and is a speciality of Dhaka. Our family cook – a Bangladeshi who lived and worked in India for a long time without a passport – swears by "Padma'r ilish," saying the hilsa of the Ganges she has here are no match to it. When the popular Indian folk-singer/composer/ scholar Kalikaprasad died an untimely death in 2016, he was equally mourned on both sides of the border.

Fabric, food, song – there is still much that binds the two Bengals in everyday life, though it has been partitioned for 73 years. They represent the quiet continuities in Bengali life, as opposed to the rupture of the political division. That division has been richly documented: in history-writing, literature, cinema. What had been lacking is the public memorialization of the Partition. The Amritsar Museum addresses that lacuna with respect to the Punjab. In Kolkata, I have initiated a project – the Kolkata Partition Museum Project (KPMP)[8] – that focuses on Bengal: aiming at both memorializing the specificity of its partition history and aftermath, and emphasizing the continuities between the two Bengals – in an effort to promote tolerance between a divided people and make a conscious attempt to remain humane. In this chapter, I will discuss how the said project intends to execute the latter.

Fabric

A part of my inheritance from my late mother is a prized "Dhakai," a muslin that originates from and is a speciality of Dhaka.

My mother was a thrifty person. Beyond the monthly expenses of her household, she saved every paisa she could. She had absolutely no indulgences – either in food, fabric, or jewellery. Even her domesticity was frugal. Only once did I see her indulging herself. The year: 1980; the reason: a "Dhakai" sari!

In our childhood, we had a neighbour from East Bengal in the housing co-operative that we grew up in. They were a big family of five brothers and three sisters and had an even bigger extended family in Dhaka who came visiting them in Calcutta all the time. (This was in the late 1970s to early 1980s, when Calcutta was yet to become Kolkata). The youngest sister of that family was close to my mother. Her nickname was "Shupu." While we addressed all Ma's friends as "mashi" (maternal aunt), Shupu was "pishi" (paternal aunt) to us. She trained in Rabindrasangeet and paired up with or assisted Ma in co-operative cultural functions for Saraswati Puja.

Shupu pishi loved dressing well and mostly wore bright saris. "Taat" – Bengal cotton – featured prominently in it, but she also had a fair collection of Dhakais. The source of that was a cousin of hers who ran a business in Dhakai saris. It was a small venture, but it did well. This cousin frequently travelled between Calcutta and Dhaka, bringing her latest collection here and selling them off before returning home. Shupu pishi's flat, next door to ours, was an important conduit for that business. I distinctly remember its drawing room being transformed into a kind of saree-shop when her cousin – a woman both tall and heavy, with an impressive personality – came visiting with her collections. I also remember her talking to Ma several times in our "landing" – the open space in front of the three flats of our floor, which was a distinctive feature of our housing complex.

I think both she and Shupu pishi persuaded Ma to buy at least one sari from her. And Ma, for once, relented. But it must have been difficult for her – giving in to this temptation. For I remember it was priced at Rs 400, a princely amount at the time. Ma had to pay it in instalments.

It was a beautiful beige-coloured sari, with a beguni (purple) paar (border) and aanchal. The border was pretty broad; and both border and aanchal were heavy with the trademark Dhakai work on it. And spread all over the sari were small flower motifs in an array of bright colours: yellow, green, purple. I loved the sari, and in my adulthood, I actually ended up wearing it more than Ma ever had. I think, for her, just possessing the sari was the important thing. We have a phrase in Bengali – "*sajatne tule rakha*" (preserving with loving care). That is what Ma did with it.

We had a Hot-Shot camera in the 1980s, with which we would sometimes have family photo sessions. In one such, we photographed Ma in her Dhakai. And then in 1995, there are several photographs of me wearing it, in our "Farewell" at Presidency College (I graduated in English Honours from there). It was thus "preserved" in other ways as well – in image and memory (the college farewell being undoubtedly one of the most memorable days of my college life).

Food

I mentioned our family cook, an economic migrant from Bangladesh, who swears by "Padma'r ilish". That instance can be infinitely multiplied. There is such intense nostalgia associated with food.

One of the most poignant passages that I've come across about food nostalgia occurs in the Bengali novel *Purba-Paschim* (East-West) by Sunil Ganguly, which is a modern prose epic of contemporary Bengali life. It covers the period from the 1930s to the 1980s; and is a story of two cities, Calcutta and Dhaka, told through the experiences of two friends, Pratap and Mamun, who are separated by the Partition.[9]

Pratap is forced to leave his home, Malkhanagar in East Bengal, after the Partition and continue living as a resident in Calcutta, where he had come initially just to study. What that entails for him and his family is a painful re-adjustment from a life of plenty to that of reduced circumstances, which does not change for decades. It is just not a question of less money, but generally, fewer resources, a cramped existence in a concrete jungle, and having to do away with an entirely different way of life. The consumption of food was a part of that.

There is a poignant food episode in the novel that is occasioned when Pratap buys his favourite fish, ilish, on a whim one evening – prompted by a childhood memory of his father bargaining with fishermen to buy four ilish, which were then shared with family and neighbours (pp. 583–584). But Pratap has no one to eat with and to appreciate the fish in his rented home in Calcutta. His sister is a widow and will not touch it; his wife, a West Bengali, is no fish lover; his son is earnestly studying for his exams and has finished his dinner early; the daughters of the house are not interested. His wife is angry at him for making her enter the kitchen again late at night, and the unwelcome fish is all but thrown away. Eventually, it is cooked, and only the couple eats it – Pratap mechanically, and Mamata, just to honour him. Pratap is hurt, and angry with his wife. But he realizes bitterly, too, "That [childhood] memory was the root cause of all trouble. If those memories can't be erased, there will be no peace in this life in Calcutta" (p. 588). Pratap's memory transcends the shadow lines of partition, reminding him of the ties between East and West Bengal; but, as the conflict over the ilish shows, that very memory also functions to interrupt and disrupt his present in Calcutta.

But there can be other kinds of food memories, too. In a guest post for the KPM website "BLOG", Sanmita Ghosh talks of culinary legacies from a 2nd/3rd generation point of view. I am reproducing it here with her permission.[10]

Born in a family that originally belonged to the Chittagong district of undivided Bengal, I was conscious of my roots and my other "desh" (country) since my childhood days ... It was my *Boro Jethu* (my father's eldest brother) who moved first, around 1945, followed by my *Mejo Jethu* (the second of the three brothers) who arrived in Calcutta in 1948. The aftermath of the Partition greatly affected the family and my father, who had stayed on with his widowed mother in the ancestral house at Dhalghat, finally moved to Calcutta in 1954. My three *Pishima*-s (paternal aunts), all senior to my father, had also migrated, following their marriages and had settled in places as diverse as Chinsurah (West Bengal), Rangoon and Bombay. My grandmother moved in with her sons at my *Boro Jethu*'s rented flat in south Calcutta around 1955 and was possibly the last one to leave our home in Dhalghat.

By the time I was born in 1974, the family no longer remained a "joint" one and the three brothers had set up their individual nuclear units. But the bond of among these three units was a strong one, and the essence of the joint family persisted. Though uprooted and now divided, the family continued to hold on to certain aspects of life that were central to it: strong sibling and familial ties and the cuisine of Chittagong.

Brought up entirely in the urban environment of south Calcutta, my connection with Chittagong strengthened over the years through the Chittagong dialect in which my father, my uncles and aunts would speak whenever they met, and the items that my aunts would cook whenever they stayed over at our place. My *Mejopishima* (who had relocated to Howrah in West Bengal during the 1950s) and my *Chhotopishima*, both being widows, would cook separately in kerosene stoves, items that were strictly vegetarian. Never having tasted my grandmother's dishes (she passed away when I was only three), my first acquaintance with authentic Chittagong cuisine was through these lip-smacking vegetarian dishes cooked by my aunts. One such item was the *posto* or poppy-seed curry (*posto* is called *morichut* in the Chittagong dialect) cooked by my *Mejopishima*. I would come back home from school, eagerly looking forward to a plateful of rice and *posto*-curry. This dish was a special one, its unique taste could never find a match with the *posto*-curries of the West Bengal variety. Cooked with potatoes and vegetables like *laudoga* (tender branches of bottle gourd) or *lal-shaak* (red spinach), *bori* (dried lentil drops) and *dhone–pata* (coriander leaves), this *posto*-curry had an other-worldly taste to it. Among the other vegetarian items that were carried over from Chittagong and found place in our kitchen was the *holud paatar dal* or *dal* cooked with turmeric leaves, a rare item, now being revived in some five-star Kolkata hotels. This dish too had a unique flavour; the aroma of the turmeric leaves mixed with *sonamoong dal*, left an unforgettable taste in the mouth when mixed with *gorom bhaat* or warm rice.

The dish that is an all-time favourite with us and with Chittagong folk living across the world is the non-vegetarian *shutki-maachh* or dried fish. Though intolerably smelly while it is being cooked, *shutki-maachh* still remains the quintessential Chittagong delicacy. Its taste is an acquired one and the residents of West Bengal find it unpalatable. But it is a dish close to our hearts, specially the *Loitya-shutki* or *Chingri-shutki*. I would never forget the taste of the *shutki–maachh* cooked by my *Borojethima* (wife of my father's eldest brother), with ingredients like mustard oil, lots of onion, garlic, red and green chillies, all of which imparted to it a rich, spicy taste. Another item that has left its indelible taste on our taste buds is the *chingri maachh* (shrimps) cooked with *kochur loti*(taro stolon), in mustard oil with garlic and chillies.

After almost about seventy years since the Ghosh family crossed the border, these dishes have continued to titillate our taste buds to date. A lot had been lost, but my grandmother's and my aunts' culinary expertise was a source of inspiration for my mother (who hailed from the Myemansingh district of undivided Bengal and knew nothing of Chittagong cuisine prior to her marriage) and my *Jethimas* (my uncles' wives), whose kitchens had produced the most authentic East Bengal dishes. Our gastronomic tastes have evolved with time, but our generation still relishes the taste of these dishes and our kitchens still churn out these. Alongside the memories of tales told by my father, uncles and aunts of our ancestral village, of our joint family at Dhalghat and of our extended family at Chittagong town, we proudly carry in us a sense of inheritance of our '*desh'-er ranna*, or authentic Chittagong cuisine.

It's not surprising that her post reached the maximum number of people when I shared it on our Facebook page – hers was the most popular post in the BLOGup to that point (i.e. in the first four months). There were several comments from friends who remembered similar cuisine being handed down from other parts of East Bengal.

Song

Bengalis are known for their love of poetry and song. That interest could not be divided with the Partition. For one, both West Bengalis (and Indians) and Bangladeshis sing national anthems that were penned by the same poet, Rabindranath Tagore – "Jana gana mana" in India and "Amar shonar bangla" in Bangladesh. In fact, Tagore songs played a crucial part in the language movement in East Pakistan: West Pakistan's clamping down on the Bengali language[11] and banning of the singing and performance of Rabindrasangeet played no small part in further strengthening their awareness of their Bengali identity and their determination to fight for it.

But Rabindrasangeet is not the only common musical treasure of the Bengalis. There are the songs of Nazrul Islam, Atul Prasad, D.L. Roy, among the twentieth-century song writers and composers. Far more importantly, perhaps, there are the folk songs of the Bauls – wandering minstrels, whose most famous exponent,

Lalom Fokir, had greatly influenced Tagore.[12] In fact, folk songs remain the most popular genre of music to this day in Bengal, being renewed in the new avatar of Bangla "bands," in new versions for post-millennials.

"Dohar" is one such band with a huge fan following in both West Bengal and Bangladesh.[13] When its lead singer/composer Kalikaprasad died an untimely death in 2017, he was equally mourned on both sides of the border. And the songs of the film he last composed music for – *Bishorjon* (which won the National Award in India for "Best Feature Film in Bengali" in 2017) – became chart busters.[14]

Kalikaprasad Bhattacharya not only sang but researched folk music at Jadavpur University. He first learnt folk music from his uncle, Ananta Bhattacharya – who, too, was a collector of folk songs and had a band of his own. The young Kalikaprasad was considerably influenced by him. Among the singers of the Baul-fokir tradition, Kalikaprasad was particularly drawn to the songs of Baul Shah Abdul Karim of Sylhet. In fact, the very first folk song that he learnt from his uncle, he later realized, was a song composed by none other than Abdul Karim; and as a college student, he discovered, to his even greater surprise, that Karim was still living! In 2000, Kalikaprasad met the "phenomenal" singer – a life-changing experience for him, of which he spoke eloquently in a TV program.[15]

It may be noted here that apart from the late Kalikaprasad, another singer – Moushumi Bhowmick – has also been collecting folk songs from both sides of Bengal, for many years now. While Kalikaprasad popularized the songs he collected (from Assam, West Bengal, and Bangladesh) through his band, Moushumi has been doing field recordings of living folk artists in their local regions and systematically archiving them in the website, "The Travelling Archive."[16]

It is probably pertinent to mention that what I have written here about songs is actually true of performative arts in general – especially the folk forms. "Jatra," or folk theatre, perhaps best exemplifies that.

Household help

My widowed father's new household is filled with abandoned women – incidentally, all from Bangladesh, and all residing now in Dattapukur in West Bengal.[17] They numbered three at one point. Now there are two. One cooks, the other cleans, and both double up as night-nurses at different places. They could never have been here if my mother was alive. She never allowed any cook for all the 44 years of her married life; and though she was certainly open to domestic help, when the local ones could not be relied on, she downright refused to hire "from the centre" because of their high hourly rates. Even with a daughter earning in dollars and dying to contribute and make them live comfortably, Ma resolutely stuck to the lifestyle that a pensioner's wife could afford.

After Ma passed away in August 2016, Diptiand Sonali (disguised names) entered Baba's life – ostensibly to take care of him and his empty home, but also ended up partially filling the void in it by making him their "meshomoshai" (uncle – maternal aunt's husband). Ever since, as with everyone else who comes within his orbit, he has been full of unsolicited advice for their health and well-being. They partly indulge this incorrigible "teacher" in him (who simply can't "retire"), partly (privately) scoff at him. They are also clearly irritated by his fussiness about vegetables and his all-new obsession with cleanliness. But they were the ones who were most distraught when, last year, he was in the ICU of a private hospital for four weeks with a kidney problem.

Baba's habitual compassion for the needy and poor is a tad bit extra for them. It stems from the fact that they are abandoned single mothers. They had briefly – at different times – shared the story of their struggle with him; and, later, in more detail with my sister and me.

Their trajectory as poor working women is not a unique one, but inspiring, nevertheless: for Dipti, it involved leaving a child on the other side of the border with her parents for a long time; for Sonali, it was having to frequently go without food for days and bear the responsibility and pain of not being able to allay her children's hunger; for both, providing the child (Dipti)/children (Sonali) a rudimentary education while doing violently exploitative and contingent work for years. But theirs is also an enabling journey – from abysmal pay to good rates, from sheer penury to being financially solvent, from living in the stinky corridor of a distant relative's house to a spacious rented room of one's own with a proper designated area for a kitchen and a separate bath, from being inexperienced and shy/afraid/anxious/ young women to emerging as self-confident and self-sufficient individuals.

Hearing their stories, I have realized that just as love has many hues, so has abandonment. Despite all that she has faced, Dipti retains a tenderness for the husband who had once loved her and nursed her during a major illness. She says she understands why he betrayed her; and then goes on to give an irrational explanation (irrational for me, very rational for her) for it: blaming it all on family intrigue and an oh-so helpless husband marrying again (without the knowledge of his first wife and child) against his choice. Sonali has faced the worst kind of physical abuse by her perpetually drunk and irresponsible husband (and eternally absent father of her sons). She is enormously relieved to have got rid of him … which was not at all easy to accomplish, as he kept coming back to claim his rights. Hence in her case, the term "abandoned" needs to be qualified: she was abandoned by her husband during their marriage, from which she actively sought to be liberate herself. She is enormously and unashamedly relieved to be alone, and to return home only to her boys. It is enough for her to love them and live for them.

They both insist on returning home every day to their children who are now adults – even when being full-time domestic help would have actually helped them earn more and spared them a lot of time and energy. So why did they not do that, I had once asked. "To keep a watchful eye", I was told – youngsters going astray being too common in their milieu.

And so, they commute every day on the Bonga local to get about three precious hours with their sons in the late afternoon. In the evening, they commute against the tide of the floating population of Kolkata. While millions leave the city to return home in far-flung towns and villages, they come to the metropolis to start their working day in the evening as night-nurses. They are both always dressed impeccably – saree pinned and pleated to perfection, hair tied up in a bun, an always bursting handbag on their shoulder. And – vermillion on their hair-parting, bindi on their forehead, sakha-pala on their wrists. I never asked them why they did that. Baba had told that part to me much before I became familiar with them and I would have guessed anyway. They retain the marital signs of Hindu (Bengali) women to protect themselves. It is the easiest armour they can carry to shield themselves from unwanted male attention and unwarranted queries on trains during daily commutes.

There are literally hundreds like them, who originally hail from border villages in Bangladesh and have come to Kolkata for better work opportunities. They mostly do caregiving work – as maids, ayahs, nannies – in private homes, but sometimes also in hospitals and nursing homes; and they are generally recruited through ayah "centres". The ones working in my home were recruited through one such centre in Salt Lake.

Seeing Kolkata partition museum project in a larger context

Promotion of tolerance

Food, fabric, song, domestic help – there is still much that connects the two Bengals in everyday life, though it has been partitioned for 73 years. The examples I have given above testify to the truth of this statement.

The reason why the Kolkata Partition Museum Project (KPMP) wishes to highlight the continuities between the two Bengals is simple. It is not a call for a utopic reunification of the two Bengals à la East and West Germany. It also has no wish to whitewash our contested histories and the religious fault lines that existed in Bengal that made Partition possible in the first place. And it certainly does not refute the fact that West Bengal (as a federal state within the Republic of India) and East Pakistan/Bangladesh have had very different postcolonial trajectories.

Instead, what KPMP simply wishes is to consciously acknowledge that there is still much that is common in our living heritage that goes beyond nationalist rhetoric (whatever that may be at any given moment). And that we need to nurture this commonality, especially in the face of increasing communalism and divisiveness. This will, we believe, both in the short term and long, help in the promotion of tolerance in our societies.

In the museum that we envision, this continuing common living heritage will be given pride of place. And in the run up to the actual museum being established, we intend to have a couple of exhibitions centred around this theme.

Can museums prevent mass violence?

It may be pertinent to discuss here whether museums can play any role in the prevention of mass violence; and in case they don't, whether they have the potential to play one.

I believe museums do have the "potential" to play a role in the prevention of mass violence. That is, however, in the realm of theory. As to whether they have actually done it is something we can answer only by giving concrete examples.

Holocaust memorials have not kept antisemitism at bay – that's the first thought that comes to mind.[18] The twentieth century has been the bloodiest of centuries. But have we really learnt our lessons from history? I am very cynical myself about this point – and it is actually my cynicism that has inspired me to do the work I am doing.

One would have thought the Holocaust would be the final horror of the twentieth century; in fact, in all time to come – but think of the genocides in Bangladesh, Cambodia, the Balkans, Rwanda in the second half of the twentieth century.[19] Are we done with it? I am not sure.

I think we need to be clear in our minds about what we mean when we talk about the potential role that museums can play in preventing mass-violence. Do we mean preventing violence in a particular geographical area or against a particular community/race? So, are we asking whether Holocaust memorials can prevent antisemitic violence; or whether Holocaust memorials can prevent genocides anywhere in the world? Since it is considered the worst of all in human history.

Could Cambodia prevent Rwanda?[20] If a Partition museum had been built in Amritsar in the early 1980s, could/would it have prevented the 1984 anti-Sikh pogroms in Delhi? An enormous amount of partition history, literature, films (all within the domain of public knowledge), and even the collective memory of 1947, with many victims still alive – could not prevent it.

After 1947, in fact, we have witnessed a vicious cycle of violence in India – in 1964, 1984, 1992, and 2002. Can a museum achieve what national history/literature/films/collective memory/family histories could not?

The Amritsar Partition Museum

While talking about KPMP, it might also be instructive to compare our effort with similar initiatives in other partitioned countries on the one hand, and to initiatives within the subcontinent on the other.

It is important to remember here that many of the partitioned countries in the world (Yugoslavia, Ireland, Korea) have "national" – and not "partition" – museums.[21] How much their partition is made a part of their national narrative, and what similarities/dissimilarities they have with our project are things that can be discussed/critiqued only after visiting/studying those museums. Something that I do intend to do.

I have, however, visited the Holocaust Memorials of Berlin – Memorial to the Murdered Jews of Europe, Jewish Museum Berlin, Topography of Terror – and they were my chief source of inspiration for KPMP. I wrote a report on the memorials for the online portal *The Wire.in* soon after visiting them in July 2016.[22]

In the subcontinent, the Amritsar Museum is the first museum to memorialize the Partition and its aftermath – 70 years after the event! It was long overdue and the Amritsar Partition Museum, housed in the right wing of the Town Hall of Amritsar, deserves credit for this initiative.

It was initiated by Lady Kishwar Desai through The Arts and Culture Heritage Trust (TAACHT). In August 2015, the Trust publicly announced itself through an exhibition held at the India International Centre, New Delhi. Two more photographic exhibitions followed in New Delhi in 2016; and in October of that year, the Museum was inaugurated in Amritsar.

It opened its doors to the public on 17 August 2017; I visited it in early December of the same year. No newspaper report had prepared me for the scale and size of APM. It is spread over 17,000 square feet on two floors and has 14 galleries. It has done amazing work within a very short time. I had a memorable experience and was impressed with the museum overall. I, however, felt that its chief lacuna lay in the fact that it did not cover the partition experience of Bengal at all. I wrote an extended report on the museum – covering both what I liked and did not – in the online portal, *The Wire.in.*[23]

The Liberation War Museum, Dhaka

Within the subcontinent, the other major history museum is the Liberation War Museum in Dhaka.[24] Going by their website and the feedback from people who have visited it, they have done a very good job. I hope to visit the museum myself in the near future.

As for the Partition, it must be remembered that, for Bangladeshis, the defining moment was 1971 – not 1947. For many, 1947 was a good thing to happen to them. For, they would otherwise always have been dominated by the Hindus in every sphere.

The main difference with the project that we are doing is that we will be taking into our ambit all the three partitions of Bengal: 1905, 1947, 1971. Their aftermath and afterlives. It goes without saying that 1947 and 1971 are related. But it all started in 1905. And 1905 had actually changed the course of the nationalist movement.

We are, however, collaborating with Bangladesh in our project. We already have the former Director (and Founding Trustee) of the Dhaka Liberation War Museum as one of our Advisors. And we are planning events that will include Bangladesh in its focus – starting with the Partition Film Fest this month.

Partition Film Fest, Kolkata, 16–19 August

KPMP is being helmed by the Kolkata Partition Museum Trust (KPM Trust). It was registered as an organization in August 2018, and it publicly announced itself at an inaugural event in February 2019.

In August 2019, it commemorated the 72nd anniversary of the Partition (and its aftermath) through a signature event: by screening Partition-related films for four days that (in keeping with KPMP's vision), included features and documentaries from both West Bengal and Bangladesh. This had never happened in Kolkata before! The event was sponsored by Tata Steel and hosted by the Jadunath Bhavan Museum and Resource Centre (a unit of the Centre for Studies in Social Sciences).

We screened a broad range of partition films from different eras of filmmaking in Bengal – from the 1950s right up to 2018. The Inaugural day featured a "classic" by Ritwik Ghatak (*Komol Gandhar*, 1961), the filmmaker who made the Partition theme his own; the second day looked at post-millennial West Bengali features on partition (*Rajkahini*, 2015, *Shankhachil*, 2016 and *Bishorjon*, 2017); the third day was (primarily) about documentaries from both West Bengal and Bangladesh (*Maati*, 2018 – this was a feature; and *Way Back Home*, 2003 and *Simantorekha*, 2017); and the fourth day focussed on feature films from Bangladesh by Akram Khan and Tanvir Mokammel (*Khancha*, 2017 and *Chitra Nadir Pare*, 1993). The Fest was rounded off with a "Masterclass" with Tanvir Mokammel on the "Problematics of Filming Bengal Partition".

While planning for this Fest, we had hoped it would help raise awareness among the youth about this defining moment of our recent history, provoke new ideas about how we can remember it, and contribute to a general public engagement with the subject beyond the specialist concerns of historians. And, in the process, take us one step closer to our ultimate aim of building a museum.

We were successful in our mission – the Fest received a fair amount of media attention both in India and Bangladesh,[25] was attended by many college and university students, a host of people from the general audience reached out to us wanting to know more about the project, and our special guests from Bangladesh showed an interest in future collaborations.

Notes

1 While speaking of the regional histories of Partition, with regard to Bengal, mention must be made of the following books: Chatterji, Joya (1994), *Bengal Divided: Hindu Communalism and Partition 1932–1947*. Cambridge: Cambridge University Press; Chatterji, Joya (2007), *The Spoils of Partition: Bengal and India, 1947–1967*. Cambridge: Cambridge University Press.

2 The feminist turn in historiography happened in the 1990s. Two seminal works were: Menon, Ritu and Kamla Bhasin (1998), *Borders & Boundaries: Women in India's Partition*. New Delhi: Kali for Women; Bagchi, Jasodhara & Subhoranjan Dasgupta (eds.) (2003), *The Trauma and the Triumph: Gender and Partition in Eastern India*. Kolkata: Stree.

3 The most influential work on de-colonization is Sekhar Bandyopadhyay's *Decolonization in South Asia: Meanings of Freedom in Post-independence West Bengal, 1947–52* (London and New York: Routledge Studies in South Asian History), 2009.

4 The most recent – and path breaking – book on migration relating to the Bengal Delta (a lot of which deals with the aftermath of Partition), is: Alexander, Claire, Joya Chatterje and Annu Jalais, *The Bengal Diaspora: Rethinking Muslim Migration* (London and New York: Routledge Contemporary South Asia Series), 2015.

5 The digital archiving of oral histories was done systematically in the last decade by "The Partition Archive", initiated by Guneeta Singh Bhalla. For more information, visit https://in.1947partitionarchive.org/. The mission statement of the Archive reads as follows: "We are concerned global citizens committed to preserving this chapter

of our collective history. We come from diverse cultural and religious backgrounds, nationalities, and professions. It is our view that a strong foundation in history will pave the way for a more enlightened future for the subcontinent and hence the world. Our core team is supported by devoted volunteers, including interns, advisers and experts who are passionate about preserving the people's history of Partition". A TED Talk by Bhalla can be watched here www.youtube.com/watch?v=j_QYPCDuFPk - Retrieving Lost Stories from the Partition of 1947 | Guneeta Singh Bhalla | TEDxAshokaUniversity

6 Following are a few useful references and links related to the work of Ritwik Ghatak: - A biopic of Ghatak, *Meghe Dhhaka Tara* ("Cloud Capped Star", 2013) www.youtube.com/watch?v=ZT5UEzQeDGg (trailer). Producer – Shree Venkatesh Films (SVF); Director Kamleshwar Mukherjee; Lead Actors – Saswata Chatterjee (as Ghatak), Ananya Chatterjee and Abir Chatterjee; An indispensable book on Ghatak – Rajadhyaksha, Ashish (1982), *Ritwik Ghatak: A Return to the Epic*, Bombay: Screen Unit; An insightful lecture by the renowned film critic and Ghatak expert, Sanjoy Mukhopadhyay (Retired Professor, Department of Film Studies, Jadavpur University), on "Construction of the Goddess in Ray's *Devi* (1960) and Ghatak's *Meghe Dhaka Tara* (1960)" www.youtube.com/watch?v=3RXozHK03II; A brilliant article by film scholar and filmmaker, Prof. Moinak Biswas (Dept. of Film Studies, Jadavpur University), "Her Mother's Son: Kinship and History in Ritwik Ghatak" (2004) www.rouge.com.au/3/ghatak.html; A brief introduction to Ghatak and a summary of his Partition trilogy aimed at a general, uninitiated audience by Dr Rituparna Roy (2016) https://scroll.in/reel/813977/all-these-years-later-nobody-has-chronicled-the-partition-like-ritw

7 Sengupta, Mihir (2005), Bishad Briksha ("The Tree of Melancholy"), Kolkata: Ananda Publishers. Sengupta had won the "Ananda Puraskar" for this novel in 2006.
It is an autobiographical narrative of a decade of the author's growing up years, from the early 1950s to early 1960s, in a Hindu family in East Pakistan.
A detailed discussion of the novel can be found in this particular session ("History Meets Literature") of the 6th edition of the Kolkata Literary Meet in 2018. www.youtube.com/watch?v=1KmPkzOTAjg
The session was moderated by Dr Rituparna Roy, and the other participants were Samim Ahmed and Aparajita Sengupta.

8 I had conceived KPMP in early 2016. Initially inspired by the Holocaust memorials of Berlin and working on the project as an independent scholar, I first formally broached the idea in an international conference (commemorating 70 years of Partition in Bengal) that I co-convened with Prof. Sekhar Bandyopadhyay and Dr Jayanta Sengupta in August 2016 at the Indian Museum, Kolkata. An Affiliated Fellowship at the International Institute for Asian Studies (https://iias.asia/profile/rituparna-roy), Leiden, during this phase (July 2017–June 2018) proved valuable as a networking platform. By August 2018, I was able to gather support for the project from a wide cross-section of people in different fields who were invested in Partition and heritage in varying ways, and got together a team which formed the Trust for the project. The KPM Trust was registered on 20 August 2018. On 26 February 2019, the Trust had its "inaugural event" at the Jadunath Bhavan Museum and Resource Centre, with renowned filmmaker Goutam Ghose as the Chief Guest of the event. From 16–19 August 2019, it commemorated the 72nd anniversary of India's partition through films. (More on this in Note 25).
More information about the ongoing work of KPMP can be found by visiting its website (https://kolkata-partition-museum.org/) and Facebook page (www.facebook.com/KPMProject/).
It may be pertinent here to also say a bit about my individual trajectory as a scholar: I am a Partition scholar who has had a long engagement with the subject. My doctoral thesis explored the evolution of the trope of Partition in literature written in English from the mid-1950s to the late 1980s (*South Asian Partition Fiction in English: from*

Khushwant Singh to Amitav Ghosh, AUP: 2010); while my postdoctoral project was a comparative study of English and (West-) Bengali partition fiction, with particular attention to the politics of nation-building on the Bengal border. A key publication for the latter was an article on the novel *Purba-Paschim*. (See Note 9).

9   Ganguly, Sunil (1995), *Purba-Paschim* (East-West), Kolkata: Ananda Publishers. Ganguly had won the "Ananda Puraskar" for this novel in 1996. It may be noted here that the "East-West" of the title refers, first, to the two divided parts of Bengal; and second, to India and the UK and US, where sections of the novel are set. Through his account of Pratap and Mamun's life in Calcutta and Dhaka respectively, Ganguli shows the aftermath of Partition on both sides of the Bengal border and the very different trajectories of the two nation states. A detailed critique of the novel can be found in Dr Rituparna Roy's article – "Postcolonial Cities across Borders: Calcutta and Dhaka in Sunil Ganguli's *Purba-Paschim*". *Special Issue ("Postcolonial Cities, South Asia") of Moving Worlds: A Journal of Transcultural Writings* 13: 2 (2013): 138–150. http://movingworlds.net/volumes/13/postcolonial-cities-south-asia/

10   The "Guest post" can be accessed here https://kolkata-partition-museum.org/desh-er-ranna-on-inheriting-the-cuisine-of-chittagong/, 17 May 2019. Dr Sanmita Ghosh is Assistant Professor in English, Hooghly Mohsin College.

11   See Schendel, Willem van (2009), *A History of Bangladesh*. Cambridge: Cambridge University Press, pp.109–115.

12   For a deeper understanding of LalonFokir's influence on Rabindranath, see Ghosh, Shantideb (1972), "Rabindranath O Banglar Baul", in *RabindrasangitVichitra* (Rabindrasangit Miscellany), Kolkata: Ananda Publishers, pp. 100–120.

13   The Wiki entry on "Dohar" -https://en.wikipedia.org/wiki/Dohar_(band) states: "Dohar has popularised Bengali and Assamese folk music. The group was co-founded by Rajib Das and Kalika Prasad Bhattacharjee on 7 August 1999. Both the members came to Kolkata from Barak Valley of Assam. The name of the band – 'Dohar' [meaning 'chorus'] – was given by Aveek Majumdar, Professor of Jadavpur University. ... Kalikaprasad Bhattacharjee and Rajib Das were both the lead singers ... of Dohar. Bhattacharya died in a road accident near Gurap village in Hooghly district on 7 March 2017, aged 47. Five other members were also injured. The remaining members of the band have continued singing under the leadership of Rajib Das."

14   "Bishorjon" – Opera Movies, 2017. Producer: Suparnokanti Karati; Director: Kaushik Ganguly; lead actors: Abir Chatterjee, Jaya Ahsan and Kaushik Ganguly. www.youtube.com/watch?time_continue=1&v=a5uepZE9I04 – Here is a popular song from the film, "Bondhu tor laaigya re", which was both composed and sung by Kalikaprasad.

15   Kalikaprasad, www.youtube.com/watch?v=SBWwZ9QZNFE- Musiana Talk | Kalikaprasad Bhattacharya remembers "Baul Shah Abdul Karim."

16   Travelling Archive: field recordings and field notes from Bengal, www. thetravellingarchive.org/. Here is the introductory section of their homepage:

> The Travelling Archive is a shared space of listening to field recordings which come out of a journey through the rich and varied folk music of Bengal, covering mainly Bangladesh and the eastern Indian state of West Bengal and some adjoining areas of Assam in the east of South Asia; even distant locations such as the Bengali/Bangladeshi neighbourhoods of East London. This journey was begun in 2003 by Kolkata-based singer and writer Moushumi Bhowmik, soon to be joined by sound recordist and sound designer Sukanta Majumdar. As the two travelled together, a map of endless possibilities began to unfurl before them. Over the years the road has taken many turns. From recording and documentation, the project has evolved to explore new ways of research and dissemination, through archiving and working with archival material; writing and publication; presentation-performance and lectures; collaboration with

museums and art galleries; even launching a record label with selections of field recordings.

17 Dipti and Sonali – This section is part of a previous post of mine ("Meshomoshai & His New Nieces", published on 17 November 2018) in my ongoing blog on Kolkata, "Kolkata Diaries" – which I started writing after relocating back to Kolkata in 2017, after a decade of living and working in the Netherlands. It can be accessed here: www.royrituparna.com/meshomoshai-new-neices/

18 An exhaustive analysis of the continuing antisemitism that we are witnessing today can be found in the essays in: *Deciphering the New Antisemitism*, edited by Alvin H. Rosenfeld, Bloomington & Indianapolis: Indiana University Press, 2015 ("Studies in Antisemitism" Series).

19 Talking of genocides, it is interesting to note that, in *Places of Pain and Shame: Dealing with Difficult Heritage* (Routledge: 2009), William Logan and Keir Reeves argue that places of massacre and genocides are now increasingly being regarded as "heritage sites"; "a far cry", they point out, "from the view of heritage that prevailed a generation ago when we were almost entirely concerned with protecting the great and beautiful creations of the past, reflections of the creative genius of humanity rather than the reverse – the destructive and cruel side of history".

20 A very moving essay on the Pol Pot regime and its aftermath in Cambodia, seen from the unique perspective of a community of dancers, can be found in the essay "Dancing in Cambodia", in Amitav Ghosh's *Dancing in Cambodia, At Large in Burma*. New Delhi: Ravi Dayal, 1998, pp. 1–53.

21 To know more about these national museums, visit the following websites: www.muzej-jugoslavije.org/en/o-nama/ (for Yugoslavia); www.museum.ie/Home (for Ireland); and www.museum.go.kr/site/eng/home (for Korea).

22 https://thewire.in/culture/holocaust-partition-berlin-memorials

23 https://thewire.in/history/the-amritsar-partition-museum-highlights-the-lesser-known-players-behind-partition

24 Bangladesh Liberation War Museum: www.liberationwarmuseumbd.org/

25 Partition Film Fest, Kolkata, 16–19 August 2019 – Two important coverages of the Fest were in "Scroll.in" (in India) & "The Dhaka Tribune" (in Bangladesh): https://scroll.in/reel/933815/kolkata-event-will-revisit-bengal-partition-through-films-from-india-bangladesh; www.dhakatribune.com/showtime/2019/08/18/partition-of-bengal-revisited-through-films-from-bangladesh-and-india

Part 7

Literature

18 The failure of secular publics and the rise of the Jewish religious public in Nathan Englander's

For the Relief of Unbearable Urges

Fuzail Asar Siddiqi

A majority of the discourse on the concept of the public sphere revolves around the need for a secular, rational subject – a participant whose religious identity does not impinge upon her ability to make a reasoned argument. Many philosophers including Richard Rorty, for example, had argued for the need to separate the religious from being introduced into the public square because he believed religion to be a "conversation stopper" (Rorty 1994). Nathan Englander's debut short-story collection *For the Relief of Unbearable Urges* traces the experience of Jewishness in America and other parts of the world spanning a period ranging from the World Wars to the modern day. In this chapter I shall be discussing five of Englander's stories, two of which are based on the Holocaust, one on the turn towards Judaism, and two that document a movement into religionist thought perhaps as an outcome of the failure of secular society and publics to prevent events like the Holocaust. Englander through his stories questions the secularization thesis, which relegates religion to the periphery in the public sphere but at the same time also questions the replacement of secular ideals with a religionist one. This chapter attempts to understand Englander's idea of the public sphere and the role of secular and religious publics in mass violence and the possible promotion of tolerance. The public sphere for Englander, as I attempt to show, can neither be wholly secular or wholly religious, and through his stories he tries to demonstrate how both in the end fail to live up to the expectations one has of them in a society that is caught up in vicious cycles of violence in different forms.

Habermas in his lecture "Religion in the Public Sphere" suggests that to participate in the public sphere the religious subject must purge his language of its religiosity into a "generally accessible language" (2006) that is comprehensible to the secular citizen. But the question that is raised is whether such a purgation cleanses the very essence of the argument of the religious subject? The second story of Englander's Holocaust section is the story entitled "The Tumblers" and can be read as an allegory of sorts to the Habermasian precondition relating to the participation in public discourse. The story revolves around the folklore of the Fools of Chelm and their antics during World War II. The stories about the Fools of Chelm are humorous tales in which the Jewish protagonists come up with absurd ways of solving problems, as the most well-known story of a man who tries to kill a fish by drowning. The stories, however, gain ironic significance in a world set in the backdrop of the World War whose moral and ethical systems themselves have turned on their heads, in a sense reliving the absurdities of the Chelm tales. The story follows a group of Chelm residents who have managed to escape the concentration camps by boarding a different train full of performers that are heading towards a theatre to stage a show for the Fuhrer. In a desperate attempt to survive, the Fools decide that they will pretend to be acrobats and perform an impromptu show. However, the absurdity of the situation is such that apart from the protagonist, Mendel, a majority of the fellow Fools are aged people unable to do such stunts. However, in a sudden turn of events the show becomes successful because the Fuhrer misunderstands the performance to be a farce mocking the Jewish race itself – "'Look,' said the voice. 'They are clumsy as Jews.' ... 'More,' called the voice. 'The farce can't have already come to its end. More!' it said" (Englander 1999, 54). The Jewish characters on display on the public stage disguised as acrobats are, in a sense, stripped of their Jewishness, masking their cultural and religious identities to be able to exist on a public forum. The allegorical significance of the episode is profound because the shedding of one's cultural and religious baggage to participate in any public forum whether in the form of a theatrical performance or a discourse and debate in the public sphere, according to Englander, will have the same effect – that of evoking laughter and mockery. The fundamental question raised is whether there can be a subject who does not invoke any cultural or religious tradition to make an argument? The Fuhrer's comments in a way also gain another level of significance in that, although the characters are masquerading as acrobats, they are nonetheless unable to completely shed their identities; they are identified as Jews on the first glance by the audience.

Englander questions the thesis of whether it is possible to participate as equals in a public setting, as subjects that are nothing more than the rational arguments that they are supposed to posit. This form of abstraction can be problematic because it assumes one's participation in the public sphere as devoid of any means of recourse to any argument based on religious resources unless purged of its religious significance. But as the case is made in Englander, it is perhaps impossible to completely deny the impact of the religious in any discourse as is evident in an allegorical reading of the Jews in "The Tumblers." In a way, Englander's imagination tries to anticipate a kind of post-secularity that recognizes the need to take into account one's religious identity as part and parcel of the rational subject in the public sphere, an argument made by Habermas in the later years of his career in "Notes on a Post-secular Society" and "Religion in the Public Sphere."

While "The Tumblers" deals with the predicament of a religious subject in a secular sphere, the first story of the collection called "The Twenty-seventh Man" highlights the tense relationship of the individual and the state, and the materials circulating in the public domain. The story is set in Stalinist Russia and traces the life and death of an unknown writer called Pinchas Pelovits. In the story, 27 Jewish writers (initially 26 but later Pelovits' name was added, supposedly by a bureaucratic error) are sentenced to death at the behest of one of Stalin's orders on the charge of circulating Zionist propaganda. The authors are writers of fiction in the Yiddish language and are seen as conspiring against the state and destabilizing its authority. Eventually, in the course of the story the captured writers are killed, even though, as is shown, the writers are not concerned about the actions of the state but spend their time in imprisonment discussing their writings and, in the end, praising Pelovits' work, which was composed mentally during the time they were in jail.

The story raises two very important questions that Englander tries to bring to the fore regarding the relationship of the state and civil society and, more importantly, the information and communication that is allowed in the public sphere. First, since all of Englander's stories revolve around Jewish protagonists, the story questions the very nature of the state, not just of Stalinist Russia, but also of the famed foundation of secularism that the modern nation-state is built upon. Englander's point is a simple one, which is if the state proclaims to not distinguish among individuals and communities then why are writers of the Jewish community the ones that are at the wrong side of its displeasure? Second, apart from just being Jewish, the arrested people are all writers of fiction, poets, and the ilk. The state's supposed racism is complemented by its dislike of writers and poets in general, a prejudice that harks back all the way to Plato and the banishment of the poet from his ideal city. The state, it becomes clear, not only wants to secularize the content circulating in the public sphere but also wants to regulate and censor any and all information that is in circulation. The end aim is therefore the very revelation and clamping down of all attempts to spread discontent against the state itself. It is a paranoia inbuilt in the very nature of the state, which forces it to compartmentalize and regulate all discourses that are in circulation in the public sphere. The protagonist – whose parents when they became too old to keep their business running sell their business to the state – was seen as a harmless, introverted man not concerned with the machinations of the state.

> Even when the business became the property of the state, Pinchas, in the dreamer's room, was left in peace: *Why bother, he's harmless, sort of a good-luck charm for the inn, no one even knows he's here, maybe he's writing a history of the place, and we'll all be made famous.* He wasn't. But who knows, maybe he would have, had his name – mumbled on the lips of travellers – not found its way onto Stalin's list.
>
> (Englander 1999, 7; emphasis original)

Englander comes to see with the rise of the modern nation-state and the coming of modernity a hypocrisy at the heart of the enterprise. He is questioning the thesis that requires religion to be merely a part of the private sphere and in a sense sees the modern state as embodying and enforcing the idea of the privatization of religious identity. However, this attempt to silence the writers' religious identities falls short because they are least concerned with bothering about the state machinery that has sentenced them to death. Their defiance is an attempt to destabilize the police order, as Rancière would put it, and introduce a democratic politics that is missing in Stalinist Russia. It is the embodiment of the very idea that Plato's banished poets also had, a destabilizing tendency that would upset the hierarchical social order that his republic was built upon. Alongside with this idea is the concept of surveillance that has actually caused the imprisonment of

244 *Fuzail Asar Siddiqi*

the writers. Pelovits' arrest is caused by the passing of his name on the "lips of travelers (sic)," and the officers who have come to arrest him were "posing as the sons of now poor landowners," a play that they believed will "tickle their superiors" (1999, 7). The whole episode, in a sense, has an air of nonchalance about it where even the arrest is by a bureaucratic error, which no one noticed since the list provided to Stalin was changed last minute to mistakenly include Pelovits' name. While Pelovits might be "harmless" the state doesn't take a chance with him, keeping in mind the possibility of a future transgression and punishes him with the excuse of preventive detention. What Englander tries to highlight in the whole affair is the continuous meddling of the state in trying to curb anything and everything that these writers have contributed into the public sphere. The old writer Zunser's remark, "never outlive your language" (1999), can be read as the state militantly attempting to enforce a monolingualism in the public sphere in the hope of complete transparency of the discourses in circulation to keep a track of any anti-state activity that might destabilize its rule and the social order.

In the very first story Englander's criticism is directed sharply at the state that suspends all ideas of secularism in persecuting Jewish authors. The story is pertinent to Englander's cause because he wants to show how the politics of the modern state is hypocritical to a great extent. The paranoia of the modern nation-state is brought to the fore because of the power of discourse that the writers being persecuted have at their disposal. Habermas in his *Structural Transformation of the Public Sphere* suggests that the political public sphere was preceded by a literary public sphere that debated and critically analysed works of art (1991, 51–57). Eventually, Habermas observes, the literary public sphere started debating political questions, which perhaps would include ideas of sovereignty and the origins of the sovereignty of the state. Englander shows in the case of Stalinist Russia the paranoia that such a public sphere can have on leaders obsessed with absolute state power. Englander shows a public of writers that do not care about the state machinery, not holding it to the high esteem expected of them, not even if it wields the power of life or death.

In the story, Pelovits, who is imprisoned in a cell with three other famous writers whom he looks up to, asks: "Are you sure I'm here for being a writer?" He is answered by another writer who says "Not just for being a writer, my friend … you are here as a subversive writer. An enemy of the state! Quite a feat for an unknown" (Englander 1999, 18). Englander highlights the potential power that the participant of a public wields when it comes to questions regarding the state or politics. Moreover, there is another pertinent point raised by Englander. Pelovits' supposed subversiveness comes from the fact that the state thinks that he is trying to take the monopoly of debating political questions away from the state. The state's paranoia and incessant need for surveillance clamps down heavily on any discussion of politics in the public sphere.

Pelovits in the story is hesitant about his position among the stalwarts of the Yiddish language he is imprisoned with. However, Zunser, another famed writer imprisoned along with them, assuages his feelings of insecurity by saying "You are not here in place of us, you are here as one of us … if it makes any difference, we welcome you as an equal" (1999, 18). The ideal secular public sphere is one where all individuals come together in a partnership of equals to discuss matters of politics and the functioning of the state. While the public sphere is a place of equals discussing issues of politics that impinges upon the state's monopoly of doing politics, the story is a reminder about the asymmetrical relationship that the participants in the public sphere share with the state.

Englander's story challenges the idea of the famed foundations of secularism that the modern nation-state is supposedly built upon. By targeting writers that are Jewish and charging them for allegedly circulating Zionist propaganda under the pretext of secularizing the content of the public sphere, Englander highlights the true agenda of the modern state, that of controlling and censoring all discourses in the public sphere. Howard Caygill in his essay "Arcanum: The Secret Life of State and Civil Society" argues that the means of functioning of the state aren't political and it hides its true anti-political agendas behind the veneer of the political. Caygill suggests that the relationship of the state and the public sphere is that of a predator and a prey, where by constant surveillance the state can reinforce its thinking on the secular public sphere and persecute people as is the case in the story as and when it wishes to do so (2015, 21–41). He shows that the state maintains its power through the method of the secret, that its mode of functioning depends on its ability to keep its secrets secret, and also maintains its monopoly on the concept of the secret by preventing it in the public sphere by constant surveillance and monitoring.

Englander's critique is aimed at the mode of functioning of the state and its methods to purge the public sphere of any activity and discourse that does not conform to its liking, using the idea of secularism as an alibi. Moreover, as Englander shows, when the relationship of the state and civil society is an asymmetrical one, a secular public sphere cannot survive if the state chooses to the employ its resources in clamping down all means of communication in the public sphere. The secular public according to Englander can survive only in ideal situations where the state does not interfere in its functioning. Englander poses the question that when the state does interfere what is the possible recourse in those cases?

Englander through his stories asks for a radical rethinking of the Enlightenment foundation of secular ideals, which he sees the modern state as adopting but having disastrous ends nonetheless. With the persecution of Jews, Englander anticipates an alternative modernity that does not relegate religion to the margins – to the private sphere – but a religious modernity of sorts to overturn the biased so-called secularism that the modern state has as its foundation. Habermas in his essay "Religion in the Public Sphere" sensed the need for a secular state that does not interfere with the lives of citizens – religious or secular. What Englander criticizes is the tendency of the state to suspend its secularism in situations of its liking to purge religious discourse when it deems fit and prosecute its practitioners. For Habermas, "in the secular state, [the] government has to be placed on a non-religious footing" (Habermas 2006, 13), not discriminating between communities and peoples. Englander's point of contention is that when the state itself has taken a stance against a religious community it has lost its secular character; the true intentions of the state therefore are hidden, according to Englander, behind the veneer of secularism – the intention itself being of total control of all forms of discourses in the public sphere as is evident from the story. In extreme cases like in the given story, the revered secular ideals of the public sphere fall flat in response to the state's overthrow of the very idea of secularism.

The shortcomings of the idea of secular publics in Englander implies a recourse to an alternative modernity that has at its core the principle of post-secularity, which believes that ethical and moral questions plaguing both the religious and secular citizen can be assuaged to a great extent by the presence of religion in the public sphere. Englander's emphasis gains its impetus from the apparent fail-ure of the secular tendencies of states and social publics to provide answers and responses to the occurrence of events like the Holocaust in modern societies – societies built on the idea of the public exercise of secular reason.

Englander in his two stories on the Holocaust tries to make a case for the failure of the ideals of secularism in the public sphere. This failure, Englander suggests, forces a community to turn towards itself, which becomes the premise of the story "The Gilgul of Park Avenue." In the story Englander shows the kind of hostility the religious subject faces even in the private sphere. The story traces the life of Charles Morton Luger, who, in a taxi ride, has an epiphanic revelation that he is, in fact, the "bearer of a Jewish soul" (1999, 109). A Gilgul is a Kabba-listic concept of the transmigration of souls, or the notion of reincarnation in Jew-ish mysticism. Charles, who is, perhaps, a non-practising Christian turns into an Orthodox Jew because he believes he has become who he really was in his earlier life. He is no more a Marrano, a Jewish man masquerading as a Christian to avoid persecution, but rather has accepted who he really is. However, for Charles the problem of accepting his Jewishness does not end there because he realizes that his wife is completely unable to believe his transformation and forces him to give up this charade and become his true self. In the meantime, Charles goes to a rabbi for help to guide him with his newfound identity. Rabbi Zalman acquaints him with the nitty-gritty details of being Jewish and advises him on how to approach the topic with his Christian wife. On finding out about his Jewishness, Sue loses her temper and thinks Charles has gone mad because he is having a midlife crisis. Charles also skips visits to his psychiatrist, which troubles the doctor too and he calls Sue to enquire about his patient. Eventually, a meeting is set up between the doctor, Charles, and Sue, but Charles also invites the Orthodox rabbi Zalman to the dinner and the evening is a heated one that results in plenty of drama and a consensus is perhaps not reached, and the story ends with Charles hoping that Sue can still "love him changed" (1999, 137).

Englander's story raises pertinent points regarding the presence of a religious subject in a non-religious setting. As in the Holocaust stories above, the religious Jewish subject cannot find solace in the private sphere, away from the omnipres-ent surveillance of the state. The freedom of religion that is supposed to be pro-vided by the state in the secular public sphere is denied to the religious subject, but he is also denied that luxury in the private comforts of his own home. Charles' first reaction on reaching home is to tell is wife what happened in the taxi but, in a moment's notice, he hesitates and makes up another story: "'You wouldn't believe my taxi ride,' he said" (1999, 111). On realizing that this is a complicated thing to talk about, he decides against telling Sue the truth: "'Nothing, just remembering.

A heck of a ride. A maniac. Taxi driver running lights. Up on the sidewalk. Took Third before the bridge traffic cleared"' (1999, 111). Finally, when Charles tells her about his choice, she reacts by saying, "Is there a punchline?" (1999, 117), suggesting that this seems like a joke. However, when she realizes that Charles is not joking she says, "If it's not a nervous breakdown, I want to know if you feel like you're clinically insane" (1999, 117). Englander tries to show the hostility even in modern times to the idea of a person deciding to accept a religion and be sincere about it. Sue's reactions, Englander suggests, is emblematic of how the modern Christian is still adverse to the idea of a person accepting Judaism of his own accord. In the story, there are layered problems that Englander highlights: (*a*) the lack of choice a person has when choosing to be religious and the hostility that one has to face because of it, and (*b*) the antagonism towards a Jewish subject from a non-practising Christian. Sue in the story denies Charles the agency to make choices in his life. In a later fight in the story where Charles is trying to explain to Sue that she should be happy that he "found God," she reacts by saying, "Exactly the problem. You didn't find *our* God. I'd have been good about it if you found our God – or even a less demanding one" (1999, 121; emphasis mine). Sue is critical of the fact that the God that Charles chooses is not the Christian God whose demands are much less taxing than the Jewish one. Sue's anger stems from the fact that Charles has made a choice to desert the Christian God for a God that can make their everyday life difficult because of dietary restrictions and religious practices. Charles' wife of 27 years is merely looking for convenience; but in her convenience she overlooks the fact that the choice is beyond her and only between Charles and his God.

She resents the fact that he is too Jewish after his so-called conversion:

Well if you have to be Jewish, why *so* Jewish? Why not like the Browns in six-K? Their kid goes to Harvard. Why? She said, closing her eyes and pressing two fingers to her temple, "why do people who find religion always have to be so goddamn extreme?

(1999, 122)

Englander shows that Sue's predicament arises from the outward presence of signs of religiosity of the religious subject. In a sense, she suggests that the religious person must hide all aspects of his religiousness. He cannot be outwardly religious in appearance and practices and must also limit all religious talk and discourse when conversing with a non-religious person even in the private sphere.

While the state clamps down on religiosity by censoring and regulating discourses in the public sphere, the private sphere is not any better according to Englander and performs the same sort of censorship on the subject who wants to be religious. When Charles refuses to abide by her strictures, she has Dr Birnbaum over for dinner to help him out of his so-called insanity. Sue employs the manipulative powers of a psychologist to change Charles' decision. The doctor, perhaps also perplexed by his actions, tries to persuade him through his own means into rethinking his religiosity. When Charles says that "it's time for me to do God-pleasing work" the doctor questions, "And God-pleasing work is living the life of the Orthodox Jew? … Are you sure it might not be something else – like gardening or meditation?" (1999, 133). Both Sue and the doctor are adamant in making Charles rethink his life choices and are rather attempting to make the choices for him. Englander uses the character of the doctor to show how the medical profession also views the religious subject; his religiousness is hinted to be a sort of madness, an ailment that requires the intervention of a psychologist. The choice to be religious is the choice of the madman according to Sue and the doctor. When the doctor's attempts to explain the situation to Charles fails, Sue tries to emotionally threaten him into abandoning his God and coming back to everyday existence. She says, "your moment of grace has passed. Real or not. It's gone now. You are left with life – daily life" (1999, 135). By invoking the idea of "daily life," Sue suggests that religion is not a permanent part of existence but only a temporary delusion, an intoxicant whose effects last for a very short time, and then daily life takes its course. Through the character of Sue, Englander points out that the non-religious person is unwilling to look beyond her own discourses. She cannot realize that for the religious subject religion is not a temporary solace ("God is for the desperate. For when there is nothing left to do" (1999, 134), as Sue puts it) but rather a whole way of life that looks beyond the limits of secular existence.

Rémi Brague in his essay "The Impossibility of Secular Society" (2013) makes a pertinent argument in regard to secular society. Following an etymological study of the word "secular," which comes from the Roman "*saeculum,*" roughly the time duration of a century, he proposes that secular societies are concerned with only a worldly existence usually ranging the life span of a person or a maximum of a hundred years or so. Moreover for a society to be secular it has to be "flat" and "closed" (Brague 2013) – flat in the sense that it doesn't privilege one group over the other and closed because its principles of equality must be immanent and not refer to an outside source for legitimation, whether it is God or something else. Englander's characters' thinking anticipates this because by invoking a Jewish tradition his ethics is necessarily not concerned with worldly, secular existence, but rather refers to an other-worldliness as its guide. His disenchantment with secular modernity – secular also in the sense of a duration of a century or a more generally worldly time – comes from the fact that it cannot think beyond a specific temporal quantity and is hence believed to be flawed because it invokes man's flawed sense of reasoning, and is also in a way a mode of thought that thinks only for short term gains. Charles is unable to explain to Sue his concern with this otherworldliness that he gets from religion, a point that Sue will not be able to understand because she is thinking of only this-worldly existence.

Before Rabbi Zalman leaves the dinner to let Sue and Charles sort it out among themselves, he makes a poignant remark: "No hope Mr. Luger. I tell you this from one Jew to another. There is no hope for the pious" (1999, 137). Zalman realizes that this so-called secular society is unwilling to take the pious religious man amongst them. The religious subject will always be an outcast in a society that claims to be secular and modern but perhaps is neither of the two. The Holocaust stories show how the Jewish subject is marginalized and persecuted in so-called secular societies. "The Gilgul of Park Avenue" attempts to highlight the problems with a man using his own agency to embrace religion but is persecuted for that too. However, in stories like "The Reunion" and the title story "For the Relief of

Unbearable Urges," which document the rise of a more religionist thinking, there is a vein of criticism of the use of religion in community life. While these stories show the shift to the use of religion as a guiding principle, and also the rise of religious ethics as a substitute for the failed secular public ethics, suggesting the loss of hope in the secular ideals of the West, Englander"s criticism is directed at both religionist thought and secular thought which he sees as failing to live up to the standard one would hope.

The title story "For the Relief of Unbearable Urges" centres around the life of a Jewish couple Dov Binyamin and his wife Chava Bayla. Bayla, who believes she is impure for months because of a prolonged menstrual cycle, refuses to touch her husband who is desperate for physical intimacy. In a bizarre twist, Binyamin goes to a Rebbe who gives him a "special dispensation" (Englander 1999, 181) to go see a prostitute "for the relief of unbearable urges" (1999, 182). Binyamin following the Rebbe's advice meets an American prostitute who, later as he finds out, has given him a venereal disease. Surprisingly, at the time of his suffering his wife's demeanour has changed and she desires intimacy, which he is unable to give because he has not told her about the encounter with the prostitute and his disease.

Englander's title story makes some very clear suggestions regarding his view of the ideals of the West. Modernity is shown to be linked with the idea of a disease. The American prostitute from which the Jewish man contracts the venereal disease, according to Englander, is the embodiment of the moral and spiritual decay of the socio-ethical systems of the West, one that was amply highlighted in his holocaust section. This story is an attempt of the Jewish individual to participate in an ethical system which is not his own; the special dispensation given to Binyamin is a chance to partake in a moral scheme outside the limits of his religion, beyond the private limitations of his Jewish faith. Such a participation in a public Western ethics has disastrous consequences for Binyamin causing not only social tension with regards his personal life with his wife, and the harm to his physical body but also to his spiritual faith. However, what occurs is a conundrum of sorts because the public exercise of religious reason is the real cause of his problems. Englander not only criticizes the ethical values of Western modernity but also implicitly ends up questioning the very system that is usually proposed as an alternative, a system whose logic of functioning has equally bad consequences for the individual. Religious reason, as the dispensation of the Rebbe demonstrates, does help in assuaging the physical desires of the body but is the cause of more moral crises and social unrest. While the reason of religion is private following its own closed ethicality, the consequences, nonetheless, are of a public nature, causing disharmony among social beings of the community.

Englander's criticism against religionist thought continues in stories like "The Reunion." The story follows the time in a mental asylum of a man named Marty who meets another by the name of Doe. Doe's brother, as Marty finds out later, is a rabbi that Marty used to go to. Rabbi Baum, as he is known, works as a counsellor holding together Marty's tense relationship with his wife, striving hard to keep the family unit together. In a counselling meeting with Marty and his wife he says:

"This is not about God," he said. "It is not about religion. What this is, is basic humanity. To shirk our responsibilities to each other as human beings is to let the family unit crumble. To hurry society as a whole on its return to dust."

(Englander 1999, 67)

However, when Marty decides to take Doe to meet with his Rabbi brother, Rabbi Baum breaks all his belief in the family bonds and forcefully asks his mentally ill brother to go away and never come back after which a fight ensues and hence the reunion Marty had hoped for never happens.

Englander shows in these stories the problems that are inherent in the rise of a religious public, a public whose arguments are based solely on religion. What was believed to be a substitute for secular reason in public and private life follows the same downward trajectory. Rabbi Baum who lectures Marty and his wife about the need to behave with compassion with each other is the first one to dismiss religious reason at the first sign of trouble when it comes to his private life.

The Rabbi preaches an ethics which he believes is not only restricted to religion but rather is a common public ethics every human is born with, a responsibility towards the other regardless of their cultural, political, and social identities. The Rabbi also makes a connection with the private and the public, where the family is a not a segregated unit separated from civil society but a part of social public existence. Society, in the Rabbi's words, becomes a collection of family units and hence blurs the line between the private life of the family and the public life of the citizen. The point Englander tries to articulate is that in a post-secular society, the private and the public merge into one, where religious reason is the guiding principle of public life and the ethical principle followed in the home and one's own religion should be the same that guides one's public existence. The Rabbi believes that at the heart of religious thought lurks a humanism that should be common to all, a humanism that secular thought never accepted as true. Such a form of public ethics is an ideal situation which never materializes in Englander's stories even if he wishes it could. The Rabbi himself is never able to practise what he preaches when it comes to accepting his own mentally ill brother, calling into question the very hypothesis he posits as the founding principle that should guide not only one's private life but also one's public existence. In a way, Englander shows that the hypocrisy of secular society's ethics is mimicked by the religious public. Whether it is the Rabbi in "The Reunion" or the advice of the Rebbe in "For the Relief of Unbearable Urges," both end up creating situations that do more harm than good. What is called into question therefore is the possibility of the existence of any form of public religious ethics that can do better than the secular ethics against which Englander raises a finger of doubt.

Englander however does not propose an alternative but shows the two extremes and the different kinds of violence inherent in both. In the last story "In This Way We Are Wise" which is about how a bombing in the heart of a city affects the individual, he ends the story by saying: "And even if a public bombing strikes you in a private way, hide that from everyone lest you be called out to lead them" (1999, 205). While Englander criticizes the powerlessness of secular and religious publics in conjuring a remedy for violence, mass violence or otherwise, his philosophy is one that has resigned to its fate and does not produce an answer that can suggest a way out of violence. However, a possible remedy can be taken from Habermas, where Englander gives up, who in the closing lines of his lecture "Religion in the Public Sphere" proposes the idea of postmetaphysical thought (2006, 18), a method that does not have secularism's stubborn attitude towards religious truth, while at the same time prepared to learn from religion while remaining strictly agnostic. A way forward as proposed by Habermas is through a middle path, through dialogue and discussion and perhaps more importantly with an open mind that is receptive to learn from the other's argument.

References

Brague, Rémi. "The Impossibility of Secular Society." *Firstthings.Com*, October 2013. www.firstthings.com/article/2013/10/the-impossibility-of-secular-society.

Caygill, Howard. "The Secret Life of State and Civil Society." In *The Public Sphere From Outside The West*, edited by Ed Divya Dwivedi and V. Sanil, 21–41. London and New York: Bloomsbury Academic, 2015.

Englander, Nathan. *For the Relief of Unbearable Urges*. London: Faber and Faber, 1999.

Habermas, Jürgen. "Religion in the Public Sphere." *European Journal of Philosophy* 14 (2006), 1–25.

Habermas, Jürgen. *The Structural Transformation of the Public Sphere*. Translated by Thomas Burger. Cambridge, MA: MIT Press, 1991.

Rorty, Richard. *Religion as Conversation Stopper*. London: Penguin Books, 1994.

Part 8

Dialogue and reconciliation

19 The 2002 Alexandria Summit and its follow-up

David Rosen

I wish to open this chapter with some musings about the relationship between religion and conflict, as the wider background to the significance of the 2002 Alexandria summit of Israeli and Palestinian religious figures.

Most modern conflicts that are portrayed as religious ones are, in fact, territorial in origin. Whether between Hindus and Muslims in Kashmir; Buddhists and Hindus in Sri Lanka; Christians and Muslims in Nigeria or Indonesia; Protestants and Catholics in Northern Ireland; or between Muslims and Jews in the Israeli/ Palestinian context; these conflicts are not doctrinal or theological in origin. They are territorial conflicts in which ethnic and religious differences are exploited and manipulated, often mercilessly.

Saint John Paul II declared that "religion is the chief antidote to violence and conflict" (*Message for the 2002 World Day of Peace*, 14). Indeed, virtually all the world's religions declare that their goal is peace, harmony, and the well-being of human society – not just tolerance, but much more.

Yet we cannot ignore the fact that not only has terrible violence been perpetrated in the name of religion; but that there are not a few adherents of religions in different parts of the world today who actually believe that conflict and violence against others is precisely what their religion demands.

The sages of the Talmudic period showed an amazing willingness for self-critique when they declared (*Babylonian Talmud, Hagigah 7a*) that Torah – used here to mean the Jewish religion as a whole – can be *sam hachayim*, the elixir of life, or *sam hamavet*, the potion of death.

So, this begs the question of why and how it is that religion is so easily exploited and abused? Almost invariably in contexts of conflict in our world, religion appears to be more part of the problem than the solution.

The eleventh-century Jewish scholar Yehudah Halevi's apologia for Judaism takes the form of a dialogue between a Jewish scholar and the King of Khazars. In the course of this discussion there is an occasion (Kuzari 1:113) when the scholar points out that while Christianity and Islam preach love and justice, in practice they perpetrate violence and oppression, whereas Jews do not behave in that manner. To which the King replies that the reason Jews do not behave in the same lamentable way is simply that they do not have the power to do so, while the others do!

In this riposte, Halevi precedes Lord Acton by many centuries in warning against the dangers of power that corrupts all aspects of life, religion included. The unholy alliance of religion with power inevitably leads to the betrayal of religion's most noble values.

This truism is very evident in human history and in our world today. The widespread apologia in the face of the manifest abuse of religion even in justifying atrocities, declare that it is not religion that is at the root of such abuse but human character that is all too easily corrupted by many factors, arguably power being the most insidious of them. Accordingly, many of us would argue that the marriage of religion to state is always dangerous and usually degenerating. Religion is far healthier when it lives in creative tension with political power.

Yet much violence in the name of religion today, actually derives from power-lessness, precisely reflecting the alienation of the marginalized.

Of course, we must not fall into the trap of assuming that religions are the same thing across confessional or geographic lines. Indeed, often the same religion can take on a very different form in one place than another; and the relationship of that religion with the society in which it functions, may vary considerably in different places from one extreme to another.

Douglas Marshall has described Religion in terms of three "B"s – Belief, Behaviour, and Belonging (*Sociological Theory, Vol. 20, No. 3*, November 2002.) Different religions may constitute different combinations or emphases of these.

The abuse of religion has often been related to the first two of these. Polemics relating to doctrine and even ritual, have led to violent clashes, and even today are used as a pretext for intolerance and even violence towards those who do not share the same beliefs and practices. Yet, as mentioned, the abuse of religion in the context of conflicts usually has far more to do with the socio-cultural territorial and political contexts in which religion functions. As much as violence in the name of religion may relate to beliefs and even practices, it generally has much more to do with "belonging".

Because religion seeks to give meaning and purpose to who we are, it is inextricably bound up with all the different components of human identity, from the most basic such as family, through the larger components of communities, ethnic groups, nations, and peoples, to the widest components of humanity and creation as a whole. These components of human identity are the building blocks of our psycho-spiritual well-being and we deny them at our peril. (Scholars studying the modern human condition have pointed out just how much the counterculture, drug abuse, violence, cults, etc. are a search for identity on the part of the disorientated who have lost traditional compasses of orientation.)

These components of our identity affirm who we are but by definition at the same time they affirm who we are not! Whether the perception of distinction and difference is viewed positively or negatively, depends overwhelmingly upon the context in which we find ourselves or perceive ourselves to be.

In contexts of conflict, identity often tends to be not just a nurturing of positive affiliation, but also a vehicle for self-righteousness and disparagement of "the other", to the point of portraying the opponent – in the words of the historian

Richard Hofstadter – as "a perfect picture of malice" (*The Paranoid Style in American Politics*, Harper's Magazine, November 1964, pp. 77–86.)

An image I find useful in explaining the behaviour of particular identities for good or bad is that of a spiral. These different components of identity are like circles within circles. When they feel secure within the wider context in which they find themselves, then they can affirm, open up and contribute to the broader context; families engaging other families; communities working together with other communities; nations contributing to the commonweal of society at large.

However, when these components of human identity do not feel comfortable in the broader context, they cut themselves off from the wider context, isolate themselves, and invariably tend to denigrate the other/s, compounding the sense of alienation.

In such situations, all too often we find that religion itself does not just assume a nurturing role for an identity under siege (or at least perceiving itself as such); but in seeking to provide self-justification, religion all too often exacerbates self-righteousness and compounds a disregard for "the other" who is demonized and even dehumanized.

In the Middle East, this phenomenon is especially intense. Everybody in our part of the world feels vulnerable and threatened. However, each group sees itself and the others in very different (invariably contradictory) paradigms! Everyone believes that they are the victims of the other's hostility and mendacity. In such conflicted contexts it is extremely difficult to get the different communities to engage one another in mutual respect for their common humanity.

In keeping with Halevi's observation, where religion does not provide a prophetic challenge to political authority but is both caught up as part of the political reality and even subordinate and subject to political authority as it is in the Middle East; institutional religion does tend to be more part of the problem than part of the solution. The role of the prophetic challenge for religious identities, to be faithful to their traditions while affirming the dignity of the other and promoting reconciliation and peace – in our part of the world, as in most contexts of conflict – has tended to be the voice of the non-establishment visionaries and activists.

Indeed, most institutional religion in our part of the world is so inextricably bound up with the power structures – with the heads of the respective Jewish and Muslim communities actually appointed by political authorities – that it is very rare for a truly prophetic voice to emerge from the institutional religious leadership of either the Jewish or Muslim communities.

And even within the local Christian minority communities, which are generally free of such direct political domination, there is an inevitable tendency to be hamstrung by the exigencies of the political realities that impose very significant restrictions and pressures upon minorities in particular and the role of their leadership.

I should mention in parentheses, so as not to give a distorted picture, that there is probably proportionately more Jewish–Muslim–Christian interfaith activity in Israel than anywhere else in the world (The Abraham Fund listed some three hundred organizations working in Arab–Jewish relations; and the Interreligious Coordinating Council in Israel contained some 70 organizations and associations promoting and/or supporting interfaith activity.) However, not only is such engagement extremely marginal to Israeli society as a whole, until recently it has hardly involved the religious establishment at all.

Yet as far as the Israeli–Palestinian conflict is concerned, not only has religion failed so far to be a significant force promoting peace; in recent decades with escalating violence, breakdown of trust, and mutual alienation, religion has been increasingly enlisted to strengthen the identities of the parties involved, to promote their respective claims while seeking to delegitimize those of the other side as aforementioned.

Accordingly, precisely because religion is associated more with partisan insularity if not downright hostility towards the "other", there has been an understandable tendency on the part of peace initiatives in the Middle East to avoid religious institutions and their authorities, seeing them as obstacles to any such peace process.

This tendency is comprehensible but terribly misguided, as it fails to address the most deep-seated dimensions of the communal identities involved and actually undermines the capacities of positive political initiatives to succeed.

Indeed, I believe this one of the factors that contributed to the failure of the Oslo Process. By way of illustration one might note that on the lawn of the White House when the famous handshake took place in September 1992 between Yasser Arafat and Yitzhak Rabin and Shimon Peres, there was no personality to be seen who represented the religious traditions, neither of the Jewish community nor of the Muslim or even Christian communities in the Holy Land, supporting the desire to find a way out of the regional conflict. The message was clear – religion is something to be kept out of the process.

This only compounded a sense of alienation on the part of the most fervently religious elements within both communities who perceived such initiatives as being against their interests and did their best to violently undermine them. In fact, the process of trying to keep religion out of the equation inevitably invites the most extremist elements to dominate the religious public discourse. Moreover, like all aspects of nature that abhors a vacuum, if the moderate voices are ignored, then the extremist ones will be the ones to be heard.

Naturally, to combat extremist violence in the name of any ideology, physical measures have to be taken to protect our societies. However, defensive action alone is not enough. If one does not want the extremist discourse to predominate, it is necessary to proactively empower the moderate voices who in most cases do represent the respective majorities.

The religious manipulation of the conflict, using religious symbols and arguments to justify carnage was especially evident during the second intifada.

The very name given to the violent uprising by the Palestinians – the Al Aqsa intifada – portrayed it as a battle for the defence of Muslim Jerusalem.

Indeed, my encounters in the Muslim world have revealed to me how much Muslims today overwhelmingly believe that this conflict in the Holy Land is over religious domination and thus involves an assault against Islam whose holy sites are in peril, threatened by Israeli malevolent intent. When I tell them that, in fact, the majority of Orthodox Jewish opinion teaches that it is prohibited for Jews to go on to the Temple mount/Haram e-Sharif; that this is the position of the Chief Rabbinate of Israel; and that, as a result, Judaism actually protects the Muslim presence on the Mount, they think I am trying to deceive them.

In keeping with this abovementioned misconception, there has been an increasing hostile denial in the Muslim world in recent times, of the religious connection between the Jewish people and Jerusalem and the Holy Land. This further exacerbates a vicious cycle and had surely played its part in the increasing number of Jewish religious nationalists visiting the Temple Mount precincts to assert historical claims.

Such a "religionization" of the conflict is very dangerous. For if this conflict is seen as what it is in essence – a territorial conflict – then it can be resolved through territorial compromise. But if it is seen as a religious conflict, between the godly and the godless, between good and evil, then we are condemned to unending bloodshed.

It was in this light, that amidst the worst violence of the second intifada in 2002, religious leaders of the Three Faith communities in the Holy Land were brought together for the first time ever in human history – in Alexandria, Egypt – to raise the voices of their respective traditions in a call for an end to violence and for the promotion of peace and reconciliation.

The then Israeli Minister of Foreign Affairs Shimon Peres and his deputy Rabbi Michael Melchior played a critical role in this initiative. But precisely because of the insecurity and mistrust that separates our communities in conflict, it required a third party to initiate this meeting. This was the then Archbishop of Canterbury, Lord George Carey, energetically supported by Canon Andrew White.

Providentially, Canterbury had an institutional relationship with Al Azhar in Cairo, the fountainhead of Islamic learning in the Arab world – indeed in the Muslim world at large – and the grand Imam of Al Azhar Sheikh Mohammed Sayyed Tantawi, encouraged by President Hosni Mubarak, agreed to host the meeting. This was crucial in facilitating the success of this initiative.

For while the chief rabbis of Israel do not represent all religious Jews in Israel, let alone in the world, nevertheless most Jews would not object to them representing Judaism for the purpose of advancing interreligious reconciliation.

Similarly, while the patriarchs of Jerusalem do not represent the whole of Christendom, their role as representatives of Christianity in an effort to promote reconciliation in the Middle East would certainly be affirmed by the Christian world at large. But in the Islamic context, the religious leadership within Palestinian society does not have the standing in the Muslim world to ensure that its voice would be heard and respected as representing Islam. Thus the need to have this major institution of Islamic learning support this process was of critical importance. In addition to giving the green light to Sheikh Tantawi to host the gathering, President Mubarak also received the participants at his palace in Cairo for a press conference at the conclusion of the summit.

Arguably the still-present impact of the 11 September 2001 attacks on the World Trade Center also played its part in this initiative, as for a brief while political leaders were eager to be seen to be on the side of constructive religious engagement.

This was, of course, particularly the case for Muslim leaders – in this context, Mubarak and especially PA Chairman Yasser Arafat. However it was also the case for the Israeli Prime Minister Ariel Sharon. It was indeed amazing that both Sharon and Arafat encouraged this initiative despite the violence in Israel and the Palestinian Territories that was taking place at the time. Indeed they both approved the text of the final declaration – perhaps the only thing they ever agreed upon!

As indicated, this summit was an historic event, as never before had heads of the different three faith communities in the Holy Land ever come together in one place. The participants included four leading sheikhs from the establishment structure of the Palestinian Authority, including both a PA minister and the head of the PA Supreme Sharia Courts; five prominent Israeli rabbis, including the Sephardic Chief Rabbi of Israel; and all patriarchs were represented, the Latin patriarch attending in person.

After much discussion we were able to agree on a text that condemned the violent abuse of religion and called for adherents of the different religions to respect the attachment of the other faiths and their sites. It urged a rejection of incitement and demonization and to promote positive education about one another. It affirmed the essential need to guarantee freedom of worship; and also called on the respective political leaders to eschew violence and return to the negotiating table; to recognize the importance of religion as a force of reconciliation; and enable Israelis and Palestinians to live in dignity and security.

Even though a "Permanent Committee for the Implementation of the Alexandria Process" was established, it did not get very far in its objectives.

It had no impact on the continuing violence, and furthermore changes in Israeli government meant that this framework was viewed as controlled by opposing partisan political interests. There was also some resentment on the part of the Christian communities that the "process" continued to be managed by external Christian parties.

Above all, one of the factors that made the Alexandria summit possible was also its weakness – namely, that the participants had been there *ad personam*. This meant that their institutions did not have ownership of any "process". When key figures left office or passed away, the continuity was lost.

Rabbi Melchior did pursue a number of important initiatives under the brand name of the Alexandria summit, but efforts to maintain a standing committee involving the official religious leadership in Israel and the PA was short lived.

As a result, a further initiative ensued involving the official religious establishments. A Council of the Religious Institutions of the Holy Land was set up comprising the Chief Rabbinate of Israel, the Palestinian Ministry of Religious Affairs and its Sharia courts, and the Patriarchs and Bishops of the recognized Churches of the Holy Land.

This Council may be described as the child of the Alexandria summit and was facilitated by the Norwegian Church through the person of Canon Trond Bakkevig (who had helped facilitate and had attended the Alexandria summit.)

The Council was founded with three declared objectives, the first of which was to facilitate ongoing communication between the religious leadership. In this regard it has been moderately successful. Indeed, when the Anglican bishop of Jerusalem faced difficulties with his residence permit, the intervention of one of the chief rabbis played a significant role in resolving the impasse.

The second goal was to combat incitement, defamation, and misrepresentation. The Council responds to any attacks on the sites or adherents in the name of all three religions and has issued statements condemning violence and calling for mutual respect between religious communities. Generally this is done on the Council's website (www.crihl.org), but there have been instances when the religious leaders gathered in solidarity with the victims at scenes of terror attacks against worshippers as we'll as acts of arson.

Last and not least, the members of the Council declared its purpose to support initiatives to bring an end to the conflict so that two peoples and three religions may live in peace and dignity.

In this regard, the Council has been an abject failure.

As indicated, the idea that religious leaders seek to pursue peace and reconciliation runs counterintuitive to the widespread perception in Israeli and Palestinian societies that view the other's religion as the source of the problem. But the main reason for the futility of such good declared intentions lies with the political authorities themselves.

In Israeli political life, religion is used and abused as a "political commodity" for partisan interests (or competing interests) and it is usually seen as something best avoided by those who have been involved in peace negotiations.

More difficult to understand is the American avoidance of Israeli and Palestinian religious leadership, evidenced in the fact that whether during the ultimately futile visits of George Mitchell, or more recently John Kerry, no Secretary of State or even special envoy met with the Council, or even any of the official Christian leaders in the Holy land, let alone those of the Jewish and Muslim communities. This, despite the fact that the Council at the highest level, had been hosted twice in Washington DC. (In fact, the only US Secretary of State to do so was Condoleezza Rice and this was not in the context of any specific peace initiative.)

This may have to do with vagaries of American separation of church and state, though I suspect again that primarily it has to do with a degree of unfamiliarity and even discomfort in the State Department regarding the religious dimension.

Of course, I do not suggest for one minute that religious figures should replace the politicians. In our part of the world, that would be far from wise (though the present impasse in the Israeli/Palestinian conflict highlights the abysmal failure of our politicians to provide any vision).

Moreover, as acknowledged, Israeli and Palestinian official religious leadership leaves much to be desired aside from being substantially subject to the political authorities and thus unlikely to provide any initiative out of the impasse of conflict.

However, all this does not mean that religious leadership is irrelevant, on the contrary. It symbolizes the very intangibles of identities that exacerbate the conflict, which can only be resolved if these dimensions are addressed. To reiterate, if we do not want religion to be part of the problem; it has to be part of the solution.

The most notable public event for the members of the Council took place two years ago at the Vatican where Pope Francis brought us together for a gathering of prayers for peace in the Holy Land in the presence of the then President of Israel Shimon Peres and Palestinian President Mahmoud Abbas. However, in this instance the deficiency was the reverse of the aforementioned problem, namely the failure to engage a relevant Israeli political authority or at least to obtain support therefrom. Such a gathering could be of significant value if it took place in the context of real negotiations.

Rabbi Michael Melchior has continued to pursue dialogue especially between Jewish and Muslim religious leaders in Israel the West bank and Gaza. This has also taken place on an international level, most notably with the three world conferences of imams and rabbis for peace that we held in Brussels, Seville, and Paris.

However, again, if such engagement does not have "buy-in" from the political echelon, its value is of little diplomatic consequence.

Nevertheless, I am convinced that engagement between Israeli and Palestinian religious figures in particular and with Arab Muslim leaders in general, can be of great value not only to the specific context. It can have profound salutary ramifications throughout the Middle East and even globally. However, for the time being, the Council of the Religious Institutions of the Holy land remains a semi-dormant body-in-waiting for a time when political leaders will seek to avail themselves of this potential.

Index

Page numbers in 'bold' indicate tables, and page numbers followed by 'n' indicate notes.

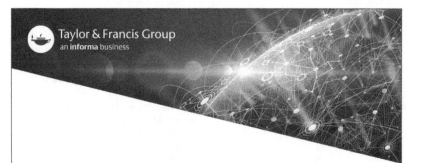